the
Resident Assistant

Applications and Strategies for Working with College Students in Residence Halls

Fifth Edition

Gregory Blimling

Appalachian State University

KENDALL/HUNT PUBLISHING COMPANY
4050 Westmark Drive   Dubucue, Iowa 52002

CONTENTS

Preface   vii

PART ONE:
The History and Foundation of Residence Halls

1. The Roles and Responsibilities of the RA
   The RA as Student   7
   The RA as Role Model   8
   The RA as Counselor   9
   The RA as Teacher   9
   The RA as Administrator   10
   Establishing Yourself with Your Residents   10
   Interpersonal Relationships and the RA   13
   What Is It Really Like?   17
   Burnout   17
   Applications
     Hall-Soccer   19
     What We Value   19
     An Unlikely Match   21
     Fourth Down and Long   21

2. The History of Residence Halls
   Roots in the British Collegiate System   24
   Origins in the United States   25
   Nineteenth Century Disregard for Student Housing   25
   Early Twentieth Century American Residence Halls   27
   Residence Halls after World War I   31
   Residence Halls in the 1930s   32
   Residence Halls during and after World War II   34

Residence Halls in the 1950s   35
Residence Halls in the 1960s   38
Residence Halls in the 1970s   39
Residence Halls in the 1980s   40
Into the Twenty-First Century   40
Conclusion   41
Applications
  How It Was Then—How It Is Now   43

3. Educational Philosophies for Residence Halls
   Need for Good Money Management   48
   Philosophies for Working with Students in Residence Halls   48
   Goals for Residence Hall Programs   51
   Summary   52
   Applications
     How Is He Doing?   53
     How Do You Do Your Job?   54

4. The Influence of Residence Halls on the Development of Students
   Comparison between Students Who Live in Residence Halls and Students Who Do Not   55
   The Influence of Residence Hall Design   57
   Ways That Residence Halls Influence Students   58
   Methods of Advancing the Growth and Development of Students Living in Residence Halls   62
   Summary   64
   Applications
   The Commuter and the Resident   66
   Friends   67

PART TWO:
Understanding and Working with College Students

5. The Growth and Development of College Students
   Biological Development   72
   Psychological Development during the
      College Years   73
   Cognitive Development   80
   Applications
      Lucy   92
      Right Meets Left   93

6. Adjusting to College
   The First Year   96
   The Sophomore and Junior Years   106
   The Senior Year   109
   Applications
      Crimes of the Heart   114
      Student Problems: Old and New   115

7. Peer Counseling
   Complaints about Counseling   118
   An Overview of Helping Skills   119
   Counseling Model   122
   Helping a Student Seek Professional
      Counseling   130
   Related Counseling Issues   133
   Advising   134
   Applications
      Understanding Yourself   136
      The Social Outsider   138

PART THREE:
Confrontation and Crisis Management

8. Behavior Problems, Confrontation, and Discipline
   Types of University Policies   142
   Disciplinary Counseling Model   144
   Confrontation Skills   150
   How to Confront an Intoxicated
      Person   152
   Tips on Disciplinary Counseling   154

Applications
   The Viking   156
   Catch Me If You Can   157

9. Mediation
   Defining Conflict Situations   159
   Management Model for Roommate
      Conflicts   160
   Analyzing Conflict Situations   161
   Applications
      Lifestyles of the Rich and Famous   164
      Why Me?   165

10. Suicide Intervention
   Causes of Suicide   168
   Symptoms of Suicidal Behavior   168
   Interviewing Potentially Suicidal
      Students   170
   Making a Referral   174
   Applications
      All Alone   176
      Quiet Desperation   177

11. Violence and Crime in Residence Halls
   Battered Women   180
   Rape   182
   Other Crimes on Campus   188
   Applications
      Loving and Fighting   192
      Without Permission   193

PART FOUR:
Social Issues

12. Food Abuse
   Bulimia   197
   Anorexia Nervosa   199
   Applications
      You Can Never Be Too Thin   201

13. Alcohol Abuse
   Short-Term Effects of Alcohol   204
   Problems Associated with Alcohol
      Abuse   207
   Causes of Alcohol Abuse in College   208

Identifying the Problem Drinker   210
Addressing Alcohol Problems   211
Low-Risk Drinking   211
Alcohol Education Programming   212
Applications
   Let the Good Times Roll   215

14. Drug Abuse
Drug Enforcement   218
Reference Section on Drugs   218
Educational Institutions and Drug
   Use   228
RAs: Counselors or Enforcers?   229
Drug Overdoses   231
Applications
   Winning through Fear and
     Intimidation   233

15. Sexuality
Contraceptives   236
Pregnancy   239
Abortion   240
HIV and AIDS   241
Other STDs   243
Healthy Relationships   252
Applications
   The Most Difficult Decision of Their
     Lives   254
   Sexual Responsibility   255

16. Sexual Orientation
Self-Disclosure   260
Homosexual Lifestyle   261
Homosexuality and the Residence
   Halls   262
Counseling Gay and Lesbian Students
   262
Applications
   Close Friends   265
   The Case of the Gay Roommates   266

17. Issues of Race and Gender
Psychosocial Development and the
   Influence of Gender and Race   270

Race and Ethnocentrism   271
Gender and Sexism   279
Applications
   Cross-Cultural Miscommunication   285
   Harassment   287

PART FIVE:
Educational Outreach

18. Educational Programming
Goals of Programming   292
Traditional Programming Model   293
Wellness Programming Model   295
How to Program   296
Conclusion   303
Applications
   Trying to Get By in Programming   306
   Program Problem Solver   307

19. Community Development
Elements of a Community   310
Types of Communities   312
How to Establish a Community   312
Conclusion   314
Applications
   Altogether   315
   The War between the Corridors   316

PART SIX:
RA Survival Skills

20. Time Management
Overplanning   322
Time   322
Conclusion   327
Applications
   Hurry, Scurry   328
   Happenstance   329

21. Study Skills
Preparing to Study   332
Basic Skills for Acquiring
   Information   337

The Studying Process   339
Test Taking   340
Academic Honesty and Dishonesty   343
Applications
  Elroy   345
  A Two-Week Vacation   347

References   349

Index   359

PREFACE

The foundation of nearly every residence hall program across the country is the resident assistant (RA) position. These student-staff members fulfill a most difficult assignment: supervising and assisting an entire floor of undergraduate students. The resident assistant is in the vanguard of the field of student development. The daily contact the RA has with students makes it possible for the RA to have a significant impact on the development of these students. The author believes that whether or not the RA is prepared to accept this responsibility is directly related to the quantity and quality of education in preparation for the position.

GOAL OF THIS BOOK

This book is designed to serve several needs.
- It will be used as a textbook in courses taught to resident assistants in colleges and universities.
- It will be used by residence hall staff for inservice education programs in institutions where courses for credit are not provided.
- It will be used as a personal manual to assist RAs in day-to-day involvement with their residents.

SCOPE

The responsibilities of RAs are similar across the country. As a result, this book provides information that should be basic to the RA positions in almost all locales. It is expected that residence hall staff on a particular campus will add to, alter, or otherwise enhance the information in such a way as to tailor usage to the individual campus environment.

NEW TO THIS EDITION

Content
The content of this edition has been updated throughout to include the most recent research available. Some of the chapters have been separated into two or more chapters so that more up-to-date information could be added for each topic.

Part One. The History and Foundation of Residence Halls
The history of residence halls provides students with background as to why colleges provide residence halls. Educational philosophies are addressed and goals are provided. Comparisons between residential students and off-campus students are given to highlight the influence of the residence halls on students.

Part Two. Understanding and Working with College Students
Part Two discusses the growth and development of students and how they adjust to college life. Peer counseling is discussed along with models to aid RAs in counseling.

Part Three. Confrontation and Crisis Management
These chapters address behavior problems and discipline and provides a model for mediation. Strategies for suicide intervention and the symptoms of suicide are given. Violence and crime in residence halls includes discussion about battered women, rape, and other crimes on campus.

Part Four. Social Issues
We have included a chapter on each of the various abuses that students inflict upon themselves—food abuse, alcohol abuse, drug abuse.

The sexuality chapter explores the various issues related to student sexuality. A new stand alone chapter on sexual orientation addresses various homosexual issues relating to college students. Race and gender have been given their own chapter in this edition so that more in-depth study could be done relative to these issues.

Part Five. Educational Outreach

Two very important aspects of the RA position—educational programming and community development—provide helpful strategies to use with residents.

Part Six. RA Survival Skills

This part highlights the skills needed to manage the myriad tasks involved with RA roles. Learning how to study and preparing to take tests are topics included with this chapter as well.

FORMAT OF BOOK

Design

This edition is presented in a new format, including size of book and page layout and design. To make the book more user-friendly for the student, many significant ideas and concepts have been brought out of the text paragraphs and highlighted as call-outs and boxed material.

Review Questions

Each chapter has review questions for the student to use to test knowledge of chapter material.

Applications

Each chapter has applications in the form of vignettes at the end of the chapter. Students can work as a group to read the vignette and come to a conclusion as to how best to handle each case.

Ask Yourself

These sections provide questions to answer before making decisions regarding various tasks involved in overseeing the residence halls.

Strategies For

Strategies are used to give tips and ideas for dealing with many issues encountered as resident assistants.

References

The references are listed by chapter at the end of the book.

Index

An index is provided for easy location of words and concepts.

ACKNOWLEDGMENTS

The Resident Assistant: Working With College Students in Residence Halls, was first published in 1981. Dr. Lawrence J. Miltenberger and I co-authored the first edition and the two revisions—1984 and 1990—that followed it. Although Dr. Miltenberger did not participate in this revision, many of the ideas, thoughts, and experiences are those that I learned from him in our working relationship and our friendship in the past twenty years.

This book has benefited from the comments and suggestions made by RAs, chief housing officers, hall directors, and others throughout the nation who have used versions of this book during the past decade. I am indebted for the assistance that I received in completing the revision. Their comments and review of certain elements of the book have been a tremendous help. I also wish to thank Rainey Ratchford for her very helpful copy editing and Elizabeth Eckler for her research assistance. This revision would not have been possible without their great assistance.

PART ONE

THE HISTORY AND FOUNDATION OF RESIDENCE HALLS

The Roles and Responsibilities of the RA

The History of Residence Halls

Philosophies for Residence Halls

The Influence of Residence Halls
on the Development of Students

CHAPTER ONE

THE ROLES AND RESPONSIBILITIES OF THE RA

©1993 PHOTODISK, INC.

You have probably heard the expression "overworked and underpaid" many times. If it ever applied to a job, that job is that of the resident assistant, or RA, as this person is commonly known. If you are now at the stage where you are contemplating becoming an RA primarily because of the financial benefits, understand that the job simply does not pay enough. You can earn more money and spend much less time doing any number of part-time jobs in college. Most RAs receive minimal remuneration, usually equal to a single room and a meal contract for the year. This simply is not enough for all the work that you will be expected to do.

What is perhaps more important is that an RA's experience in college is uniquely different from that of other students. As an RA, you cannot always be a part of group activities in the living unit. Some students in the unit will ostracize you because of the authority that you represent. You will be intentionally left out of some group discussions and often not invited to share in the "inside information." Many tasks will be required of you, and some will force

3

you to reorder your personal priorities. You will be among the first students back to school in the fall of the year and among the last to leave in the spring. The same will be true of each vacation period.

Other students and the student affairs staff will place great demands on both your personal time and study time. Many activities with which you want to involve yourself must take second place to duty nights, working at the information desk, or advising students in the living unit. Even your friendship patterns will be somewhat defined by the residents that you are assigned to advise. You assume all of these demands, requirements, and expectations when you accept the responsibility of being an RA. It is not an easy job. Think very carefully before you accept it.

RA EDUCATIONAL SKILLS

To fulfill the educational mission of residence halls,
RAs need to acquire knowledge and skills in the following areas:

Skills	Scope
Conceptual Application	A basic understanding of human development, including the concepts and strategies necessary to help students in their development and growth toward adulthood
Counseling	Listening, referring people for additional help, empathizing, and helping others resolve problems
Basic Information	Knowledge of the services and procedures on your campus, rules and policies of the residence halls, and knowledge of academic and social survival skills
Administrative	Good organization, paperwork management, time management, and follow-through on projects started or assigned
Teaching	Two types required: programming skills and role-modeling skills. More traditional teaching skills may also be required for instructors (of other RAs or students)
Leadership	Setting objectives, motivating others, and supporting others in becoming leaders themselves
Crisis Management	The ability to view a crisis situation and control it effectively. Requires self-confidence, calmness, knowledge and direction of resources, good judgment, practice, and often good relational skills
Relational	Understanding of oneself and others and specific knowledge about such areas as motivation, sexuality, and behavioral problems. Requires the ability to react freely and communicate with others in a personal, inviting way

EXPECTATIONS OF THE RA

From campus to campus the responsibilities of RAs vary.
The following are responsibilities common to most RAs throughout the country:

Administrative

1. Prepares necessary reports and maintains records
2. Assists with public relations by being able to explain residence hall programs and staff duties to faculty, guests, parents, and students
3. Assists with room checks as required by hall operations
4. Assists with communications among staff members, students, and residence program leaders
5. Keeps residence hall director informed of major plans developed by students
6. Maintains good liaison relationship with housekeeping personnel
7. Regularly staffs the hall information desk

Institutional Representation

1. Sets an example by adhering to rules and regulations of the college or university
2. Knows the institution's and residence hall's regulations
3. Knows and explains the rationale for institution's rules and regulations
4. Informs students of institutional expectations
5. Encourages students to confront other students about violations
6. Assists in individual growth toward accountability
7. Knows and interprets the institution's philosophy of discipline
8. Reports behavioral infractions according to institutional policies
9. Supports, or does not openly disagree with, the institution's regulations

Residence Hall Environment

1. Helps students develop respect for each other's rights and freedoms
2. Helps students develop respect for private and institutional property
3. Encourages residents to attend residence hall and institutional programs
4. Encourages faculty to visit and talk informally with residents
5. Knows and communicates well with the residents
6. Is tolerant of different lifestyles
7. Encourages an atmosphere conducive to study
8. Promotes a feeling of community among residents

Individual Student Assistance

1. Becomes aware of individual student goals, abilities, and potential for achievement
2. Becomes aware of socially isolated students and helps them make friends and become a part of the campus community

(continued)

Individual Student Assistance—cont'd

3. Becomes aware of attitudes and behavior patterns of the residents on his or her floor
4. Knows resources in the campus community to help students
5. Refers students for help when they need it
6. Becomes aware of adjustment problems that new students experience
7. Makes himself or herself available for casual contacts and develops a pattern of available times for students to visit
8. Applies good listening and counseling skills
9. Applies good interpersonal skills
10. Becomes aware of his or her own strengths and weaknesses (is self-aware)
11. Shows concern for people and their problems
12. Follows up with students who have had a problem to see the results and to learn whether additional assistance should be given
13. Assists students with class scheduling as requested
14. Assists students in developing effective study habits

Hall Government Programs

1. Encourages students to take responsibility for residence hall programs
2. Helps students get involved with university clubs and organizations
3. Provides creative suggestions for hall programs
4. Initiates activities and programs by personal attendance

Information and Referrals

Keeps current on information about:
1. Sexually transmitted diseases
2. Suicide prevention techniques and referral services
3. University services and programs
4. Alcohol and drug education programs and behavior indicating the need for referral
5. Issues of student wellness and healthy lifestyl behaviors
6. Relationship violence, acquaintance rape, and about appropriate referral services

Parts adapted from Elizabeth A. Greenleaf, *Undergraduate Students as Members of the Residence Hall Staff* (Washington, D.C.: NAWDAC, 1967).

Though the responsibilities are great and the demands that will be placed on you throughout the academic year may be even greater, you also will benefit from this experience. The RA fills a unique role as a teacher and a leader that few students are privileged to experience. No other group of students receives the training, assistance, and attention that you will. This is an opportunity to grow, to learn, and to experience responsibility in a work situation.

Your first responsibility as an RA is to your studies.

THE RA AS STUDENT

The first role the RA has is that of a student. Although most RAs rank their educational goals as top priority, their responsibilities as students usually come to take second place to the RA position. This is unfortunate. The first responsibility of the RA should be to his or her studies. However, RAs often find their studies pushed to a second priority, and the RA position becomes all-consuming. People place unreasonable demands on RAs' time, and wishing to do a good job, many RAs find an increasing amount of their time spent working with other people's problems while their own studies are neglected.

Though some RAs find that the additional responsibilities make them better budget their time, many find that they enjoy being an RA much more than they enjoy being a student. They put all their time and energy into being an excellent RA, while their grades slip. Obviously, no one benefits if the RA loses the position because of poor grades. So when you take time to study and pursue important academic interests, you will be fulfilling one of the student affairs staff expectations for you as an RA.

Part of the limits to your availability can be explained in your first floor meeting. You should reinforce that you are available, that you are accessible, and that you want to be consulted about matters of concern to the residents. At the same time, you should make the point that you, too, are a student who needs to study. Close your door when you are studying and leave it open when you are not. An open door is an invitation to be interrupted.

Some residents will want all of your attention and will often spend their time in your room procrastinating. These people can consume monumental amounts of your study time. This can create a difficult situation, because you do not want to alienate your residents by refusing to spend time with them. You must find a balance between your personal priorities—that is, your studies and your own social life—and the needs of your residents. Do not be afraid occasionally to post a note on your door asking people not to disturb you for an hour or two unless it is an emergency. In the event of a crisis, you will be interrupted. If a problem needs your attention, your residents will need to consider it pressing enough to interrupt you during your study time.

Many routine questions can wait until you take a break or have finished your studying. If you have established a positive relationship with your residents, you will find that they will interrupt you only for truly important discussions. When you are not studying and are in your room, leave your door open so that the students will feel welcome to come and talk with you. You will find that students will contact you at the times you are available.

THE RA AS ROLE MODEL

Perhaps your most influential role as an RA is that of role model. By virtue of your position as a residence hall staff person, students know that you have certain characteristics that the university values. New freshmen view you as a model to emulate. This is one of the reasons for providing undergraduate RAs in undergraduate residence halls.

At one time, graduate students were used as RAs for undergraduate halls because these older students were thought to be able to assert more control over undergraduates and provide better counseling. However, appropriate role models are ones with which students can easily identify. If the role models are too far removed from what the individuals believe they can become, the role models have less influence. The standards and behavior exhibited by the role models must be perceived as attainable. Much of the behavior and many of the accomplishments of graduate students are not seen as attainable by undergraduates.

Undergraduate RAs have an advantage in that their experience is not too far removed from the experiences of incoming freshmen. The incoming freshmen can usually identify more easily with undergraduate RAs than with older graduate students.

As an RA, you model behavior that others will come to assume as appropriate for students in college. If you have good study skills, new students in your living unit are more likely to develop good study skills as well. Likewise, if you spend most of your time throwing a Frisbee up and down the hallway, drinking beer with people in your living unit, or continually find that your time is occupied by your boyfriend or girlfriend, you are setting an entirely different example of behavior.

As an RA you are expected to live by the rules and policies that your institution has set. Unless you can abide by them, do not expect your residents to do so. If you cannot abide by these policies, do not

RA ROLES

- Student
- Role Model
- Counselor
- Teacher
- Administrator

consider becoming an RA. When you accept responsibility as an RA, you also make a commitment to the position as it is defined. If you disagree with the administration's policies or regulations, try to change them through the appropriate supervisory channels. If you cannot change them and still cannot live with them, resign. Do not do yourself, the institution, and your residents a disservice by not enforcing the rules or by pretending that the policies and regulations do not exist.

Understand from the outset that your RA position extends outside your residence hall and onto the campus. This does not mean that you go about campus enforcing random rules and regulations, advising students on this and that, and asserting your staff position in places where it is not welcomed. It does mean that your role-modeling responsibility carries beyond your living unit. If you believe that you shed the cloak of RA when you leave your living unit, you are mistaken. While on campus—and at some universities off campus as well—you are expected to conduct yourself as a member of the staff. Amazingly, many RAs believe that as soon as they leave the residence hall they can become as wild and reckless as they please. Not only is this practice illogical, it is irresponsible.

Nor should you misuse your role as an RA. Perhaps the classic example of misusing one's position as an RA comes in writing editorials for the school newspaper. As a student you are entitled to submit whatever opinion you wish to your newspaper. Your position as an RA need not enter into it. Some RAs, however, send in their editorials and sign their names and their position title as though they were making official policy statements. Unless you have been elected to make an official policy statement for your residence programs office, avoid attaching your position to your personal opinions. Remember that the views you hold as an RA do not necessarily reflect the views of every other RA in your hall or institution as a whole.

Your role as a model for other students is one of the most important duties that you will assume. Handle the responsibility carefully and with the respect it deserves.

THE RA AS COUNSELOR

The third role of the RA is that of a counselor, consultant, or advisor. The word *counselor* may be a misnomer. The RA might more appropriately be considered to have a helping role. This function is an important part of being an RA. Students undergo many adjustments, stresses, and crises throughout the academic year. They are separated from their families, the comfortable and familiar surroundings of their homes, and their established friends. They are asked to live among a group of peers whom they do not know and asked to study and produce more than they have ever had to before. At the same time, they are undergoing tremendous psychological adjustments in their transition to adulthood. In the day-to-day living environment of the residence hall, many of these growth experiences, emotional traumas, and crises come to light. In residence halls students challenge each other's values. Students' knowledge of themselves and their ability to work with other people will be tested. For students accustomed to a quiet, private environment, a group living situation can be threatening and difficult. As an RA you are expected to help students through this experience.

Think for a moment how many challenges are placed before a student just within the first two weeks of college. Think back to your own experiences when you entered college. You did not know how to register for classes, how to get a meal pass, what to do if you were ill, or whom to see if you were experiencing a problem with a professor. Simple issues like these can become real problems for students who want to be accepted and are afraid to ask someone for help. New students fear that they will be labeled as less mature, less intelligent, or not part of the group. You are the person with this information and the one responsible for seeing that students get it. Providing information and helping are important functions of the RA position and among the primary reasons for its existence.

To provide such information in a counseling framework, you must establish a positive, friendly relationship with every person in your living unit—not selectively with only those you like, but an open, understanding, and warm relationship with each person in the unit. You must be accessible to everyone. You must be viewed as fair, consistent, and knowledgeable about the institution. Only after they know you as a person will students come to you with their problems. People do not share personal information with people they do not know and trust.

The helping role can be taken one step further. The RA has the best opportunity to help students who are experiencing minor problems and to identify students who are experiencing major problems. Identification of students who are undergoing personal crisis or severe depression can literally save someone's life.

THE RA AS TEACHER

The fourth role that the RA assumes is that of a teacher. This role includes teaching in a formal sense, not simply the informal teaching involved in role modeling. The RA teaches: (1) general information about the university, about events happening on campus, and about services offered; (2) by inviting speakers to the living unit in conjunction with residents, thereby creating a situation in which formal learning takes place; (3) group-process skills in floor meetings, in groups planning activities, in floor elections, through student activities within the building, and through intramural activities; (4) values, both through his or her own personal behavior and through late-night discussions (bull sessions) in which such issues as sex, religion, politics, and career plans are discussed. The RA is an agent in this teaching process and at the same time becomes a learner; for not only does he or she challenge other students' values, but his or her own values are also challenged.

Of all these teaching roles, educational programming is probably the most visible sign of teaching. It is the time in which the RA has the opportunity to bring a host of different ideas to the collective experience of the members of his or her floor.

THE RA AS ADMINISTRATOR

Most RAs have a set of administrative duties they must perform. Check-in, check-out, filing incident reports, and performing other administrative duties for the housing and residence life office are common to the RA position. Although the administrative duties are not the central reason why universities employ RAs, the administrative duties are important to the function of the residence halls. Accurate and reliable information and records provided by RAs help insure the efficient and effective management of residence halls. When residence halls are managed well, the cost of living in a residence hall is reduced and students benefit. Repairs and maintenance issues that occur in the normal operation of residence halls are more quickly addressed when the RA initiates the process to have these items attended to.

Good administration is a matter of organization, discipline, and the application of knowledge about structures and procedures for specific situations. It is an important skill to learn, and the RA position provides you with an opportunity to learn it. RAs who are poor administrators usually are poor time managers and are poorly organized. These deficiencies usually result in greater student dissatisfaction with residence hall living and with the RA. Enough conflicts arise in a residence hall setting without adding to it the conflicts which arise from poor administration and poor communication about administrative procedures and processes. You, as the RA, can be of great assistance in helping the university to maintain a high level of student satisfaction and to provide the best and most reliable services to your residents.

ESTABLISHING YOURSELF WITH YOUR RESIDENTS

No matter how well you have prepared yourself to help students with their problems, unless students are willing to discuss their concerns with you, you may not have an opportunity to use those skills. The opinion that your residents have of you is important to your success. If they view you as a person solely concerned with the enforcement of college policies, concerned only about yourself and your friends, or concerned only with the prestige and authority of the RA position, this will affect their willingness to share their concerns with you.

First Impressions and the Start of School

The first few days of the academic term are critical in establishing yourself with your residents. The first impression you make on your new residents will have a lingering effect; it will either lay the foundation for further contacts or create barriers to them. Some RAs begin this process during the summer, before the school year, by contacting each of their residents by mail. Although this is a time-consuming process, the early expression of concern may pay off in better relationships later.

Make an aggressive attempt to contact your residents as they arrive. Within the first week, you should have met and learned something about each resident. Many RAs make a list of the residents' names and room numbers on a floor diagram and keep it with them until they have committed it to memory. The list can also be used as a check to ensure that you have met each of the residents. By the time of the first floor meeting, you should have met and talked with each person in your unit, if only briefly.

In the following few weeks, you should make a point to stop at each student's room for a few minutes to become more familiar with them. People like to talk about themselves and what they do. Share things about yourself; tell them about your hobbies, your interests, your college major, and anything else that interests you.

Part of what you do in establishing yourself is to develop a sense of belonging among the members of your floor. You do this by finding ways for people in your living unit to interact. Dinner is always a good opportunity to have a group of your residents get to know one another. Make certain, especially during the first few weeks, that you invite some of the new residents in the unit to have dinner with you and any of the other residents with whom you usually dine. It is important that you make an effort to include all residents in your living unit as part of the group.

Once you have made the initial contact, follow up with each student. If a resident tells you that he or she is taking a math class or is trying to locate a particular building, make certain that you ask about that particular topic when you next see him or her. You really have several goals to accomplish during these first few days. First, learn the names of your residents. Second, learn their backgrounds. Third, learn something unique about them as individuals. And, fourth, learn something you can follow up on later. This follow-up is an important way to demonstrate that you care.

These initial contacts will be important in helping you establish the respect of your residents. This respect can more easily be lost than acquired. Contact, recognition, reinforcement, and similar forms of support must continue throughout the academic year.

Establishing and Enforcing Policies

Students are not compelled by college policy to contact you for assistance, to respect you, or for the most part, to follow your directions. Your residents do not report to you, and you do not have supervisory responsibility for them. Instead, your authority in the living units is derived primarily from the authority that the students are willing to give you. To the extent that your residents respect you, recognize your competence, and come to you for information and assistance, you have authority in your living unit. It is true that you can make a disciplinary referral, but chances are that any other student at your institution can make the same referral.

You do have some authority by virtue of the responsibilities assigned to you and the fact that the institution recognizes your authority to intervene in certain situations. The point is that your effectiveness in the RA position depends on how students view you in that role. If you attempt to present yourself as perfect, unapproachable, always correct, and puritanical, it is likely that few of your residents will come to you with their concerns for fear that you will condemn them or at least lose respect for them. On the other hand, if you conduct yourself in a drunken, rowdy, and slovenly manner, students likely will feel that you are unable to handle your own problems, let alone theirs.

The respect of your residents is an important element in performing your job. It is not always easily gained, but it is easily lost. Being respected and being liked need not be mutually exclusive.

The issue of being liked and being respected always seems to play a critical role in the area of policy enforcement. Some RAs confuse being liked with being lenient about the enforcement of policies. Once you have explained the policies, the rationale behind them, and the institution's instructions to you on their enforcement, you have taken the first step in establishing the expectations for enforcement of these policies.

One good way to undermine your credibility is to inform your residents of the institution's policies and then add your commentary on the policies with which you agree and those with which you do not agree. "The university told me to enforce the marijuana policy. I personally disagree with it, but I have to enforce it." You are sending out a dual message to your residents. You have told them that you are doing something in which you do not believe. This is a difficult position for other people to respect. An easier position to respect is "The university has this policy; the reason for this policy is . . ." If somebody asks you if you agree or disagree with the policy, your stock answer should be, "My personal beliefs about these policies are not an issue" or, "Yes, I believe in this policy and I have found it to be supported by most of the other staff." The fact that you agree or disagree with a particular policy really is not the issue. If you have accepted the responsibility of the job, you have accepted the responsibility to carry out the policies.

During the first few weeks, some students may feel a need to challenge your enforcement of policies. This is a testing period. Students will try to determine how strict you are, how sincere you are about enforcement, and what the real behavioral boundaries are. This testing is like testing the enforcement of the speed limit. The speed limit may be posted at 55 mph, but chances are good that one will not be ticketed until traveling 60 or 65 mph.

Some students need to determine the tolerance limits of behavior. If you allow Frisbee wars in the hallways at the beginning of the year, or allow people to hit golf balls or play soccer in the hallway, play their stereos loud enough to rattle the bathroom fixtures in buildings two blocks away, flood the hallway with water, or to throw toilet paper from the bathroom windows, then be prepared to permit this kind of behavior throughout the year. It is much easier to set reasonable limits at the start of the year than to stop excessive behavior once it has begun.

It is more important that people feel that you treat everyone equally, that you are consistent, and that you are fair than to have them believe you are doing them a favor by letting them do what they want. You need to communicate to your residents that a group-living situation carries with it special duties to respect the rights of others.

This means some restrictions on personal freedom. In a community-living situation, people simply do not have the personal freedom to play their stereos as loud as they wish until whatever hour they choose. Some students are selfish and will not want to acknowledge these limitations on their freedom. Chances are that your relationship with them will become strained as you help them develop this understanding.

Availability

Being available to all of the residents of your living unit is a complex task. If you spend the majority of your time with a small clique of people, you run the risk of alienating other segments of the unit. The same applies to spending most of your time with other staff members, as is often the case. You must balance your personal need for comradeship with the needs of your residents, which is not an easy task.

Students are sensitive. If they continually see you in the company of other RAs, they begin seeing you as a member of an elite club in which they cannot participate. This is difficult for RAs, who often find that their closest and most supportive associations are with other RAs. It is equally difficult for the hall director, who wants to establish a spirit of unity among the staff yet wants to ensure that the needs of the building residents are met. If all the RAs congregate in one or two of the RAs' rooms, you are not spending your available time with your residents. You will then be viewed as an outsider who only comes to the living unit to deal with behavior problems, to change the bulletin board, or to enforce regulations. In some cases this can develop into a "we-them" mentality about working with students in the hall that lessens students' willingness to approach RAs for assistance. You must become part of the living unit, a part of the team. It is not an easy job. It takes time and continued effort.

Confidentiality

Confidentiality is essential. Probably the quickest way to lose the respect of your residents and to ruin opportunities to help students with personal problems is to begin sharing a student's personal problems with other members of the floor. Although the individual to whom you are speaking may feel good about you taking him or her into your confidence, he or she will be wondering if you share what he or she tells you with others.

Inevitably, if you violate a student's confidence, it gets back to that student. Not only will that person probably never trust you again with any important information, but chances are that that person's friends will not trust you either.

The only person with whom you should legitimately share these confidences is the hall director. Occasionally some information may be shared with other members of the RA staff, but only when there is a legitimate reason for them to have this information. The indiscriminate sharing of information can quickly generate a lack of trust among the residents in your unit. This is another reason why continual association with the other RAs in the building helps engender a feeling among the residents that the RAs are an exclusive group who get together and share information about their units. No one wants his or her personal feelings, beliefs, or confidences shared with large groups of people. If students have shared personal information with you, they do not expect you to share it with every other person on the staff.

Again, if you require advice about a shared confidence, consult the hall director. There may be no need to share certain confidential information with the hall director, but the confidential information that you receive should be considered available to your hall director. You do not keep secrets from the person who hired you, has responsibility for your actions, has trained you, and who is interested in achieving the same objectives you are. If you do not believe that you can share certain confidential information with your hall director, either you should not have agreed to accept the information or you have a problem *in your relationship with your hall director that must be resolved.*

The best way to establish yourself with residents in your living unit is to be yourself. After all, one of the factors that gained you the position was your personality and your ability to get along with other people. Let that come forth. Be sincere and honest about yourself. Do not try to assume any superficiality about your job, what you will be doing during the year, or your authority. Be open, be yourself, and be available.

Remember that not everyone will like you, but that is not your goal. Your goal is to let everyone know that you care and are concerned about them as individuals, that you are willing to help, that you have information and training to help them if they choose to take advantage of it, and that you are available to them.

INTERPERSONAL RELATIONSHIPS AND THE RA

As an RA you may find that some of your relationships with students in your living unit are not of the quality you would like. It is difficult for RAs to establish interpersonal relationships with their residents. Students often feel that to get close to the RA is a form of seeking favoritism. Other students may discourage this behavior by teasing students who are attempting to establish close relationships with their RAs. If you do not establish close relationships in your living unit, the problem may not be with you but with your position.

Often RAs become so consumed with being an RA that they neglect their own needs for recreation and escape. You should develop friendships in your living unit and among the RAs, but also outside of the residence hall. These friendships may help you maintain some objectivity about what you are doing and can provide a much needed retreat from the subtle pressures of residence hall work.

Dear Brad:

I'm a month into my RA job, and it's not at all what I expected. Some of it's fun but some of it's a drag. Our hall director is new this year and is trying to do a good job. He seems like a pretty nice guy, and I think he'll be good to work with. The RA staff this year is great. Everyone seems so motivated and there is a lot of competition to see who can do the best job with the start of the year. Three of the RAs are returning from last year and have been a real help in telling us how to handle a lot of the details of the job.

I met all the residents the first day they arrived but have not had a chance to get to know all their names. I hope to do that in the next few weeks, but it's hard with all the other things I have to do. What's surprising is that the floor has divided up into small groups. The guys at one end of the floor don't know the guys at the other end of the floor, and there seems to be a couple of groups in the middle that gravitate toward one side or the other. I wish I could get everybody together in a large group, but I'm not sure this is going to be possible.

At the first floor meeting, I was the only person who talked. I tried to get the students to interact and to share some personal information about themselves, but most of the guys seemed uninterested or unwilling to do that. Half of them I had to drag out of their rooms to go to the meeting. There are about four guys on the floor who I suspect I'm going to have trouble with. I know they've been drinking in their room, but I haven't caught them. They seem to be pretty arrogant and want to play "tough guy" all the time. I think I also have a group of guys on the floor who have been smoking dope. It's only a matter of time until I catch them. I spoke with them the other day and told them that I thought I smelled marijuana smoke coming from the room and re-minded them of the university's policy. The students denied it and said they were just burning incense—right, like I'm going to believe that. I really don't want to start the year off by busting a bunch of people, but I'm not sure I'll have much of an alternative.

We have a bunch of guys who turned out for the floor's intramural soccer team. Some are really good. Soccer seems to be the most popular sport here on the floor. We only had five guys who were interested in flag football and had to join up with one of the other floors to form a team.

The RA job is really cutting into my study time. I had duty last weekend and spent about three hours at the main desk and the rest of the time in my room in case there was a problem in the residence hall. You can't get any studying done at the main desk because people keep coming by and bothering you. Twice last Saturday night I got called out, once because a guy was drunk and loud and had to be written up because he was keeping everybody else awake. It wasn't on my floor. The second call was at about 3:30 in the morning. The police department had a report that some people on one of the floors were throwing stuff out of the bathroom windows. I went to that room but didn't find anyone. It was obvious they had thrown a bunch of stuff out the window onto the ground.

(continued)

I think some of the guys are developing some trust in me. I've had two of the new students, freshmen, come by to just chat and spend some time in my room. One of them began talking about his family life and what a hard time he had at home with his parents. I think the guy needs some counseling and tried to talk him into going over to talk to somebody in the counseling center, but he said he didn't want to do that. My guess is that by the end of the semester I'll get him over there to talk with somebody. Another guy on the floor is having problems with his girlfriend; she dumped him. He's kind of freaked out about it. He was really drunk the other night and was feeling really sorry for himself. I went down to talk with him, along with his roommate and some other guys. We shared some of our own date problems and I think that made him feel better.

Two of the guys on my floor are gay. They're roommates and are pretty open about the fact that they're gay. Most of the guys are pretty cool about it. A couple of the new guys, freshmen, were doing the macho routine and making jokes about fags and queers. I had a talk with them. I told them I didn't want to get this kind of stuff started on the floor and that it was none of their business what these guys did. I tried to explain to them what I had learned in RA training about sexual orientation, but these students weren't in the mood to listen. One of them kept quoting Bible verses and the other kept talking about what he would do if they got close to him. I made it clear to both of them what I would do if they harassed these guys—that they would be sent to the dean of students' office for discipline. I think that got their attention, but I'll have to wait and see.

That's all for now. I'll write again soon.

Luke

Dear Lisa,

Midterms are only a week away, and I can't believe how much studying I have to do. The women on my floor this year have been just great. Our floor is leading in intramural soccer, and two of the women on my floor were elected to the SGA senate. Both are very sharp. We've had a few roommate conflicts this semester but nothing too serious. The major problem seems to be that the university assigned the sloppiest students with the neatest students. It's so hard to work these things out because both sides can make good points about their freedom to live in their room the way they want to. I worked hard to try to develop some roommate agreements between them, and I think I have things worked out for the time being.

I've gotten somewhat behind in my studying because there's been so much to do as an RA. I've already put on three programs this semester and still have two more to do to meet the programming requirement. I think there's just too many programs expected of us. Attendance at the programs has been o.k. but not great. I think the best program we did was a self-defense demonstration

(continued)

that we did with two other floors. The person we brought in showed us really easy things we can do to defend ourselves if we're attacked.

I exchanged duty nights with several of the other RAs over the last couple of weeks so I could have some free time around midterms. I hope this was good planning on my part, but now I'm behind in some of my studying. My thinking was that if I could arrange a block of time without interruptions from the RA job I would be able to really focus on my courses during the exam period. Last weekend I was on duty and it seemed I lost the whole weekend as far as studying goes. We had two problems last weekend that just seemed to consume all of my time. First, one of my residents and her boyfriend got into a big fight. He had been drinking and began yelling and pushing her around. Her roommate came and got me. He was totally out of control and slammed the door in my face. I was afraid for her safety and had to call the police. As soon as he found out I called the police, he left the building. When the police officer arrived, I gave him the report and room number but nothing was done. My resident, Susan, didn't want anything done to him and wasn't willing to sign an official complaint. The incident will get referred to the hall director, and I hope she'll refer it on to the student discipline office. She's been pretty good about those things, and I like working with her. We also had a drug bust last weekend, and since I was the RA on duty I had to be there. While I was making rounds, it was obvious that a bunch of people were in a room smoking dope. I called the hall director, and she came to the room. This was on the floor right below me, and the RA for that floor had gone home for the weekend. This was the first time I had to do a drug bust, and I didn't like it very much. I couldn't believe how well my hall director handled it. She did everything by the book and I didn't have to get too involved. She told me I will have to testify at the student disciplinary hearing as a witness to what transpired. I'm not looking forward to it, but it goes with the job.

I'm still dealing with one of the women from my floor who didn't get a bid at sorority rush. She was so upset that I thought she would leave school. I've talked with her at least half a dozen times about the process and told her not to worry about it, that most of the students here aren't in a sorority, that it really didn't make any difference. She was an emotional wreck for about a week. Her parents came down and spent the weekend with her, and the hall director talked with her twice. Things seem a little better, but I'm not convinced she'll make it this semester. The real problem seems to be that the girls that live across the hall and the girls next to her were all pledged to sororities and have been going out to do a lot of things with their sorority. I talked with them privately and asked them not to flaunt their sorority involvement in front of this girl because she is feeling so bad. They understood and have talked to her about everything. It's possible that she will get pledged in the second semester when the sororities aren't limited by quotas.

Well, I have to get on with my studying. I'm doing reasonably well in most of my engineering courses but have to really put in the time to keep up. I'm not sure I'll be able to do the RA job next year. The courses I have to take in my

(continued)

junior year look unbelievably difficult. With all the administrative duties they expect me to do, all the things that my residents need me to do, and the two projects I've agreed to help with for the Key Club, I literally have no time left. Despite all this, I enjoy my job and have learned more than I thought I would. The other RAs in the building have been a great support and we've become close friends. I started dating one of the other RAs, but we have to be careful not to spend too much time together in each other's rooms, because then our residents won't come in and talk with us. We're working it out. Write when you can.
Your friend,
Gwen

WHAT IS IT REALLY LIKE?

The RA position may be one you have to live to truly understand. Following are two letters based on comments made by RAs over a number of years. The letters attempt to describe what it is really like.

BURNOUT

College is a very hectic time in a person's life. It is even more so because of your responsibilities as an RA. You must not only contend with the day-to-day pressures of academic work but also with stress associated with the intensity of personal relations strained by your responsibilities and magnified by living with students that you are trained to assist.

Everyone needs quiet time each day—time in which you know that you will not be interrupted. This might be an hour set aside just for you to do whatever you want. If it is only for 15 minutes at the end of the day, it may help you to relieve some of the stress and deal with your job and other people's problems more objectively.

Psychologists have found that a person undergoing a series of major stresses in a short period of time can become overstressed or burned out. Some major stress producers include a major job promotion, marriage, divorce, and a death in the family.

An accumulation of too many of these major stress producers in a short period of time can overstress a person. Taking on a series of new leadership roles or committing to more than you can do will also lead to burnout.

As an RA, you are a good candidate for burnout. People tend to place great demands on your time. School, parents, job expectations, the expectations of your residents, and your career objective can all be sources of stress; if you live in a hall that has frequent discipline problems with students or that is loud and congested, these factors will cause you stress, the accumulation of which may cause burnout.

You have two choices. You can stay in the RA position and find effective coping mechanisms (such as exercise, meditation, biofeedback, or counseling) or you can separate yourself from the stress (quit your job). Spend time thinking about what steps you are willing to take to avoid burnout.

Stress affects everyone. The key to dealing with it is to recognize when you are under stress and learn what situations produce stress for you. If you can learn to cope with and prevent stress in yourself, you can more efficiently accomplish your goals. The regular practice of a relaxation technique or exercise will not only combat and relieve stress but may also provide additional benefits. Effectively dealing with stress enhances your health, general well-being, and productivity. Not confronting it can only lead to problems.

CONCLUSION

The RA position is one of the most comprehensive roles in the student affairs division. No student problem escapes the RA's involvement. This job is one of the most difficult student positions to hold and to perform well. To be called to do so many tasks, to hold so many responsibilities, and to be accountable for so many other people during the time when you are shaping your own education is one of the greatest challenges you will face during early adulthood.

REVIEW

1. What are four reasons why someone may not want to become an RA.

2. What are four benefits of becoming an RA.

3. What are the four major roles of an RA?

4. Which of the roles do you believe is most important? Why?

5. What do you believe is the most unrealistic expectation students have of RAs? Why?

6. What do you believe is the most unrealistic expectation college administrators have of RAs? Why?

7. What are the conceptual application skills that RAs need?

APPLICATIONS

HALL-SOCCER

Norwood was the RA on Four-West. This floor had over half of the residents return to the floor from the previous year. It had the reputation of being rowdy, but also of having a strong sense of community among the residents. The RA on the floor last year was very popular with the residents and made many friends. This was Norwood's first year as an RA, and he wanted to be as well liked as last year's RA and to do a good job for the university.

About halfway through the second week of the semester, Norwood returned to his floor and found about fifteen of his residents in the hallway and lounge playing hall-soccer. This game had been invented by the residents and involved kicking a soccer ball down the corridor and into the lounge where a goal consisting of the sofa and two chairs had been erected. The game stopped when they saw Norwood. Mike, one of the men who had lived on the floor for the past two years and who was very popular with the other residents, was holding the ball when Norwood appeared. Norwood asked what they were doing, and Mike explained that they were playing hall-soccer. He told Norwood that they played all last year and play the game at least three or four nights a week for several hours at a time. The scuffed walls and broken light fixtures bore proof of Mike's statement.

WHAT WOULD YOU DO?

1. Norwood does not know what to do. If he stops the game, he believes that he will lose the friendship of most of the residents and may break a floor tradition which gives the residents a chance to interact. What would you do if you were Norwood?

2. What, if anything, could Norwood have done to avoid this happening?

WHAT WE VALUE

Claudine was a first-year RA and was a member of a campus group that took an activist stand opposing abortion. They believed that any effort necessary to save the life of an unborn child was justified. She was a warm and personable individual who was well liked in the residence hall. In fact, her warm personality and outgoing style were two of the reasons she was selected as an RA.

When the residence halls opened in the fall semester, Claudine wore a button that said "Abortion is Murder." To every student who obtained a key, she handed an antiabortion pamphlet that had been produced by the organization to which she belonged. The bulletin board on her floor had a series of photographs showing fetuses that had been aborted at different stages of pregnancy. During the fall semester, her programming effort for her floor included a lecture about abortion conducted by two women who headed the local antiabortion effort.

During the first two weeks of class, Claudine went door-to-door among the residents in the building asking them to sign a petition opposing abortion. She and several other students wrote letters to the editor of the student newspaper about abortion. Claudine did not indicate in her letter to the editor that she was an RA; the letter she wrote was signed only with her name and the residence hall where she lived.

In her first floor meeting, Claudine encouraged students who had any questions about abortion to discuss them with her. She said that she knew a lot about this issue and that if anybody was thinking about having an abortion to please come to her so she could give them information. She said that she had been trained as a peer counselor by the university and as an abortion educator by one of the organizations to which she belonged. She was willing and eager to share her time and energy in helping any young women who needed her support and help with handling an unwanted pregnancy.

WHAT WOULD YOU DO?

1. If you were a student on Claudine's residence hall floor, how would you feel about Claudine asking you to sign a petition?

2. If you or a female friend were considering having an abortion, is Claudine a person you would seek out to discuss this issue? Why or why not?

3. Should residence life officials intercede and inform Claudine that she should curtail her antiabortion activities while she is an RA? Why or why not?

4. Do you believe that Claudine can be objective in counseling students about abortions and in referring them to resources in the counseling center or health center that may have a different perspective?

5. How would you feel about living on Claudine's floor as one of her residents?

AN UNLIKELY MATCH

Norwood asked Claudine to go to a party with him off campus. While at the party, they each saw several people they knew, including several of their residents. The drinking age in the state was 21, and the people having the party had legally purchased a keg of beer. Norwood and Claudine were both 19 years old, but both drank alcohol occasionally. The university prohibited alcohol on campus, and RAs were expected to enforce this policy in the residence halls.

Claudine and Norwood both saw several of their underage residents drinking alcohol, but neither one commented to the other about it. Claudine stopped and talked with one of her residents. While she was talking, Norwood got himself and Claudine each a beer. Norwood came to where Claudine and her resident were standing and handed her the beer.

WHAT WOULD YOU DO?

1. What should Claudine do? Should she accept the beer?

2. Should Claudine report Norwood to his hall director for drinking alcohol at the off-campus party where some of his residents are also drinking?

3. Should Claudine report the illegal use of alcohol by her residents at the off-campus party to her hall director?

4. Would your response to the above questions be different if Norwood offered Claudine marijuana, and marijuana was being smoked by a number of the party guests including Claudine's residents and Norwood's residents? Why or why not?

FOURTH DOWN AND LONG

Juan was a new RA in a men's residence hall. He was responsible for a floor of approximately 40 men. He wanted to do a good job as an RA and to be liked by his residents. The first week of school he organized a large group of his residents to go off campus with him to a private club where they serve beer or wine to people over 18—which is legal in private clubs in his state. He also had men from his floor in his room most of the time playing cards and socializing.

At the beginning of the year, Juan told his residents that he wanted them to have a good time in college and that he would always be available to them. He told them that university regulations did not permit alcohol in undergraduate residence halls, that marijuana and all other drugs were forbidden, and that there should be quiet hours each school evening from 8:00 P.M. to 8:00 A.M. He told his residents that he was not going to be a cop, and as long as he did not see anything, they would be all right.

Juan would usually watch Monday night football in the room of his former roommate who lived on another floor in the same building. In the privacy of his roommate's room, he and his old roommate would usually have a few beers while they enjoyed the game. About halfway into the semester, his roommate was ill and not able to watch Monday night football with Juan. Juan went to the library instead, to study for midterm exams. He returned about 10:00 P.M. When he entered the building, he met the duty RA who said he got a complaint about the noise on Juan's floor and was on his way to check on it.

When the two RAs entered the floor, they saw about 20 of Juan's residents in the floor lounge drunk and yelling about the football game they were watching on TV. One of the older residents had purchased a pony-keg of beer with money he had collected from the other residents. When the duty RA asked what was going on, the residents told him to stop interrupting the game, that they did this every Monday night, and to mind his own business.

WHAT WOULD YOU DO?

1. Should the duty RA report this unauthorized party and violation of the alcohol regulations to the hall director? Why or why not?

2. Juan asks the duty RA not to report the situation to the hall director because of previous complaints about him and Juan is afraid that he will be fired. Juan promises he will talk to his residents about the situation. If you were the duty RA, would you still report the situation? Why or why not?

3. What should Juan do? Should he report the students to the hall director? Why or why not?

4. If Juan reports the students, he is afraid the residents will stop liking him and will not come to him when they have problems. Is Juan right? Why or why not?

5. Is it possible to be both liked and respected by students when you are an RA? If you answer yes, explain how to do this. If you answer no, explain why this is not possible.

6. What could Juan have done to avoid this situation?

CHAPTER TWO

THE HISTORY OF RESIDENCE HALLS

©1998 PHOTODISK, INC.

R esidence halls owe their origin to the housing problem created during the Middle Ages by thousands of "wandering students"[1] flocking to universities in Bologna, Paris, and Oxford. The number of these students was considerable:

In 1262 at Bologna, the faculties were lecturing to 10,000 students—twice as many students as there were people living in the

local town. In 1257, there were 30,000 students enrolled at the University of Paris. There were more students than townspeople. And so it has been down through the ages. Any time that a group of learned men band together for the purpose of imparting knowledge, the youth of that age gather about them, sometimes in numbers which create very difficult problems in the field of housing.[2]

The sheer numbers of these otherwise home-less young men, most of whom were only 14 or 15 years old, created considerable problems in the customarily small cities of the early to mid-1200s. As it was, "the number of students was so much in excess of any possible provision for them that they lived in tents, they camped in the fields, in fact some places they burrowed into the sides of hills."[3] In time, students moved from living with schoolmasters and townspeople to rented houses that became known as "hostels" in Bologna, *"paedagogies"* in Paris, "halls" or "colleges" at Oxford, and *"Bursen"* at German universities. For the most part, the residents of these houses were self-governing. However, by the mid-1400s these houses had come under the control of university authorities.

ROOTS IN THE BRITISH COLLEGIATE SYSTEM

Many of the students attending Oxford and Cambridge Universities in the Middle Ages were poor. To assist these students, Oxford University established *domus pauperum* (endowed hostels) as charitable institutions. The endowed halls, which subsequently appeared at Cambridge, came to be known as colleges. This system of colleges flourished from the fourteenth to the eighteenth century throughout most of Europe.

During the 1800s, this system of colleges began to vanish in continental Europe. In Germany, clerics who followed Martin Luther expressed concern over any institution that housed students in anything that remotely resembled the monkish orders of the Catholic monasteries. The *Bursen* resembled the living arrangement of Catholic monasteries too closely, and the Germans abandoned this form of student housing.

The French Revolution further sealed the fate of college-operated housing for students in continental Europe. A new class of students were now attending universities and most did not have money for housing. The collegiate system of colleges and halls, which had its origin at the University of Paris, grew to maturity in England but survived only at Oxford and Cambridge.[4]

Dormitories

Originally taken from the word *dormant*, meaning "to sleep," *dormitory* literally means "a place to sleep." Although at one time colleges and universities had large sleeping rooms known as dormitories, most institutions abandoned this form of housing. The use of the word *dormitory* is inappropriate to describe contemporary residence halls because they are now used for studying, socializing, educational programs, and other activities in addition to sleep.

Charles F. Thwing, president of Western Reserve University and Adelbert College, explained how the word *dormitory* first came into being:

> *The word "dormitory," in its present meaning, is a new word in academic language; in its present meaning standing for a building used by a college for housing students. Mullinger, the historical of Cambridge, uses the word in contrast with* study *in speaking of a student of his university of about the year 1550. The present meaning was formerly taken by the "hostel" or "college" or "hall." The hostel of the English universities of three hundred years ago was a lodging house under the charge of a principal, where students resided at their own cost. The word was never transferred to America. . . . The word* college, *as applied to a building, has been the favorite word in American academic usage. . . . The brick row at Yale of eight buildings was composed of colleges, though* hall *was the term applied in the earlier time. . . . Hall is still used and to it have*

been added house *or* cottage *or* halls of residence, *especially as applied to women's colleges. Dormitory has within fifty years come into good use. It can hardly be called a fitting word except for those who wish, in their earnestness or wit, to represent the college as torpid.*[5]

ORIGINS IN THE UNITED STATES

When the English colonized North America, they brought with them the traditions and concepts of education learned in England. In 1636, the Congregationalists founded Harvard University using as their model what they had known as students at Oxford and Cambridge. Of the original nine colonial colleges (Harvard College, New Jersey University, Yale University, College of William and Mary, King's College, Philadelphia Academy, College of Rhode Island, Queens College, and Dartmouth College), all but two were founded by graduates of either Oxford or Cambridge. The College of William and Mary was founded by James Blair, a graduate of Edinburgh University, and the Philadelphia Academy was founded by Benjamin Franklin. According to W. H. Cowley, "The British background of the prerevolutionary college organizers had more to do with the establishment of residential colleges in America than any other factor."[6]

The collegiate system of Oxford and Cambridge focused on building a student's character and intellect to develop a member of the English gentry who was both a scholar and a gentleman. The residential colleges were the focus of this learning. The faculty worked closely with students serving as role models and mentors.

Unfortunately, the American system of residence halls did not provide students with this same intellectual atmosphere and social spirit. Part of this is due to the abandonment of the class system of England and part to the pioneering fashion in which the American colleges grew.[7] Students as young as 13 and 14 attended American institutions. Attending college frequently required traveling great distances during a period of time when travel was difficult and often dangerous, so living and boarding at the college was a necessity.

Unlike the English system of residential colleges, faculty at American colleges were expected to assume all manner of duties, from proctoring residence halls to classroom instruction. At Oxford and Cambridge, deans, proctors, and beadles had been employed to attend to these affairs, leaving the faculty free to engage students in scholarship and expose them to the social rules of being English gentlemen. Responsibility for student discipline was one of the more practical reasons why the collegiate system of residential colleges had such difficulty in becoming established in America.[8] The disciplinary conflict between faculty and students was cited as one of the primary reasons residence halls in American colleges never came to serve as the core of the educational program as they did in England. According to Cowley,

In America, . . . the faculty member living in the dormitory became the student's natural enemy. Circumstances made him a martinet, and conscientiously he lived up to his responsibilities. The results are well known. Student riots and rebellions against the faculty have bespattered the historical records of every college up until the inception of athletics and extracurricular activities in the last decade of the nineteenth century.[9]

NINETEENTH CENTURY DISREGARD FOR STUDENT HOUSING

The nineteenth century was a difficult time for American colleges. Historian Frederick

Rudolph described some of the problems associated with residence hall living in the 1800s:

In the commons room of the dormitory at South Carolina College in 1833, two students at the same moment grabbed for a plate of trout. Only one of them survived the duel that ensued. Among the victims of the collegiate way were the boy that died in the duel at Dickinson, the students who were shot at Miami of Ohio, the professor who was killed at the University of Virginia, the president of Oakland College in Mississippi who was stabbed to death by a student, the student who was stabbed at Illinois College, the students who were stabbed and killed at the University of Missouri, the president and professor who were stoned at the University of Georgia, and the University of North Carolina. For this misfortune these victims of the college life could thank the dormitory, the time house of incarceration and infamy that sustained the collegiate way.[10]

It is little wonder that in 1852, President Henry Tappen of the University of Michigan converted one of the university's residence halls into classrooms. Tappen gave this rationale: "The dormitory system is objectionable in itself. By withdrawing young men from the influence of domestic circles and separating them from the community, they are often led to contract evil habits and are prone to fall into disorderly conduct."[11]

Tappen was not alone in his condemnation of "dormitory" life. Presidents Francis Wayland at Brown University and Frederick Barnard at Columbia University shared his sentiments about residence halls. Tappen and many other educators came to embrace the "Prussian system of education," which placed no value on what students did outside the classroom. Faculty educated at German universities fought to replace the "overbearing paternalism of their clerical predecessors, and . . . [substituted] impersonalism."[12] Student housing and social life were viewed as beyond the concern of the university, which was to expand the fields of knowledge and train the minds of young scholars. Following the Civil War, many German scholars and Americans trained in German universities joined the faculties of American institutions, which further ingrained this educational philosophy into the character of American colleges.

American colleges attempted to regulate student behavior by imposing prescriptive sets of rules. In 1870 one small denominational and coeducational college published its rules in a small book, which President Kolbe of Drexel University read to the Eighteenth Annual Conference of the National Association of Deans and Advisers of Men in 1936. President Kolbe quoted the following rules for students of the 1870s:

1. *Students are expected to be kind and respectful to others.*
2. *Students, while connected with the college, are strictly forbidden the use of intoxicating liquors and tobacco, profanity, or indecent language on the college premises, or so far as the college has any jurisdiction.*
3. *Students must refrain from all improprieties in the halls, boisterous talking, or scuffling.*
4. *Young men and women are not allowed to take rides or walks without permission.*
5. *No student will fire gunpowder in college buildings, or on the premises, or engage in card playing or any other form of gambling in college, or in the city, or commit injuries upon the person or property of any student.*
6. *The faculty shall have the authority to visit and search any room in college, using force if necessary to enter, and assess all damages occasioned by the violation upon the offender.*[13]

In 1862 Congress passed the Land Grant College Act, which established 69 state colleges. This act and other legislation encouraging state-supported higher education assured the preeminence of secular education in the United States.[14] A second factor contributing to secular education was the gradual dissolution of religious affiliation at such institutions as Harvard, Yale, Princeton, and Columbia at approximately this same time.[15] The result of this secularization was a loosening of the controls that the institutions wished or chose to exercise over students. The rigid codes of obedience and hours of compulsory chapel were replaced by conduct regulations that granted students greater freedoms. With the lessened concern for student welfare and a freeing of students from the control of clerics, much of the violence associated with student behavior vanished.

In time this diminished concern for residence halls took its toll on the facilities available for student housing. *Ill-kept, disheveled, rat-infested,* and *dilapidated* are appropriate adjectives to describe college-owned student housing in the late 1800s. Students lived where they could. Townspeople, faculty, and the presidents of colleges all boarded students. Other places that served as housing in this period included the basement of the town meeting house for students attending Hiram College and the attic of the first building constructed at Oberlin College. At Amherst College the same rooms were used as bedrooms, classrooms, study halls, and chapel.[16] Most of the residence halls built earlier in the century were still in operation, but they were not well maintained.

Some students who were dissatisfied with these living conditions took refuge in privately owned housing that had been established in a few communities, organized or joined a fraternity with residential functions, or found other accommodations. At the turn of the twentieth century, Thwing explained that:

Most state universities have declined to accept special responsibility for the domestic interests of students. These men and women have been left in no small degree to shift for themselves. Funds given by the state or by the individual have been required for the erection of libraries, laboratories, and other halls. The ordinary home has opened its doors to students, glad to avail itself of the means of increasing income, and students have not been loath to accept.[17]

The attacks on residence halls and the collegiate way were most pronounced at the Eastern colleges; Midwestern and Western colleges appear to have been largely indifferent.

EARLY TWENTIETH CENTURY AMERICAN RESIDENCE HALLS

The collegiate system of residential colleges was not easily vanquished. Some kept alive the idea that colleges should educate both the character and intellect, as in English colleges. Arthur T. Hadley, president of Yale; William Rainey Harper, president of the University of Chicago; A. Lawrence Lowell, president of Harvard; and Woodrow Wilson, president of Princeton, all spoke on behalf of the English residential system and the importance of the collegiate experience. The rebirth of interest in student housing started at Yale, where an adherence to "the English philosophy that the communal life of students has high educational value"[18] remained.

The Quadrangle Plan

In 1907, while president of Princeton, Woodrow Wilson suggested that residence halls be joined to form quadrangles and that unmarried faculty be housed with students in what he termed the Quadrangle Plan. His plan was motivated by a desire to disband the powerful men's social clubs at Princeton by substituting residence halls that would be under the control of the university.

Although Wilson's plan initially met with the approval of the Princeton University trustees, it ultimately fell under attack from the men's social clubs and the influential alumni of these organizations who opposed it. But as Shay pointed out, "Wilson had lost the Battle at Princeton, but helped the War for the Residence Hall."[19] The debate over the residential system of colleges sparked discussion at other universities which later served as inspiration for an expansion of college-owned residence halls at Harvard.[20]

The comments of Richard C. Hughes, president of Ripon College, are typical of this philosophy supporting residence halls and the value of the collegiate experience:

The purpose of a college education is not only to educate the student in formal disciplines, but to aid him in discovering his own powers and to train him in the best use of these powers for effective work in life; in other words, to discover the profession or calling in life for which he is best fitted and to prepare him to be a good citizen. A large part of this most important work is done outside of the classroom and laboratory, during the hours when the student mingles freely with his fellows, expresses himself without restraint, and takes on the habit of thought and speech and life of the crowd with which he associates. The education of the classroom may be training in one direction while education of his chums in the dormitory is training him in the opposite direction. In other words, the first factor in solving the problem is to recognize that for good or evil, success or failure, life in the dormitory is a powerful influence in the life of a student. The strongest lines of social influence are always horizontal. We are more powerfully affected by the opinions of our peers than by those of our superiors. The student will listen with respect to the teaching of the faculty, but he will accurately imitate the language and life of his chums.[21]

Student Activities

At the turn of the century, in most universities, the vivid recollections of the old residence halls with their myriad problems and manifold abuses had mellowed into pleasant recollections and funny stories of days long past,[22] thus lessening the objections of faculty who had often worked as tutors or proctors in these halls. There was also a revival in student activities and increased attention to college life. It was marked in the late 1800s by such activities as intercollegiate athletics, which Cowley dated as beginning with a boat race between Yale and Harvard in 1852 on Lake Winnipesaukee.[23] Intercollegiate football games followed 17 years later. Other activities associated with college life included an increase in student participation in social clubs, student publications, drama clubs, and intercollegiate debates.

Revival of Residence Halls

Edmond J. James, president of the University of Illinois, upon laying the cornerstone of the first women's residence hall at that institution, gave the following reasons for the revival of residence halls at American universities in the early 1990s:

1. *In the first place, the people outside may not keep up an adequate supply of rooms, and the prices for rooms may be excessive. . . . The addition of university residence halls will tend to relieve this pressure, and even if they do not take all of the students, . . . they will do something to relieve the situation. . . .*
2. *A second reason is that they will do something to help standardize the conditions of life. A student needs for his work as peculiar and distinct a room and equipment as the grocery man needs for his, as the iron man needs for his work . . . and it is very difficult to get*

people who rent rooms to students to understand that point of view and to provide the proper kinds of furniture and equipment.

3. *A third reason which is often assigned for the university residence hall is to be found in the fact that it offers a certain kind of social organization which is not so easily supplied by the students if they live at random throughout the houses of the community.*

4. *While we are getting our university education, our knowledge of Latin and chemistry, and other subjects, we ought to be getting a lot of other things that help to make a civilized people. We ought to be acquiring polished manners. We ought to be acquiring a certain ability to live easily and efficiently, so to speak, with our fellow men. . . . And residence halls properly constructed, properly organized, properly administered, can do something toward crystallizing and helping to form and shape what may be called the social life of the student body.*

5. *Another reason sometimes assigned is that students who live scattered about through the towns do not get in touch with the university spirit. Some people come here . . . and insist that they would not send their boys or girls to institutions which could not provide what they called the opportunity for the development of college spirit. And so they insist upon a kind of institutional life which the college dormitory may develop. . . . A student who comes to the university and lives here four years and goes away without having increased his desire for profitable and wholesome human companionship will certainly have lost one of the greatest opportunities which college life can bring.*[24]

Women's Colleges. One cannot overlook the importance of women's colleges and the role they played in the revival of residence halls. It was one thing to let men fend for themselves in a community and quite another to permit the same liberty to women. Women's colleges such as Vassar, Smith, and Mount Holyoke all were founded in the late nineteenth century and all were strictly residential.

Marion Talbot, a professor at the University of Chicago, believed that women's residence halls held great potential for educating young women. She thought residence halls should be organized to "bring all into relation with all and to have all recognize the privilege and obligation" associated with living in a community.[25] In addition, this sense of community responsibility could be realized through such activities as learning the social graces, exercises in hospitality, participation in some charity, interest in the affairs of the university, and cooperation in a common interest such as setting quiet hours for the house or determining how Sundays should be observed. Talbot observed that these residence hall experiences, and others like them, lead to "the opportunity to acquire that power of expression, that facility in social intercourse, that ability to meet situations of an unusual and unexpected character, that dignity and poise, which ensure that the intellectual and scholarly results of the academic experience will be made available in full measure."[26]

Administrators. Most faculty and administrators at colleges and universities were men. Findlay noted that when women joined institutions that had been exclusively for men, "it turned out that women's problems were frequently of a different nature than those of men students. Convention required a stricter supervision of women than was expected of men. These facts, together with the earlier establishment of women's dormitories and the influence of the American Association of Collegiate Alumnae in its desire for a special adviser for women students—all served to bring into existence a new administrative officer—earlier called 'the lady principal' or preceptress."[27] These female administrators soon came to be known as deans of women, preceding the deans of men on most campuses. In 1902, at Northwestern University, deans of women entered into a national association, which they called the National Association of Women Deans. Cowley observed that this organization was a "powerful influence, especially in the direction of bringing the attention of administrators to the housing of women students"[28]

Deans of men on most campuses were appointed later, between about 1910 and 1930, but unlike the appointment of deans of women, deans of men were not appointed principally over concern for housing male students. According to a survey of all the institutions affiliated with the National Association of Deans of Men 1936–1937, the reasons for establishing the office of dean of men and the number of institutions giving that reason were as follows:

The survey shows that problems with housing were among the reasons for appointing a dean of men at a college; however, it was not one of the principal reasons for establishing this office. Rather, the administrative press presented by increased enrollments, although not entirely unrelated to the need for housing, was the most-often-cited reason for establishing this position.

Fraternities.   Another influence supporting the revival of residence halls in this period was the increasing disparity in wealth between those students from rich families and those from poorer ones. This inequity was often the distinction between those who could afford to live in private dormitories or fraternities and those who were forced to live in the meager accommodations offered by the college. Charles W. Eliot, president of Harvard University, took exception to this situation because it developed a form of caste system and perpetuated cliques of students from the same backgrounds. In commenting on the differences between private residence halls (established in

Reasons for Establishing Deans of Men	Number of Votes
1. Increased enrollment	47
2. Need for adviser of men (counseling)	36
3. Extracurricular development (and centralization)	33
4. Administrative reorganization	30
5. Relief for the president or general administration	27
6. Influence of the dean of women's work	22
7. Housing problems	13
8. Request of students	11
9. Enlarged service for the institution	9
10. Discipline	5
11. Study of other college programs	5
12. Had been doing it unofficially	5
13. Campus morale demanded it	4
14. Aftermath of the war	3

Twelve other causes were given, for each of which only one or two votes are offered.[29]

Cambridge in the late 1800s and early 1900s as investment properties by private individuals to cater to the wealthier students) and the college residence halls at Harvard, Eliot wrote:

I like better to have the youth go into the college dormitories. . . . The college dormitories are not occupied by any one class of students at all. They are occupied in the most promiscuous manner as regards the classes from which their occupants have come, and they are occupied in a completely democratic manner as regards the school from which the occupants have come and the parts of the country from which they come. In these private dormitories there is a great deal of grouping by sets of fellows who have known each other before, who, for instance, have come from St. Paul's school, or from some other boarding school in some other part of the country. For my own part, I prefer the breaking up of those groups when they come to college, but is a very natural thing that in the private dormitories they seek precisely to create or prolong the life of these groups formed elsewhere. It is merely a case of birds of a feather flocking together.[30]

Fraternities became influential organizations on many campuses. They went from secret societies to social bodies with lodges and, eventually, to democratically run houses. Birdseye defended fraternities, writing that they were "homebuilding agencies, wherein many rich and influential alumni and earnest and energetic undergraduates are laboring together to erect college homes and thereby solve to a limited extent the modern problems in the college family life arising out of increasing numbers and changed dormitory and social conditions."[31] Fraternities were so successful as to cause some universities, like Amherst, to stop construction of residence halls for lack of student interest.[32] However, this same "success"

of the fraternity system catering to the needs of a particular class of students was viewed by others as antithetical to the democratic principles of egalitarianism that were central to the educational mission of many state universities and religious colleges. Shay noted that because access to fraternities was "based upon grounds which were repugnant to the American concept of democratic life, wealth—and high social standing . . . [fraternities] . . . acted as a stimulus to the development of college residences not so much because it was a model institution, but because it came to be seen as an unhealthy influence which might wither away if the college provided residence halls."[33]

RESIDENCE HALLS AFTER WORLD WAR I

Following World War I, enrollments at colleges and universities increased. By the mid-1920s, many institutions were experiencing overcrowding due to increased enrollment. Some institutions began to build more residence halls. In 1926 the Virginia State Board of Education authorized $1 million of state funds for "dormitory needs" of state institutions under the Noel Act.[34] Similarly, President Coffman of the University of Minnesota, after being denied state funds, embarked on a plan—which was successful at other universities—of selling bonds to finance residence halls.[35]

Harvard's House Plan

The most popular approach to organizing residence halls at this time was to establish residential colleges which were usually composed of a group of halls segregated by gender and by class standing. This plan was proposed by a committee of the faculty at the University of Michigan in 1927.[36] The most popular and well published of these new plans was Harvard University's house plan. Harvard president A. Lawrence Lowell, like his predecessor Charles Eliot, objected to the "cliques [of students] based upon similarity of origin and upon wealth" and believed that "great masses of unorganized young men, not yet engaged in definite careers, are prone to superficial currents of thought and interest, to the detriment of the personal intellectual progress that ought to dominate mature men seeking higher education."[37] A gift of $3 million from Edward S. Harkness, a graduate of Yale University (class of 1897), made it possible for Harvard to build two houses. Harkness earlier had made this same offer to Yale, but the faculty committee established to study the idea did not respond in time to meet Harkness's deadline; he then took to Harvard his offer to build residence colleges similar to those at Cambridge University.

The aim of the Harvard house plan was to "bring into contact a body of students with diverse interests who will by attrition provoke one another to think on many subjects, and will have a corporate spirit."[38] Each house was a cross-section of students selected from the students who resided the previous year in one of the freshmen residence halls that Harvard established in 1911. Upperclassmen and faculty residing in the houses selected students based on applications and interviews. President Lowell intended for the plan to encourage scholarship, intellectual interests, and increased personal attention. Perhaps most of all, Lowell envisioned that the houses would become communities of scholarship dedicated to enhancing the learning process. He believed that through what he called the "spirit of emulation" and informal group discussions that would grow from the day-to-day contacts naturally occurring among students and faculty living together, the residence houses would enhance the formal classroom instruction "with all men not destitute of mental appetite."[39]

Yale University established residential quadrangles in December 1929, principally because the undergraduate schools were so overcrowded that life at Yale had lost some of the important benefits of smaller classes.[40] Although the problem of overcrowding was recognized earlier, it had become acute and relief was needed.

RESIDENCE HALLS IN THE 1930S

Inadequate housing facilities for students seemed to be the rule rather than the exception. A 1931 survey of 44 of the 52 land grant institutions showed housing facilities existed for approximately 15 percent of the 136,000 students. Two institutions (the University of Nebraska and Colorado Agricultural College) had no residence halls, and eight were still waiting for state legislatures to make appropriations. The other institutions surveyed had either constructed residence halls through issuing bonds, by establishing non-profit corporations, or by some other creative financing arrangement.[41]

Life in the residence halls during this period emphasized making the college residence hall a "home." The college authorities believed it was their responsibility to mold a student's character. The courts also recognized this as the responsibility of colleges. As early as 1913 in *Gott* v. *Berea College,* the courts held that college authorities were to act *in loco parentis* (in lieu of parents). The court stated that "College authorities stand *in loco parentis* concerning the physical and moral welfare and mental training of the pupils, and we are unable to see why, to that end, they may not make any rule or regulation for the government or betterment of their pupils that a parent could for the same purpose."[42]

This concept came to be a guiding principle for much of the early work with students outside of the classroom. Some of the residence hall regulations for women at Louisiana State University in 1934 illustrate the scope of control which the colleges sought to exercise over the daily lives of students while serving in lieu of parents.

1. *Smith Hall residents are under regulations from the time they register in the university until they sign out to leave for their homes at the close of school.*

2. *Smith Hall residents who leave the campus for any reason are required to sign out on the register in the general office, stating destination, time of leaving, and expected time of return, and sign in immediately upon return to the campus. Each student must sign for herself.*

3. *Women students who have permission to attend a dance or a special function must return to Smith Hall within fifteen minutes after the time set for closing, or leaving, such functions.*

4. *Women students are not to visit a house where men reside exclusively, unless a chaperone approved by the dean of women is present.*

5. *Students are held responsible for the conditions of their rooms at all times, subject to daily inspection.*[43]

Other regulations included a 10:30 P.M. curfew on weekdays and a midnight curfew on weekends, a roll call in the residence hall each night at 8:15 P.M., and a requirement that all lights be out and students in bed by 11:15 P.M. on school nights. Regulations for men were often more liberal, but they too had curfews, room inspections, and roll calls, and men were usually required to sign in and sign out when leaving the campus.

Concern with shaping the lives of students was also reflected in "The Student Personnel Point of View," issued by the American Council on Education in 1937 to express the philosophical purposes and functions of student personnel administrators during this time. In this statement, 23 functions or services were enumerated as the responsibility of student personnel practitioners. Included among these was an acknowledgment that student personnel administrators were responsible for "assisting the student to reach his maximum effectiveness through clarification of his purpose, improvement of study methods, speech habits, personal appearance, manners, etc., and through progression in religious, emotional, social development, and other nonacademic personal and group relationships."[44]

Life in the residence halls cannot be viewed apart from life on campus and the influence of national social and economic upheaval. The 1930s were a time of social change and economic confusion. There was strong sentiment favoring socialism and communism as viable economic systems for the country. "Calls to use teachers and students as tools in a process of social reconstruction stood side by side with concern for teacher and student freedom."[45] Extracurricular activities on campus became so important that Cowley and Waller defended such activities, writing, "Other factors, of course, contributed to the widespread opinion that the campus has seemed to swallow up the classroom. These include the values of activities in educating for a competitive world, the consonance of activities, education, and Babbitry, and so forth. Our fundamental point, however, is unchanged: The function of all student organizations must be canvassed and evaluated in terms of the fulfillment of human purpose."[46]

Development of Low-Cost Student Housing

Low-cost student housing was developed in the late 1930s as a means to assist those less able to afford higher education and as a way to meet the demands of the increased number of students enrolled. At the University of Wisconsin, for example, enrollment increased from 8,000 students in 1935 to 11,400 students in 1938. To meet the increased demand for housing and the needs of low-income students, the university constructed cooperative housing facilities with varied rents based on the services supplied by the university. Rates for these low-cost residence halls ranged from $70 per year (optional food service and the students responsible for all housekeeping) to $96 per year for room and $245 per year for food with daily maid service.[47]

Iowa State University opened a "cooperative dormitory" for women students in 1922 and a second one in 1938 to accommodate women who required reduced living expenses in order to attend college. These accommodations were run on a cooperative basis in which the women planned, cooked, and served their own meals and performed other household tasks. The room rent was approximately the same as the traditional residence halls at the university—approximately $32.00 per quarter—but the women in the cooperative hall paid about half the board rate, amounting to a savings of approximately $2.25 per week.[48]

Public higher education benefited from government-sponsored work forces such as the WPA. Stewart said that between 1931 and 1941, "publicly supported universities and colleges in America have launched such a gigantic program of construction for student housing as to constitute one of the major developments in American educational history."[49] He estimated that institutions of higher education invested in excess of $150 million, matched by the federal government, for the construction of student housing facilities. Universities, supported by government subsidies, reduced or eliminated tuition and fees for many students unable to pay.

The Independent Men's Association at the University of Oklahoma was organized to help integrate nonfraternity men into the mainstream of campus life. Findlay explained the plight of many students during the early thirties when he described the organization.

The Depression gave the university an increasing number of nonfraternity men who were attempting a college education "on a shoe string." A large portion of these men were leaving school at the end of nine months—maladjusted, disappointed with their experience, still unacquainted with their fellow students, and poorer in health than when they first set foot on campus. Their slim pocketbooks did not permit attendance at the usual social events. Many did not attend a party or a social function all year.

When scholastic troubles came on, there was no chapter preceptor or tutor available for them and they had no money with which to hire the services of a private tutor.[50]

RESIDENCE HALLS DURING AND AFTER WORLD WAR II

During the war years, college campuses saw most young men leave to join the armed services or prepare to become officers through the Reserve Officers' Training Corps active on most campuses. To participate fully in these programs, universities were expected to provide some form of housing facility, offering yet another incentive for constructing residence halls.

Sixty percent of veterans eligible to enroll in institutions of higher education after World War II did so within approximately two years of the end of the war. The GI Bill made attending college financially possible for 25 percent more veterans than would have been able to attend without government support.[51] The students who returned to campus after the war were different from those who had left. They were older, more experienced, and more serious about their studies. Many campus restrictions designed to "parent" students were out of place when applied to veterans. Campus organizations that flourished before the war seemed frivolous to many students following their experiences of war and the loss of loved ones.

The surge of this new breed of student caused housing problems. For the first time on many campuses, colleges were asked to provide housing not only for students but also for the families that accompanied them. The federal government responded to the needs of war veterans by making temporary housing available to servicemen. In June 1945 an amendment to the Lanham Act, which had been established to provide temporary housing during the war years, allowed universities to seek financial support for the housing of students.

To meet the demands for housing, colleges developed temporary quarters for married students. Often these took the form of converted barracks or trailer parks. The University of Illinois housed about 300 veterans in the gymnasium and secured "275 temporary shelter-type houses" from the Public Housing Authority.[52] The University of Michigan was able to place most of their single veterans in one of nine residence halls, but had problems integrating students with families.[53]

The problems associated with the increased need for student housing was impetus for S. Earl Thompson, director of housing at the University of Illinois, to call on the housing officers at other universities to attend the first National Housing Conference held at the University of Illinois in 1949. In 1951 the housing officers, attending what became an annual meeting, formed an association; they subsequently adopted the name of the National Association of College and University Housing Officers.[54] Later the organization changed its name to the Association of College and University Housing Officers—International.

Universities were reluctant to undertake the construction of permanent structures after the war, believing that the influx of older students was temporary and that in time campuses would return to the pastoral academic communities of the prewar years.

Although the direct influence of veteran enrollment rose and fell in a relatively short time—the decline beginning in about 1952 and lasting until about 1955—a return to the small prewar colleges did not happen.[55] Francis Brown, staff associate for the American Council on Education, forecast the problem facing higher education in his 1951 address to the National Association of Deans of Men. He said:

If you look at the long range future, in terms purely of the matter of births, an appalling situation faces higher education. The present 18-year olds were born in 1932 and 1933— take 1932 as illustrative. During the year 1932 there were 2,059,000 babies born in the entire United States. In 1947 there were 3,656,000 babies born in the United States. In the last six months of 1950 there were more than 2,000,000 babies born, indicating more than a 100 percent increase in the birthrate at the present time, as contrasted with the declining birthrate of the 1930s. . . .

But one wonders what this means. We are seeing it now in elementary schools. It will move into the high school, and by 1956 and 1957 it will begin to strike the colleges. This is not a bulge in the birthrate. It is apparently a permanent and continuing plateau that turns only upward.[56]

Mr. Brown's forecasts for enrollment increases came to pass. In 1946, institutions of higher education in the United States enrolled 2,078,095 students. By 1957 enrollments had increased by approximately one third to 3,036,938 students.[57] To meet this increase, universities built new residence halls. But these were not the small, quaint halls steeped in tradition and built to encourage companionship within the community of scholarship; instead, buildings were constructed to meet demands for housing large numbers of students. Decisions were often made on the basis of cost-per-square-foot assessments and a formula that allowed residence halls to generate enough funds to pay for the bonds sold to build the facility and to cover the operating costs of the building. The idea was to make the residence halls self-financing—a financial auxiliary of the university. According to Shay, this self-financing idea was an "unfortunate policy . . . [which forced] many an unhappy administrator to choose between providing a rigid institutional environment or charging exorbitant rents which impecunious students cannot afford. Most administrators have tried to split the difference, resulting in our brightly colored barracks with opulent lounges which can hardly be classified as educational facilities."[58]

Traditionless Period

Unseem called the period after 1950 in which there was a surge in building residence halls the "traditionless period." She described the characteristics of student housing built in this period:

1. *The number of students housed within any unit has increased. The units are sometimes grouped together in complexes, and occasionally the complexes are coeducational.*
2. *The halls are managed by professionals or what I have called members of professionalizing occupations: housemothers have become resident advisers, janitors and cleaning people have become maintenance personnel. . . .*
3. *Services to students have increased both in quantity and quality. The bare minimum provided in a dormitory room has increased to include lamp fixtures, bedspreads, built-ins, and venetian blinds.*

4. *Investments must be protected, accounted for, managed, and organized. And to do this students have to be managed, too. Rules and regulations have become more depersonalized and, from the point of view of students, seem to be imposed by the professional staff rather than learned from students and self-enforced.*
5. *With the increase in campus size, more services and activities that were once on central campus have had to be decentralized. . . .*
6. *Much the same standardization has happened and will continue to happen in residence halls as has occurred in other organized-administered activities of modern mass society. I sometimes call this the "Residence Hall Beautiful" or the Howard Johnson syndrome, for residence halls are repeatable from coast to coast.*
7. *In some of the freshmen halls, in the absence of traditions, adolescent behavior tends to take over; and this must be managed and controlled by the professional staff.*[59]

These new buildings lost much of the aesthetic appeal of the smaller residence halls of the past. Shay described them as "gilded barracks with glamorous appurtenances . . . far less home-like than many of the halls built as WPA projects in the late 1930s."[60]

Personnel

The personnel who managed the residence halls had also changed. Cowley said in 1957 that "three kinds of people engaged in student personnel services professionally: the humanitarians, the administrators, and the scientists, more especially psychologists."[61] The first group of student personnel administrators, those who founded the field, he described as coming from the ranks of humanitarians (and some as distorted sentimentalists). But the second wave, and the ones Cowley described as predominating the student personnel field in 1957, were administrators. He said that "by and large, those who have come into the field during the past 25 years to administer the huge coordinated programs that have been developed have been appointed primarily because of their administrative ability rather than because of any compelling interest in students. They are primarily executives in charge of large and important operations."[62] Those who came from backgrounds in psychology, Cowley noted, had been in the student personnel field since about World War I, but in 1957 were just beginning to be a force within the field still dominated by the "administrative types." And, to some extent, the predominance of the "administrative types" may help explain why universities built the high-rise, sterile environments of concrete and glass and expected students to enjoy the experience of residing in them.

Those individuals who worked with students as resident counselors or hall directors were not insensitive to the needs of students. Indeed, much of the literature of the late 1940s and 1950s was concerned with the counseling and advising of students.[63] However, these people were not the administrators who usually made the decisions about construction of facilities. On most campuses such decisions were left to top administrators, architects, and those in the college business office.

Counselors. Residence counselors were engaged in helping students learn social skills that would give them greater flexibility in social and professional situations. Typical of this approach was a book written by Irene Pierson, social director of the Illini Union, entitled *Campus Cues*. The book was written to help "those who are unknowing in the area of manners to gain information and [to reassure] those who have good manners that they know and are doing what is socially acceptable."[64] In it Pierson detailed for both men and women how they should act by answering some of the questions that have plagued college students for generations, such as:

Question: Is it considered correct to kiss the girl on the first date?

Answer. If you try to kiss every girl you go out with, you could be labeled as promiscuous and thus admit that you are not at all particular. It is rare to get to know a girl really well enough on that date to consider a good-night kiss proper.[65]

And:

Question: What is the correct procedure when a girl has a Saturday night date and her boy friend from out of town pops in a half hour before time for the date?

Answer: Tell the boy friend you have plans for the evening and cannot break them as you do not want the reputation of being a person who is not dependable. The boy friend was inconsiderate in not calling in advance. You could have been out to dinner and not have been located by him all evening.[66]

Effects of Communist Threats

The late 1950s were also a time in which many in the United States felt threatened by Communism in Europe and the Far East. On October 4, 1957, Americans learned that the USSR had launched a space satellite called Sputnik into orbit around the earth. By early November, the Eisenhower administration had found a palatable explanation to offer the American public for the USSR's advanced technology, and the U.S. Office of Education released a report—prepared eighteen months earlier—describing the emphasis on science, math, and engineering in the curriculum of the educational system of the USSR. The *New York Times* recounted this information to the American public on November 11. On November 13, President Eisenhower told the nation the reason the USSR had a space satellite and the United States did not was that the USSR was able to produce 80,000 engineers to our 30,000 and that their educational system emphasized math, science, and engineering.[67] Eisenhower called on Congress to expand the National Science Foundation (established in 1950) and requested the enactment of a number of special educational programs in math, science, and engineering as temporary emergency measures.[68] Out of this was born the National Defense Education Act of 1958 (NDEA), which was an unprecedented expansion of the involvement of the federal government into higher education.

RESIDENCE HALLS IN THE 1960S

In the 10 years following the NDEA, enrollments on college campuses more than doubled, going from a national student enrollment of 3,226,038 in 1958 to an enrollment of 6,928,115 in 1968.[69] This increase in enrollment cannot be attributed solely to the NDEA; it was also the predicted result of the "baby boom," that is, the higher birthrate following World War II.

The increase in enrollments helped create the community college movement, transformed many state colleges and normal schools (two-year teachers' colleges) into comprehensive universities, expanded the size and character of large state universities, and increased the number of professional schools.[70] With these changes came a continuing increase in the size and number of residence halls to meet the increased demand for housing.

Involvement of the Federal Government

Higher education was changing throughout the 1960s in large part due to the increasing involvement of the federal government, which provided special funds to students and universities as part of President Johnson's War on Poverty and as a result of the Civil Rights movement. Educational programs such as the Higher Education Facilities Act and the Higher Education Amendments Act changed the character of higher education.

Federal interventions in higher education brought a different kind of student to campus and significantly increased enrollment in institutions of higher education. Of particular importance to the construction of residence halls was the Higher Education Facilities Act of 1963, which gave universities access to low-interest government loans to build residence halls. Many of the high-rise residence halls standing on campuses today were built with loans authorized under this act. Among the items that could be funded under this act were building fixtures, defined as any items built-in or otherwise permanently attached to the building structure. The reason that many residence halls have built-in beds, desks, and dresser drawers can be traced to the provisions of this act, which permitted these "fixtures" to be financed through the loan authorization.

These structures were of the same sterile variety begun in the late 1950s. Bess wrote of the residence halls being built at this time that:

With the recent rapid growth in higher education, huge complexes of dormitory residences have been built with little thought to the ways in which residence life might be integrated into academic life. Often beset by unwieldy state and federal restrictions on costs per square foot, institutions have cut financial corners by creating space-saving devices without thinking about the educational life of students, let alone their personal living space. The typical long corridors, bolted down furniture, monolithic exteriors, and cramped lounge spaces are cases in point.[71]

Student Rebellion

It is little wonder that students rebelled against living in residence halls. Most students did not like life in the halls with their rules and policies.[72] Van der Ryn and Silverstein suggested that "the need for independence, a diversity of activities and friends are characteristics of successful student living. And yet, it is the search for these conditions that drives many students out of the dormitory."[73]

This was a time when students were dissenting against the established practices of universities and the government. Sentiment against the Vietnam war was strong, and students questioned the value of traditional education and sought approaches more "relevant" to the issues of the day.

By this time, public universities were prohibited from exercising their disciplinary authority over students without affording them due process.[74] In 1962, policies regulating student behavior in the residence halls included strictly enforced curfews for men and women, sign-in and sign-out logs, strictly enforced dress codes, strict rules governing the use of alcohol, and limited visitation privileges for men and women; by 1972, the policies no longer included curfews or dress codes, reflected more tolerant attitudes about student drinking, and allowed open visitation and even coed residence halls.

Residence hall counselors and undergraduate students, serving as peer counselors or resident assistants (RAs), accepted as their principal roles that of counselor and adviser. They were educated in understanding the psychological problems of college students, in drug-use intervention, suicide prevention, counseling skills, and similar psycho-

social and developmental issues. Housing officers defined their relationship with students by a housing contract that students were required to sign upon requesting to live in a residence hall. Access to a student's room changed from an unchallenged right of the university to one defined by the housing contract and dictated by court cases related to warrantless searches.

Students challenged in court the university regulations that required students to reside in residence halls. In *Prostrollo* v. *University of South Dakota*, the court rejected the university's original argument that students must live in the residence halls during their freshmen and sophomore years to ensure that enough money was generated to pay the bond obligations. On appeal the university emphasized the educational programs and benefits to be derived from living in a residence hall; the court reversed the original decision, thereby upholding the right of universities to require on-campus residence for reasons related to the educational benefits to be gained by exposure to this environment.[75]

RESIDENCE HALLS IN THE 1970S

In 1977 Mayhew noted that "residence halls during the 1970s appear to be considerably more popular with students than they were from approximately 1965 to 1970, although the significance of this shift is difficult to gauge."[76] In the mid-1970s, many financially pressed students sought to live in residence halls for the economic advantages they offered over the rising costs of off-campus apartments and utilities. Some universities experienced an increase in student housing, while others—predominantly comprehensive state universities without easy access to urban areas—experienced marked housing declines.

Students of the seventies were described by Levine as more narcissistic, career oriented, less concerned with social issues, and disillusioned

Some students are not enthused about living in residence halls because they feel restricted in their lifestyles.

with the credibility of established social institutions such as higher education, church, and the family. He characterized the students of this time as "Going First Class on the Titanic," noting that they believed they would survive and be economically successful, while believing other students would experience significant economic hardships.[77]

RESIDENCE HALLS IN THE 1980S

In a 1981 survey, over 60 percent of freshmen entering college planned to live in a college-owned residence hall, although this was the preferred residence for only about 46 percent. The difference is accounted for by the number who preferred to live in an apartment off-campus but for some reason were unable to.[78] Little changed when the same national survey was conducted with 1985 freshmen: Almost 60 percent of the freshmen students planned to live in residence halls, with only 42 percent actually preferring this option.[79] When comparing freshman students of the 1980s to those who had been surveyed in the late 1960s and throughout the 1970s, researchers found that by 1986, autonomy was of greater importance to entering freshmen; students resented institutional attempts to monitor their behaviors or influence their values.[80] This trend may help

explain the lack of enthusiasm for living in residence halls.

INTO THE TWENTY-FIRST CENTURY

Students in the 1990s have demanded more from their residence halls. As housing divisions have complied with students' requests for private baths, floor kitchens, air conditioning, and cable television, RAs have worked harder to create opportunities for students to meet and learn from one another. In-room Internet access has provided students with the option of global communication but has significantly hindered them from becoming acquainted with other students in their halls.

The emphases for residence hall administration in the 1990s have been to provide comfortable living areas as well as to promote communities for learning. Learning communities are formed when student affairs divisions have had to forge collaborative partnerships within the institution and to become more intentional about creating opportunities for student learning, particularly within residence halls. Such initiatives have fostered: the development of the whole student; the acquisition of values and skills associated with responsibility, citizenship, and work ethic; and the celebration of diversity within the community.[81]

Technology of the 90s enables students to escape crowded labs and do assignments on their own schedules.

Blimling identified six challenges confronting residence life and housing that have implications for residence life staff as the next century approaches:

1. *Multiculturalism:* Anticipated enrollment increases for underrepresented groups will challenge higher education to further involve these students in the life of the campus and to design programs that meet their needs.

2. *Student mental health problems:* Research shows that more students with more severe psychopathologies are attending universities than in the past and that more students are confronting problems associated with eating disorders, substance abuse, sexual abuse, and dysfunctional families.

3. *Campus violence:* Violence against women, hate crimes, and other criminal behavior has increased on college campuses and will continue to present problems in the future.

4. *Changing student attitudes:* In 1991, more incoming freshmen had already participated in an organized demonstration than had at any time in the twenty previous years. Also, more incoming freshmen in 1991 anticipated that they would participate in demonstrations during college than at any time in the previous

RA STAFF CHALLENGES

- Multiculturalism
- Student Mental Health
- Campus Violence
- Student Attitudes
- Accountability
- Facilities

twenty years. Probable issues of concern include ecological issues, multiculturalism, sexual violence, and women's issues.

5. *Accountability:* Higher education is being asked to be more accountable for educational outcomes associated with all its programs, including residence halls.

6. *Residence hall facilities:* Many high-rise residence halls have inherent design problems that are counterproductive to the educational interests of students and will require redesign and renovation.[82]

CONCLUSION

History reveals that residence halls have been both the herald of and the bane of higher education. At times residence halls were viewed as the focus of building a student's character through the companionship of faculty and fellow students seeking to be scholars and gentlemen. Later it became synonymous with all manner of hedonistic and insidious activities of wayward youths. There was a revival of residence hall construction for all the cherished educational reasons and a reorganization into high-rise sterile structures for all the wrong reasons.

The pattern of the evolution of residence halls has been essentially one of reacting to other influences in history. Although in the early development of residence halls they were acknowledged and promoted as an important educational tool, in recent years their growth has been predicated on enrollment trends and considered on many campuses as a service provided for students. The same enrollment-driven expansion that fostered the often-cursed high-rise residence halls was also the genesis of a new commitment to the education of students living in residence halls.

Because of the complexities associated with fulfilling a commitment to have residence halls become a meaningful part of a student's education, practitioners in residence hall work have had to become more sophisticated in their approaches to structuring these peer environments and more analytical in assessing the value of the residence hall environment.

REVIEW

1. List two reasons for the decline of residence halls in continental Europe after the early 1800s.

2. What was the most important reason for the establishment of residence halls at America's nine original colonial colleges?

3. What is the "residential college concept," and how did it influence the creation of residence halls?

4. List three reasons for the collapse of the residential college concept in the mid-1800s.

5. What effect did the collapse of the residential college concept have on student housing?

6. Give four reasons for the rebirth of residence halls in the early twentieth century.

7. What role did women's colleges play in the rebirth of residence halls in the early 1900s?

8. What is the *Student Personnel Point of View?*

9. Give two reasons for the construction of residence halls following World War II.

10. What is *ACUHO* and when was it established?

11. Between 1958 and 1968 enrollments at colleges and universities doubled. Give two reasons for this increase.

12. What does *in loco parentis* mean, and how does it relate to the student-institutional relationship after 1961?

13. Give three reasons for changes in the student-institution relationship during the 1960s.

14. Give three major differences in the philosophy of working with students in residence halls after the 1960s.

APPLICATIONS

HOW IT WAS THEN—HOW IT IS NOW

Below are lists of some of the policies which governed student behavior in the residence halls of a major state university in 1938. Read the policies and respond to the questions which follow.

For Girls

A girl's character is always reflected in the way she lives. Your relations among girls in your dormitory will be continually used as a yardstick to the judgment of your true self. To help you achieve a moral standard the Dean of Women, together with the hall house mothers, have offered the following helpful suggestions.

There is a mailbox in every dormitory for the posting of letters. Have all special delivery letters and telegrams addressed to the dormitory and not to boxes.

Read the bulletin boards every day to see if you have a special delivery or telegram, also to observe notices from the Dean of Women regarding special permissions, etc.

Never leave the dormitory overnight without getting special permission from the Dean of Women. A letter from your parents must always be sent to the Dean of Women giving special permission for each time you spend a weekend night in town with friends. Remember to sign a visiting permit card in the dormitory office on return.

Be sure to be in your room for check-up at eight o'clock Monday, Tuesday, Wednesday and Thursday nights. Friday, Saturday and Sunday nights are open nights.

Guests are permitted on Friday and Saturday nights. Be sure to register your guest with your housemother. Be sure to introduce your men friends to your housemother. Always rise when an older person speaks to you or enters the room.

Study hour is held Monday, Tuesday, Wednesday and Thursday nights. Visiting in friends' rooms, radios, and loud talking is not permitted at this time. Turn off lights at 11:15 P.M. unless special permission is received.

Form the habit of signing the hall registers when leaving the campus in the daytime and when leaving the dormitory at night.

Ask your men friends not to call at the dormitory before 1:00 P.M. any day except Sunday.

Do not use the telephone any longer than five minutes. Do not use it during study hour.

Always have your room neat and attractive. Keep the furniture in the room free of all scars and stains. Regard all regulations, keep your rooms neat, and strive to get on the Honor Roll. This entitles a girl to an open Wednesday once every three weeks.

Send your laundry out through the chutes of each hall, and call for it at the laundry room in the basement.

Your trunk must be unpacked within 24 hours after your arrival at the University. Put your name on it and send it to the storage room. Trunks are not allowed to remain in the rooms.

Do all your pressing in the pressing rooms. Be careful to always turn off the iron.

Report to the Infirmary in Smith Hall when ill.

Do not keep valuables in the dormitory.

Be sure to have your own room key.

Go to all dormitory meetings.

Go to the candlelight service each Thursday night at 10:00 P.M. in Smith Hall Reception Room.

Budget your time and money carefully.

Wear your hat and gloves to church and afternoon teas. If you are a hostess at an afternoon tea, wear a long afternoon dress, not an evening dress.

Buy your meal tickets from the Auditor's Office in the Alumni Building.

Remember to ask questions when in doubt.

Remember to show good taste in every way on the campus.

How to live rightly is a problem which all men must face as they enter the University. Each newcomer should try to establish orderly habits immediately. The following information will be of some assistance to men who wish to lead well-balanced lives.

Know your cadet regulations.*

Men who wish to go home frequently over weekends should obtain a letter from their parents authorizing them to do so. Absences from inspections during that time are then automatically excused if intention to take advantage of the weekend privilege is given your first sergeant.

Your first sergeant cannot excuse you from any formation or inspection whatsoever. All excuses accepted by him are first handled through the commandant's office. If you do not want to be refused, never ask him for a privilege he cannot grant.

Study hour is not only a military regulation which must be conscientiously met, but is a time when each man has the opportunity to think of his friends about him who are studying. Be certain that you do not disturb anyone. Absolute quiet begins at 7:30 P.M., and visits are ended.

Your 7:30 A.M. inspections should always be passed by leaving a clean and neat room. Get the habit of hanging up your clothes and get up early enough to sweep thoroughly.

Watch your bulletin board. If your name is always on the right side, you are becoming a success. Strive to make each situation a stepping stone.

When in uniform you are no longer John Doe, but you are a living tribute to the United States of America—any slight in the wearing of your uniform is a blight on your reputation, on your alma mater, and an insult to your country. Be proud, therefore, and wear it correctly.

WHAT WOULD YOU DO?

1. List at least five differences between the policies governing women students in the residence halls in 1938 and today.
2. List at least five differences between the policies governing men in the residence halls in 1938 and today.

---

*Note: The Morell Land Act required that men attending a land grant college complete two years of compulsory enrollment in the REserve Officers' Training Corps (ROTC) as a condition of attendance.

3. Are there any differences in the policies from 1938 governing male students and female students? If so, give examples.

4. After reading the case study, do you note a difference between the overall philosophy in working with college students in 1938 and the philosophy your institution holds for working with students today? If so, describe the principal differences.

5. Given the brief description of the residence hall policies of 1938, how would you feel about being an RA in 1938? Do you think that the role of the RA has changed? If so, in what ways?

CHAPTER THREE

EDUCATIONAL PHILOSOPHIES FOR RESIDENCE HALLS

©1998 PHCTODISK, INC.

Before examining a philosophy to guide residence halls, some realities of operating a residence hall system must be addressed. At public universities most residence halls are considered to be auxiliary organizations; that is, they have self-generated funds and receive little or no state support. Construction of residence halls at public universities is usually financed through a bond issue offered by the state government or through a special loan program offered by the federal government. The fees students pay to live in residence halls cover the operation of the halls and help retire the bonded indebtedness or loan.

Private institutions usually take a similar approach to the operation of residence halls—that is, they must be self-supporting. At private institutions, wealthy alumni sometimes fund construction of residence halls; more often, the money is borrowed from a lending agency, from the institution's endowment, or from the federal government. Such loans are repaid, with interest, from monies generated by the fees students pay. At both public and private institutions residence hall income is usually supplemented by renting rooms to conference groups in the summer.

NEED FOR GOOD MONEY MANAGEMENT

This all means that the first responsibility of the director of residence life or housing is to be a good money manager. No matter how laudable the director's intentions may be, or how educationally directed he or she wishes to be, a large part of what occurs in residence halls is dictated by the financial stability of the residence hall program as a whole. Resident assistants (RAs) and other staff members are an expense incurred in the operation of residence halls, just like the bond retirement expense or cost of utilities. When the cost of housing is determined, the cost of professional staff and RAs are factored into the overall cost residents are asked to bear. Therefore, students are purchasing the services and skills of RAs and residence life professional staff.

Effective residence hall programs have developed a balance between the operating expenses and financial reserves. If a director were to operate a residence hall without a continuing process of maintenance, refurbishment, staff training, and renovation, the residence halls, like any other resource, would be depleted. The physical environment and social atmosphere of the building would soon drive students away, and the financial stability of the residence halls would be disrupted.

By the same token, if the director were to establish exorbitant rental rates for rooms, students would seek accommodations elsewhere. Student housing is a cost that people consider along with tuition when they select an institution. Even if the institution has a requirement that students live in residence halls for one year, the cost of this is a factor in the overall financial attractiveness of the institution when the institution recruits new students. Thus, a balance must be struck between operating expenses and the fees students are willing to pay for a residence hall room, educational programs, and residence services.

PHILOSOPHIES FOR WORKING WITH STUDENTS IN RESIDENCE HALLS

Throughout history, residence halls have been guided by many philosophies. In the early years, residence halls were viewed as a necessity and as a method for controlling the behavior of students. They were considered an extension of the educational philosophy of the school and were used to help instill piety and obedience in students. As noted in Chapter 2, the philosophy toward students in residence halls changed with the imposition of the German model of higher education. In this context, residence halls were viewed merely as places of residence having no influence on the institution's relationship with students.

Today four philosophies, or approaches, exist in residence halls. The lines of demarcation between approaches are not always clear, as some characteristics are shared by several philosophies.

The Student Services Approach

One of the early philosophies for guiding the experience of students in residence halls holds that residence halls are a *student service* provided by the university. In this view, residence halls fall into the same category as services provided by the health center or dining services. As a service, residence halls must be managed effectively and efficiently. This may also be referred to as a *business approach,* because it views residence halls first and foremost as a business, appropriately managed in the best interest of students. Educational programs, RAs, intramurals, and hall government are services provided to the student.

An extension of this student services approach is a greater emphasis on consumerism. The belief is that residence halls should be operated in a businesslike manner, marketed to students, and those services with the greatest student appeal should be retained, whereas those of less interest to students should be eliminated.

The Custodial Care and Moral Development Approach

Some private universities and colleges use what can best be described as a *custodial care and moral development approach* to running residence halls. The living environment of students is used as an extension of the philosophy or dogma of the institution. With this approach, residents may be restricted from having radios or televisions in their rooms. They may be forbidden to smoke cigarettes or to drink alcoholic beverages on campus and may be subject to periodic room inspections, curfews, dress codes, and nonvisitation periods.

The idea behind this philosophy is that by controlling behavior of the residents, residence halls instill or model values consistent with the values of the institution. The rules by which students live create a social environment that supports and fosters what the institution believes to be a healthy environment for students. Students are therefore exposed to fewer temptations and more positive examples.

The Student Learning Approach

The *student learning approach* to residence halls has been part of residents' education for many years; however, the Student Learning Imperative (SLI) provides a recent framework which allows this philosophy to be more clearly articulated. According to the SLI, student learning includes concepts such as personal development, student development, and other components of "learning." Five elements are characteristic of student affairs organizations committed to student learning:

1. The student affairs mission complements the institutional mission and accepts student learning and personal development as the primary goal of the programs and services.

2. Resources are allocated to encourage student learning.

3. Student affairs professionals collaborate with other institutional agents to advance student learning.

4. Student affairs divisions include educators who are experts on students, their environment, and the teaching and learning process.

5. The policies and programs are based on research on student learning and institutionally specific assessment data on what advances student learning.[1]

Within the residence halls, the policies, programs, and practices of the staff are focused on advancing dimensions of learning in students. Hall government, RAs, and residence hall programming exist to promote the educational environment in the residence halls in a manner that will most readily advance the learning of students. The focus of this philosophy is on maintaining the components that contribute to a positive educational environment in the residence halls and that directly impact dimensions of student learning. For example, training helps RAs develop a variety of skills so that they can respond to the demands placed on them by residents and maintain an environment on their residence hall floors that will support the learning objectives of the institution.

PHILOSOPHIES OF
RESIDENCE HALLS

- Student Services
- Custodial Care and Moral Development
- Student Learning
- Student Development

The Student Development Approach

The *student development approach* is characterized by the following:

1. Acceptance of the belief that individuals develop in stages that are sequential, cumulative, increasingly complex, and qualitatively different
2. Acceptance of the student as the principal agent for change
3. A belief that the role of residence hall staff is to assist students in accomplishing goals that they have set for themselves
4. A recognition that one must consider the development of the whole individual—intellectually, physically, emotionally, and spiritually

Residence hall programs adopting this approach may begin by assessing students' personal goals through testing or through personal interviews. A plan may be designed for each student, based on opportunities in the residence halls, to help that student accomplish the goals he or she has set for himself or herself. Students may receive feedback about their progress through testing and records of participation in educational experiences in the residence hall. New goals are then set with individual students based upon the progress they have made toward attainment of their goals.

Using this approach requires a strong theoretical knowledge of experiences that facilitate cognitive, psychosocial, and moral development. The assessment techniques and interpretation of instruments require professional training and experience. Consequently, this approach requires professional staff who work individually and in small groups with students. RAs generally help implement educational programs, counsel students, and give feedback to professional staff on the progress of individual students and groups.

A somewhat less intense approach to student development often occurs in the residence halls. The recognition of students' developmental issues guides decision making in designing educational programs and interventions to enhance the social environment of a residence hall.

Central to the student development approach is a commitment to the intellectual, cultural, and personal development of students. This philosophy is grounded in the belief that students' education must include their intellectual, physical, spiritual, moral, and emotional growth and development. Experience in the classroom and life outside the classroom contribute to this development. The student development philosophy combines the in-class and out-of-class experience of students to educate the whole person.

A Blend of Approaches

Most college campuses employ a mixture of approaches rather than one philosophy for working with students in residence halls. The approaches reflect the orientation or attitudes of the people operating the residence halls. A residence hall philosophy combines the experiences that the

Many different activities can enrich a student's educational experiences.

student population and professional staff bring to that campus environment. It is blended with the tradition and heritage of the residence hall system on the campus, and with the educational philosophy and mission of that institution.

If residence halls do not adopt a philosophy of education, universities have no real justification for supporting them. Residence halls are surely easier to operate as hotels than as an extension of the educational mission of the institution. Were residence halls not provided on college campuses, in most communities the private sector would respond with low-cost housing for students. Residence halls exist on most campuses only because the college community believes in their educational value.

The involvement of students in the experience of education through the residence halls and in other ways enriches the quality of their educational experience. This involvement helps sustain the students' intellectual pursuits throughout college.

How does this discussion apply to you as an RA? It reveals the reason that the university employs you. You help facilitate the education of students outside the classroom. This is why your institution spends time training you in human relations skills, crisis management, counseling techniques, and the other skills necessary to aid students in their personal development. Your function is to serve as a catalyst, an identifier of services, a role model, and as an informal assessor of students' strengths and weaknesses.

GOALS FOR RESIDENCE HALL PROGRAMS

If the philosophy of residence halls is educational, it must be directed to accomplish educational goals. In 1986, the Council for the Advancement of Standards for Student Services/ Development Programs (CAS) issued a set of standards and guidelines for student personnel programs on college campuses: "The housing and residential life program is an integral part of the educational purpose of the institution. Its mission must include provision for educational programs and services, residential facilities, management services, and, where appropriate, food services."[2]

The CAS identified four goals to accomplish this mission.

The first two of these goals are of particular importance to you as an RA because they define the standards for your living conditions and for your educational purpose in residence halls.

Educational Goals of Residence Halls

Residence halls serve an important educational purpose, and they best serve the needs of students and the university community when the educational goals of the residence hall program include the following:

1. The primary goal of residence halls is to assist students with their personal growth and development.

2. Residence halls should be appealing places to live. They should be places where students feel

CAS STANDARDS AND GUIDELINES

- a residential community that encourages both individual and community development and learning;

- reasonably priced safe and secure facilities that are clean, attractive, well-maintained, and comfortable;

- management services that ensure the orderly and effective administration and operation of all aspects of the program; and, where appropriate,

- food, dining facilities, and related services that effectively meet institutional and residential life program goals.[3]

comfortable and at home. Not only should physical facilities be comfortable and well-maintained, but the social climate of each living unit also must be appealing and comfortable. Residence halls should be as free as possible from noises from other people's rooms, practical jokes, general disruptions, irritations, and distractions.

3. Students should be given as much freedom as possible in the decoration and control of their individual rooms. The need to have control over one's territory is a basic human need. The residence hall room represents this territory.

4. Living in a residence hall should teach students tolerance for others, skills in group living, and a sense of responsibility to the community. Through the residence hall experience, students should develop the ability to interact with peers and to contribute as a member of a group. Residence halls should help students learn the necessary human relations skills to socialize and work with others. In exchanges with other students, students should have the opportunity to explore their own values, share ideas, and receive feedback. Older students and the RA should serve as models for new students.

5. The focus of administration in the residence halls should be primarily educational. Managerial functions are necessary for a positive educational environment, but these functions should not become the focus of administration or the goal of the residence hall program.

SUMMARY

Four philosophical approaches to working with students in residence halls were identified in this chapter. The student services approach views residence halls as one of many student services provided on a college campus. The moral development approach is based on the belief that institutional control of student behavior is a way of modeling a particular set of values which helps students acquire these values. The student learning approach focuses on advancing student learning through direct learning interventions (e.g., programs, special lifestyle units) and by maintaining an environment that encourages students to learn. The student development approach is based on human development theory and focuses on helping students identify and obtain goals consistent with their personal objectives and their stage of maturation.

These philosophical approaches are not mutually exclusive. The more common pattern is a combination of them based on the history and traditions of the institution.

REVIEW

1. What is the first responsibility of the director of residence life or housing?

2. Give one characteristic of the *student services approach*.

3. Give one characteristic of the *custodial care and moral development approach*.

4. Give two characteristics of the *student learning approach*.

5. Give two characteristics of the *student development approach*.

6. Give two characteristics of the *wellness approach*.

7. How would you classify the approach to working with students in residence halls used at your institution?

8. The Council for the Advancement of Standards for Student Services/Development Programs established a mission for residence life programs. In it are four goals to accomplish this mission. Briefly describe three of these goals.

9. Why is it important to the overall educational atmosphere that the residential facilities are well maintained?

10. What is the primary goal of residence halls?

APPLICATIONS

HOW IS HE DOING?

Biff was in his second year as an RA at Julian University. He took the job last year because he thought it would look good on his resumé and would help him get into law school. He stayed for the second year because of the resumé and because he liked the extra money it gave him for buying clothes.

Biff was a very conscientious RA. He was meticulous about his record keeping. Students in his living unit were always checked-in correctly. Biff always filed reports on time and returned all of the surveys and other information the hall director required of him. He regularly inspected students' rooms for lounge furniture and was prompt about getting light bulbs replaced and items repaired in the living unit. Biff also kept room hours posted on his door. Students who wanted to see him could sign up for an appointment or could complete a service request form which he kept in a folder on the outside of his room.

Biff was in his room most nights after about 10:00 P.M. or was on duty somewhere in the building. No programming was required in the residence hall, so Biff did not do any. He knew most of the students in his unit and believed that students would contact him when they needed something. Unless they contacted him, he thought it best to leave them alone.

WHAT WOULD YOU DO?

1. How would you describe Biff's philosophy for working with students?
2. What are Biff's strengths as an RA?
3. What are Biff's weaknesses as an RA?
4. Is Biff's philosophy of working with students in the residence halls consistent with the goals of residence halls as expressed by the Council for the Advancement of Standards for Student Services/Development Programs? If not, how is it consistent and how is it inconsistent?

HOW DO YOU DO YOUR JOB?

1. You have been asked by the residence life department of your institution to talk to a group of new RAs about your philosophy for working with students in the residence halls. Give a brief statement of your philosophy.

2. One of the new RAs asks you to give some examples of group educational and development opportunities you provide for students living on your floor. List four.

CHAPTER FOUR

THE INFLUENCE OF RESIDENCE HALLS ON THE DEVELOPMENT OF STUDENTS

Are residence halls influential in the development of students? Do they aid students in academic pursuits, help students integrate their personal values, and, in general, provide an environment that contributes to students' overall growth toward maturity? Researchers have found evidence that residence halls do all these things.

COMPARISONS BETWEEN STUDENTS WHO LIVE IN RESIDENCE HALLS AND STUDENTS WHO DO NOT

A statistical combination of all the research on residence halls does not indicate that residence halls have a significant influence on students in the intellectual areas of academic performance, study habits, or values.[1] Although some studies do show residence halls have a positive influence in these areas, the sum total of research does not support this conclusion. Among the reasons for these differences in study findings is that students who choose to live in residence halls generally come from more affluent family backgrounds and are usually better prepared for college. Studies that control for initial differences generally do not show that living in residence halls, compared to living off campus have a significant influence on academic performance.

The sum total of residence hall research does indicate that residence halls have a positive influence on students in the nonintellectual areas of perception of the campus social climate, participation in extracurricular activities, likelihood of graduating from college, and personal growth and development.

The college experience of residence hall students and off-campus students are likely to be

Students who live in residence halls are most apt to be aware of social activities on campus.

most similar in the intellectual areas associated with the classroom activities and least similar in the nonintellectual areas associated with out-of-classroom activities. Chickering made this observation when he compared residence hall students with commuter students.[2] He concluded that residence hall students were more likely to experience immediate changes in the nonintellectual areas because the differences between high school and college were greatest in these areas; changes in the intellectual areas occurred more slowly because the experience of residents and commuters was most similar in these areas.

A synthesis of over 20 years of empirical research revealed seven areas in which residence halls had a significant influence on students.

Retention. Students who live on campus are more likely to graduate from college than students who do not live on campus. They are more likely to have greater expectations for academic achievement and are more likely to remain in college and graduate.

Participation in Extracurricular Activities. The residence hall environment also permits students to become involved in more campus activities. This is, in part, an issue of proximity. If a student

AREAS OF INFLUENCE OF RESIDENCE HALLS OVER STUDENTS

- Retention
- Participation in extracurricular activities
- Perception of the campus social climate
- Satisfaction with the college
- Personal growth and development
- Interpersonal relationships
- Faculty interaction[3]

lives on campus, their involvement in the activities that take place on campus is simply easier. Through this involvement and working with their peers, students gain important skills and experiences that aid them throughout their lives. For example, students learn to work with others in small groups, manage budgets, express their ideas in formal committee meetings, negotiate with members of the administration, develop and follow through on projects, and manage others. These are functionally transferable skills; therefore, these skills can be applied to many different situations in both the work world and daily life.

Perception of the Campus Social Climate. Students who live in residence halls have a more positive perception of the campus social climate. These students feel that the campus environment is more comfortable, more academic, more supportive, and generally more enjoyable. Generally they are more satisfied with their college experience. They feel better about themselves, what they accomplish, and the quality of their education.

Personal Growth and Development. Living on campus also facilitates personal growth and development. Residence hall students mature more quickly because they are forced to meet more challenges and thus have more opportunities to grow and become independent. Because they are away from home, they must assume more responsibility for themselves.

Interpersonal Relationships. Living in a residence hall builds strong friendships. Interpersonal relationships between students who live in residence halls are strong because of shared experiences. Living with one another allows residence hall students to have greater interaction with each other and make more and stronger friendships than students who live off campus. This finding merely reflects the opportunities these students have to interact. These interpersonal relationships

force students to develop greater tolerance for different cultures and lifestyles. Cultural biases exist when people have limited experience with people of other cultural heritages. The residence hall living environment helps break down these cultural stereotypes by forcing students to experience cultural diversity.

Faculty Interaction. Finally, students who live in residence halls have more faculty interaction than students who live off campus. This occurs partially because faculty are invited into the residence halls to meet with students and partially because residence halls are located on the campus and students can more easily mingle with faculty in informal situations. Residence hall professional staff also serve in this faculty interaction role. Interaction with both faculty and staff provides for the opportunity for mentoring relationships and for academic discussions and exploration of ideas.

THE INFLUENCE OF RESIDENCE HALL DESIGN

Residence halls are not all alike. The architectural design of some buildings invite students to interact with one another and have a warm and supportive atmosphere, whereas others seem to be sterile and institutional. The architectural designs of buildings do influence students. Research shows that satisfaction with the residence hall is inversely related to the size of the building: The larger the building—the greater the student density—the less satisfied students tend to be with living there.[4] Long, double-loaded corridors tend to isolate students and make them feel unwelcome. High-rise buildings and buildings with more than two students assigned to a room also tend to decrease satisfaction. Ideal residential situations are those with suite living arrangements, shortened corridors, and buildings that have no more than four levels.

Institutional policies regulating residence hall living can help students increase their satisfaction with the living situation. Where students are allowed to personalize their rooms, and the residence hall living unit is allowed to personalize the common space (floor lounge, hallway), students feel more a part of the residence hall environment. The more a student can invest of himself or herself into the environment, the more likely the student is to feel comfortable in that environment.

Limitations on what students can physically do to their rooms are necessary. It is unreasonable for students to so alter a room that it becomes unacceptable for future inhabitants. It is also unreasonable for students to endanger others by personalizing their room or common space with items that could create safety and fire hazards. Whatever institutional policies are adopted to increase student satisfaction must be balanced by the need to maintain a safe, clean, and orderly building for the current inhabitants and for those who will occupy that facility in the future.

Residence halls have a positive influence upon the lives of students. Students who live in residence halls develop social and interpersonal skills more rapidly, and come closer to a level of self-actualization than students who have not had this experience. But how does living in a residence hall help accomplish these goals? What is unique about this experience? Perhaps most importantly, how can the environment be shaped to increase, enhance, or ensure attainment of these important educational objectives?

WAYS THAT RESIDENCE HALLS INFLUENCE STUDENTS

Family Background

One of the key reasons that residence hall students accomplish more has less to do with the residence hall program or staff than with the students themselves. In some of the early work on the development of college students, Newcomb found that a student's background was the most important factor in determining success or failure in college.[5] Nothing the college can do inside or outside the classroom has as much influence on the ability to achieve as a student's experiences prior to college. Early childhood development (i.e., opportunities to learn), prepares the individual for future learning—both emotionally and intellectually.

Generally, students who attend residential colleges and live on campus come from somewhat more affluent backgrounds than commuter students. These residential students are often afforded more developmental advantages prior to college, more often have parents who attended college, and more often associate with peers who plan to attend college. These background factors contribute to the overall development of students, their motivations, and their ability to cope with an environment of ideas. The residential experiences further enhance these developmental advantages.

Leaving Home

As important as family background is to students, the break with it is an important new step and a critical phase in the maturation process, which is not experienced by students who remain at home and attend college. The very act of moving into a new environment, free from parental influences and former friends, provides students with new opportunities to learn. Meanwhile, the commuter students' environment remains relatively unchanged. They are not faced with the same challenges of adjusting to a new environment with a new pattern of social role expectations.

Peer-Group Influence

Of all the factors that influence student development in college, the peer group is the most powerful.[6] Classroom instruction, course of study, and association with members of the faculty will not be as important to a student's personal development, values, career expectations, and desire to complete college or to go on to graduate school as the other students with whom he or she associates.

In a residence hall, it is possible to predict who will make up a student's peer group—defined here as that group of students with whom the person commonly chooses to associate. A number of studies have shown that in a residential setting, a student's friends, his or her *primary peer group*, will be determined most by the opportunities that students have to interact.[7] Students who live in close proximity are generally afforded the most opportunities to interact with one another; thus, one determinant of a student's primary peer group is who lives close to that student.

Other factors obviously enter into friendship selection. Common interests, the size of the living unit, the location of a student's room in relation to the traffic pattern in the living unit, homogeneity of the group, and isolation of the group all play important roles in increasing opportunities for individuals to interact and select their primary peer group.

Once selected, the peer group is critical in the student's development and growth. It carries so much influence because it acts as what Whittaker described as the intermediate social environment between the family and society.[8] Peer groups acquire an almost parental role by setting standards of expected conduct and holding the power to reward and punish. The rewards offered by peers consist mostly of emotional support and esteem or influence within the group through acceptance. The punishments of the group, such as ridicule, isolation, reprimand, or ostracism, are also emotional.

The residential experience heightens this peer-group influence. The similarity of backgrounds, the frequent and continual interaction by virtue of proximity, and similar academic and career goals contribute to the intensification of this influence in the residence halls.

Fraternities and Sororities. Fraternities and sororities serve this same peer-support function. These organizations formalize the experience through rituals and ceremonies. Rituals serve as rites of passage into the organized group; however, most importantly, they serve to increase the commonality of experiences among the group members. Pledge pranks, hazing, and similar activities are used by the organization to solidify the group and promote group trust, although hazing usually has the opposite effect.

Informal Rituals. Students in residence halls generally do not have formal rites, but they do have informal rituals that serve the same function. The experience of preparing for midterm and final examinations, of getting intoxicated together, of participating in intramural sports together, of undergoing the same social pressures for dating, of working together on a particular program or a student government project, and of simple physical contact through proximity and interaction serve the same function. Compare for a minute the experience of a practical joke played in a residence hall a group of students and a fraternity prank. Both groups of students share in the same secretive adventure and undergo much the same unifying experience by selective inclusion into responsibility for the act. The difference between a group of students in a residence hall having a shaving-cream fight, secretly discharging fireworks, or some similar activity within the residence hall is little different from the "kidnapping" of an active member of a fraternity or sorority by the pledge class, the stealing of a composite picture of a particular fraternity or sorority, or the painting of the fraternity or sorority's letters in a prominent place on campus. The action of the group, at the exclusion of others, promotes trust, confidence, mutual dependence, and community, further solidifying the group.

Roommates often become lifelong friends.

COURTESY OF UNIVERSITY OF DUBUQUE

Roommate Influence

One element of influence in a student's peer environment is the student's roommate. During the freshman year, the roommate is a particularly important influence. Heath studied the influence of roommates in a male residence hall and found that roommates forced individuals to become more tolerant, more understanding, more expressive, and either increased or retarded the individual's maturity.[9] Vreeland went further, taking the position that freshman roommates who were also good friends could be identified as the primary force for attitude change in college.[10]

Attitudes, values, and maturity are not the only things affected by a student's roommate. Murray found that a student's grades will deviate from predicted grades, either higher or lower, in the same direction the student's roommate's grades deviate.[11] In other words, if one roommate does well academically, the chances are better for the other roommate to do well. Conversely, if one student in the room does poorly, chances are better that the other student in the room will also do poorly. Sommer provided one rationale for this observation in similar studying habits. He found that if one roommate was studying, there was a 75 percent chance that the other roommate would

also be studying. Conversely, there was only approximately a 33 percent chance that the student would be studying alone.[12]

Differences in roommates' academic performances may be associated with the students' academic performance prior to their room assignment. Blai matched roommates on the basis of high school academic performance. When there was a small degree of difference between roommates in their academic performance (i.e., high-achieving student matched with an above-average student), the tendency was for the student of lower academic achievement to perform better than expected. When the roommate match resulted in a high degree of difference in past academic performance (i.e., high-achieving student matched with a below-average student), the tendency was for the student of lower aca-demic performance to do worse than expected.[13] These findings suggest that when the margin of difference is small, the better student models good study habits and challenges the weaker student, but when the margin of difference is too great, the weaker student does not view the academic performance of the better student as attainable and performs worse than expected.

Ainsworth and Maynard studied the relationship between personality characteristics and academic performance.[14] The results of their study tend to support those of Blai. Ainsworth and

Maynard found that average and below-average students earned higher-than-predicted grade point averages when paired with high-achieving students with similar personality profiles. Without similarity in personality profiles, high-achieving students tended to perform at lower levels than predicted. Average students who scored high on the intellectual orientation subscale of the personality inventory overachieved regardless of their roommate's personality.

Some research has shown that highly dissatisfied roommates are significantly more likely to have lower academic performance than roommates with little dissatisfaction.[15] If differences in personality profiles are associated with dissatisfaction, then these findings would support those of Ainsworth and Maynard. However, studies exploring the direct relationship between the academic performance of roommates, randomly assigned, have found little or no support for roommate influence on academic performance.[16]

The Influence of the RA

Resident assistants (RAs) are another developmental influence in residence halls. This was the conclusion of a study by Zirkle and Hudson at Pennsylvania State University.[17] In this study, the researchers compared the influence of counselor-oriented RAs and administrator-oriented RAs on the development of maturity in freshman males.

They found a significant relationship between the RA's behavior and the development of maturity. Students who lived in a unit with a counselor-oriented RA had significantly higher maturity scores than students with an administrator-oriented RA. The researchers also measured the effect of not having an RA and found that units with RAs, whether counselor- or administrator-oriented, yielded significantly higher maturity levels than did units without an RA. Students with a counselor-oriented RA also had significantly higher grade point averages than did students living either with an administrator-oriented RA or without an RA.

The students in the counselor-oriented units, as compared with the other groups, had generally more positive environments. Zirkle and Hudson reported that students who lived on floors with counselor-oriented RAs

1. had more contacts with resident assistants concerning theft prevention, personal concerns, and informal matters;

2. had lower assessments for physical damage to the unit;

3. made more room changes within the unit and fewer requests to move out of the unit;

4. had considerably more unit activities;

5. felt they knew their resident assistant better, saw him more as a counselor and friend, and preferred to have him as their resident assistant again.[18]

The researchers concluded that "The behavior of the resident assistant has a significant effect upon student development. And this carries implications which are important to the role of the residence hall staff member and, more specifically, to the resident assistant in the total university educational program."[19]

These five important developmental factors—the student's background, the experience of moving into a residence hall, the student's association with a group of peers, the student's roommate, and the influence of the RA—must be viewed in the context of other environmental factors. These factors include the physical condition of the building; the predominance of students within a particular academic discipline; the composition of the residence hall (male, female, or coed); the rules, policies, and regulations of the university; the location of the university; the selectivity of the institution; the size of the institution; and a number of other factors. These all contribute to the overall impact that the residence hall environment has on an individual student at a particular college or university.

METHODS OF ADVANCING THE GROWTH AND DEVELOPMENT OF STUDENTS LIVING IN RESIDENCE HALLS

Residence halls are the intermediate peer environment by which students are invited to membership in the university or college community. Residence halls do this formally and informally. This section examines methods used in residence halls to facilitate development in students.

Involvement

Researchers have concluded that involvement is central to the education of students.[20] The National Institute for Education's Study Group on the Conditions of Excellence concluded in their report that (1) the amount of student learning and personal development associated with any educational program is directly proportional to the quality or quantity of student involvement in that program, and (2) the effectiveness of any educational policy or practice is directly related to the capacity of that policy or practice to increase student involvement and learning.[21] Pascarella and Terenzini reached a similar conclusion after analyzing over twenty years of empirical research on the effects of college on students. They found that the magnitude of a student's effort and involvement in both academic and cocurricular activities was central to a student's success in college. "The greater the effort and personal investment a student makes, the greater the likelihood of educational and personal returns on the investment across the spectrum of college outcomes."[22]

Involvement is essential to advancing the growth and development of students because it requires them to invest something of themselves in the process. When students involve themselves in

the college environment, they are committing something of themselves to their own education. They have begun to become part of a community. People are more satisfied and more motivated to achieve when they feel part of that which is trying to be achieved. Involvement requires commitment, and this commitment means that the participants become shareholders in the success of the project undertaken. Involvement in residence hall activities is a form of commitment. Through the investment of personal energy that comes through involvement, students learn skills such as working in groups, how to organize their thoughts and ideas, how to manage a budget, how to assess needs, and how to set goals. Often involvement in these programs and activities leads to career opportunities after graduation.

Integration of the In-Class and Out-of-Class Experience

Residence halls integrate the in-class and out-of-class experience. This is done to the extent that informal discussions about academic matters take place in residence halls. It also happens through informal tutoring that occurs when an upperclass student helps a freshman or sophomore, or when political issues or major social issues are discussed in small groups in late-night discussions. These discussions can be some of the most rewarding and involving aspects of living in a residence hall.

These experiences help to join what takes place in the classroom with what takes place outside of the classroom. Students in these environments are called on to defend their point of view and examine in-depth issues they may have taken for granted. Questions about premarital sex, drug use, the existence of God, and so on, are now approached on a rational basis rather than with a rote response from a prescriptive set of rules that

> **METHODS OF ASSISTING STUDENT DEVELOPMENT**
>
> - Involvement
> - Integration
> - Intervention
> - Community
> - Optimum Dissonance
> - Role Modeling
> - Adult Roles

students have been taught to follow regardless of rationale.

Living and learning centers—residence halls incorporating some form of classroom instruction and usually employing a process for selecting their residents—are good examples of a formal blend of the in-class and out-of-class experience available in residence halls. Mortimer and Boyer have both described living and learning centers as a model for integrating the in-class and out-of-class learning experience of students.[23]

Learning does not stop when a student leaves the classroom. It is the mulling over of ideas, the exploration of these ideas, and their application to real-life situations that enhances learning. Because students living in residence halls are focused on the same objective, academic discussions that enrich the classroom experience are a natural outgrowth.

Direct Intervention

Residence halls also provide the opportunity for direct intervention, such as counseling, with students. When a student is depressed, has a behavior problem, or fails to meet normal social expectations, RAs and other staff are available to counsel the student. Sometimes this counseling comes in the form of referring students for psychotherapy, which may give students permission to confront some long-term personality problems. Such intervention is a crucial element in students' overall education, including both their intellectual development and their personality development.

Community

A fourth method used to achieve educational objectives is the development of a sense of community in the residence halls. Community is a sense of mutual support and acceptance among a group of people. It offers a safe environment for students to experiment with different roles and lifestyles. It also transmits a sense of institutional culture. This institutional culture represents those experiences and commitments that are valued in the community. Such concepts as academic integrity, tolerance, compassion, honor, and trustworthiness that the educational community represents should be transmitted through the experience of working and living together in the academic community.

Optimum Dissonance

Sanford described the principle of *optimum dissonance* as the balance between a challenge and the support to meet that challenge.[24] The educational environment presents many challenges for students; competition for grades, fulfilling the expectations of parents and oneself, and financial stress, are just a few examples.

Associations that students make in the residence halls (through friendships and mutual experiences) offer support to meet the challenges of the environment. These relationships provide individual students with feedback, a sense of acceptance, and nurture. When students are stressed, have self-doubts, or overextend themselves, this support gives them the opportunity to get reinforcement and encouragement and to expel their frustrations in the safety of mutually supportive friendships.

Role Modeling

Role modeling is another method by which students learn. RAs help set examples, give feedback, and help mentor individual student growth and development. What RAs do and how they do it set an informal standard for others. Role modeling by the senior staff in a building also demonstrates for students what is appropriate and what is inappropriate, how to act and how not to act.

Adult Roles

Erikson identified four experiences people need in young adulthood to help them develop appropriate adult roles:

1. experimentation with different roles and lifestyles
2. freedom to choose activities and experience the consequences of those choices
3. involvement in what can be seen as meaningful achievement
4. time for reflection and introspection[25]

Residence halls provide the opportunity for all four of these experiences. Because students are separated from parents, they can more easily become independent and experiment with different roles and lifestyles to determine what fits them and what does not. Residence halls also provide the opportunity to be alone and to do nothing. Students can reflect on what they want to accomplish and have an opportunity to examine their feelings.

When students make decisions, colleges hold them accountable for those decisions. When these decisions are good, generally students are rewarded. When the decision is bad, students receive counseling and experience the consequences of those decisions. This kind of give and take helps students set reasonable boundaries for themselves.

The peer environment of the residence hall provides feedback to students. If students are being disruptive or have poor social skills, other students are quick to identify these deficiencies. There is no more critical judge of a person's behavior than a group of his or her peers. This feedback helps students gauge and refine their social interaction skills and their own standards for behavior.

SUMMARY

Living in residence halls has a positive influence on the educational achievement and personal growth of students. Much of this academic and personal growth can be attributed to family background, the decision to live in a residence hall, the peer group that exists within the residence hall, the student's roommate, and the influence of the RA. Residence halls can facilitate student growth and development using various proven methods.

REVIEW

1. When one combines all the research on residence halls, what are four of the areas in which residence halls seem to have the greatest influence on students?

2. What influence does architectural design have on student satisfaction with the residence hall experience and on the social climate of the hall?

3. What influence, if any, does family background have on the differences between students who live in residence halls and students who live at home with parents while attending college?

4. List four ways in which the residence hall experience influences students.

5. What factor has the greatest influence on a student's development in college?

6. List three areas in which a person's college roommate influences his or her development.

7. Give three examples of how the RA influences the development of students in the residence halls.

8. Which personal style (counselor- or administrator-oriented) of the RA is likely to have the greatest influence on students' maturity and satisfaction? Why?

9. What is a living and learning center?

10. List five methods for advancing the growth and development of students in the residence halls.

11. What is *optimum dissonance?*

12. According to Erikson, what four forms of experience do people need to have in young adulthood to help them develop appropriate adult roles?

APPLICATIONS

THE COMMUTER AND THE RESIDENT

Missy and Bambi were new freshmen at Tara College. They knew each other from leadership camp where they had been roommates for a week. They met again at freshmen orientation. Missy's home was about fifteen miles from Tara College, so she decided to commute to college and live at home with her parents. She chose Tara College for several reasons, but most of all because it offered her the most financial aid. Her parents both worked; her mother was a secretary at a local high school and her father was a roofing contractor. Neither of Missy's parents had the opportunity to attend college. Missy worked part-time off campus. She decided to keep her job to help with expenses and for personal spending money.

Bambi lived thirty miles from Tara College, but she decided to live on campus in one of the coed residence halls. She was also receiving some financial aid, but she came to Tara College because both her mother and father were graduates. Like Missy's parents, both of Bambi's parents worked. Her mother was a teacher and her father was a reporter with a local newspaper. Part of Bambi's financial aid included a work-study job on campus.

Bambi enjoyed Tara College. She and her roommate became good friends with several other women who lived on their floor. Bambi was elected as the floor representative to residence hall government. She was also active in the hall intramural activities and joined a student organization which supported environmental protection. Bambi had a number of social acquaintances and dated frequently. She also had a season ticket to the campus performing arts program which she and some of the other women from her floor had purchased together at the beginning of the year. Academically, Bambi did well. When she had difficulty with an assignment she could usually find someone in her living unit to help her, or she could go to the residence hall library or the main college library.

Missy also enjoyed Tara College, but found it difficult to spend as much time there as she would have liked. Between classes she would go either to the student union or to the library. Sometimes she would meet someone she knew from class or from high school and they would spend some time talking, but most of the time she either studied on campus or found other things to do between classes. She scheduled her classes to leave her afternoons as free as possible so that she could work.

Missy joined a campus club in history but had difficulty making their meetings. She also was unable to make most of their field trips because of her job. Most of her free time was spent with several friends from high school who chose to remain at home and work rather than go to college. Missy had a boyfriend whom she dated throughout most of high school and who was working as an apprentice electrician. She dated him exclusively. Academically, Missy was doing well, but she spent at least four to five hours each night to keep up in her classes. The branch library was about five miles from her home. It contained some of the materials she needed. She could use this library or drive to campus to use the main college library. Professors were usually available by appointment or after class to help her with assignments, and she tried to anticipate any problems with assignments far enough in advance so that she could make arrangements to see one of her professors for help.

WHAT WOULD YOU DO?

1. Who do you believe has the best chance of graduating from college, Missy or Bambi? Why?
2. In what important ways are Missy's college experiences different from those of Bambi?
3. What could Missy do to improve the quality of her college experience?

FRIENDS

Buddy and Floyd were roommates at Big South University. They met for the first time during the fall semester when they moved into the residence hall. Floyd was a National Merit Scholarship recipient and was given a full tuition waiver at Big South University. The scholarship would be continued as long as Floyd maintained a 3.0 grade point average (a B average).

Buddy was a reasonably good student in high school but he was not nearly the caliber of student that Floyd was. Buddy was an outstanding athlete in school, and was voted the most popular guy in his senior class. Everyone liked Buddy, and Buddy liked everyone. He was good looking and had a very active social life. One of Buddy's skills was organizing and having parties. His good interpersonal and social skills made him the quintessential host or party guest.

Floyd admired Buddy. Although Floyd was reasonably good-looking, he lacked the social confidence and poise which seemed to come so naturally to Buddy. Because of Buddy's interpersonal skills, Floyd and Buddy's room became the social focus of activities on the floor. There was always someone in their room talking, watching a football game, or playing cards. Seldom did any of this activity break up before 1:00 A.M. During times the room was occupied by others, Buddy was either talking on the telephone, or Floyd was taking messages for him. Buddy was also thinking about pledging a fraternity, and two fraternities were rushing him very hard. They also rushed Floyd, but he thought it might be because he was Buddy's roommate. This simply added to the confusion. At least one night each weekend, Floyd found himself sleeping in either the floor lounge or in someone else's room, because Buddy usually brought his date back to the room where they would spend most of the night together.

Although Floyd realized that all of this activity was detracting from his school work, he liked Buddy and the other men on the floor. He wanted to be a part of the group and enjoyed the attention from the people who were constantly in and out of his room. This experience did have some benefits for Floyd; he felt more self-confident, was more comfortable in groups, and had made some friends. His social life had also improved. He had been on several double dates with Buddy and his girlfriend, and was beginning to develop a relationship with one woman in particular.

Midterm grades were sent home to Floyd's and Buddy's parents. Floyd's grade point average was 2.2. Buddy's was also 2.2, which he thought was fine. His parents, knowing Buddy's strengths and weaknesses, thought it was acceptable. Floyd's parents, though, were very concerned. They realized that Floyd would lose his scholarship if his grades did not improve. They called the dean of students at Big South University, who called the hall director, who talked to Buddy and Floyd's RA. The hall director wanted the RA's recommendation on what to do, if anything, about Floyd, his new lifestyle, and his roommate.

WHAT WOULD YOU DO?

1. If you were Floyd and Buddy's RA what recommendation(s) would you make to the hall director?
2. Is Buddy at fault for the negative study environment in Buddy and Floyd's room? Why or why not?
3. How has Floyd benefitted? Do these benefits outweigh the poor academic performance?
4. Floyd's parents have suggested that he be moved to a "study floor" in another building, where study hours are strictly enforced, or that he be given a single room someplace on campus. What do you think about these ideas?

PART TWO

UNDERSTANDING AND WORKING WITH COLLEGE STUDENTS

The Growth and Development of College Students

Adjusting to College

Peer Counseling

CHAPTER FIVE

THE GROWTH AND DEVELOPMENT OF COLLEGE STUDENTS

©1998 PHOTODISK, INC.

This chapter considers the biological, psychological, and social development of traditional-aged college students—those between the ages of 18 and 24. The focus is on "normal" development during these years. *Normal* means the average behavioral changes, or those the majority of college students experience.

If you think of a normal distribution curve, the term includes those responses that fall within one standard deviation above or below the mean for any particular group.

Each person moves through development at his or her own pace. Maturation is influenced by individual differences that may accelerate or retard the process of development. Social factors, biological factors, and experience play roles in the pace at which one matures.

BIOLOGICAL DEVELOPMENT

During the years of young adulthood men and women biologically are becoming adults. Women begin puberty somewhere between the ages of 8 and 13, and men start puberty approximately two years later—between the ages of 10 and 15. Puberty is the period when a person becomes physically mature enough to reproduce. It involves developing secondary sexual characteristics associated with gender and with hormonal changes in the body.

Physically, women reach their full height at about the age of 17. Men lag behind and do not reach their full height until about the age of 21. Men and women grow differently during this period of adolescence. Men's shoulders grow wider and their chest cavity expands while their legs and forearms grow longer. Women grow wider in the pelvic area, ostensibly to enhance their ability to bear children, and their breasts, legs, arms, and torso develop.

Uneven Growth Patterns

Growth is not necessarily proportional throughout the entire adolescent period. Different portions of the body grow at different rates; therefore, some portions of the body may reach maturity faster than others. Typically the extremities, head, hands, and feet reach maturity prior to the legs, arms, and trunk of the body. This constantly fluctuating size leads to a decrease in motor skill coordination as the individual is learning to adapt to the changing size of his or her body. The description of the "awkward adolescent" is a reflection of this uneven growth toward maturity.

Recent generations have seen a trend (known as the *secular trend*) toward increasing size and earlier sexual maturity. Zastrow and Kirst-Ashman noted that sons are likely to be as much as one inch taller and ten pounds heavier than their fathers, and daughters will be between one-half to one full inch taller than their mothers and approximately two pounds heavier. Menstruation is occurring in women of the current generation about 10 months earlier than it did for their mothers. The secular trend is worldwide. The reason for this trend appears to be related to better nutrition, better standards of living, and possibly the dominance of genes for tallness and rapid maturation. For the time being, this trend for increased size seems to have stabilized in the American population.[1]

During college, men and women approach their physical prime, reaching their full muscular development generally between the ages of 25 and 30. Top physical speed, dexterity, and overall strength generally continue to increase until about the age of 30, when a gradual decline begins. Eyesight and hearing continue to improve and are best at about the age of 20.[2] For the most part, college students are in good health and generally have a high energy level.

Health issues that interfere with good health are heavy drinking, drug use, and stress. The major causes of death among college students are auto accidents and suicides. In a high percentage of cases, alcohol use is involved with both causes of death.

Psychological Adaptation to Physical Development

In the 1950s a longitudinal study on the influence of late and early maturation in men and women showed that boys who matured early were viewed by others as more physically attractive, were treated more like adults, and were more likely to be chosen as school leaders. In contrast, late-maturing boys were viewed as less physically attractive, more tense, and more involved in attention-getting behavior. But, they were also more flexible and more capable of confronting periods of uncertainty. For women, the results were less clear. Early maturation seemed to be associated with some psychological benefits related to attractiveness and feelings of maturity; however, no noticeable negative effect was associated with late maturation in women.[3]

In 1981 Blyth, Bulcroft, and Simmons conducted a study in Wisconsin on early and late maturation. They found that boys who matured early had a higher self-concept, were generally less satisfied with their overall physical development, tended to be more popular with girls, and participated in more school activities during high school. The same study found that early-maturing girls were also less satisfied with their bodies than late maturers, were more often in dating relationships with boys, and had more behavior problems during middle school.[4]

The short-term implications of early and late maturation appear to affect self-concept and early identity formation. Early maturers generally had greater self-esteem, and some evidence indicates that early maturers may have been pushed prematurely into decisions about identity.[5] These differences appear to be short-lived. By the age of 30 there are generally no significant differences in physical size, educational attainment, marital status, socioeconomic status, or in the number of children per family unit. One benefit to late maturing may be that late maturers are forced to deal with ambiguity in adolescence and to develop an increased tolerance for uncertainty. As a result they tend to be somewhat more flexible.

PSYCHOLOGICAL DEVELOPMENT DURING THE COLLEGE YEARS

One of the most dynamic periods of psychological growth occurs during the college years. In this period young adults begin to integrate their identity, enhance their intellectual development, and internalize a personal set of beliefs and values. As people mature, they change. Sanford defined *change* as "a system that is altered from a previous state."[6] Two forms of change take place as a person matures. The first is *growth,* which Sanford described as an expansion of the personality by addition of parts or expansion of existing parts. The second is *development,* defined as the process of organizing with increasing complexity. Both forms—growth and development—occur simultaneously throughout a person's life.

Development is driven by two forces: epigenesis and social role expectations.[7] *Epigenesis* is an internal evolutionary "clock" that biologically and psychologically pushes us towards maturity. Puberty is one example of this clock or internal force which drives the individual forward. *Social role expectations* are behaviors that are culturally associated with a person's age and gender. As we grow older, society expects us to be increasingly independent, less impulsive, and more in control

GENERAL CHARACTERISTICS OF DEVELOPMENT

1. Development is continuous.
2. Development is a process, not a state.
3. Development has order.
4. Development moves from general to specific and from simple to more complex.
5. Development has characteristics associated with specific age levels.
6. Both heredity and the environment influence development.
7. Development occurs in the context of interactions between the individual and the environment, rather than through internal processes of maturation alone.

of our lives. When a person's behavior conflicts with the social role expectations for him or her at a particular age, the person experiences a *developmental crisis*. These crises are good. They force people to evaluate their current behavior and pattern of thinking, and to adjust them to meet new social role expectations. All of this simply means that society has come to expect more mature behavior from people as they grow older, and that society defines how people are expected to behave at different periods in their lives. Epigenesis complements this process.

Development follows a logical sequence of stages. At each stage, people work to resolve the same or similar issues. These issues are referred to as *developmental tasks* and have a logic to their progression. For example, when children are very young, parents establish and enforce a bedtime. As a child grows older, this bedtime may get moved to a later time of the evening, but is still enforced. By the time the child reaches high school, typically parents no longer enforce any bedtime and leave this decision to the child. However, parents of high schoolers usually establish a curfew for when their children must return home. As the child grows older, the curfew is generally withdrawn, and the time in which a single person may be expected back in the parents' home is left to the discretion of the young adult, with the understanding that some basic courtesies are respected in the family home.

The culture in which psychosocial development occurs influences the individual. Because cultures vary widely, different social influences may accelerate or retard different forms of development. Environment and social role expectations combine to influence development. For example, it is unusual to find a young man at the age of 17 living in a Midwestern town who does not have a driver's license. Having a drivers' license is one of the first symbols of entering adulthood and provides the opportunity to have greater freedom. However, it is not at all unusual to find a young man from New York City, Queens, or Brooklyn who does not have a driver's license. Public transportation in New York City is such that a driver's license is not a necessity, and the environment does not demand that families own automobiles. Freedom may come earlier as parents permit their children greater liberty in the use of the subway system and other public transportation. Thus, the issue of autonomy can be advanced or retarded by the interplay of the social and physical environment and its influence on the individual.

Development changes qualitatively as well, meaning that it is not simply an adding on of more responsibility; the complexity of organization also increases at each stage in development. Psychosocial stages are also concerned with content issues. Experience with certain social issues such as dating, defining appropriate sex roles, marriage, and family influences a person's development.

Although some of this discussion may seem to indicate that development is segmented—that is, one part of the person develops while the rest remains stagnate—this is not the case. Development is unitary; it involves the whole person. Elements of a personality develop in interaction with other characteristics of the individual. The process of change has order and develops a foundation for successive developmental changes.

College offers students the opportunity to socialize with a variety of people and model the roles of a variety of different lifestyles. Separated from parents and in many ways on their own, students also have the opportunity to experience the consequences of their actions. The grades a person achieves and the successes and failures are owned by the individual. A college education is viewed by society as a meaningful achievement. Acquisition of a degree and working toward a career goal are consistent with a need to be involved in a meaningful experience. Finally, the college environment is ideal for providing time for reflection and introspection. Although many college students are pressed for time, without doubt most still have the option to have a large portion of unstructured leisure time available.

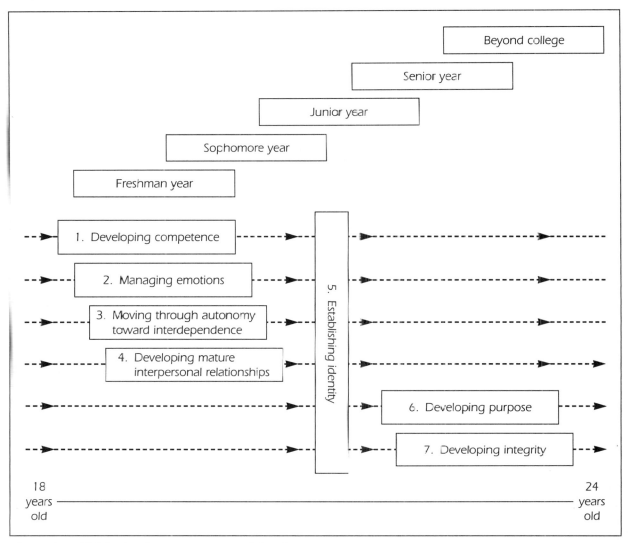

Figure 5.1   *Chickering's seven vectors of development.*

Chickering's Theory of Psychosocial Development in College Students

Authur Chickering studied the psychosocial development of college students and later collaborated with Linda Reisser. Their research revealed seven vectors of development (Figure 5.1) that students work on throughout the college years.[8] A *vector* is a theme or a recurring issue that tends to drive growth and development in the personality. At certain periods in a person's life, societal expectations come into conflict with a person's usual pattern of behavior. The clash between a person's current behavior and new age-related role expectations causes a developmental crisis. This crisis creates an inbalance that the person needs to correct by adjusting his or her behavior and integrating this change into his or her personality. These seven vectors begin in early childhood and extend throughout a person's life. The seven vectors Chickering and Reisser identified are:

This time provides the opportunity for reflection and introspection.

The interaction of students living together provides regular feedback to the individual, time for reflection and introspection, and late-night discussions with other students. It also provides the opportunity to live alone or with a roommate in an environment controlled mostly by the individual. This environment allows a person to choose among a number of activities and to experience the consequences of choices made in this environment.

Developing Competence.   When students arrive at a university, they are usually uncertain about how they will fit into this new environment. It is an environment that they have yet to master and presents for them a number of uncertainties. The first task that students must accomplish is to develop competence in the environment. Students work on three forms of competence. First is intellectual competence. Students must come to believe that they are intelligent enough to compete in the university environment. They do this by consulting with their peers, getting feedback from instructors, and measuring this progress by performance on tests. One response often heard from new students is, "It's not as hard as I thought it would be." This response is most likely the result of somebody who had high expectations for great academic demands and found that the students with whom he or she was competing and the instructor's demands were geared for freshman-level academic performance.

While working on intellectual competence, students also explore their physical/manual competence. This refers to whether students view themselves as though they are as strong as, as attractive as, as physically developed as the other students attending the university. This is an issue of fitting in, determining whether one possesses the same athletic skills, manual dexterity skills, and other normal physical skills which other students possess.

The third competency issue is interpersonal competence. Students need to feel that they belong. They need to develop confidence in their relationships with peers, develop strong social networks, develop dating relationships, and similar forms of social interaction that signify peer acceptance. Participation in clubs and organizations, election to residence hall government, and establishment of friendships with roommates and others in the living unit give the person feedback about how he or she fits into the peer environment. Through this interaction, the person develops a sense of control or competency.

These three forms of competency—intellectual, physical/manual, and interpersonal—form an overall sense of competence or self-confidence, which is one of the first building blocks in students' overall move toward establishing a working identity structure. These competencies are formed through the process of differentiation followed by a process of integration. First the individual examines how he or she is different from other students. In some cases this will mean that the person performs better than peers, and in other cases it means that the person is not functioning as well as peers. Through the process of trial and error, feedback, and comparison, a person begins to develop a concept of where he or she fits in relation to others. This information is integrated into one's overall self-concept, forming one element in the person's identity. Competition with others and

Participating in sports provides a common bond for fitting in with peers.

success in mastering academic work help to reinforce and build these identity structures.

Managing Emotions.   Two processes occur in the evolution of emotional development during the college years. The first is moving from controlling one's own behavior because of external influence to a process of controlling behavior through internal processes. Children do what is right based upon external controls, generally through authority exercised by the school or parents. In adolescence, peer standards tend to control the same kind of behavior. Right and wrong are often defined by the external source of peer norms. However, as people mature, they come to accept increasing responsibility for their actions. This is a shift in *locus of control* from external sources being responsible for actions to an acceptance of the self as responsible for actions.

The second process, differentiation and integration, has four steps: (1) awareness of one's emotions, (2) acting on emotions, (3) receiving feedback on actions, and (4) exercising internal control of actions and integrating emotions. As an example, take a young man learning to control his aggressive behavior. First he becomes aware that he gets angry. He controls his anger principally due to external sources such as the social rules of school or the imposition of authority. At some point he acts on this emotion, perhaps by striking

someone. He will receive feedback about this aggressive action. This feedback may come from friends or authorities who reason with him about the propriety of his conduct for his age. Peers may encourage or discourage this form of action. As a person grows older, this form of aggressive behavior is strongly discouraged, and punitive action is taken by society for those who are unable to control their actions. Eventually, through a process of reasoning, feedback, and having to confront the consequences of his action, the person internalizes appropriate responses to aggressive feelings.

During college, people learn to confront a wide range of emotions, not as children but as adults. Emotions such as love, rejection, grief, anger, and lust are among those which a person must learn to understand and integrate. People will comment that someone "is not acting like himself" because they have a concept or definition of other people; when someone does not respond as expected, they are likely to get feedback about how the behavior has changed. In other words, others define for a person how he or she is perceived and how people have come to expect the person to act. This feedback process helps the individual maintain and establish identity and sets expectations for how one is to control his or her emotions.

The process of managing emotions is actually

about increasing awareness of feelings and learning how to understand and trust these feelings. The only way this can be accomplished is by experiencing these emotions, receiving feedback on them, and integrating this information into the self-concept.

Moving through Autonomy toward Interdependence. The vector of autonomy is a recurring issue throughout life, as are the other vectors identified by Chickering and Reisser. As early as the age of two, children begin differentiating themselves from others and take greater control over their lives. The process of autonomy consists of three elements. First is developing emotional independence. When people become emotionally independent, they accept responsibility for themselves and lessen the need for emotional approval from family and peers. People come to realize that they are ultimately responsible for themselves and that although the recognition of friends and family is important, it is less important than the

College students generally are willing to share parts of themselves with their friends.

individual's own sense of what is right. The second element of autonomy is what Chickering and Reisser described as "instrumental independence." Being instrumentally independent means that a person has become responsible for himself or herself and that the person has control of his or her environment. This usually involves being financially independent—employed—and having one's own residence. The integration of emotional independence and instrumental independence forms the third element of autonomy, which Chickering and Reisser described as "interdependence." This is a realization of independence and of one's responsibility for contributing positively to one's community.

For college students, the process of autonomy is a process of breaking away from parents emotionally and financially. College both helps and hinders this process. It helps the process, because it allows students to move away from home and therefore free themselves from parental control. Residence halls provide an excellent intermediate peer environment in the transition between parental control and total independence.

College also hinders the maturation process, because it is expensive and requires a substantial time commitment. Parents are usually involved in providing some financial support to students for college. This financial support inhibits the development of instrumental independence. As long as students are dependent on parents for the money to survive, the apartments or residence halls in which they live, and the cars they may drive, students cannot be truly independent. Only after people become financially responsible for themselves can they become mature to the point of interdependence.

Developing Mature Interpersonal Relationships. As people come to know more about themselves, they feel more secure in relationships. Chickering and Reisser observed that as people mature, the depth and intimacy of their relationships are enhanced. People retain belief in fewer stereotypes, are generally more tolerant of the views of others, and have fewer superficial relationships. Friendships are based on greater trust, and there is more openness and freedom to express one's innermost feelings. Part of the process of developing mature interpersonal relationships involves understanding and accepting differences in others—accepting others for who they are.

Women generally have had greater freedom to do this throughout their lives and have less difficulty developing their interpersonal relationships. The situation is different for men. Men are taught to be competitive with each other. It is difficult for them to share openly in friendships for fear that these expressions of emotion will be viewed as weakness. Men are generally much more selective about those with whom they share their most intimate feelings. Often this level of intimacy is reserved only for a special female companion with whom they feel secure, or perhaps one close male friend with whom they have shared many experiences.

People are not really prepared to participate fully in interpersonal relationships until they know themselves and feel secure in who they are. As this self-confidence and self-knowledge increases, people become less vulnerable and more willing to take emotional risks by sharing parts of themselves with others.

During maturation there is a shift toward greater trust, independence, and individuality. People should become less anxious, more secure, less defensive, and more friendly. They are often more spontaneous and more respectful of other people. General cultural stereotypes are broken down, and there is an increasing tolerance for a range of different people.

Establishing Identity. Like the other vectors, establishing identity is a process begun in childhood. The college years are part of the period most critical to forming identity. The first four vectors—competence, managing emotions, moving through autonomy toward interdependence, and develop-

ing mature interpersonal relationships—form the framework for the establishment of an identity. They are necessary but not sufficient conditions for identity development.

The process of maturing and developing in these four areas helps people bring definition to their personality. For young adults to discover who they are, they must first separate or differentiate themselves from others. Only by doing so can they begin to integrate their successes and failures and develop a self-image or self-concept. Chickering described *identity* as confidence in one's ability to maintain inner sameness and continuity. It involves recognizing one's physical needs and limitations and developing comfort with one's body and appearance, sexual identity, and gender.

Once a person has established a self-image and formed an identity structure, the person is prepared to move toward expanding and enriching this identity. During the college years and throughout his or her 20s a person works on resolving issues connected with the last two vectors: developing purpose and developing integrity.

Developing Purpose. Career and vocational plans do not wait until the latter part of college. Most high school students and first-year college students wrestle with what they want to do with their lives. However, by the junior or senior year in college, career decision-making is pressed by the rapidly approaching graduation date. Another way to express this is that the social demands of the environment create a crisis that the student must confront. Wrestling with the crisis of a vocational choice forces students to assess their strengths and to develop the beginnings of a commitment to a particular vocation. By the time students are ready to graduate, most have a general idea about how they might wish to earn a living.

As people make decisions about vocations, they are also enhancing their self-knowledge about avocational interests, the lifestyle that they would like to have, and the things that they hold to be important—their values. If a person is committed to important social issues, such as the needs of the homeless, this particular value commitment may influence their career choice. If an individual wants a high-status position and a high-profile, luxurious lifestyle, he or she may choose a different profession. Some people are able to successfully integrate vocational, avocational, lifestyle, and value commitments into an occupation. A person who is interested in being outside and working with nature, who enjoys backpacking and camping, might, for example, choose a career in forestry, as a conservationist, or perhaps with the U.S. Park Service. A person who is interested in animals and nature might choose a position as a veterinarian or as a zoologist.

The goal of this vector—clarifying purpose—in the college years is to integrate the four elements of purpose: vocational commitment, avocational interests, lifestyle, and values, into an initial commitment for adulthood. As with identity and the other vectors, a person's purpose in life and overall career changes and matures as he or she develops. College is devoted to the integration of the initial commitment, and life after college is focused on exploring and confirming these initial commitments.

Developing Integrity. The last of the seven vectors is integrity. It consists of humanizing and personalizing values and developing congruence between them. Humanizing values is a process of making rule-governed beliefs that guide society applicable to the human condition. It is a shift in how we view rule-governed behavior. It reflects a general liberalizing of values from a position where they are considered absolute to a position where they are considered to be relative. People come to learn that certain social rules may not always be consistent with the purpose for which they were designed. As people apply these beliefs and rules to their own lives, they come to accept or commit to those standards most consistent with their developing sense of values.

The humanizing of values also involves the internalization of these values. A person no longer considers them to be values to be held by others, but internalizes these values as his or her own. This follows a shift in locus of control.

Personalizing values occurs as values are applied to one's own life circumstances. It is an integration of what a person believes with how a person acts. A person may, for example, believe that stealing is wrong but be arrested for shoplifting in the bookstore. This incongruence may reflect a failure to personalize values and integrate what one believes with how one acts. This integration is a process of developing congruence between beliefs and actions.

Integrity is not something that a person achieves. It is a continuing process of moral growth and development. Although this is a continuing concern throughout college, many value issues are not resolved until after college. In part, integrity is the result of experience with ethical dilemmas confronted in life. The extent to which one's behavior reflects personal values is a complex internal process. Research suggests that as a person's stage of moral development increases, he or she is more likely to act in a manner consistent with those values.[9] In other words, moral development fosters greater consistency between beliefs and actions.

COGNITIVE DEVELOPMENT

Cognitive development is concerned with increasingly complex structures or methods of reasoning. The characteristics of cognitive developmental stages are as follows:

• The stages form an invariant sequence. Issues at lower stages must be resolved in order to move to a higher stage of development. Moving from a lower stage of development to a higher stage is not possible without passing through the intermediate steps.

- The stages are arranged in a hierarchy, moving from simple to complex. In the early years, cognitive issues are resolved in a simplistic form. As a person gains experience, he or she may find more complex methods of reasoning and move to a higher stage.

- The sequence of cognitive development is universal. Regardless of culture or social issues, cognitive development follows a pattern or sequence inherent to the human life cycle. Social influences can affect the rate and the likelihood of reaching high levels of cognitive reasoning, but without these social or cultural influences, the potential to achieve higher stages is the same, regardless of culture.

- Stages are qualitatively different. This means that different issues are resolved and new forms of reasoning are confronted at each stage.

- Cognitive developmental stages are concerned with the structure or complexity of reasoning, rather than the content of the judgments made. It is not so much the decision a person makes, but the reasoning or structure of the judgment used to make the decision that reflects cognitive development. Cognitive development is the process of acquiring increasingly complex reasoning at each stage.

Cognitive development occurs through *adaptation,* which is a process of change to adjust or fit into one's surrounding environment. It is composed of the processes of assimilation and accommodation. *Assimilation* is the process by which one acquires and integrates new information into a thought structure. As one gathers new information and experiences, these events are held not only in the conscious awareness, but are also used to help shape one's thinking. As this information is accumulated, it is used as experimental information in similar problem-solving situations. *Accommodation* is the process of adaptation used when a person's perception and actions are changed to use a more abstract or higher level of reasoning. Assimilation involves taking in and storing information, and accommodation

applies this information in more complex forms of reasoning.

Perry's Theory of Cognitive Development in College Students

William Perry was interested in how the reasoning of students changed as a result of their exposure to the classroom learning situation and the college environment. Through his research, Perry found three major stages, each composed of three positions. He defined a position as a structure representing a mode or central tendency through which a person perceives the world at a given time.[13]

Dualism. *Dualism* is the first sequence of positions students encounter in their intellectual growth in college. In this stage, students see information classified as either right or wrong. They have little tolerance for ambiguity and attribute knowledge of "truth" to those in positions of authority. When two authorities disagree, one authority is usually seen as a bad authority (Position 2) and later, when two good authorities disagree, a new category of "not yet known" is assigned to those areas where knowledge is uncertain (Position 3).

Although the Perry scheme does not examine behavior directly, certain behavioral patterns can be identified within each level of development. In dualism, Widick and Simpson characterized students as

- experiencing stress when uncertainty is encountered

- having difficulty in resolving interpretative tasks such as essays

- perceiving instructors as knowing the truth

- attaching disproportionate importance to evaluations[11]

At this level, students believe all knowledge is known, Professors supposedly have the right

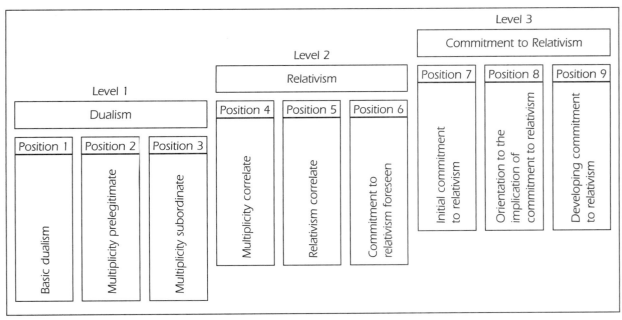

Figure 5.2. *Perry's stages of intellectual and ethical development in college students.*

answers. The role of a student is to study and learn from those who hold the truth. As a person develops in this stage of dualism, he or she moves from a period of uncertainty to a period of increasing acceptance that it is legitimate to feel uncertain about some events.

Relativism. Through the process of grappling with issues that have no right or wrong answer, a student reaches the stage where he or she is willing to accept that not all information is known and that it is legitimate to be uncertain. In *relativism,* the concept of absolute rights and wrongs—held in dualism—are replaced by the legitimacy of uncertainty (Position 4). Students are inclined to believe that people have a right to their own opinions and that no answer is any more valid than anyone else's.

In Position 5, knowledge is seen as certain only within context and relativistic assumptions of knowledge, and values begin to be linked to issues of self-identity. Knowledge and values are contextual and authorities are seen as ways to help

a person reach his or her own decision as to what answers are correct. However, there are no absolute criteria for making these decisions.

In Position 6, students see the necessity for orienting themselves to make commitments where there is no certain right answer. They recognize that many questions have multiple answers and that authorities are useful in selecting among the alternatives. The important aspect of this position is that students have come to accept uncertainty and are willing to commit even when they are uncertain.

Widick and Simpson noted that during the stage of relativism: students experienced
- an emphasis on intuition
- development of the capacity to perform complex analytic tasks with some skill
- more internalized learning
- a lessened concern with pleasing instructors[12]

Commitment to Relativism. At the level of a *commitment to relativism* (Positions 7, 8, and 9), students focus on clarifying their place in the world by exploring careers, marriage, and lifestyle. This level is characterized by self-discovery, commitment, balancing of priorities, and (in Position 9) a search for or the beginning of a synthesis in issues of ethics and integrity.

In Position 7 students make an initial commitment in some areas such as career, marriage, and lifestyle. In Position 8 they experience implications of these commitments and explore the responsibility associated with them. Finally, in Position 9 adults experience and affirm those commitments consistent with their identity and reassess or change commitments to meet that changing identity.

Perry acknowledged that Positions 7, 8, and 9 may be circular as opposed to linear. People throughout their adult life may reexamine these same issues as they fulfill other dimensions of their life. Thus, Positions 7, 8, and 9 may simply be a cycle created as people experience different issues of commitment throughout their lives.

In 1981 Perry introduced a stylistic variation evident throughout the scheme, but particularly important in Position 4.[13] Students appear to approach the stage of relativism by viewing authorities either as role models to be followed or as adversaries to be debated. Moore described the different methods of cognitive adaptation. "The adhering student struggles with the transition from being a dependent learner to becoming an independent one; the oppositional student struggles with the temptation to stay in the apparent 'freedom' of the 'do your own thing' perspective."[14] Both groups of students depend on the authority figure, but in different ways—the adhering student for support and as a role model, the oppositional student for a challenge and for contrast.

Perry's scheme differs from many of the other developmental approaches in that it provides alternatives to development through *escape, temporizing,* and *retreat.* In retreat, a student confronted by too much challenge and not enough support may retreat to the security and certainty of basic dualism. Students who fail to make a commitment

in the stage of relativism may escape into a relativistic way of viewing the world. They do not need to commit to uncertainty. Finally, some students temporize by remaining in a position because they are hesitant or unprepared to advance.

Conditions that tend to facilitate intellectual development include affective involvement, which involves empathizing with others and placing oneself in the role of another. Being confronted with new challenges, having the ability to process the encounter, and getting feedback regarding issues of uncertainty assist with development. Other dimensions of personality such as ego style and identity formation may further enhance or retard intellectual development.

Kohlberg's Theory of Moral Development

Lawrence Kohlberg's research blended the work of John Dewey and Jean Piaget into a new way of thinking about how people develop the capacity to make moral judgments.[15] Kohlberg broke from the traditional view of moral development, which held that as people mature they absorb or internalize the cultural values around them. This view, sometimes referred to as *childhood socialization* or the *anthropological perspective,* continues to have support.

Kohlberg proposed that there are three levels of moral reasoning (*preconventional, conventional,* and *postconventional),* each consisting of two substages. Figure 5.3 illustrates the movement from Stage 1 reasoning to Stage 6 reasoning by showing the primary considerations (egocentrism, sociocentrism, and allocentrism) in making a moral judgment at each of Kohlberg's stages.

Preconventional Level (Egocentrism). At the preconventional level, children are attentive to the cultural rules defined by their parents. They tend to interpret what is right by the physical consequences of their actions. Rewards and punish-

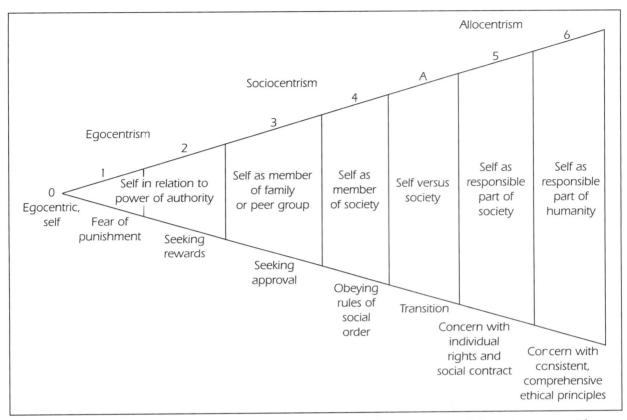

Figure 5.3. *The move from egocentrism to allocentrism and the expansion of the primary considera-tion in moral reasoning in Kohlberg's model.*

ment tend to dictate what is right and what is wrong. Stage 1 is the "punishment-and-obedience orientation" (fear of punishment). In this stage children are consumed with avoidance of punishment and defer their judgment to a parent or anyone with authority. There is no reasoning about the underlying moral order supporting this decision, only a response to authority or punishment.

In Stage 2, "the instrumental relativistic orientation" (seeking rewards), moral reasoning is based on self-gratification or hedonistic values. Moral decisions are based on issues of reciprocity, equal sharing, and quid pro quo.

Conventional Level (Sociocentrism). At the conventional level of morality, a person relinquishes moral judgments to the expectations of the social group. Initially this is the family group, followed by the peer group, and finally some type of cultural or social order. Moral decisions conform to the social norm or model expectations in the particular social order regardless of the consequences. There is loyalty to the group, support for it, identification with it, and internal justification for it. The conventional level of morality comprises stages 3 and 4.

Stage 3 is the "interpersonal-concordance or good-boy, nice-girl orientation" (seeking approval). Morally correct decisions are decisions that please others. There is a concern with the stereotypes of what is good and what is bad or what the majority would do in a particular case. The focus is on being a good or nice person. The standard of what a good boy or good girl would do in a particular situation is internalized. Such statements as "Nice girls don't" characterize the kind of judgments that would be made at this stage.

At Stage 4, "the law-and-order orientation" (obeying rules of social order), moral decisions are determined by fixed rules for the purpose of maintaining the social order. The correct decision is one that follows the rules, fulfills duty, or upholds the social authority structure. As a member of society, one has a duty to maintain the laws of the community because the law has been created by a legitimate order and is necessary for maintaining the social order.

Postconventional Level (Allocentrism). In this level there is a shift to principled thinking and an effort to internalize and personalize values. Morally correct decisions conform to the individual's concept of justice. These decisions occur apart from consideration of the response to authority or the need to conform one's opinions to those of a group. Stages 5 and 6 compose this level of moral reasoning.

Stage 5 is the "social-contract, legalistic orientation" (concern with individual rights and social contract). Morally correct actions uphold individual rights as agreed upon in the society. The decision-making process and democratic decision making are emphasized. Without this form of decision making, what is right is viewed as a matter of personal opinion or choice. When decisions are not made through the democratic and legal process, social contracts between individuals are the binding force of what is morally correct.

The highest stage of moral reasoning is Stage 6, "the universal ethical-principle orientation" (concern with consistent, comprehensive ethical principles). Morally correct decisions conform to one's own conscience, consistent with a valid set of ethical principles that are logically comprehensive, universal, and consistently held. Decisions are made on the basis of principles, not on the basis of rules. These decisions are based on deontic principles of fairness, equality, human rights, and dignity.

These three levels of moral reasoning also may be viewed as movement from a focus on egocentric issues in early childhood (Stages 1 and 2) to a focus on the social environment (Stages 3 and 4) to a focus on allocentristic or other-directed values (Stages 5 and 6). This shows development as a move from self-interest to interest in others. Kohlberg's theory is consistent with the developmental concept of moving from simple issues to more complex issues.

Moral Development in the College Years

Moral development in the college years has been described by Gilligan as a "shift from moral ideology to ethical responsibility."[16] The source of the shift is a realization of the relativity of moral values brought about by the wider exposure to ideas and influences in the college environment.

Most college students are in Kohlberg's Stage 3 of moral reasoning, in which what is right is determined by the peer group. If one's peers believe that a certain behavior is correct, for all practical purposes the person holding loyalty to that group will act accordingly. As the person moves away from dependence on the peer group and comes to rely on his or her own judgment, there is a shift to adherence to moral judgments based on principles of law and order. This is Stage 4 reasoning. Most people in our society are Stage 4 reasoners. A greater exposure to education and the conflicting values in a college community press many students to advance to consider moral judgments on the basis of ethical principles (seen in Stages 5 and 6).

During college, students move from the recognition of external sources of authority for moral decisions to an acceptance of their personal authority and responsibility for moral judgments. It is a shift from letting others determine what is right and simply following those dictates, to accepting responsibility for their own actions and acting in accordance with an internally held, valid set of principles.

One might question whether students who exhibit some of the most outrageous behavior in residence halls are making progress in their moral development. At one point, Kohlberg and Kramer believed that some students actually regressed after entering college. Their research showed that some students began making decisions[17] based on hedonistic self-interests without consideration for others. Upon closer examination, Kohlberg concluded that it was not regression that these students experienced when they entered college. Rather, it was a transitional period when some students experienced a conflict between the relativity of moral principles (conventional morality) and a commitment to ethical principles based on social contracts in a legalistic orientation (postconventional morality).[18]

This period of transition, marked by hedonistic behavior, permits students to increase their awareness of the concepts of equality and individual rights, their understanding of the collective functioning of humanity, and their knowledge of and concern for objective criteria for moral judgments.[19] It also allows a psychological moratorium that gives students the freedom to integrate conventional moral reasoning and establish a framework for Stage 5 reasoning based on ethical principles.[20] Because students are still struggling with internalizing the principles for ethical judgments, they substitute personal and subjective criteria for these decisions. Thus, these students appear to lack values or moral judgment. A more accurate description would be that they are in the process of developing principled thinking.

Carol Gilligan's Theory of Moral Development in Women

Carol Gilligan studied the relationship between moral reasoning and moral behavior using women as subjects. She discovered in her research that women may make moral judgments in ways that differ from those described by Kohlberg. Kohlberg's theory is based on the concept of justice. In contrast, Gilligan's theory is based on the concept of caring. Gilligan contended that women emphasize relationships between persons and how they fit into a particular moral dilemma.[21] Women seek first to understand the needs of others and to respond to those needs rather than to respond first to self-interests. The moral dilemmas that they face tend to be viewed in the context of relationship, collaboration, preventing physical or psychological harm, or restoring friendships. One example cited by Gilligan as symbolic of this caring voice in women which defines their moral judgment is taken from a story in the Old Testament. In this story, two women and a child are brought before Solomon. He is asked to determine which of the two women is the mother of the child. Both claim that they are the mother. Solomon offers a solution by calling for a sword to divide the baby in half. The true mother speaks up and surrenders her claim to her son to save the life of the child. Solomon recognizes that only a mother would make this sacrifice and declares her to be the rightful mother of the child. The story illustrates the nature of moral action that Gilligan believes women use to define their behavior—self-sacrifice and placing the well-being of others ahead of their own interests.

Gilligan described three levels of moral development and two transitional periods.

Level 1: Orientation to Personal Survival.
At this level women focus on their self-interests. The needs and well-being of others are not a principal concern. Women are interested primarily in issues of personal survival and practical issues concerned with what is best for them.

Transition 1: Transition from Personal Selfishness to Responsibility.
In the first transition women move from consideration only of self-

interest to a recognition of the interests of others. In this transition women begin to acknowledge that their actions affect others and that they have a responsibility not only to themselves but also to others.

Level 2: Goodness and Self-Sacrifice.

Self-sacrifice is considered to be morally superior to the expression of personal needs, interests, or wants. Women tend to be more dependent on what other people think of them at this stage. Some women are conflicted over accepting responsibility for their own actions and social pressure to make a decision. Generally, other people's needs are put above their own needs.

Transition 2: From Goodness to Reality.

In this transition women integrate Level 1, Transition 1, and Level 2 reasoning. They become more objective about their individual situations and tend to develop independence from the social influences of other people's opinions. They develop a more global understanding and acceptance of everyone's well-being. This includes themselves, and their own wants, needs, and personal survival.

Level 3: The Morality of Nonviolent Responsibility.

At the third level, women accept responsibility for making their own judgments and the repercussions associated with these actions. Their reasoning has advanced beyond the concerns of others to a new level where their own needs are as valued as the needs of others. Moral judgments are based on weighing various consequences of actions and acceptance of personal responsibility for making those decisions. The single most important moral construct that operates through-out this level is the desire to minimize hurt—emotional or physical—to oneself or to anyone else. It can best be described as "do no harm to thyself or to others."

Social Development in the College Years

College influences students in two ways: formally and informally. Formal influences are those specifically designed by the university to inform or change a student in a specific way. These include classroom lectures, counseling sessions, and orientation programs. Of equal importance in a college environment are the informal influences. These include informal interactions with faculty, discussions with friends in the residence hall, dating experiences, and the scholarly atmosphere of the institution.

The process of influence is known as *socialization*. It is the system by which a person learns the social rules for interacting in the community. These rules of interaction, called *norms,* define acceptable behavior within the group and set standards for individuals seeking membership with that group. As prospective members come to understand the social behavior associated with membership, they come to accept these group standards so that they can gain group acceptance. The more an individual is integrated into the group, the more that person will conform to the normative standards of the group.[22]

Student's Peer Group.

The single most important developmental influence upon values, career aspirations, and overall adjustments is a student's peer group. It sets the standards for interaction, acceptable behavior, and approval. It also acts as a mirror to reflect the images that students will create for themselves. Residence halls are one of the most important places for these peer groups to operate. Friendships formed in the residence halls help students meet new socioacademic demands; learn their way around campus; combat feelings of loneliness; provide tension relief as students talk about common concerns; and through informal discussions in the residence halls, provide orientation to classes, teachers, and types of courses to be taken.[23]

Part of the interaction in a residence hall is controlled by the physical environment. If the living unit is constructed in such a way as to form small isolated groups in the unit, chances are the smaller groups will form the initial peer groups for individuals. According to Chickering, "The interior design and architectural arrangements concerning placement of living units and the nature of their location in relation to one another influences the choice of friends, the groups joined, and the diversity of persons with whom significant encounters can occur."[24] Without question, one effect of residence halls is that they create chances for students to have contact with one another. The day-to-day living situation of eating together, using the same washroom facilities, and other casual contacts give students a chance to become acquainted and to influence one another's attitudes and beliefs.

Researchers have found that students who live close to one another are more likely to form and maintain friendships than students who live further apart.[25] These friendships are likely to be formed in college and to be maintained throughout college and beyond. Not all college students participate in a special clique; however, all are influenced to a greater or lesser degree by the general peer environment. Some students simply prefer to be loners, but most students identify with other students. Part of the reason for this may be that they believe that other students share their personal values, interests, background, and experience.[26] Friends and peer groups "give each other emotional support and also serve as important points of reference for young people to compare their beliefs, values, attitudes, and abilities."[27]

Friendships are formed on a number of bases. Proximity, similarity of values, reciprocity and mutual trust, compatibility, duration of acquaintanceship, and admiration of the friend's good qualities significantly influence the selection and maintenance of friendships.[28] The frequency of shared interactions and of common experiences helps maintain these friendships. Such interchange provides an opportunity to share relationships and to develop linkages of trust. These commonly shared experiences reaffirm for students how they are similar and help students develop a bond of mutual support and confidence. With greater confidence come greater trust and self-disclosure.

A variety of different peer socializing agents are found within the undergraduate experience. The two that seem to exert the most influence are reference groups and primary peer groups. A *reference group* is a group with which the person wishes to be associated. In a college community this might be a fraternity or a sorority, a varsity athletic team, student government, or some other recognition group on the campus. The *primary peer group* may be the same as the reference group; however, it may be different. The primary peer group is composed of those people with whom the individual most closely associates. This might include an individual's roommate, persons in close proximity to this person's residence hall room, or others counted among the student's closest friends. Both the primary peer group and the reference group exert an influence on students.

Most students do not identify directly with the larger culture of the university. Through intermediate social environments, students gain a sense of identification with the larger normative environment of the university. A student's reference group or primary peer group becomes the intermediate social environment through which he or she identifies with this larger university environment. This is why peer groups are so important during the college years. They are the bridge between the family as a controlling agent and the larger adult community.

A person's peer group tends to be most important in influencing beliefs, opinions, and dress. They are most likely to set normative standards for one's appearance, resolving school-centered dilemmas, and in seeking advice on dating relationships. They also help shape opinions about a variety of issues, including political candidates, academic courses, and popular school activities. However, family background and parental opinions carry more weight in making complicated moral judgments that have long-range implications. Students tend to maintain their values concerning marriage, career selection, family commitments, and sense of honor and duty throughout their college careers.

Residence halls provide a natural place for primary peer groups to form. Feldman and Newcomb were among the first researchers to examine the influence of peer groups in residence halls. They described the peer group as the most important agent for change operating within residence halls. They summarized the ways in which peer groups influence students as follows:

- As part of the intermediate stage between the family and the larger postcollege world, the college peer group may help the individual student through the crisis of achieving independence from home.

- Under certain conditions . . . the peer group can support and facilitate the academic-intellectual goals of the college.

- The peer group offers general emotional support to the student; it fulfills needs not met by the curriculum, the classroom, or the faculty.

- The college peer group can provide for the student an occasion for and practice in getting along with people whose background, interests, and orientations are different from his or her own.

- Through value reinforcement, the peer group can provide support for not changing. Yet, it can also challenge old values, provide intellectual stimulation and act as a sounding board for new points of view, present new information and new experiences to the students, help clarify new self-definitions, suggest new career possibilities, and provide emotional support for students who are changing.

- The peer group can offer an alternative source of gratification and a positive self-image, along with rewarding a variety of nonacademic interests for students who are disappointed or not completely successful academically. Friends and social ties may also serve to discourage voluntary withdrawal from college for other than academic reasons.

- College peer group relations can be significant to students in their postcollege careers—not only because they provide general social training but also because of the development of personal ties that may reappear later in the career of the former student.[29]

Residence halls influence students by virtue of intensifying or defining the perimeters of the peer environment. Differences between students living in different types of undergraduate residence halls in part represent the different background characteristics of students, which are intensified as peer groups form.

Perhaps the most dynamic aspect of the residence hall environment is its potential as a means of organizing the critically important peer environment. The power of this peer environment is to influence students by helping to shape beliefs, career direction, and lifestyle among other dimensions of personal growth and development.[30] Of the three major influences determining a student's success in college—family background, the peer group, and tutelage—only the student's family background is more important to the student's success than the student's peer group. Once a student reaches college, the peer group is the major determinant of success or failure, more important than information learned in the classroom.[31] And, the residence hall is an important component in determining how this peer group is formed and who composes it.[32]

When one considers the potential for structuring associations by the mere assignment of students to live in close proximity to one another, and thus determining at least one level of the peer environment, the importance of residence halls to the overall influence of college takes on increased meaning.

1. In section A, Chickering's seven vectors of development in college are given. Section B contains a list of developmental issues students exhibit during the college years. Match the vectors with the behaviors. Vectors are used more than once.

   Section A: Chickering's Seven Vectors
   A. Developing Competence
   B. Managing Emotions
   C. Developing Autonomy
   D. Establishing Identity
   E. Freeing Interpersonal Feelings
   F. Developing Purpose
   G. Developing Integrity

   Section B: Developmental Issues
   _____ 1. A freshman who refuses to talk with her parents
   _____ 2. A junior who is spending all his free time with his girlfriend
   _____ 3. A freshman who is concerned with fitting in with the other students
   _____ 4. A sophomore who cannot control his temper
   _____ 5. A sophomore male who is homophobic
   _____ 6. A junior who is searching for a college major
   _____ 7. A student from the student judicial committee who gets caught shoplifting in the campus bookstore
   _____ 8. A freshman who is worried about being as intelligent as the other students in his classes
   _____ 9. A sophomore student who wants to live in an off-campus apartment
   _____ 10. A freshman who continually violates college regulations
   _____ 11. A sophomore who enters a college-sponsored co-op program in which she alternately works one semester and attends college one semester
   _____ 12. A student who announces his engagement
   _____ 13. A freshman who is overly concerned about her appearance
   _____ 14. A student who spends much of his time proving to others how much he can drink, how tough he is, and how brave he can be
   _____ 15. A freshman who is concerned because he cannot decide on a college major

2. Define *growth* as it is used in the text.
3. Define *development* as it is used in the text.
4. What two forces drive development?
5. Explain *developmental crisis.*
6. Give three characteristics associated with development.
7. Give three characteristics associated with cognitive development.
8. Cognitive development occurs through a process of adaptation. What are the two adaptive processes in cognitive development and how is each defined?
9. List the three major periods of cognitive development that Perry identified in college students.
10. List Kohlberg's six stages of moral development.
11. In Kohlberg's theory of moral development most college students are in what stage of moral development?
12. What are the three major stages of moral development in women identified in Gilligan's theory?

APPLICATIONS

LUCY

Lucy was a freshman at State University. She was a little overwhelmed by the size of the university, which had 40,000 students and about 7,000 faculty and other employees. Her hometown had only 7,000 people, and her entire high school graduating class had fewer students than the number of women living on her residence hall floor. Lucy came to State because it offered the state's only agriculture degree.

Lucy did not make friends easily. She was somewhat shy and hoped that the experience of going to college would help her with her shyness. Her scheduled roommate never showed, leaving Lucy with a single room and the possibility of having someone assigned to the room later in the semester. She lived in a residence hall at the end of a long double-loaded corridor which had about 45 women on it, and she kept to herself the first two weeks of school.

By the end of the first month of classes, Lucy still had not made any friends in the residence hall. She got up in the morning, went to classes, and came back to her room and stayed there. She was very unhappy and was thinking about going home. The residence hall handbook instructed students who were having a problem to consult their RA. She went to the RA's room to tell her that she thought she wanted to leave school and that she wanted to know the procedure for withdrawing from State University.

WHAT WOULD YOU DO?

1. If you were Lucy's RA, what questions would you ask and how would you counsel her?
2. Is there anything that Lucy's RA could have done to have helped Lucy make friends early in the semester? If so, what?
3. What major developmental issues does Lucy seem to be confronting?
4. How can the RA help Lucy address these developmental issues?

RIGHT MEETS LEFT

Hans is a freshman who lives in a single room in an all-male residence hall of about 300 men. He went to a military high school and is very precise about everything. He keeps his closet and his other belongings in impeccable order. Hans has very conservative political views and proudly displays in his room an American flag and a photograph of a U.S. Marine Corps recruiting poster. Although he has not yet decided if he wants to join the ROTC, he is giving it serious thought. On most topics Hans has a strong opinion. The classes he likes best are math and science. He likes philosophy and history least because the professors in these courses won't give him a "straight answer" to his questions. Hans does not fit in with most of the other students on the floor and has become somewhat of a joke.

Asher is a freshman who lives on the same residence hall floor as Hans—about five rooms away. Asher is quite different from Hans. He wears blue jeans with holes in the knees, one silver earring, and usually a T-shirt with the name of some type of heavy-metal rock group on it. Asher believes that everyone should have the right to do his or her own thing. He does not like most of the rules in the residence hall but abides by them because he does not want to get into trouble. Asher has an American flag which he uses as a rug in his room. Asher intends to major in philosophy. He likes philosophy because he believes that it allows everyone to have their own opinions about things.

One day Hans was in his room studying when he heard heavy-metal music coming from Asher's room. When he went to Asher's room, the door was open and he saw Asher dancing on the American flag. Screaming above the music, Hans got Asher's attention. He asked Asher to turn down the music, which Asher did. Hans then told Asher that he thought Asher was a degenerate for dancing on the American flag and that only a communist drug fiend would ever show such disrespect for the flag. Asher acknowledged that he did occasionally use drugs and had not yet decided if he was a communist or an anarchist. He told Hans that when he decided what he was, he would get back to him but until then, Hans could "stay the hell out of his way." Some words and threats were exchanged, and Hans left and went back to his room, whereupon Asher turned his music up twice as loud.

That night someone forced pennies against the lock to Hans's room, making it impossible for him to open it from the inside. Bottle rockets and shaving cream were then shot under the door, followed by a bucket of water under the door. When the RA returned to his floor he found Hans screaming in his room and pounding on the door. No one was in the hall, but most of the residents were awake and in their rooms with their doors open. Most were laughing. When the RA let Hans out of his room, Hans was furious and suspected Asher of the vandalism. He started down to Asher's room to confront him. Asher did not answer the door, but stayed inside listening to his music.

WHAT WOULD YOU DO?

1. If you were the RA what would you do?
2. Based on the facts of the case study, what would be your best guess as to Hans's stage of cognitive development (using Perry's scheme) and why?
3. Based on the facts of the case study, what would be your best guess as to Asher's stage of cognitive development (using Perry's scheme) and why?
4. What, if anything, could the RA do to facilitate the cognitive growth of both students?
5. How could the RA best resolve the conflict between Asher and Hans before it escalates into more serious pranks?

CHAPTER SIX

ADJUSTING TO COLLEGE

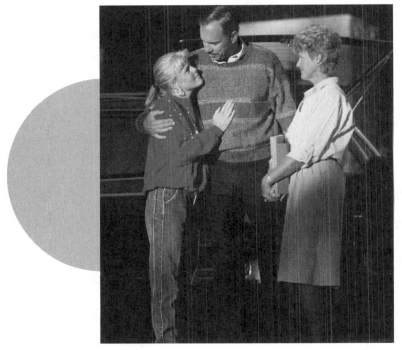

©1998 PHOTODISK, INC.

The theories of development reviewed in the previous chapter reveal a pattern of growth during the college years and beyond. In this chapter, developmental stages evident in each of the undergraduate years are examined in relation to adjustment problems students experience in college and the residence hall environment. As the overall scheme for this chronological development unfolds, remember that individual students vary in the pace of development.

The important fact to note from developmental theories is that the development of an individual involves a complex system of interrelationships and experiences based on physiological maturation, environment, and personality factors. Development is a continuous process and has no absolute starting and finishing points. It is a loose-knit, fluid interchange of events, circumstances, and developmental cycles. None of these developmental stages takes place in a void. No two people move through them at the same pace or with the same experiences. As an RA, you need to understand the types of development that are taking place.

The particular developmental task most in evidence at a given time defines much of the student's relationship to the institution.[1] If you can identify this developmental task, you should be able to anticipate the adjustment difficulties a student will be experiencing in the residence hall at that time. Your ability to recognize developmental issues and to understand the experience of students will help you respond appropriately to students experiencing problems.

THE FIRST YEAR

Attending a college or university for the first time is a threatening and frightening experience for many students. The familiar environments of home and high school are gone. In place of these is a new and formidable experience. Professors with doctoral degrees, maps for navigating around the campus, a library with hundreds of thousands of volumes, and hundreds or thousands of new fellow students confront the entering freshman, who is thrust into this environment and expected to survive. This experience challenges the individual's personal security, need for acceptance, and need for physical comfort. Not only are new students uncertain of this unfamiliar environment, but they are filled with doubt about succeeding in meeting the expectations of their parents, teachers, friends, and themselves.

Many students entering the residence hall environment for the first time project the attitude that they know everything there is to know about that environment. They have difficulty admitting that they are not in control and may be uncertain about how they will fit in with others in the residence halls. For men this seems to be especially true. Men, as defined by our culture, are supposed to be self-reliant, exhibit independence, and confront new tasks with little difficulty. The freshman male often has difficulty admitting that he really does not understand everything about his new environment. To ask simple questions such as "Where is the dining hall?" or "What do I do if I get locked out of my room?" is an admission that he is not in control of his environment. When one's ego is fragile and one's self-image is closely tied to the perceptions of other students, a person may be reluctant to ask simple and basic questions.

This new environment presents a major adjustment for students. Freshman year is often the first time they have been on their own away from their friends and families. They want to be accepted by their peers and want to make college a successful experience.

In these early days of meeting other people, students tell other people who they are through their past experiences and through what their parents do. Students use these reference points because their identity has been tied to these signposts for so long. Students who are dissatisfied with their background, dissatisfied with themselves, or feel a need to enhance their images will embellish their backgrounds and experiences when they describe them to other people. They may claim that their parents are much wealthier than they really are, that they were tremendous athletes in high school, or that they were heavily involved in some recognition group for intellectual achievement. By communicating this to other people, the student hopes to establish a more favorable impression and to gain the acceptance and approval of others.

Almost all students go through an adjustment phase when they enter the residence hall environment. Most are secure enough to adapt and establish an open and honest relationship with their peers. Some will rely on various forms of embellishment to bolster their identity and enhance their security.

Transition to College

In this transition into college, students go through what Rossi identified as an adaptation phase of four to eight weeks.[2] In this period, students make some major transitional adjustments to set a pattern for future interaction, values, and success in this environment. Rossi concluded that

Massive socialization effects occurred during the initial few weeks of entry into the institution in question, that effects were greatest among those individuals who were most oriented toward their peers, and that changes beyond the early weeks were relatively slight, as long as the individual remained in the institution in question. Indeed, the major shift in value emphasis occurred during the period between September and November, indicating that socialization to the normative system of the school occurred in a short period of time and involved changes of considerable magnitude. Changes of similar magnitude did not occur among upperclassmen, sophomore, junior, and senior classes being essentially alike in their value orientation.[3]

Thus, most socialization takes place within approximately the first six weeks of entry into the institution. Students appear to come to college with a set of expectations that they are willing to change to conform to the prevailing group behavioral norms. The socialization process appears to be faster for female students than for male students and may, at first, influence academic performance by shifting grades downward.

Levitz and Noel described the first two or six weeks of the fall semester as the most critical transition period for freshmen.[4] Almost half of all students who drop out during the freshman year do so during this period. Studies show that, of those students who drop out during this transitional period in the fall semester, more than half

Female students seem to adjust to college life easier than male students.

have not had any significant contact with a residence life staff member, faculty member, or advisor.[5] Levitz and Noel concluded that a "caring attitude of faculty and staff is the most potent retention force on campus."[6]

Meeting the expectations of the peer group is an important developmental factor for the new student. In these first few weeks of adaptation to the new residence hall environment, freshmen learn to conform to the normative modes of interaction in the living unit and to emulate roles set by their peers. These patterns of interaction or models of how to cope with this new environment are set by upper-class students in the residence halls. Freshmen conform to the group standard by emulating the behavior of the older and more experienced students. As these standards of behavior are set during the first few weeks, they come to form the expected role behavior within this new environment.

Another way of viewing this adaptation process of conformity or patterning is to view it as "habits." People are creatures of habit and soon develop a routine of studying, eating, sleeping, and socializing at predictable times each day. Much of a successful cafeteria operation depends on this routine or habit. Probably the cafeteria manager at your institution can tell you with precision when the meal hour will be the busiest, approximately what percentage of the total number of students eating in that cafeteria will eat a particular meal, and even the approximate number of servings of each entree that will be requested for a given menu combination.

Students who develop the habit of studying between certain hours every evening and in a particular location every evening will tend to continue this pattern of behavior throughout the year. Likewise, people who exercise at a particular time during the day will tend to continue this pattern of behavior as long as their schedule permits. Once the pattern is established, it becomes difficult to break.

This has some interesting implications for what you as an RA can do during the first few weeks after the new student enters the residence hall. If the student enters an environment in which studying is respected and that offers a supportive community of openness and trust, a pattern will likely develop that will serve you and your residents throughout the academic year. Programs and other activities help integrate the floor during these first few weeks. Likewise, if noisy, disruptive, and otherwise prohibited types of behavior are allowed to go unchallenged during these first few weeks, this will probably establish a pattern of expected behavior and create an entirely different type of living environment.

Part of the interaction in the living unit is controlled by the physical environment. If the living unit is constructed in such a way as to form small isolated groups in the unit, chances are that smaller groups will form the initial peer groups for individuals. Chickering explained that (1) "friendships and memberships in various groups or subcultures influence development, and (2) . . . interior design in architectural arrangements concerning placement of living units and the nature of their location in relation to one another influence the choice of friends, the groups joined, and the diversity of persons with whom significant encounters can occur."[7]

Precollege acquaintanceships, similarity of attitudes, common interests, size of the group, the homogeneity of the group membership, and the relative isolation of the group all contribute both to the formation of the peer group and to the degree of influence it has on its members. The peer group is a significant influence in the lives of freshmen making the transition into college and helps set a pattern of behavior within the first few weeks that greatly influences their direction for the first year in college.

Tolerance

Freshmen tend to view situations as either right or wrong. Students who have not learned to share, to compromise, and to accept other people's views will experience interpersonal conflicts. The residence hall is one of the best places for students to learn to be tolerant. Learning to live with others in such close proximity, to accept the necessary inconveniences of noise, to adhere to regulated eating hours, and to cope with other people's annoying habits all contribute to helping the individual become more tolerant.

Tolerance is a necessary step toward maturation. Unless a person can learn to compromise, accept other people's views, and express his or her satisfaction or dissatisfaction with the behavior of other people, he or she will have difficulty moving to a level of maturity and personal identity.

FORCES OF ATTRITION IN THE FRESHMAN YEAR

1. **Academic boredom:** In particular, freshmen who have not yet decided on their major often become bored with academic assignments. Some students feel a lack of challenge in courses and others are bored because of poor teaching in the classroom.

2. **Irrelevancy:** Many students believe that the information they are receiving in classes is irrelevant because they do not understand how the information links to practical issues related to their career objectives. Part of this feeling develops when teachers and advisors fail to interpret for students how the information they are learning in the classroom will be useful to them in later life.

3. **Limited or unrealistic expectations of college:** Many students enter college with no realistic idea of what to expect. They have a wait-and-see attitude and base their judgment of the college experience as they progress through it. Because of this attitude, some students fail to involve themselves in college. They are never drawn into full membership within the institution.

4. **Academic unpreparedness:** Although some students come to college more academically prepared than other students, some also come to college significantly underprepared. These students usually experience difficulty in basic skills, which makes academic work overly challenging and stressful.

5. **Transition or adjustment difficulties:** During the freshman transitional period, students develop a support system to replace the one they had during high school. If they fail to develop friends or contacts with residence life staff and college faculty, students feel somewhat alienated and are more vulnerable to leaving.

6. **Lack of certainty about a major and/or a career:** Students who are uncertain about their academic major can become easily frustrated by college, lacking a direction or goal. They feel uncertain and confused about why they are in college and what they want to accomplish. Being tentative about career choices does not, in itself, present a problem; only when students cannot narrow their options nor bring into focus how their efforts in the classroom relate to what they want to accomplish in later life do problems develop.

7. **Dissonance or incompatibility:** Not all students who enter a particular university belong at that university. Sometimes a mismatch between the student and the institution exists. Social, academic, geographic, and other factors enter into how well a student fits with a particular institution. Incompatibility between the student and the institution increases the student's chance of leaving. Similarly, situations involving students who want to pursue careers for which they are not qualified based on how they are performing in the classroom (such as students who wish to be physicians but have substandard performance in premed courses) create cognitive dissonance for them. This frustration sometimes leads to attrition.

(Levitz and Noel, 1989, pp. 67-70)

Break in Child-Parent Relationship

As students adapt to their new environment through conformity with peer expectations, they begin to break with parents and enter a world defined by their peers. The establishment of independence from parents is a necessary step in discovering one's identity.

All people operate at three different levels: parent, adult, and child.[8] The parent level is the critical, judging, caring, and protective level of a person's personality. The adult level is the mature and cooperative side. It is concerned with transforming stimuli into information and integrating that information based on experiences. The child represents the seeing, hearing, feeling, and understanding part of the person.

When students enter college, their relationship with parents is one of child to parent, with the parent holding certain authority or control over the child. Through the process of maturation and autonomy that occurs during the college years, students change the relationship with their parents. It moves from a child-to-parent to an adult-to-adult relationship. The transition requires that students and their parents make changes. These changes are difficult for both. Parents often have difficulty relinquishing control and allowing their children to take risks and have increased independence. Most of this difficulty is due to the parents' desire to ensure the well-being and success of their children. Students also have trouble establishing this new relationship. They may demand greater autonomy and freedom than they are prepared for, and they may find themselves wanting their parents to shelter and protect them while at the same time demanding increased independence and autonomy. The transitional experience is difficult for all involved parties.

Researchers have explained the cycles of this transition with parents as follows:

Almost inescapable during the transition from high school to college is a change in perception of one's parents. It begins, generally, when parents are seen as having attributes such as usually being right, being somewhat different from other adults, and having some peculiar power and influence over one's behavior. Then uncertainties about the parents and their ideas arise— some ambiguity about how controlling or permissive they are going to be during the first year of college, some questions about dependence and independence relating to them. Parents are generally seen more and more realistically, feelings about them which were previously suppressed find expression, and the relationship changes from that of child-to-parent to that of adult-to-adult. The parents are perceived more objectively and compared with parents of close friends. The student's attitude toward them moves in the direction of understanding and acceptance in spite of their failures, weaknesses, and biases, which are now more evident than before.[9]

One of the most common problems for freshmen is the break in the child-parent relationship. This break is the result of the increasing autonomy of the student. It is a necessary part of growing up and self-discovery; to discover who he or she is, each person must separate from parents. This can be difficult for college students, because many rely on their parents for financial support. The lack of financial independence subjects students to some degree of control by their parents. As students mature and learn to handle greater degrees of freedom, they learn to respond on a more adult level to their parents. This does not mean that parents will respond likewise; parents also must learn to accept the new relationship with their children. The more protective and involved the parents are with the student, the longer this adjustment will take. Many students, however, are able to resolve this conflict by the end of the sophomore year. Some students and parents take longer. In either case, the resolution of this conflict is necessary to a student's growth and eventual maturity. As the RA, you may support students in establishing a more positive adult-to-adult relationship with parents by sharing with them your personal experiences and how you have progressed in this development.

Value Exploration

Students enter college with values most similar to those of their parents. Seeking a sense of belonging in their peer group, they explore the value systems of their peers and experiment with different beliefs and attitudes. College offers an opportunity to try different attitudes, beliefs, and values. This is the time of life to find values and beliefs that fit and modify those that do not.

Most students have had experience making decisions for themselves that involve an assessment of their beliefs and values. These experiences force students to make decisions about why they hold the beliefs that they do. Some students have not had many of these experiences, and when they are placed in a new environment apart from the security of their parents and home life, they often experience value conflicts. If students are unable to understand the difference between what they were taught and the values being expressed by peers, they can undergo a crisis in their value system.

One of two things could result from this crisis. First, the student may need to undergo psychotherapy and be removed from the environment until he or she has developed sufficient coping mechanisms to deal with the conflicts in values. The second alternative is for the student to seek a new value system and adopt it. Such students are drawn to some of the fundamentalist religious groups, cult groups, and charismatic groups in which they no longer need to make value decisions for themselves. The group prescribes what is correct and why. It provides emotional support and a sense of belonging that reassures and reinforces the values offered by the group. Life becomes simpler, and the student is again able to function.

Self-Esteem Needs

Self-esteem is generally described as the gap between one's self-image and one's self-expectations. When one moves into a new environment, one's image and expectations often change. In the transition to college, students must retain a strong ego identity and a strong sense of self-worth. Their confidence can be easily undermined in a new environment in which basic emotional security and self-esteem can be challenged by peers and the new environment. Students need the comfort and support of other people to reaffirm their self-worth and self-image. As an RA, your support and encouragement can assist these students. Your friendship and support could be critical to helping students maintain a positive self-image and increase their self-concept.

Need for Support

Helping students persist during their first year in college requires focus on academic, personal, and social adjustments. RAs help with the latter two forms of adjustment—personal and social. To connect, freshmen need a supportive environment that allows them to ask questions, receive feedback, and feel competent in their new environment. Levitz and Noel explained it this way: "Residence advisors, peer assistants, and well-trained staff members in campus offices can also contribute to a supportive environment for students. In a supportive climate, newly enrolled freshmen will not feel too intimidated to ask those 'dumb questions' about academic expectations, college procedures, social concerns, or the location and purpose of specific campus resources."[10]

Roommate Reaction

On the day new students arrive in the residence halls, students who have not specified a particular roommate get to meet their assigned roommates. This can be a tense situation, particularly if the new roommate is of a different ethnic or racial background. Having parents present during this first encounter generally complicates any problem between the roommates. Students frequently are able to resolve conflicts within the first two weeks. Roommates often recognize that they share many of the same interests and many of the same apprehensions. They usually become friends. This, however, is not always the case. Some roommate matches are just not as agreeable as others. Sometimes the lifestyle differences are too divergent, and the two students cannot reach a compromise. In these cases, a roommate change is needed.

As an RA, you can best assist in resolving these situations by assuring all parties involved that the university will seek to reach a workable solution for everyone within a reasonable time after the move-in rush. You can be of great assistance by knowing the policies and following the procedures that your institution may have regarding these conflicts. Most importantly, you need to know the rationale behind the policies. Parents and students will question you. Although they will likely seek higher authorities to challenge any decision or interpretation you may make, you can lend credibility to yourself and to your superiors if you can articulate the policies and the reasons behind them.

Once the parents are gone, attempt to discuss the situation openly with the students. In subsequent days, attempt to involve the students in common experiences that can help them get to know one another. Athletic events, discussion groups, dining together, and other mutual experiences may reinforce their common interests and encourage the relationship.

If the two students are unable to resolve their conflicts, having them reside together serves no purpose. It is disruptive to them as individuals, to their development and growth, and possibly to the living unit as a whole.

Conflicts

Conflicts can arise naturally in any group situation, but they seem to be accentuated when groups of students are asked to live together in close proximity. The conflicts that arise between roommates are usually minor and usually indicate a difference in communication style, lifestyle, or personality type. Roommate conflicts and conflicts with other students in the living unit are common for freshmen. The resident hall often is the first experience students have had with small-group living among nonrelatives. Often the lack of privacy and the irresponsible acts of a few individuals conflict with the need for privacy and the need to retreat from the stress and congestion of college. Group intensity infringes on territorial needs and the drive to maximize control over one's environment. As students develop greater tolerance and greater interpersonal skills, conflicts will be more quickly resolved. Patterns of acceptable behavior emerge naturally from the group as norms become established in the living unit.

Academic Adjustment

Adjusting to the new academic environment with its demands for studying, more intense competition, and enhanced critical thinking skills is both frightening and anxiety producing for students. The anxiety and apprehension surrounding students' first college examinations can evoke stress, frustration, fear, and questions of self-worth. Excessive drinking, disruptive behavior, and other stress reactions, such as depression, panic, and avoidance, are common.

Reaction to Freedom

Independence carries with it newfound freedom. No longer does the student need to report his or her whereabouts to parents. No longer does anyone challenge or monitor the student's behavior. Freedom, independence, and self-determination are all dropped on the student in a relatively short period of time.

Students react to this new freedom by testing the boundaries through trial and experimentation. Students who have not had much freedom may not have sufficient experience in disciplining their own behavior and, as a result, may abuse this freedom. Frequently, such behavior is disruptive to the living unit or personally destructive. As the RA, you can assist by being observant and by being available to students. If a student evidences negative social behavior, other members of the living unit will usually discourage it or at least bring it to your attention.

Evidence of students experiencing problems with this newfound freedom includes a decline in grades, poor time management, procrastination, and excessive socializing. These behaviors can be used as a basis for initiating counseling intervention to explore with students their lack of self-discipline and its effects on their academic goals.

Homesickness

Common to freshmen is a sense of loss or feeling of aloneness known as homesickness. It stems from an absence of attachment with the family. Depression can emerge as a reaction to this sense of loss. Though most students experience some homesickness, few students are willing to admit it. Students equate homesickness with a lack of maturity and with ties to the affirmation of the child-parent relationship. Most students are able to overcome this homesickness through a short weekend visit at home or through support of close friends at college. Those who are unable to cope with the depression of homesickness can develop a sense of complacency about college life and may need to return home until they are emotionally ready to make the break.

Extreme Introversion and Extreme Extroversion

Students having difficulty in establishing relationships may exhibit one of two common behaviors—extreme introversion or extreme extroversion. Introversion is a common reaction from the student who has difficulty establishing relationships with peers. The simplest solution, as students may interpret it, is to remove themselves from the group. It is easy to do. Introverted students may limit contact with other students, spend time away from their living unit, watch television, or simply remain alone in their rooms. These students may feel insecure and perhaps somewhat frightened about the college experience. Some students simply take longer to establish positive peer relationships. They may be somewhat shy and retiring at the beginning of the school year but soon learn sufficient skills to interact with the other members of the living group.

Students who never seek this interaction are not afforded the opportunities to learn important social skills necessary for their development. Skills such as how to engage others in conversation, how to tell a joke, and how to participate in a group are all part of the social learning experience that comes through contacts with peers. Perhaps most importantly, these students who opt out of interacting with others will not experience the support that peers can offer nor receive the feedback they need for their own growth.

Extremely extroverted students are the other side of the coin. They wish to participate in the group so much that they try too insistently. Through their extroverted, sometimes compulsive, behavior, they force themselves on others to the extent that students begin to ostracize them. Often these students have what are best described as "awkward social skills," which cause them to do or say inappropriate things. Unfortunately, the harder these students try to become part of the group, the more apprehensive the group becomes. These students can develop a reputation for being overbearing and obnoxious and may be left out of many group activities. Although a student may establish many contacts at the beginning of the year, as people get to know the extremely extroverted student, they move further and further away from him or her. As with the introverted student, the extroverted student has not learned an acceptable style of interaction within the peer group and overcompensates for the deficiency.

As the RA, you are in a position to observe both types of students and to assist them in developing skills that will benefit them in their interactions with others. All too often, the outstretched hand of the RA is clung to permanently by students who have been ostracized by the group. They come to sit in the RA's room for prolonged hours, occupying much of the RA's time and inhibiting other students from making casual contact. These students can consume much of your free time because you are the one person who seems to care about them. If you become their constant companion, you may hinder their development. Though they may acquire important skills by using you as a model, their protracted contacts with you may be an escape from establishing positive relationships with other people within the living unit. Your challenge is to be supportive and nurturing to these students and, over time, encourage them to become more independent from you.

In these situations, talk with the student about his or her interaction with other people. The discussion should center on ways in which the student might interact with the group. You can suggest that other students include those who have not been accepted by the group. Activities, informal discussions, and similar common experiences will increase contact for these students and assist them in developing better relationships. Some of these students may need assistance from a professional staff member. Do not be afraid to discuss the situation with your residence hall director and make a referral if needed.

Difficulties with Dating Relationships

During late adolescence and early adulthood, students are discovering their own sexual identity. Students often experience some difficulty with their dating partners. The college social situation places an emphasis on dating and intimacy. Part of students' self-concept and self-esteem are defined by these relationships. Because students at this stage have not usually solidified their identity, they have difficulty sharing themselves intimately with another person. Because students have not fully developed the capacity to achieve a compassionate relationship of personal intimacy, their relationships often lack the depth and emotional vitality that they are seeking. Students may substitute a number of brief, unsatisfying sexual encounters, but these seldom satisfy the need for intimacy. In fact, these encounters may trivialize intimacy and make it more difficult to achieve.

Initially, much of the dating relationship centers on having an appropriate personality interaction, being a "good date." Good conversation, the way one dresses, a pleasing personality, and other more superficial qualities are important in the initial stages of these relationships. The dating relationship has a positive effect upon the individual's human-relations development. Specifically, it teaches good interpersonal skills with members of the opposite sex; it develops social courtesies and skills; it aids in discovering more about one's own identity; it provides occasional sexual experience; and it fosters a level of intimacy that would not otherwise be available.[11]

For most people, dating begins in high school and seems to blossom in the first year of college, becoming a major influence on a person's development, self-image, and self-esteem. Dating relationships can be anxiety-producing situations for both men and women. Physical attractiveness, personality, status, and other issues related to one's identity and image are drawn into question. Not having a date for the weekend can be a traumatic experience for both men and women. Developing the self-confidence to request a date, with the possibility of being rejected, is difficult. Of equal difficulty is waiting to be asked for a date or not having a socially acceptable means to contact a person one would like to know better. Many traditional gender roles dictating who should ask whom for a date have changed, allowing both sexes greater freedom.

You will observe the stress and anxiety students have about dating. Some students will be confident and will date frequently. Others will consistently have difficulty establishing such contacts. These students may lack self-confidence or social/dating skills or have a poor self-image. Simply put, the student may not know how to meet somebody or may not have occasion to meet a potential date in a setting that could initiate a date. Prescribed social roles in dating for men and women compound this situation. On the one hand, a man may be reluctant to ask a woman out for fear that she may be dating someone else or that he may not have enough money to support the type of dating relationship that he believes is appropriate. The female student may be in a worse predicament. She may be reluctant to contact a man for a date for fear of seeming too forward.

You may be able to talk candidly with students experiencing difficulties in establishing social relationships. You can tell students that deceptive tactics, witty one-liners, and contrived schemes are often viewed as somewhat corny. The open, honest, and straightforward approach with an individual usually works best. Also, sharing the cost of the date and women initiating dates are now socially acceptable.

Fears of Homosexuality

Men in particular undergo a crisis in discovering their sexuality that often includes wondering whether they may be attracted to other males. Some may experiment with casual sexual contacts with other males, and some may overcompensate by continually declaring loudly and publicly how heterosexual their relationships are. Although the majority of students are able to establish a satisfying sexual identity, some students experience much anxiety in resolving this issue.

One view of the homosexual issue is to see the individual in terms of how satisfied the individual is with himself or herself. People are sexual: some people are heterosexual, some are homosexual, and some are bisexual. In this view, the important factor is how satisfied students are with their sexual identity and how comfortable they are with the lifestyle it presents. When students experience a conflict between what they believe they want and what they perceive they are, then they often need to address this issue through professional counseling.

By being an understanding listener, you may help the student better understand some of the questions surrounding sexuality. If early in the year you berate a certain sexual orientation or defend your own sexual identity to students in your unit, you may lose a student who needs to talk with you.

Suicide

The difficulty of handling autonomy and independence in college may cause students to cry out for help through attention-getting devices such as attempting suicide. The issue of suicide is discussed in a later chapter. You should be particularly aware of this problem in the initial stage of settling into the residence hall situation, although it is present among college students throughout their education.

Financial Problems

Financial problems can be frightening to new students. While at home, students may have had certain financial constraints, but probably were never faced with worrying over whether they would have enough money to eat. Students who have irresponsibly spent their money in the first few weeks of the month or who did not have enough money to begin with (depending on the cafeteria arrangements at your institution) may not have sufficient money to buy food at some point in the academic term. Though some students may be able to borrow money or to get additional funds from their families, some students cannot.

Other Problems

Illness, family problems, and general personal problems are always present among students. In today's high-pressure college environment, few students can afford to miss more than one week of classes and hope to catch up. These problems are not specific to freshmen, but they may present special problems for students who have never had to cope with them independent of the support of their parents. Think back to the time you were first sick in college and your parents were not available to comfort you. It can be lonely being ill and on your own in college.

Personal problems such as roommate conflicts, exams, a physical impairment, or having to spend a birthday alone for the first time can be a mild trauma for a new student. Students will experience some of these problems in this initial stage of adjustment. As the RA, you need to be sensitive to these needs and lend your support, assistance, and experience in guiding students through these difficulties.

THE SOPHOMORE AND JUNIOR YEARS

As students reach the end of their sophomore year and start their junior year, they should be well on their way to defining a new relationship with their parents, establishing a sexual identity, and beginning to examine what they believe and what they value. They should have established some tolerance and the ability to interact with other members of the peer group. Intellectually, they should be less authoritarian and have a more open-minded acceptance of other points of view.

Students are now beginning to question what they have accomplished and what lies ahead. Most students are starting to study in their chosen major, having completed many of the core course requirements. They have been able to stay in college until this point and have learned much about existence within the system, including how to register, how to select classes, and how to use the college catalog and bulletin. Students should feel somewhat more comfortable with the college environment and should have established a support group of friends on whom they may rely. If they have defined no other identity for themselves than that they are college students, they have an interim identity that satisfies their need for the time. High school seems far behind, and there might even be some disdain toward those people who inquire what they did when they were in high school. Their identity and self-concept at this point are tied to college. Many students have started to identify attainable role models in the educational community to emulate. Students are more confident in their abilities to cope with a new environment and more secure in what lies ahead and what they have already accomplished.

Emotional Growth

As students come to understand themselves better, they increase their capability to move from responding only to their own wants and desires to accepting others in an intimate and sharing relationship. As students mature, they learn to experience free interpersonal relationships, enhancing their ability to share with others and to become less self-centered and more other-centered.

As students come to feel more secure in their relationships with dating partners and as they become more intimate, greater security and confidence lessens the need for outward signs of physical affection. As Chickering pointed out, "Although the interpersonal ties are stronger—again with persons of both sexes—they are considerably loosened and less binding. Couples do not have to walk with arms around each other or even hold hands. Public necking—that vehicle for personal declaration of attractiveness and likability—and mutually supportive commitments and assurances are no longer required. Physical intimacy plays its important part. But again, for most students the context is one of respect, commitment, and love. Sexual intercourse in the absence of such feelings is infrequent."[12]

The development of this capacity for intimate contacts and a sense of loving between people carries a concomitant ability not only to love but to know how to accept love from other people. Students begin to accept other people in a common union of understanding and mutual commitment. People become more secure about releasing intimate and personal information about themselves. They learn to share their own life and experiences, desires, needs, wants, and frustrations with others in a union of caring and emotional support.

This period of emotional development takes time. The person moves from a level of self-commitment and self-exploration to a new level of personal acceptance. This state of intimacy is not an absolute, but a period of growth.

Value Identification and Clarification

By their junior year, students have confronted many of their attitudes, beliefs, and values. They have been forced to defend, question, abandon, or reevaluate many of the opinions that they held upon entering college. During their sophomore and junior years, students attempt to find a resolution to some of these value questions by sorting out what they believe and why. Vital issues of the day and questions about drugs, sex, religion, and politics take on increased importance during late-night discussions as students attempt to sort out how they feel and what they believe. Values often change from conservative, authoritarian positions to increased liberalism. Though students emerge from college with a value system somewhat more liberal than that of their parents, overall, students' values tend to be most similar to those of their parents.[13]

Intimacy and Broken Relationships

One of the most common adjustment problems at the end of the first year and the beginning of the second year is the termination of a dating relationship that was developed in the first year of college. Frequently, students develop an intimate relationship with another person shortly after arriving at college. Because students left high school having established a familiar and comfortable network of parents, friends, teachers, and peers, one of the first things they wish to do in college is to reestablish a network of associations. Some students do this by investing themselves emotionally in one person. Through this relationship, students are able to establish a sense of balance in their lives and gain temporary stability in their personal lives during this first year of transition in college. As students mature, they begin to find that these initial relationships are restrictive, holding them back from exploring other dimensions of their personality and expanding their acquaintanceships and network of associations. By the end of the freshman year or into the beginning of the sophomore year, these relationships begin to break down. Often they start with the desire on the part of one or both people in the relationship to "date other people." A typical trauma comes during the breakup of these initial transitional relationships that develop during the first year in college. A student can feel jealousy, rejection, and a sense of being alone. Because people grow at different rates, one person in a relationship may wish to end it while the other person wishes to keep it. This usually presents conflicts for both parties and requires a considerable investment of emotional energy on the part of both.

An extension of this problem is students who arrive at college expecting to maintain dating relationships begun in high school. These individuals expect to continue their relationship while one is in college and the other is in high school or when the two attend different colleges. Most of the time, these relationships fail. Students grow, develop other interests, and change. New friends, new opportunities, and new social opportunities tend to make people grow apart from one another. Relationships are difficult to sustain without regular contact. Students discover this during their first year, and often these relationships break up over the summer when the two people have more opportunities to spend time with one another.

As an RA, you will see many students experiencing feelings of rejection. When a student is closely tied to another by feelings of emotion, intimacy, and compassion, the break in this relationship can sever much of the student's self-esteem and sense of security. The loss and feeling of rejection can become all-consuming. It can halt the forward progress of an individual's development and bring the person into an emotional crisis that impedes functioning. Common responses to these situations include failure to attend classes, lethargic attitude about life, depression, loneliness, despair, frustration, feelings of abandonment, and often desire for revenge.

Your contact with the student in a counseling relationship may be the only assistance you can offer, other than referring the student to counseling with a member of the professional staff. You must not become an intermediary between the two parties; you would find this role untenable as you could easily be drawn into the controversy. You can be of the greatest assistance to the student by remaining objective, not taking sides, and helping the student think through the situation. Offer empathy but not pity. Offer support but not advice. Be very careful not to agree with any negative appraisal of the other individual, no matter what your personal feelings are. Remember that the person did care for that individual at one time.

Sophomore Slump

Somewhere toward the end of the sophomore year, many students experience what is sometimes called a "sophomore slump." This is best described as a sense of depression or a questioning about being in college. With approximately two years of college behind and at least two more years of college ahead, many students question the basic worth of their education and what they wish to accomplish in life. One of the questions for many sophomores at this halfway point centers on the utility and application of material that they have already learned. They question the worth of some information they have acquired and seek greater control over their lives. A feeling of impatience sets in. For students who are uncertain about completing college, this is a time of reappraisal and reevaluation.

Students usually resolve these questions themselves. As an RA, you should not attempt to sell a particular point of view, although you might believe you are doing students a service by attempting to convince them to stay in college. A particular student might benefit from being out of college for a time. Students occasionally "stop out" of college for a year or so after their sophomore year to experience other aspects of life. Many return; others find greater satisfaction in life outside of college. Students must work through these issues and decide for themselves. As an RA, you can help students define the problem and offer perspective, support, and insight on how you have resolved these issues for yourself.

The Apartment Quest

Many colleges and universities have a one or two year *parietal policy* that requires students to stay in residence halls for the freshman and sometimes the sophomore year—or until they achieve a given number of academic credits. Two philosophies support this rule. One contends that at least one year of residential learning provides the basic foundation for social skills and other important developmental skills for the great majority of students. A second philosophy maintains that most of these skills are learned in the freshman year and that the learning takes place primarily through interaction with upper-division students. Sophomores model appropriate behavior for the incoming freshmen, who in turn pass it on the following year to the next freshmen. The retention of the sophomores in the residence halls is a way of transmitting these skills from one generation of college students to the next.

In either case, by the end of their sophomore year many students are seriously considering a move from the residence halls into apartments. Though students justify their move by blaming the food in the cafeteria, the noise in the residence hall, or the belief that it is less expensive to live in an apartment than it is to live in the residence halls, the real issue is independence. Nothing seems to epitomize independence more than having one's own apartment. It presents a new freedom, a new lifestyle, and a new experience.

Most students probably benefit from having their own apartment after the sophomore year. It requires the development of some new skills in working with people and meeting the demands of utility and telephone bills, food purchasing and preparation, and cleaning for themselves.

One reason students remain in residence halls is a sense of community in the living unit. Students who enjoy the experience of associating with other members of the living unit may envision the same type of interpersonal community environment the following year. You may wish to invite someone to a floor meeting to speak about apartment living during the spring semester when most students begin their apartment search. Students should know about contracts, leases, damage deposits, subleasing, pets, utilities, vacations, and landlords. Consumer protection agencies, the student ombudsman office, or the dean of students' office might be good resources.

THE SENIOR YEAR

As students complete their junior year and begin their senior year, they should begin to feel comfortable with themselves and be on their way to clarifying their values, accepting a sex role, establishing an adult-to-adult relationship with their parents, and developing tolerance for different lifestyles. Intellectually, students should begin to relate to "truth" in the context of values and evidence. Students' critical thinking, analytical abilities, and abstract reasoning skills should all have increased. The end of four or five years of college by no means heralds the end of the search for identity, but students are usually not in crisis about it. People continually discover new dimensions within themselves and continue to learn and grow throughout their life.

As you might expect, most of the adjustment difficulties associated with the latter part of the junior year and throughout the senior year revolve around career decisions and career anxiety. For many seniors, their previous four years have revolved around the college community, their identity closely tied to being part of the collegiate environment. In the college years, students come to know that environment, to depend on it, to identify themselves with the label "college student," and to develop a sense of security within that community.

Facing graduation, students are confronted with a threat to their security. Within a period of a few months, they may be in a new environment. This challenge to identity is the catalyst for a developmental crisis. It is an opportunity for students to grow.

Values

From the freshman to the sophomore year, students move from values of idealism to values of increasing realism. This increasing sense of realism is reflected in a decrease in rigid, inflexible views of the world. As students' experiences increase, they gain a better perspective and recognize the limiting variables in resolving complex issues. This might be described as a period of learning to accept the world around them with an increasingly realistic perspective.

Career Planning

Much of the senior year is concerned with the selection of a career and life work. Students often enter college with a concept of what they believe they would like to do and use college as an opportunity to refine their general interests into a career direction. Research suggests that career decision-making can occur as early as age 14 and continues until around the age of 25.[14] The exploration period has been described as follows:

1. *crystallization of a vocational preference*
2. *specifying a vocational preference*
3. *implementation of the preference*
4. *stabilization in the chosen vocation*

5. *consolidation of one's status within the vocation*
6. *advancing in the occupation*[15]

The first step, firming up vocational preferences, occurs in high school and in the first couple of years in college. Specifying and implementing such preferences are usually concerns of the junior and senior years. The task of the senior year is implementing the vocational preference. Miller and Prince described this process of career decision-making as

examining the world of work, understanding the abilities, interests, and values that are needed in various occupations, synthesizing facts and knowledge about oneself and the world of work, and committing oneself to the career and beginning to implement a vocational decision. Finally, a plan for the future that balances vocational aspirations, a vocational interest, and family concerns must be developed along with a sense of direction to identify the next steps and make a tentative commitment to future plans.[16]

The careers and vocations people select are based on a combination of factors, one of which is the job market. Colleges and universities experienced an increase in the number of students interested in the sciences and engineering when the job market called for more engineers and scientists. A similar increase in the number of students entering the field of education occurred when there was a shortage of teachers in the occupational market. Later, the interest was in accounting and functions related to management and business. The job market plays an important role in helping someone select an occupation. However, of equal importance is how students feel about themselves and what they believe they can accomplish. Persons who see themselves as shy and retiring are unlikely to picture themselves in an aggressive occupation such as sales and marketing. People come to make decisions about their vocations on the basis of many factors, including their self-perceptions, the availability of jobs, their status needs, other people's expectations of them, previous role models, and job opportunities.

As an RA and a student, you are no doubt aware of the frequency with which students change academic majors. Astin explained that "these changes are more systematic than random; students who change majors or career plans usually change to related fields. Fields differ markedly in their retention and recruitment of students, with business and law generally showing the greatest gains and science and engineering the greatest losses in the undergraduate years."[17]

Job anxiety is an extension of career-decision problems. The anxiety is centered around pending decisions of other people. Will a student be offered a job with a particular company or be accepted in graduate school with an assistantship? Will he or she need to take a job of lower status or attend a graduate school of lower status? Job anxiety mounts even for students who have been offered positions or graduate assistantships at excellent universities. Often they are reluctant to accept these offers, hoping that something better will come along. The anxiety, stress, and tension mount as the year progresses and the jobs appear to be fewer and fewer. The news media often carry stories about how many college students will be out of work this year; at the same time, one begins to hear about friends who have acquired responsible positions. This is a difficult and stressful time for all. Many students are gripped with a type of panic that affects other students as the anxiety of one student feeds off the anxiety of others.

Often, students view their entire success or failure in college in terms of their ability to find employment in a particular occupation. This can be especially threatening for a humanities or social sciences major who may have been more interested in acquiring a liberal education than in pursuing a specific vocational interest. Fears of getting into graduate school—especially law school and medical programs—tend to raise the stress and anxiety among seniors.

Students vying for a limited number of positions in business management and related areas may become very competitive. Reports abound of students violating university placement office procedures to ensure a scheduled appointment with a favored firm. The anxiety preceding and following interviews creates stress. As you know from your own experience, people have a tendency to relieve this stress and anxiety through heightened reactions to situations and people. People in these stressed situations can be aggressive, competitive, and difficult. Alcohol abuse is common, and many students show physical signs of stress.

Separation and Loss

Most students who are completing college find their college experience generally satisfying. They recall with nostalgia their freshman days, their first date, and memorable moments on campus. After all, for the past four years or more, much of their lives has been directly related to the campus environment. It has been their home. They feel warm and comfortable and very good about the college environment as a whole. They may question different aspects of their education, disdain the administration, and curse some of their instructors, but most will look on their time in college with very fond memories. Some students may feel a sense of relief in finally leaving, but most seniors feel a sense of loss as they depart from close friends and recall their experiences. When asked "If you had to do it over again, would you attend the same institution?" over 80 percent of all graduating students answer yes.[18]

Self-confidence

The anxiety, stress, and emotional involvement in departing from college can attack a person's self-confidence. The student's self-image, self-esteem, and status needs, as well as other people's expectations of him or her, all seem to come together at one time. If students have many positive, reinforcing experiences from interviews and friends, this may have a tendency to accentuate their self-confidence and encourage them. However, the opposite is often true. Students may have one or two very stressful job interviews, parents calling with questions about postcollege plans, relatives and friends with expectations of success, and their own expectations for themselves. Students in this period need emotional support to make it through some very anxious situations.

Other Problems

Stress and anxiety can become contagious and trigger similar feelings in other people. As an RA, you need to be aware of the pressure that is confronting seniors and make yourself available to them for emotional support and for counseling. You must carefully assess when it is appropriate for you to inquire about the decisions and issues confronting them at that particular point in their lives. Asking questions can produce heightened anxiety; disclosing a lack of success in job placement is difficult for many people. Make students aware of the counseling opportunities on campus and of any career planning and placement workshops available to assist them with some of these decisions. They will need your support and friendship and your positive reinforcement during this time.

RA Anxieties

RAs experience some of these same anxieties and crises as they move into their own senior year.

You will find that your interest in education and a subsequent career, as well as your maturity level, exceed those of many students in your living unit. So it may be very easy to lose patience and become intolerant of certain activities. Be careful not to take your anxieties and tensions out on the students in your unit. You will need to employ some personal coping mechanisms and seek support among the other RAs. Some schools do not permit graduating seniors to assume the position of RA for this very reason.

The best way to decrease anxiety about job placement and other related graduation plans is to plan early. Put together a resume, contact the placement office, and do your job search early. These steps will help ensure some confidence for yourself as you approach job interview situations. As other people's anxiety mounts, you will be able to maintain confidence in your preparation and will be ahead of many who wait until late in the spring term to begin searching for a job or graduate school after graduation.

REVIEW

1. Indicate when the following adjustment problems are most likely to occur: freshman year (F), sophomore or junior years (S/J), or senior year (S).
   a. homesickness
   b. problems with parents
   c. intimacy
   d. marital plans
   e. doubt over whether or not to continue in college
   f. authoritarian personality
   g. boyfriend/girlfriend conflicts
   h. pressure to live off campus
   i. stabilization of a vocational preference
   j. sex-role identification problem

2. When a freshman begins living in a residence hall, he or she goes through an adaptation phase. How long is this period and what is its importance to the RA?

3. What role does the architectural or environmental design of a residence hall play in the maintenance of peer groups?

4. In the freshman year, most students experience a "break in the child-parent relationship." What is meant by this phrase and what is its function in a student's development?

5. What are some of the advantages and disadvantages to assigning freshmen to live in the same residence halls with upper-class students (i.e., sophomores, juniors, and seniors)?

6. If new roommates react negatively to each other when they first meet, what can the RA do in subsequent weeks to help them adjust?

7. If roommates continue to have problems after two or three weeks, what is likely to be the best course of action and why?

8. What is "sophomore slump" and what are some of the reasons it may occur?

9. What is the primary reason students want to move from the residence hall into an apartment during the sophomore or junior year? Is there a good educational reason for letting students move from the residence halls after the first or second year? Explain why or why not.

APPLICATIONS

CRIMES OF THE HEART

David was a criminal justice major. He enjoyed the first year of college, but the second year was just not as interesting. It seemed like it would take forever for him to finish the core course requirements of his college. He had taken only two courses in his major, and he enjoyed them. The foreign language requirement and the advanced math requirement were giving him the most difficulty. He had dropped both last semester because he could not keep up.

If it were not for Carol, he might have just dropped out of college and joined a police force someplace. Carol was a student he met at the beginning of the fall semester, and they had been dating regularly ever since.

One night David returned to the residence hall and saw Carol standing in front of the hall talking with another man. They were laughing and seemed to be having a good time. David was jealous. He watched them for awhile, then approached them. He was polite, but it was evident that he found this situation stressful. When the other young man left, David began to quiz Carol about him. His questions were so intense that Carol got angry and told him that she wasn't some criminal and to stop the third-degree questioning. David got angry and the two had a major fight which ended in Carol telling him she never wanted to see him again.

David returned to his room, frustrated and upset. His roommate tried to console him with statements like, "You were too good for her," and "There are a lot of fish in the sea—learn to play the field."

During the following week, David tried to call Carol at least a dozen times. She spoke to him only once. She told him that it was not just the fight they had that made her break off the relationship, but other things also bothered her. She told him that he was a nice guy and that she hoped that they could just be good friends. David fell into a deep depression. He stopped eating and stopped going to classes.

David came back to the room one afternoon and told his roommate that he had decided to drop out of college and was giving serious thought to joining the Marine Corps. He planned to meet with a recruiter tomorrow. He was not going to tell his parents, because it was his decision and he didn't want them to try and interfere.

David's roommate was concerned and went to talk with the RA. He told the RA the whole story.

WHAT WOULD YOU DO?

1. If you were David's RA what would you do?
2. What developmental issues is David confronting?
3. Do you think the college should allow David to withdraw and join the Marine Corps without someone from the college talking with his parents?
4. What adjustment problems is David experiencing?
5. List three things the RA could do to help David with his personal adjustment.
6. What are some of the potentially positive and negative outcomes of David's decision to leave college and join the Marine Corps?

STUDENT PROBLEMS: OLD AND NEW

Rhoda Orme acted as a "dormitory counselor" (hall director) at Barnard College after a number of years working as an instructor and academic dean at Bradford Junior College. From her experience she observed that the most common student problems among freshman women in 1950 were the following:

1. Having to supervise personally one's own activities without being checked on, as at home
2. Feeling lonely because one is afraid at first to talk confidentially to new friends
3. Finding oneself to be a little frog in a big pond, the opposite of the situation in a small-town high school
4. Finding out that college life is not as glamorous as one imagined
5. Trying to decide what to do about an unlikable girl who sticks close
6. Wasting too much time in "bull sessions" and bridge games, and then letting work pile up because there is no check-up in class
7. Resisting the temptation to ask advice about many details from a roommate, as one did from family at home
8. Not being able to figure out "what the professor wants"
9. Finding it hard to compete with girls who have had wide social experiences[19]

WHAT WOULD YOU DO?

1. Are these problems of the 1950s still problems for most students today? If so, which three do you believe are the most significant problems? If you do not believe these issues are problems for most students, what do you believe has changed so that these issues are no longer major concerns?

2. List the five problems you believe are most common among freshmen.

3. Do you believe that male and female freshmen have different kinds of problems during their first year? If so, what are these differences?

4. Choose any three of the common student problems Rhoda Orme observed and identify the psychosocial or cognitive developmental issue each one reflects.

CHAPTER SEVEN

PEER COUNSELING

©1998 PHOTODISK, INC.

Some RAs join a residence hall staff expecting to become full-time counselors. RAs do some counseling in the form of active listening. They do some advising in the form of providing information, and they do some referral counseling to help students seek assistance from a professional counselor or psychologist. RAs do not do psychological analysis or clinical counseling. Psychology majors sometimes view this helping relationship as an opportunity to try their ability to diagnose and assist troubled students. The skills necessary to do this take many years to develop. An RA is neither expected nor trained to do this.

The RA is best viewed as a peer counselor, a helper, or a skilled listener. Many of the skills needed to perform this counseling role cannot be taught in the short time students remain in the RA position. For this reason, RAs should be chosen on the basis of their human relations skills. Sensitivity toward others, an ability to work in groups, an accepting personality, and a desire to help others are the qualities needed to fulfill the counseling responsibilities of the RA position. Every

RA must have these qualities to some degree. A person can always be taught the operational procedures needed to manage the residence hall, to report emergencies, or to apply first aid. However, they cannot be taught to develop a personality that makes other students want to know them and the sensitivity to work compassionately with other students in a time of emotional crisis.

If you did not possess these qualities, you would not have been chosen as an RA. However, having these qualities is not enough. The key is knowing how to transform these qualities into skills. This chapter will help you do this by providing you with some counseling techniques, some counseling strategies, a counseling model, and some tips on counseling.

COMPLAINTS ABOUT COUNSELING

The most common complaints heard from RAs about counseling are (1) most students contact the RA for relatively trivial or routine matters like unlocking doors or asking other students to turn down their stereos; (2) RAs are not always certain when they are counseling a student and when they are simply having a good discussion; and (3) RAs believe they are given too much theory and not enough practical information. These complaints are supportable.

Complaint One. Most of the requests that an RA receives are for routine tasks, like opening doors or giving information. These requests are important. How you handle them can demonstrate to students either that you are available to help or that you would prefer not to be bothered. Students can easily assume that if you are too busy to help with small matters, you are too busy to help with something major. It is a matter of trust. You must demonstrate to students that you are interested in them as individuals. If you fail to do this, students are unlikely to be interested in contacting you for any assistance.

Complaint Two. Although it is not really very important to define the specifics of a helping contact as it differs from a discussion, many RAs feel a need to establish parameters for defining these situations. For discussion purposes, a *counseling encounter* is an act of helping another person cope with an emotion, a personal problem, stress, or a crisis by assisting in decision making and helping to return the person to an improved emotional state. Counseling contacts will come from one of three sources: (1) the student will initiate the contact; (2) you will observe behavior in a student that indicates the need for some form of counseling intervention; or (3) a resident of your living unit or another staff person will inform you of behavior that indicates the need for counseling intervention.

Complaint Three. The third complaint heard from RAs is that they are given too much theory and not enough practical information. A modification of this complaint is that the techniques they have been taught are superficial, simplistic, and artificial. Some of this is probably true. It is difficult to teach people how to transform personal qualities into skills until they have some basic understanding of exactly what they need to do. On the other hand, a review of major counseling theories and counseling approaches is best reserved for those who are interested in counseling as a profession. It is easy to become bogged down with conflicting theories and schools of thought on counseling; yet there needs to be a pattern or model to follow.

The helping-skills or counseling model used in this chapter is composed of three phases. The first phase is to become aware of your own feelings, motivations, values, strengths, and weaknesses as you prepare yourself to help others. The second phase is to establish yourself with the residents in your living unit in a way that will encourage students to contact you for assistance with personal problems. The third phase is a five-step helping-skills model. In the last two sections of this chapter, the model is modified to suggest a method for giving advice and for making a referral for professional counseling.

AN OVERVIEW OF HELPING SKILLS

Most problems students experience in college are products of the maturation process, adjustment to a new environment, or normal stress. Few of these require the assistance of a professional counselor. General depression, anxiety, stress, disappointment, rejection, and grief are normal; they are the kinds of feelings that you, an RA with helping skills, should be capable of handling. These problems will be brought about by many of the same experiences you have had. Even though a problem may stem from feelings of inadequacy, difficulty with class assignments, or problems with parents, money, or a significant other, it can usually be discussed and some method of coping with it uncovered.

Problems can be resolved alone or with the help of a friend. Talking about the problem with another person can be all the help needed. There is something special, a type of emotional catharsis, in sharing a problem with another person; it is almost as though one no longer carries the burden alone. The sympathy and understanding expressed by another can often help a troubled individual cope with the problem.

Although you can help with most problems, not all students will share their problems with you. Though you may never be confronted by a student who is contemplating his or her own death, the probability that this will occur in your unit is higher than you may realize. One of your residents will probably experience some type of serious emotional problem during the academic year as a result of breaking up with a significant other. Your ability to respond to these situations may be crucial to the student's ability to function. Many of the skills you develop through your RA training will be used daily. Some, however, are really preparation for the one or perhaps two times that you may be called on for some serious counseling during the year. These one or two times might make the difference between life and death for the student involved.

Preparing Yourself to Help

Confidence. The very nature of the helping relationship places you in a position of authority: The student comes to you seeking assistance with a problem. Many undergraduate RAs, not previously exposed to this degree of responsibility, feel a sense of ambiguity. They lack the basic

Counseling often takes place in an informal, relaxed atmosphere.

self-confidence to enter into an exchange with the student for fear that they may say or do something that will make a student's situation worse.

This is a reasonable reaction, but, for the most part, unfounded. There is very little that you, as a reasonably prudent RA, could say that would do irreparable harm to the student. Most of the situations that you will encounter will be situations you can handle. The types of problems that students experience in college are similar to the types of problems that people experience in all walks of life; most of them are not unique, special, or overly serious.

However, you may encounter situations during the year for which you are not prepared. As you come to recognize your ability to help students, you must also recognize your limitations. Remember that you can help students most of the time; in situations in which you are uncertain, ask the hall director for guidance. Later in this chapter, conditions under which you should seek the support of a professional counselor and making a counseling referral are discussed.

Attitudes, Beliefs, and Values. As an RA, you are in a position to influence the attitudes, beliefs, and values of students during a critical time in their lives. In a counseling encounter, the influence is magnified by virtue of the helping rela-tionship. Therefore, you must accept one of the basic canons of counseling: Do not judge other people's values by your own.

RAs are selected in part based on personal skills, motivations, and values that coincide with the institution's approach to working with students in residence halls. Except in the case of some religiously affiliated institutions, RAs are chosen to model tolerance, not to teach beliefs or values. Though RAs may reflect their values in their day-to-day interactions with students, they generally do not have the responsibility to advance a particular set of beliefs.

To enter into a helping relationship with a student, you must first become aware of what you believe, not superficially, but what you really believe. Issues such as sex, religion, politics, interracial dating, and similar topics will confront you in many forms through your contacts with students. If, for example, you do not approve of interracial dating, you are entitled to this belief, just as other students are entitled to theirs. When students come to you for counseling, they are not coming for your judgment of their behavior. They are coming to receive help with a problem. Consider the following example. A woman in your living unit becomes pregnant and thinks an abortion may be the best course of action. You personally find abortion unacceptable. How can you

Remaining non-judgmental and objective is critical in counseling students.

best help her? Will it help her if you condemn her for what she is contemplating or if you try to prevent the abortion? You have two choices. First, you could try to remain as objective as possible and facilitate the student's own decision-making process—help her consider her options and facilitate a referral to a mental health professional at your institution. Second, you could tell her that you personally have some strong feelings about this subject and refer her to someone who could be more objective.

Either of these approaches is acceptable. Sometimes people have strong feelings about a particular topic and they cannot be objective. They sometimes cannot divorce themselves from values that judge the right or wrong of certain actions. In these situations, the only option is to be open about your feelings and tell the person that you cannot be objective enough to help with the decision.

The counseling relationship should be nonjudgmental. You should maintain your own values, but refrain from expressing them and instructing others to abide by them.

It is not always easy to remain nonjudgmental. Sometimes you may think you are helping people when you are actually attempting to push your view of the world. Perhaps the classic example is with a student contemplating resigning from college. When the student comes to the RA to discuss the issue, the RA takes the position of trying to convince the student to stay in school. This position is based on the premise that it is better to attend college than not to attend college and that it is bad to drop out. This may or may not be true. The RA may set out on a well-intentioned quest to help the student stay in college. The person who should be making this decision and who should be in the midst of the evaluation is the student, not the RA. Not only is it presumptuous of the RA to assume that he or she is more capable of determining what is best for the student, but it places the RA in the position of assuming responsibility for the actions of the other person.

If you are to help other students with their personal problems, you must know yourself and know what you believe and how strongly you feel about these beliefs. Becoming aware of your attitudes and beliefs is a continual process and may require you to participate in some self-discovery workshops with other staff members and students. Once you know what you believe, you can work to control these beliefs in your counseling encounters.

Motivation.   What is the motivation to help another person with a personal problem? Ideally, it is associated with a basic sensitivity to others, the desire to alleviate suffering, and perhaps the knowledge that the other person trusts you enough to share his or her problem. It is satisfying to help others with their problems and to have knowledge that they wished to share something of themselves with you.

The helping role of the counselor is primarily one of an understanding, often sympathetic, facilitator of the student's own thinking and ideas. Many times you will feel as though you could simply dispense your wisdom on the particular topic and resolve the student's problem. Seldom will this be the case.

An inexperienced RA could easily confuse the role of counselor with that of problem solver. Usually problem solving does not help students. They are left with the solution to a particular problem and not the skills to resolve similar problems in the future. One of your goals should be to help students develop these skills for themselves. If they do not, they may contact you with every problem that arises.

Remember, it is always simpler to give advice than to stimulate ideas in others. If you find yourself falling into the role of guru, consider who is receiving the most benefit from the relationship—you or the students.

Objectivity.   As an RA, you will have many demands placed on your time. If you are liked and trusted by your residents, they will bring you a number of their problems. People who are sensitive to the needs of others are susceptible to falling into the trap of accepting other people's problems as their own. If you are to remain a viable resource for students in your hall, you must remain objective and retain some degree of emotional detachment. You can never accept responsibility for someone else's problem or someone else's decision. Each student is responsible for his or her problem. Most people do not have enough time or emotional fortitude to accept responsibility for the problems and actions of an entire living unit of college students. You will be of help to your residents only so long as you can be objective and assist them with their own decision making.

As you enter into a helping relationship with a student, you must understand yourself, your strengths and limitations, your values, and your motivations. Recognize that you are capable of helping students with most of their problems, but that you are not the problem solver. Help them work through their own problems, recognizing that not all problems have a solution.

COUNSELING MODEL

The goal of all helping skills encounters is to help students make positive, self-directed choices about their own lives that aid them in their development and return them to their previous state or an improved state in which they can again function. This goal can be accomplished through the following five-stage model (see figure 7.1): (1) precounseling, (2) listening, (3) problem identification and analysis, (4) resolution, and (5) follow-up.

COUNSELING
MODEL

- Precounseling
- Listening
- Problem Identification and Analysis
- Resolution
- Follow-up

Precounseling Stage

This is the stage in which the student has either sought your assistance with a problem, someone has told you about a problem a student is experiencing, or you have observed something about a student's behavior that needs to be discussed. In the latter two situations, you will be initiating the counseling. In these circumstances, you will need to explain the reason for your inquiry. These inquiries can be simple expressions of the behavior you have observed. For example: "John, I have observed that you appear depressed and moody recently. Is something bothering you?" Or: "John, is everything going all right for you? I noticed that you have not been attending classes recently and don't seem to be acting like yourself." Such statements invite students to disclose their problem, if they have one. They also show that you care.

When someone has told you about a problem that one of your residents is experiencing, it is appropriate for you to explain by saying something like, "I was talking with X the other day, and she told me that you and your boyfriend broke up. How are you feeling about that? Is everything all right?" Or: "The hall director told me that you were not pledged by the sorority in which you were interested. I was sorry to hear about it. How do you feel about what happened?" These questions reveal to the student the source and substance of your information.

An open-ended question ("How are you feeling about . . . ?") will invite more than a yes or no answer. If the person wishes to talk, he or she has the opportunity. In both these cases—observed and reported behavior—you can prepare beforehand. You can think of areas you may wish to explore with the student, and you can plan the time to contact the student.

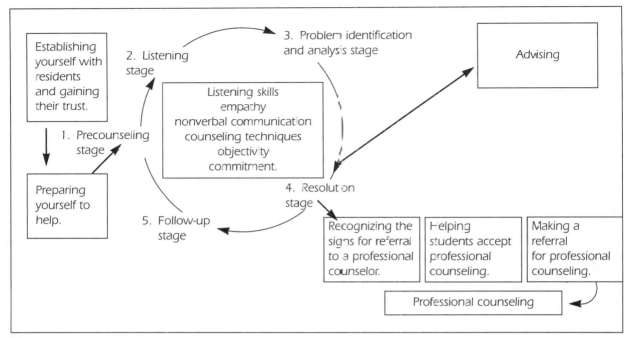

Figure 7.1

If the student approaches you with a problem, you will not have the opportunity to think about the problem beforehand or possibly to set the time and place for the discussion. You do, however, have the right to request that the student select another time. You may find yourself in the middle of an important class assignment, late for an important meeting, or so frustrated that you simply cannot assist the student at that particular time. Every time a student comes to you with a problem, you need not drop everything and deal with it at that precise moment. Some students will come and sit in your room and simply spend time procrastinating. This wastes both your time and theirs. Other students run to the RA with every petty problem they have. You soon will find such students to be a nuisance.

You can decide to see the student immediately or postpone discussing the problem until a more convenient time. Chances are that the first encounters will be the most meaningful. If a student comes to you for the first time with a problem, if at all possible try to see that student and help him or her with the problem. However, each decision needs to be made independently. It should be based on what you know about the individual, his or her emotional state at the time, how often he or she comes to you with problems, and how important the completion of your own work is at that moment. You must also assess some things from the person's tone and physical manner at the time. A woman who continually runs to you for emotional support, often crying, may not need your attention as much as a woman who does not come to you often and is somber and lacks much emotion. You must begin making some subjective decisions about the individual and how important the particular problem is.

It is appropriate, based on your responses to the above questions, to ask the student if the problem requires your immediate attention or if it can wait until you have more time or are better able to assist. Remember that you will not be able to give your full attention to helping if your attention is focused on studying for an examination or completing a paper. You will be trying to get the problem resolved quickly so that you can continue with what you really want to do. Both you and the student would be better served if you set a time later—the same day if at all possible—to discuss the problem. Most students will understand if you explain that you have something that must be completed.

Assuming that you decide that a student's problem is important enough to set aside what you have been doing, perhaps turn off your stereo or television, your first step in the counseling exchange is to make the person feel welcome. You would probably do so anyway, whether you had invited the student to your room to discuss an observed problem or if the student just stopped by. Making the person feel comfortable requires just a little more effort when the purpose is counseling.

Set the Environment for the Exchange. Close the door, physically push aside what you were doing, and sit directly across from the person. If another person is in the room when the student comes in and is not discussing an important problem with you, ask the other person to leave.

The visitor, understanding your role, will not be offended. In no case should you try to discuss a serious subject with a student in front of another person. If the telephone rings during the conversation or if there is a knock at the door, answer it very briefly. Tell the caller that you have someone with you and that you will return the call. This is a way of reinforcing to the student with a problem that he or she is the central focus of your concern. Probably nothing is more irritating for a troubled student discussing a serious problem than to have the conversation interrupted by a telephone call and the person with whom he or she is sharing the information spend an extended time on the telephone. This conveys disinterest.

Be Conscious of the Nonverbal Clues You Are Sending. If you lie down on your bed and stare at the ceiling or sit behind your desk, you could be nonverbally communicating disinterest or placing a barrier to intimacy between you and the other person. The same applies to assuming any physically superior position relative to the student seeking help. If you sit on the desk or tower above the person, you are conveying a superiority that may further inhibit the student from expressing his or her feelings.

The proper counseling posture is to sit directly across from the student. Your posture should be open—meaning that neither your arms nor your legs should be crossed. Nonverbally, having your arms or legs crossed could communicate that you are closed off from the other person. Your eyes should focus on the other person's face. If you have trouble looking into the other person's eyes, try looking just slightly above them at the eyebrows. You may find this less intense. Try to project a feeling of being relaxed and open, yet attentive and interested in the other person. Your voice should be calming, tranquil, and soothing, but not a whisper. Your entire demeanor should convey acceptance, comfort, and understanding. This mode helps the person feel more comfortable with you and more willing to share his or her problem.

Listening Stage

This is the stage in which the student talks and you listen. It is an opportunity for the student to describe how he or she views the problem. You in turn are periodically telling the person how you are interpreting the situation being described. Although people describe clearly how they view what is happening, you are trying to understand the student's frame of reference to understand the view being described. Whether you agree with the viewpoint being presented is not important; the important thing is that you listen and understand what is being said. In this communication you need to determine what the student sees as the problem and views as the reason or cause, as well as how the student is currently coping. To determine these things, you first must be a good listener.

Communicating is a difficult process. It requires the person sending the message to confirm that the message being sent is the one being received. It requires the receiver to confirm that he or she has received the message that was intended. Thus, good listening is an active process. Messages are sent, received, and confirmed by each of the parties.

To do this you must know how to listen. Hearing what somebody is saying is not the same as truly listening to what is said. This two-way process means that you must check the meaning of certain words. If the student claims to be hated by his or her roommate, that only tells you that the student perceives a conflict with the roommate. Appropriate questions for you to ask in this situation are "What do you mean by 'hates you'?" and "What makes you believe that?" Communication only takes place when both of you understand and have a common meaning for the words, phrases, and situations that are being described.

"Being yourself" means exactly that. Be natural about your actions and your relationship to the other person. Do not try to be psychoanalytic, use unnecessary complex terms, or attempt to impress the person with your knowledge. The student is looking for a friend and someone who can help. You should refrain from giving the impression that you are doing a psychological counseling session. Your goal is not to make a diagnosis but to help the person cope with the problem. If a student needs professional assistance, your role is to make a referral, as described later in this chapter.

"Talk less and listen more" is a good rule of thumb. This is a chance for the student to paint a picture for you of what is happening and for you to understand. The student at this point is the teacher instructing you. You, in turn, are trying to understand the subject matter or the view that the student is painting. You can only do this if you give the student time to discuss the problem.

The amount of time, however, is not the issue. Some students will be able to paint a clear and accurate picture for you in a relatively short time. Others will need to add a quantity of elaborate and nonuseful detail. You may help the student move through the explanation with questions such as, "How does that particular event affect the problem?" Or, "Yes, I am familiar with that area, go on."

Questions that clarify the situation are a simple but important method of communicating to students that you are understanding what they are saying. Feed back the information that has been given you. Some stock phrases and questions you should make part of your listening technique are: "What I hear you saying is . . ." "If I understand you correctly, you are saying . . . " "Did you say . . . ?" "What do you mean by . . . ?"

These restatements and questions clarify and, most important, give the student information on what you are perceiving. Sometimes this is enough for the student to gain perspective on the problem. You are asking questions that help the student clarify the situation by feeding back or reflecting what he or she has said. This reflection of ideas and perceptions is important in gaining a mutual understanding of what is being said as well as establishing a different viewpoint for the student.

Open-ended questions help the student elaborate in more detail any areas you do not understand or areas in which you believe the student has made some incorrect assumptions. Closed questions can be answered with one or two words; open-ended questions need a more complete response. For example, if you ask a student, "What is your major?" the student may easily respond, "My major is . . ." You could ask that same question and receive more information by asking, "Why did you choose your current major?" Open-ended questions are best for follow-up information. Follow-up questions are ones such as, "Tell me more about . . ." or "How do you believe the situation would have been different if you had . . . ?" Remember, most of the counseling session will be spent with the other person doing the talking and working through the problem. You will be asking appropriate questions to help clarify the problem.

Be careful not to deviate from the subject being discussed. Help the student keep to the problem at hand. When you ask questions, ask only those that directly relate to the problem. This will help eliminate diversion and help the student focus on the problem.

While talking with the student, you must have good attending skills—those nonverbal or subverbal indications by which you let a person know that you understand. Good attending skills are essential. They confirm that you understand what has been said.

If used appropriately, these techniques will aid in the communication process and facilitate listening. If you are acknowledging the receipt of information and asking questions of clarification, you become an active participant in the listening process. As a participant, you contribute as well as receive by confirming the information that is given. This interchange is esential to effective listening.

Empathy. The ability to empathize with another individual is closely associated with interpersonal communication. Empathy takes place when two people share in the same sensory experience at an emotional level. Empathy requires the ability to attune yourself to the sensory and verbal cues expressed by another person to the extent that you experience someone else's feelings as your own. You do this by projecting yourself into the experience of the other person. The ability to empathize is based on the ability to understand and accurately read cues individuals give about their internal state. Verbal symbols and expressions of emotions are cues to interpret how a person is experiencing a particular internal issue. Of equal importance are nonverbal cues such as eye movement, body language, voice inflection, and key word phraseology, which provide a deeper understanding of another person's communication.

By accurately reading a person's body language, a trained therapist can determine whether the person is suppressing information or is afraid, sad, embarrassed, or happy. This information aids in interpreting and responding accurately to the experience of another person. The more information one has about a person, the more accurate the understanding of the experience being communicated.

Using Good Attending Skills

- Nod your head to communicate that you understand and are soliciting more information or that you are giving approval to the individual. To see this technique work, sit down across from a friend and, while he or she is talking, nod casually throughout the discussion. Part of the way through, simply quit nodding and only look at him or her. Your friend will either begin going into more detail or may ask you if you understand what he or she is saying. In our culture, we need reassurance or confirmation that the other person hears and understands what we are saying.

- Use hand gestures, such as the rotation of one hand in a certain way, to express the feeling of approval.

- Use facial expressions—smiles, frowns, and such—to express that you understand and approve or disapprove. You need not say anything, just show the appropriate facial expression to get the person to continue talking.

- Use subverbals such as "uh huh" or another similar form of subverbal sound to communicate understanding.

- Assume an open accepting posture to convey interest and sympathy.

There are two steps to empathizing. First, your must be able to predict and understand the motives and attitudes of the other person. The prediction is based on understanding the individual, and what rewards, behaviors, and experiences this person has had and finds satisfying.

The second step is learning to communicate you understanding of what the person is saying. This feedback has the quality of reaffirming what you are hearing and seeing. Not only must this communication provide understanding, it also must be rewarding. The reward comes from the knowledge that the other person understands and shares those feelings. This means that if the person is relating a sad, stressful situation, the person empathizing with that experience may feel similar emotions. He or she also may show depression, cry, or get angry. This is the psychophysiological level at which the deepest empathy takes place.

Problem Identification and Analysis

Once the student has explained his or her perception of the problem, its cause, and how he or she is coping with it—and you understand and believe you have a fairly accurate picture—you can then begin to analyze the elements of the problem (not the student). In this stage you will be helping the student direct attention to specific elements of the problem. The basic techniques used are questioning and sharing of personal experiences.

Four steps are accomplished in this stage:

1. Restate the problem as you understand it.
2. Analyze the problem to determine if the student's perception is accurate.
3. Develop options for managing or resolving the problem.
4. Determine the student's expectations for the ideal and the realistic resolutions to the problem.

Review. First, reiterate or review with the student the problem as you see it with the student. Establish your perception of the problem, confirming the three basic elements of (1) the cause, (2) the perception of the problem as the student sees it, and (3) how the student is currently coping with it. You are trying to confirm that you are talking about the same problem and that you understand.

Analyze.   Second, analyze the problem to determine the accuracy of the students' perception. This should be done through a series of questions and confrontations. Through questioning and answering you attempt to have the person acknowledge realities that may conflict with the person's perception of the event. Never assume that you know more about the problem than the student does. You do have a base of personal experiences on which to draw, and it may be appropriate to point out that what the student is experiencing is not abnormal and that many people have expressed similar problems.

Be careful, however, when expressing views about comparable problems, that you do not minimize the student's problem. An example is students who receive poor grades on their papers. The students may believe that their professors have negative opinions of them, so the students may try to shift the responsibility for poor performance to the professor. Questions you might appropriately ask would be, "What makes you believe the professor picked on you specifically? Have you spoken with the professor about the situation? Do you believe that this is a good example of your ability? Do you feel that the paper could have been better than it was? Have you had an opportunity to see anyone else's paper? Are you certain that no one else has received a similar grade for a similar performance?"

Use confrontation to point out inconsistencies in what the student has said. Such statements as "On the one hand you have said . . . , but on the other hand you have also said . . ." are attempts to establish a consistent line of reasoning. Such comments help students gain a clearer perspective on the way they are viewing the problem. You have the advantage in that you have some distance from the problem and can be more objective. When students become emotionally involved in a problem, they can lose perspective and not always realize the inconsistencies in their reasoning. In the example of students who receive poor grades on a paper, you may have inquired earlier how they had performed previously and found that they had done well. You then could suggest the conflict in logic as follows: "You have done well on all your past examinations and papers, yet you say that the professor is out to get you. Why is that? Does that seem consistent to you?"

In analyzing the problem, three conclusions are possible: (1) the student may be relaying accurate information and is perceiving the problem

Ask Yourself . . .

- Does the student have any control over what is happening? Often he or she does not. A good case in point might be the student who is experiencing frustration and anxiety because of financial problems created by the late arrival of a financial aid check. The student has little control over the cause of the problem. However, he or she may have alternatives that you could explore.

- Is any action on the part of the student necessary or indicated? Sometimes the best course of action is to do nothing. This is usually an alternative.

- If some action could be taken to help the situation, what types of action are possible? If a student experiences financial problems because of not receiving a financial aid check, other courses of action might include a part-time job, a loan from another source, or an extension on a payment that is due.

- What resources can the student bring to bear on the situation?

- What are the consequences of each proposed action? What is the worst that could happen, the best that could happen, and the probability of each?

correctly, (2) the student has a distorted perception of the problem and thus may be relating distorted information, and (3) the student may have relayed accurate information but may have misperceived the problem.

Develop Options.   Having helped the student analyze the problem, the third step is to develop options for managing or resolving the problem and to explore consequences of these options.

When discussing options with the student, you may make suggestions, but most suggestions and alternatives should be analyzed by the student. Do not fall into the trap of trying to answer the questions, "What do you think I should do?" or "What would you do if you were me?" The student is asking for your advice for you to make a decision. This is usually inappropriate. Your responses should be, "The question is what do *you* think you should do, not what *I* think you should do." Appropriate questions are, "Now that we are at this point, what do you believe you can do about the situation? What alternatives do you see available? What resources do you have to deal with it?" Suggestions that you might make could be derived from your experience within the institution. Such suggestions as, "Have you considered trying to get an emergency student loan from the dean of students office?" Or, "I know there are part-time jobs available in the cafeteria; have you considered working there?"

Determine Ideal and Realistic Resolutions. The last step in the problem identification and analysis stage is to determine with the student what he or she believes to be the ideal outcome and whether this outcome is realistic. Specifically, what would it take to achieve the ideal resolution? Because what is ideal is not always realistic, it is also important to establish the likelihood of the desired outcome. Does the student have the resources to achieve it? Is it actually within the realm of probability?

Resolution Stage

In the resolution stage, have students reiterate the alternatives, plan how they intend to implement action if necessary, and develop a time frame in which the action will be initiated. Confirm with students the action that will take place. When students leave your room, they should feel that several alternatives are available and that they have a definite course of action. This is the ideal situation. Sometimes it will not be possible to reach this desired end. Students you counsel should feel that they have worked through their own problem with your help. Make sure that students understand that you have a continued interest in what happens. Invite the students back to talk with you after they have taken the proposed action. By doing so, you establish a foundation for the follow-up stage.

Follow-Up Stage

Use the follow-up stage as a check to ensure that students attempt to implement the course of action they identified during counseling sessions. Confirm with students again that you care and have a continued interest. This follow-up should be informal and might be accomplished by stopping by the students' rooms. However, you are the one who should make the effort. That may mean asking students to have dinner with you or making a point of asking them to stop by your room for a few minutes.

The follow-up need only be a one-time encounter for most situations. For some students who are having prolonged difficulties, you may need to continue these follow-ups. This applies particularly to people who are under severe emotional strain, such as might occur when students break up with someone they have been dating for a long time. Your continued support and interest will be helpful. Be careful, however, not to reinforce that depression or sorrow. If students find that they get attention for depression, it may reinforce the behavior.

If enough people reinforce negative emotional states, students may become more depressed.

Many of the emotional problems that students undergo simply take time for them to work out. If you observe in your follow-up that a student is not coping with the problem effectively and that it is impairing his or her ability to function, you should initiate a counseling discussion with the student to make a referral to a professional counselor or professional staff person. Professional counselors or therapists should be able to give students some additional help in coping with their situations.

HELPING A STUDENT SEEK PROFESSIONAL COUNSELING

A referral to professional counseling should be made when it becomes apparent that the student is experiencing a severe emotional problem with which he or she cannot cope. Behavior that you observe, that is reported to you by another person, or that the student describes may indicate the need for such a referral.

In working with a student who has apparent need for professional guidance or who is experiencing an emotional crisis with which you cannot assist, your goal is to have the student agree to see a professional counselor and actually keep the counseling appointment. Many students are reluctant to seek professional assistance for fear that they may be viewed as "mentally ill." Although this label serves no purpose within the context of a helping relationship, it may be one of the greatest barriers you will need to overcome in having the student seek professional counseling.

The three steps to making a referral for professional counseling are: (1) recognize the signs that a student needs referral, (2) help the student recognize and accept the need for professional counseling, and (3) make the referral.

Recognize the Signs for Referral

As noted earlier in this chapter, students are able to resolve most of the difficulties they experience with the assistance of a friend or with some help from you. However, some students will need professional help with their problems. Identifying these students can be particularly difficult, because the college environment naturally lends itself to the acceptance of behavior that in another

STRATEGIES FOR

Counseling

- Develop the skills of empathy, acceptance, attending behavior, and reflection.

- Be confident in your ability.

- Learn to listen to what the person is actually saying.

- Don't take notes.

- Make the person feel comfortable.

- Learn to ask open-ended questions.

- Learn to give feedback responses.

- Care about the person with whom you are talking.

- Share personal experiences when appropriate.

- Be authentic and sincere about your emotions and express them to the student.

- Keep confidences.

- Do not make decisions for the individual.

- Show acceptance of the individual.

- Do not give advice.

- Help the student to understand that feelings are normal.

- Acknowledge responses that the student makes, such as crying.

Some students must
be referred to a
professional counselor.

environment would be out of the ordinary. Students are experiencing conflicts and crises in both their identity and their values. Some of the common signs of emotional problems, such as erratic sleep patterns and eating habits, are difficult to interpret within the college environment. Following are some of the signs people use to signal a need for assistance. This list is not meant to be definitive or the only criteria on which to base a decision to make a referral. The behavior listed is intended solely to assist you in developing a common-sense approach to identifying signals for help in the unique environment of the college residence hall.

- *Poor emotional control* can be exhibited in different forms. Open hostility and belligerence toward people for no apparent reason, exaggerated outbursts of emotion disproportionate to the event, and uncontrolled crying or laughter at inappropriate times are some common signs of poor emotional control. The repeated or prolonged occurrence of these incidents over several days may signal the need for help. This is especially true when the behavior deviates radically from the person's normal personality or is tangential to or follows a difficult emotional time, such as the loss of a parent or rejection by another significant person.

- *Excessive moodiness* or worry is another sign the person may be experiencing a problem. Anxiety, stress, and depression are normal outlets in a person's emotional cycle. A person who is anxious and feels under stress during final exam time may be expressing a very normal emotion. It is natural to worry occasionally. Extreme cases are people who spend an inordinate amount of time worrying about very trivial or insignificant matters, such as whether or not there will be enough forks in the cafeteria line. Preoccupation with or unnatural attention to detail is often a sign that the person needs assistance.

- *Sleeping and eating habits that change dramatically* are also a sign that the person is not coping well with some problem. A student who suddenly begins sleeping 18 hours a day and missing classes is probably experiencing some difficulty. The opposite is also true. The student who develops insomnia and begins taking catnaps during class or at other times also may be experiencing a problem. Eating can be another sign—excessive or continual eating or abstaining from food for prolonged periods of time. Some erratic behavior may occur naturally. The student who has been studying or partying for three days may need to get some additional rest. Someone on a crash diet

STEPS FOR REFERRALS

- Recognize Signs
- Help Student Recognize and Accept
- Make the Referral

may not eat for several days. It is important for you to recognize this behavior within the context of the surrounding situation and in relation to the individual's normal patterns.

- *An unnatural preoccupation with personal health* may be a sign of needing help. The person who constantly complains about the most minor ailment and continually seeks pills and medical advice from other residents may have emotional, rather than physical, problems.

- *People who express a universal mistrust or paranoia about others* may need help. This is a form of insecurity in which people claim that others are continually talking about them or are plotting against them, or similar unsubstantial claims.

- *Persistent and continued depression*—for more than one week—is generally not normal. This could be serious if the person stops talking about the future and begins viewing life as holding only more of the same joyless existence. A student reaching this state of depression is in serious need of attention and is possibly suicidal.

- *Students who talk openly about suicide* are signaling a need for professional help. Such discussions are to be taken seriously and are a call for help and support.

If the answer to any of these questions indicates that the student needs help, make the referral. Share with the residence hall director your perceptions and evaluation and gain the director's assistance in working with the student. Remember, the psychological health of students and their active progress toward growing and accomplishing both academic and personal goals are the common purposes for which both you and your hall director are working.

Help Students Recognize and Accept the Need for Professional Counseling

In making the referral, make two facts clear to the student. First, the student needs to understand that seeking assistance from a professional counselor is not an indication of mental illness. To overcome the student's reluctance, you may need to reassure him or her that all counseling records are confidential and protected by federal law. The institution will not remove the student from school, nor will it record on any of the student's transcripts that he or she has seen a counselor. A common fear is that a decision to seek help will become public and that the student will subsequently be viewed as unstable. It is a breach of professional ethics for a counselor to discuss a student's problem with anyone other than another professional counselor, unless the student seems likely to harm himself or herself or others. The second fact the student must accept is that he or she needs assistance. If you can help alleviate the stigma of seeing a counselor by communicating the first fact well, you will have a better chance of getting the student to acknowledge need of professional assistance.

Listen to the student with interest and empathy. Do not encourage the person if he or she talks of bizarre or strange events taking place or bizarre actions that he or she may like to carry out. Your goal in listening is to determine a frame of reference from which to help the student reach a decision about seeking additional help. Specifically, question the student about the behavior that he or she has exhibited. Inquire as to whether he or she feels satisfied with what is taking place and if the situation could be better. Never argue or in any way try to convince the person that your perception of reality is correct and his or her perception is not. Confront the student only with logic and understanding.

You are not attempting to diagnose the cause of the problem but trying to help the student reach a decision about seeking further help. The techniques of confrontation, open-ended questions, and questions related to the student's goals are appropriate. Reiterate the behavior the student exhibited and ask how he or she feels about the behavior. During this questioning, attempt to have the student acknowledge a willingness to seek additional help.

If you believe that a student needs professional counseling, talk over this perception with your hall director. In most situations, your hall director should be involved, if only in confirming the institutional referral procedure or suggesting a particular counselor to whom you may make the referral.

Making the Referral

If the student accepts the idea of seeing a professional counselor, have the student state the specific action he or she will take. In most situations the student is responsible for making contact with the counselor. On some occasions, you may assist the student by literally accompanying him or her to the counseling center, but for the most part you want the student to take the necessary steps in making the appointment and going to the counseling center.

One technique to confirm the agreed-upon behavior of seeing a counselor is to have the student state the specific behavior he or she will accomplish and the time frame during which it will be accomplished. For example, "I will call Dr. Smith tomorrow morning for an appointment to discuss my problem, and I will attend the counseling session we agree on." Have the student repeat this in exact terms. This becomes a kind of verbal commitment or bond between you and the student.

You will need to follow up with the student to ensure that he or she has kept the commitment. If he or she has not, the follow-up reinforces this verbal bond and may prompt the agreed-upon action. Sometimes this follow-up offers the student the needed opportunity to share with you the events of the counseling session. You can supply some feedback to the student and listen to what the student has to say about the counseling session.

Contact with the counselor, once the referral has been made, is generally not a good idea unless the counselor asks you for your help or feedback about the student's behavior. What transpires be-

tween the student and the counselor should remain limited to them, unless the student chooses to share the information with you.

RELATED COUNSELING ISSUES

RAs occasionally have difficulty responding to students' crying. With men, the emotion is viewed as unmasculine, because our society tells men that they must withhold these emotions. Society permits women to express emotion through crying more openly and freely. If a student begins to cry when explaining a problem, do not be embarrassed or ignore what is obvious to both of you. Offer the student a tissue and some consoling words to confirm that this expression of emotion is acceptable and is nothing about which to be embarrassed. Crying is a natural emotion for many people and can be a healthy way of relieving the tension and anxiety of a difficult situation.

Listen carefully to what a person says. If you listen, you will find that most people tell you exactly what is troubling them. Usually you do not need to look for hidden meanings; this problem, after all, is the reason that the person came to talk with you. Being a good listener and a sympathetic friend as an RA are the key elements of helping.

Learn to empathize with the student. Empathy is an important medium of support. It not only helps you understand what the person is experiencing, but confirms for the student your concern. Many counseling tips simply involve learning to empathize with other people.

Be confident in your ability to work with the student. You were selected to be an RA because of your skills in working with people and with groups.

Do not evaluate how well you are liked on the floor by how many people come to you with personal problems. The occasion to help a student with a personal problem may arise only a few times within your living unit in an academic year. When it does arise, you must be trained and confident in your ability to handle the situation.

Remember that most problems students experience are normal, everyday difficulties related to depression, fear, anxiety, stress, lack of self-confidence, interpersonal relationships, and rejection. Each of these could be a crisis for an individual. People learn and grow from solving crises in their lives, and the ability to solve and handle crises helps them handle future problems. These crises represent development and growth in the individual.

Be aware of your feelings about a student you counsel. Hostility, recent problems you have had with him or her, or stereotypes will color your perception of what the individual tells you. Try to erase these images and listen to the student. This will help enable you to see the picture that the student is painting for you.

STRATEGIES FOR

Giving Advice

- Do not give advice to people who do not seek it or who do not want it. Often your interjection of "If I were you . . ." is not at all welcome. It is better to wait until your opinion is asked and then to give it only if it is appropriate.

- If a person asks for advice and it is appropriate to give it, do so in confidence. This allows the person to disagree and does not make the person feel as if he or she is following directions.

- Never give advice using such words as *don't* and *shouldn't*.

- Present advice as suggestions. Use phrases such as, "Have you ever thought about trying . . ." or "You might try . . . ."

- Use personal experiences in making suggestions. This provides the listener with a base for your authority in making the suggestions, and it reveals some personal information about you so the conversation is less one-sided.

- If you choose to give advice, give it cautiously and sparingly. Remember, no one likes to be told what to do or how to do it.

ADVISING

Advising is the act of giving information and suggesting a specific course of action for an individual to take. At times you, as an RA, will do just this. Advising should be infrequent, but there are some obvious times it is necessary.

It is appropriate for you, as an RA, to advise someone who comes to you with a request for specific information. An example might be when a student asks you where to get financial assistance. You can advise the student of any emergency loan programs the university has, job opportunities, and financial aid. You can share other types of information, such as not to take an overload of academic hours in the spring quarter when there are many activities. Other areas in which you might advise are directly related to personal safety, such as not walking alone at night in dimly lit areas or not keeping large sums of money in the room. These are appropriate areas in which advice is worthwhile.

As a general rule, advise only when the student requests specific information, when the person's safety or security is at stake, when the issue is of no emotional consequence, or when the results of your advice cannot injure or harm the individual.

People are always ready to give advice, yet few people are willing to accept it. Even though many people solicit advice and suggestions, people seldom put them to use.

REVIEW

1. Below is a list of situations you might encounter as an RA. From the information provided, would you: (A) initiate a counseling contact with the student, (B) contact and counsel with the student and refer the student to the hall director, (C) contact and counsel with the student and refer the student to the campus mental health or counseling center, or (D) not take any action at this time?

    a. Paul is very depressed about breaking up with a girl he has been dating for the past year. He seems depressed and angry about the situation.

    b. Violet is spending much of her time at college bars. Her usual pattern of behavior is to get intoxicated and then bring a man back to her single room in the residence hall and spend the night with him. She has been bringing a different man back to her room almost every night.

    c. Bud has the reputation of being very difficult. He is suspicious of others and given to violent, unexplained outbursts of emotion.

    d. Lucy did not do as well as she expected on her midterm grades. She was expecting to get a 3.5 grade point average or better, and she received a 3.0. She thinks her parents will be angry with her and has been depressed most of the day.

    e. Carruth's brother died in an automobile accident earlier in the semester. He seemed fine when he first returned to the residence hall, but recently he has retreated from activities with other students and has been keeping to himself.

    f. You suspect that one of your residents, Ernest, is gay because you saw him walking out of a gay bar near the campus and passionately embrace and kiss another male. You are almost certain that his roommate is not gay and that he does not know that Ernest is.

    g. Barbara has been spreading rumors about another student on the floor. This gossip is malicious, and if it gets back to the person who she is talking about, it would both hurt her feelings and result in some form of retaliation.

    h. Frances and three other women from your living unit went though sorority rush together. Frances was the only one not to get a bid to a sorority.

    i. You are in the shower room when you observe one of your residents who is pledging a fraternity remove his clothes and reveal a series of welts across his buttocks and thighs.

    j. Nancy took a long weekend and went on a three-day retreat with a religious group of some kind. She returned to the residence hall and has been telling everyone that she has experienced a revelation in her life. She has given away all of her records and CDs and has been spending most of her time with people from this religious group or reading the Bible.

    k. Norman has been very depressed for the past two weeks after breaking up with his girlfriend. He has stopped going to classes and has recently given away his most prized possessions. The past couple of days he has appeared much happier.

    l. Sheila is White and her new roommate is Black. It is the first week of school, and the two never seem to do anything together. They eat with different groups in the cafeteria and do not appear to be spending much time together.

2. Define an "open-ended" question and give an example of one.

3. What is the first step in the counseling exchange with a student and what kinds of physical steps can you take to set the environment for this exchange?

4. What is the proper counseling posture and why?

5. What are the five stages of counseling as defined in the text?

6. What is the goal of the helping skills encounter with students?

7. Give three examples of counseling techniques you use in the listening stage of counseling.

8. What are the four steps to be accomplished in the problem identification and analysis stage?

9. When should you refer a student to professional counseling?

10. What three behavioral signs may indicate a need for professional counseling?

11. How does advising differ from counseling?

APPLICATIONS

UNDERSTANDING YOURSELF

For each category, list the numbers of the statements with which you **disagree.**

A. RACE
1. I would have a person of another race as a friend.
2. I would have a person of another race as a roommate.
3. I would date a person of another race.
4. I would consider marrying a person of another race.
5. As an RA I can be objective in working with a student of another race.

B. RELIGION
1. I would have a person of another religion as a friend.
2. I would have a person of another religion as a roommate.
3. I would date a person of another religion.
4. I would consider marrying a person of another religion.
5. As an RA I can be objective in working with students who have different religious beliefs than my own.

C. ABORTION
1. I would have a person who had an abortion as a friend.
2. I would have a person who had an abortion or who encouraged his girlfriend to have an abortion as a roommate.
3. I would date a person who had an abortion or who encouraged his girlfriend to have an abortion.

4. I would consider marrying a person who had an abortion or who encouraged his girlfriend to have an abortion.
5. As an RA I can be objective in working with students who have had an abortion or who encouraged their girlfriends to have an abortion.

D. OBESITY
1. I would have an obese person as a friend.
2. I would have an obese person as a roommate.
3. I would date an obese person.
4. I would consider marrying an obese person.
5. As an RA I can be objective in working with obese students.

E. HOMOSEXUALITY
1. I would have a homosexual person as a friend.
2. I would have a homosexual person as a roommate.
3. I would date a person of the same gender.
4. I would consider engaging in a long-term sexual relationship with a person of the same gender.
5. As an RA I can be objective in working with homosexual students.

F. DRUGS (i.e., illegal drugs such as marijuana, cocaine, and speed)
1. I would have a person who used drugs as a friend.
2. I would have a person who used drugs as a roommate.
3. I would date a person who used drugs.
4. I would consider marrying a person who used drugs.
5. As an RA I can be objective in working with students who used drugs outside of the residence halls.

G. ANTI-AMERICANISM (Defined as a strong dislike of the United States government and capitalism, and critical of American culture)
1. I would have an anti-American international student as a friend.
2. I would have an anti-American international student as a roommate.
3. I would date an anti-American international student.
4. I would consider marrying an anti-American international student.
5. As an RA I can be objective in working with anti-American international students.

H. PHYSICAL HANDICAPS (e.g., paraplegia)
1. I would have a physically handicapped student as a friend.
2. I would have a physically handicapped student as a roommate.
3. I would date a physically handicapped student.
4. I would consider marrying a physically handicapped student.
5. As an RA I can be objective in working with a physically handicapped student.

I. BLINDNESS
1. I would have a blind student as a friend.
2. I would have a blind student as a roommate.
3. I would date a blind student.
4. I would consider marrying a blind student.
5. As an RA I can be objective in working with a blind student.

THE SOCIAL OUTSIDER

Ruby is a sophomore in a large state university. She selected the university because it had a program in fashion design in which she was interested. Ruby does not have good social skills and frequently seems to say the wrong thing at the wrong time. The other women on her residence hall floor don't like her. She just doesn't fit in. She wears exotic clothes. She overuses makeup, and her personal hygiene needs attention. Her roommate transferred to another room as soon as she had the opportunity. She couldn't stand being around Ruby because of Ruby's lack of personal hygiene and the immense clutter that Ruby had in the room.

Ruby's attitude about the other women on the floor is, "If they don't like me, I won't like them." She ignores them. She goes to class alone, eats alone, and comes back to her room, closes the door, and watches TV alone. Needless to say, Ruby does not date and does not fit in well with the other students who are in the fashion design program.

Ruby has become increasingly depressed. She has decided to make some changes in her life but doesn't know how. As she has become increasingly depressed, she has started binge eating. She does not want to get any fatter than she is; that might interfere with her career goals in fashion design.

One night after dinner, the RA entered the bathroom and heard Ruby vomiting in one of the stalls. When the RA asked Ruby if she was sick, Ruby indicated that she was ill. Two nights later, the RA saw Ruby enter the bathroom after dinner and, after waiting a few minutes, followed her in. Again she heard Ruby vomiting in a toilet stall. She asked Ruby if she was ill, and again Ruby indicated that she was.

WHAT WOULD YOU DO?

1. What should Ruby's RA do, if anything?
2. How would you go about making a counseling contact with Ruby? What are some of the open-ended questions you could use to help Ruby discuss some of the issues she is probably facing?
3. List three things that you could say to Ruby or do for her that would help her seek professional counseling to address what appears to be bulimic behavior.
4. The other women on the floor often make fun of Ruby. Should the RA say anything to the other women about their behavior? What should the RA say or do, if anything?

PART THREE

CONFRONTATION AND CRISIS MANAGEMENT

Behavior Problems, Confrontation, and Discipline

Mediation

Suicide Intervention

Violence and Crime in Residence Halls

CHAPTER EIGHT

BEHAVIOR PROBLEMS, CONFRONTATION, AND DISCIPLINE

ounseling is not an excuse for discipline, yet you can approach a disciplinary situation within the framework of a helping relationship. Some students feel a need to challenge college policies by breaking rules or infringing upon the rights of others. As an RA, you have an obligation to the institution and to other students in your living unit to enforce the policies that the college community has agreed upon to guide its interaction. A particular policy may not always seem to help students adjust to the responsibilities of college. Experience has shown that learning to interact within a residence hall environment aids students both in accepting accountability for their actions and in developing respect for the rights of others.

TYPES OF UNIVERSITY POLICIES

Some institutions retain rules and regulations based on an *in loco parentis* philosophy; however, the majority of colleges have abandoned most of these in favor of policies based on a community standard of behavior in five major areas: (1) regulations concerning the health, safety, and well-being of the college community; (2) landlord-lessee policies; (3) federal, state, and local laws; (4) regulations designed for the unique situations provided by small-group living; and (5) regulations concerning the academic mission of the institution.

Health and Safety Regulations

Colleges have an obligation to protect the health, safety, and well-being of students, faculty, and staff. Policies in this area concern security within individual buildings, possession of dangerous weapons on campus, state health codes, fire regulations, and similar security or safety precautions. The rationale behind the prohibition against hot plates in student rooms, as one example, is usually determined by fire code regulations, and the policy prohibiting animals in the hall is usually determined by health code regulations.

Most residence halls have operational policies that require outer doors to be secured at a certain time each evening, that requires visitors of the opposite sex to be escorted by a resident of the building, and that prohibit students from making duplicate keys for their rooms or exterior doors. In recent years, a number of colleges and universities have reported rapes by strangers occurring within residence halls. Thefts of private and college property are not uncommon in residence halls with little or no security. Clearly, institutions must enforce these regulations.

Landlord-Lessee Regulations

The second category of regulations is landlord-lessee regulations. Provisions for the contractual relationship between students and institutions cover these policies. Regulations such as not permitting students to keep animals in the residence hall may be both a health regulation and a contractual obligation students assume when entering the residence hall. Other landlord-lessee regulations include students paying for room damages or damage to public areas, check-in and check-out procedures, contract periods of the room (such as requiring that the room be vacated during academic vacation periods), and the right of the institution to inspect rooms for the purpose of enforcing health and safety regulations. Most policies in the landlord-lessee relationship may be considered extradisciplinary, meaning that institutions have chosen to regard infractions not as disciplinary violations, but as contractual violations that may carry the imposition of a fine. Noncompliance with regulations could mean termination of the contract or a similar penalty.

Federal, State, and Local Laws

Educational institutions generally accept responsibility for enforcing federal, state, and municipal laws through various means and with various degrees of dedication. Laws against major crimes such as theft, battery, possession of dangerous drugs, extortion, and similar violations are usually enforced by institutions.

Laws regulating the use of both alcohol and marijuana have undergone dramatic changes. Possession of small quantities of marijuana was once considered a felony in many states. Now, most states have made possession of small quantities of marijuana a misdemeanor. College administrators are faced with a paradoxical situation. On the one hand, they do not want to place RAs in an enforcement role within the residence hall; on the other hand, they wish to provide an environment that is educationally sound and that reflects the basic educational interests of all members of the university community. This is a difficult task. Some college administrators believe that the strict enforcement of alcohol and marijuana regulations provides the type of living environment that is most conducive to the educational goals of students. The reasons given for the enforcement of these regulations are:

1. The institution is accountable to the state, the alumni, the faculty, and future student generations.
2. Not to enforce these policies gives tacit approval for the violation of institutional policy and the law.
3. Failure to enforce policies related to drug use encourages such behavior and promotes an environment that is not conducive to the educational interests of the institution and the student population as a whole.
4. The university must stand for certain values both in theory and application.
5. Nonenforcement of laws related to marijuana and other drugs encourages the introduction of even more dangerous behavior connected with drug trafficking.

Occasionally administrators take an opposing philosophy. They assert that it is not the institution's duty to monitor an individual student's behavior and that they have more important concerns than victimless crimes such as the use of marijuana or alcohol. These administrators argue that:

1. Marijuana and alcohol are socially acceptable drugs to many college students.
2. RAs are trained as counselors, not police agents; therefore, they should not involve themselves with the identification and enforcement of law violations, except to protect the immediate well-being, safety, and security of residents in the unit.
3. The use of alcohol or marijuana is a victimless crime in which no one suffers.

4. The use of these substances is a personal choice that a student must make independently.
5. The university cannot enforce such rules and regulations, because it does not have the technical or legal capability to do so.
6. Because students are adults, police agents have the duty to enforce such laws, as they would for any other adult members living within the community at large.

Small-Group Living Regulations

The fourth area in which institutions make regulations is in small-group living (i.e., residence halls, cooperatives, fraternities, and sororities). This type of living requires regulations to help maintain an environment consistent with the mission of the institution. Policies regulating quiet hours, conduct in the hallways, noise, and similar environmental concerns are designed to enable all students to benefit from the environment without infringing on the rights of other students. This is the area in which most of an RA's time is spent—helping people cooperate and learn to live together. Some students believe they have a right to express themselves, even to the point of infringing on others' rights. This does not necessarily mean that the RA must personally confront each violation. Other students live there too. RAs are not employed to fight all the battles. Students should themselves ask offending students to comply with some reasonable noise or conduct level. Only when this course of action has failed should the responsibility fall to the RA.

Academic Regulations

The last area in which universities make rules and regulations concerns the educational mission of the institution. Academic rules and regulations seldom come under the purview of the RA. Violations of these rules include academic dishonesty, cheating, plagiarism, falsification of information, disregarding lawful directions of college officials, or failure to comply with rules related to the process or function of the institution.

DISCIPLINARY COUNSELING MODEL

Students are more likely to respond cooperatively or to avoid a confrontation when they respect you and your position. Confronting people with their behavior and referring them for disciplinary action is difficult. Unfortunately, it must be done if the residence hall environment and the rights of others are to be ensured.

The model used for a disciplinary encounter is similar to the one used for the helping-skills form of counseling discussed in the previous chapter. The major differences are in the dynamics of the disciplinary exchange and the student's perception of you. In most disciplinary encounters, you will confront a student with some alleged violation of regulations, and the student will probably view you as an adversary. Figure 8.1 illustrates the disciplinary counseling model. It has five steps: (1) collect the facts, (2) approach the

student, (3) listen to the student, (4) take the necessary action, and (5) follow up.

Step 1: Collect the Facts

Before accusing anyone of violating university regulations, make sure your facts are accurate. Often students who relate information about the behavior of another student will not want others to know who provided this information. An interesting attitude in our culture holds that it is more honorable to protect people who have violated the law than it is to hold these people accountable. Those who provide information about people who break the law are called "informers" and "stool pigeons."

Although some students will report others and follow through with the charge, frequently you will receive the information thirdhand with the proviso that you not reveal your source. Some circumstances allow you to accept information under these conditions, but in general you should be reluctant to do so. As a rule, when students wish to share some information with the under-

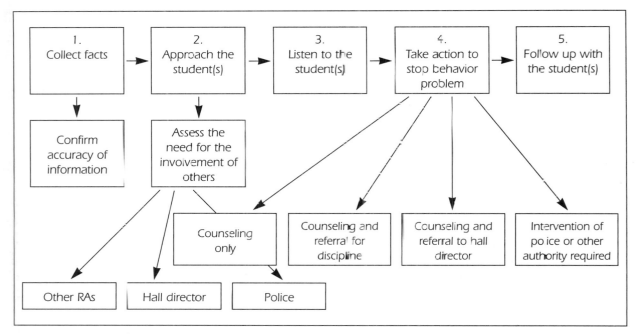

Figure 8.1. *Disciplinary counseling model.*

standing that you will not pass it on to anyone else, you should tell them that you cannot offer this guarantee. After all, they may tell you that their roommate just robbed a bank or is selling drugs out of their room. Should you be approached with the provision that the information must remain secret, tell the person that he or she will need to trust your judgment about whether or not this information will need to be passed on to someone else.

You can talk with the student who allegedly violated the regulation without revealing the source of your information. However, the credibility of your facts will be in question. Also, you will have insufficient information to make a referral for disciplinary action to a college official. Neither of these points preclude you from approaching the alleged violator with the information you have. This person may be very open about the situation and admit his or her involvement. If the person does not, you have had the opportunity to discuss the behavior, a step that may have some positive benefit.

Step 2: Approach the Student

Approach is a better word for this action than *confront*. The difference is your perception. If you approach the student with the attitude that this will be a confrontation, you may develop a mindset that could be counterproductive.

Conflicts between students and college policies are common. In these conflict situations, you should try to act as an arbitrator between the student and college policy. This is a particularly difficult role because a student who violates a policy may view you as an agent for enforcement. In actuality, the conflict is not between you and the student but between the policy and the student's behavior. You can take steps to deescalate conflicts of this type and to remove yourself as an agent in the conflict.

Sometimes, in the heat of anger, students are not reasonable. Once a student has been informed of the behavior problem and the policy you believe may have been violated, you need not subject yourself to any abuse from that student.

Deescalating Conflict

- At the beginning of the academic year, explain college policies and the reasons behind each one.

- When a student appears to have violated a college policy, reexplain the policy and the reason for it to the student as well as the process that the university has established to determine if a policy has been violated.

- Explain to the student that, as an RA, your role in this process is not to determine if a student did or did not violate a policy. Your role is to identify behavior that may be in violation of college policy and report it to those who have responsibility for making this decision.

- Explain your responsibility as an RA and that you are required to report certain behavior as part of your duties. Remind the student that the process is designed to be fair and to insure that students are not unjustly sanctioned for infractions of college policy.

If a student is angry and wishes to vent his or her hostility and make disparaging remarks about you, it is usually best to remove yourself from the situation. Do not engage the student in a debate, a yelling contest, or an exchange of threats. Walk away from these situations. Tell the student that when he or she calms down, you will be available to talk about the situation.

At some point these conflict situations are out of your hands. Once you have reported the alleged violation to your hall director or another staff person, it becomes that person's responsibility to follow through with the situation. Although your involvement may not end at the point at which you make your disciplinary referral, you will not be responsible for determining if the student did or did not violate college policy.

One of the factors in a productive exchange is to engage the student in a meaningful dialogue concerning the alleged incident. If other people are present, the dialogue can become a group discussion or an audience debate. Neither of these multi-person interchanges is productive; both you and the student lose in these situations. If you cannot isolate the student and must approach him or her while others are present, deal only with terminating the offending behavior (e.g., yelling, playing

the stereo loud, or damaging property). Do not attempt to go beyond this until you can find some opportunity to engage the student in a one-to-one discussion about the behavior.

Following are some responses you can expect from students when you approach them with an alleged violation.

The Big Lie. One response students use is to claim that the event never took place, to deny that they were involved, and to challenge you to prove in some legalistic framework that they are responsible. With this response, students are often aggressive, hostile, and somewhat threatening. You can only relate the information you have and attempt to bring the issue to a level of common understanding. You may tell the student that you cannot resolve the situation at this point and that you will refer it to someone who can. This is probably the only course of action available to you.

When students use the big lie, you may become aggravated. Usually there is sufficient information to catch the students in their lie. Unfortunately, you will not have the opportunity to resolve the situation and will need to refer the student for discipline.

Misdirection. Students sometimes attempt to change the subject or minimize the consequences of their actions. This response is used to divert attention from the issue at hand. Students may try to lead you into a discussion about the general correctness or incorrectness of a particular institutional policy. Keep the discussion on track. Bring students back to the issue if they react philosophically.

Third-Degree Questioning. A version of the big lie is third-degree questioning. In this response, students challenge the information you received and your observations. Such questions as "How do you know that?" or "What makes you believe that?" or "Can you prove that?" are raised. Some students want to examine every element of the information and to place you on the defensive by demanding that you explain to them in detail every aspect. They will attempt to refute and argue with you over every minor point. Do not argue over nitpicky details that are probably irrelevant to what took place. You are only trying to determine the violator's view of what actually occurred.

The Hostile Response. You can expect personal hostility from some students you approach.

Students may become hostile and challenge your motives for questioning their behavior. They may suggest that you have singled them out because of some personal hatred. This defense technique is intended to change the subject and to delay the issue at hand. Do not feel that you must justify your actions or your motives. Simply relate the behavior that you observed and question the person on why the behavior took place. It is enough to deny an accusation of personal dislike once, and it does little good to engage in a verbal exchange about past events or your perceptions of them.

Contrition. Admission of guilt and a true act of contrition are other techniques. Some students will openly confess their involvement in some type of negative behavior and tell you they are sorry that they caused any problem. Their goal here is that you should accept their contrition and not make any further disciplinary referral. In minor situations, and based on your perception of the individual, this might be appropriate. However, it can create a situation in which students may feel that, even after repeated offenses, they can evade accountability by admitting guilt and saying they are sorry. Because students say they regret their actions does not necessarily mean

It's important to analyze the reason for conflict in order for mediation to be successful in resolving issues.

that you should not make a referral. Admission of guilt is not the goal of disciplinary counseling.

Remember, the process itself is educational. Part of this process is an examination of values and the decision-making processes that led to the behavior. The process of a disciplinary hearing—including waiting for the hearing—can be educational.

Shifting Guilt.   Students who admit guilt sometimes plead with their RA not to make a referral to higher authorities. This is an attempt to make the RA accept some guilt for doing his or her job and making a disciplinary referral. If a student commits a violation serious enough to demand disciplinary action, do not place yourself in the position of determining guilt or innocence. Students should be treated fairly and consistently. Some of the educational benefit can best be achieved through a session with professional staff who are trained to help students examine the values that led them to violate campus regulations.

Step 3: Listen to the Student

Establishing a meaningful dialogue with a student during a disciplinary encounter is as much a goal as it is a technique. You want to reach a point where the student is willing to discuss the situation with you. Given the circumstances, establishing a meaningful dialogue can be difficult. You can do this, however, if you approach the student as an equal, as an adult peer.

Students do not want to hear a lecture from you, nor do they want to be chastised or criticized. The approach you should use is the same approach you would use with a friend. You are not the students' parent and should not give them parental commands. The establishment of a meaningful dialogue means exactly that: a dialogue, an exchange of ideas with a give-and-take response.

Listen to students' explanations of what took place. Use the same general listening techniques in the chapter on counseling. You want students to tell you the truth about what actually took place. This may not be easy. Students may fear reprisal in the form of a disciplinary referral for the violation, or they might be afraid that you will lose respect for them.

Defense mechanisms are common reactions in a disciplinary encounter. *Defense mechanisms* are attempts to explain behavior that cannot be excused in any other way. They are used by a person who feels threatened or insecure. Defense mechanisms help people protect their self-image or egos. Examples of defense mechanisms are repression, anxiety, compartmentalization, compensation, rationalization, and projection. The latter two, rationalization and projection, are probably the most common defenses used by students in a disciplinary encounter.

Rationalization is the attempt to justify one's behavior with excuses that offer a more acceptable motive for the behavior. The person denies accountability for the action, contending that it was justified because of special circumstances. For example, the student who is discovered to have stolen a book from another student may say that he or she was only borrowing the book for a short time to prepare for a test.

Projection is another way a person may reject responsibility for his or her behavior. In projection, the person attempts to justify his or her behavior by attributing the same actions to everyone else. The all-too-common excuse of "everyone else does it" is offered as justification for the behavior. The implication is that if everyone else is violating a particular policy, such violations must be acceptable. The truth is probably that a few other people do violate the policy, but when their actions come to the attention of the staff, those offenders are also held accountable.

Your objective is to help students understand the faulty reasoning in offering these justifications. Willingness to accept responsibility is related to students' maturity. As students' values mature and as they develop personal ethical standards of conduct, their willingness to accept responsibility for their actions increases. If the consequences of a disciplinary encounter are great, such as arrest or suspension from college, the person is less likely to be willing to accept responsibility.

Your role is to help students better accept responsibility for their behavior. Your objective is to assist them in sorting through what took place and reach an understanding about their future behavior. You are the facilitator of the students' own review of the situation and an objective guide in the process.

Step 4: Take Action

If the student clearly is in violation of a regulation of such a nature that you must make a disciplinary referral to a college official, inform the student of your decision. If you are not able to determine the facts of a situation and there is a discrepancy between what you believe to be true and what the student is willing to admit, make a disciplinary referral to resolve the disparity. You may not need to make a referral for a first-time violation of a minor regulation, but you should discuss the violation with the offending student and inform him or her that such conduct is not acceptable and that continued violation could lead to disciplinary action.

RA disciplinary referral is regarded as punishment by most students. Realistically, it is the method that colleges use to educate students about their behavior. True, students might be placed on probationary status or perhaps suspended from school for a period of time. These actions, however, are educational. They state to students that their conduct is not acceptable in the college community. When students do not achieve academically, they flunk out of school. Similarly, if students fail to abide by the regulations that guide behavior, they have not fulfilled this aspect of their education.

By making a referral to the appropriate offi-cial, you are indicating that a particular student's conduct needs to be reviewed to determine if it is consistent with the expectations of the college community. If it is not, the official, through whatever process the school has adopted, will help the student bring his or her behavior within acceptable limits. If residence halls are to be part of the educational process, and a student's conduct violates the reasonable standards used to guide conduct within this small-group living situation, then the student has failed this part of his or her education and should be held accountable.

Step 5: Follow Up

If you make a disciplinary referral, chances are that your relationship with the student involved will be strained. You have two options: you can continue to perpetuate the animosity, or you can make an effort to discuss the difficulty in the hope of reaching some common understanding. The only acceptable choice is the latter. After all, you probably will be living in the same unit, and it is better to get feelings like these out in the open and discuss them. The longer you wait to deal with the conflict, the more hostility will build up between the two of you. Although it is easy to say that students should not take the referral as a personal affront, most students do. How you handle the follow-up can help appease the student's ego and help you remain above the immaturity and petty bickering that is likely to follow.

One of the more difficult aspects of a disciplinary referral is remaining objective. Your responsibilities are to bring alleged violations to the attention of the appropriate staff person, to assist students in understanding the reasons for referral, and to help students accept accountability for their behavior. This is where your involvement ends.

If students are found to be in violation of a regulation but very little action is taken, you should not feel betrayed. Students may believe they have beaten the system or beaten you. You may feel that you lost and the student won. If you let yourself get caught up in this "win-lose" philosophy by becoming ego-involved in the outcome, you defeat the purpose of the educational process. Remember, the *process* is educational.

Students returning from a disciplinary hearing usually need to reestablish themselves with their peer group in the living unit. They may allege that nothing happened to them, that they beat the system, or that in some other way they "won." They will probably attempt to minimize any action that was taken. You must maintain the confidentiality of any information you have about the hearing. This may be difficult, especially when you know that the student is lying about his or her case. You must remember that students have the right to disclose whatever facts about themselves they choose, whereas you do not have the right to disclose any such facts about them. Although you may feel that your credibility is at stake among your residents, in truth your credibility and personal integrity would be compromised more by sharing confidences.

Disciplinary encounters may place you in a defensive position. Try to remain above the personal attacks or practical jokes that may follow a particular disciplinary referral. Chances are, if you accomplish your task well, the student will feel that your actions were justified and will respect you for taking the action. This can only be accomplished if you do not make the encounter a personal confrontation. The goal is not to see the student punished, but to help the student develop mature behavior.

CONFRONTATION SKILLS

There is no set of rules to tell you how to respond to a particular disciplinary encounter. You can, however, develop skills in confrontation that will be of assistance to you in many of your personal interactions. RAs find the first few confrontations with students difficult. With experi-

ence they gain self-confidence in their ability to handle these situations. Few ever feel comfortable or enjoy the actual exchange.

One way to feel more comfortable is to develop your assertiveness. Assertive behavior confirms individual rights in a nonthreatening, non-defensive manner. It is open, honest, direct, nonaggressive, and communicates a person's beliefs or opinions. Assertive behavior does not require other social skills such as compassion, empathy, or persuasion. It is most simply viewed as a statement of the individual's rights, beliefs, attitudes, feelings, opinions, and similar forms of personal expression.

Assertive communication is different from aggressive or passive communication. Aggressive responses attack the other person or in some way infringe on the other person's rights. Passive communication permits another person to take advantage of your rights. To be inconvenienced, to be compelled to do something through a sense of guilt, or to be taken advantage of is to be passive. In letting people take advantage of you, you are sacrificing your time or duty.

If somebody asks you to perform a special favor, being assertive does not mean necessarily that you must refuse. It only means that if you do not wish to comply with the request, you state this and do not comply with the request. You are in control of your own life and you are not compelled to perform special services for individuals that unreasonably infringe on you. Because you are an RA, certain duties are expected of you; some may inconvenience you. Performing these duties is not being passive; it is fulfilling the expectations of your position.

Assertive Confrontation

Three assertive techniques should be part of your disciplinary counseling skills. The first is called *assertive confrontation*.[1] It follows a simple four-step pattern:

1. Describe the person's behavior in objective terms.
2. Describe how this behavior affects you or others within the unit.
3. Describe how you feel about the behavior.
4. Describe how you would like the person to correct their behavior.

Some examples of this are:

"John, your stereo is very loud. The noise is preventing people on the floor from studying. I feel the stereo is too loud, and I would like you to turn it down."

"John, I saw you put glue in the lock of another student's room. Unless it is cleaned out before it hardens, a locksmith will be called to repair the lock at your expense. I do not believe you have a right to damage university property or to inconvenience this other student. I would like you to clean out the lock and ensure that it is in working order. I will discuss this situation with the hall director for possible disciplinary action."

Commitment Confronted

Another form of assertive confrontation is the *commitment confronted technique*. It emerges when a student has made a commitment for a certain type of behavior and then does not comply with the commitment. This may follow a discussion that you had earlier with the student about the behavior. This technique follows a similar format:

1. State the observed behavior.
2. State the student's commitment.
3. Present the contradiction.
4. State how you feel.
5. State the behavior you would like to see take place.
6. State the steps you will take.

An example of this form of confrontation is:

"John, I observed you drinking beer in the floor lounge. Because you are under twenty-one the university doesn't permit this. The last time this took place, you gave me your word that it would not happen again. I do not understand why you gave me your word if you did not intend to follow through. I am angry that I cannot trust you and accept you at your word. I am disappointed that you did not keep your word. You need to get the beer out of the residence hall, and I will be discussing this situation with the hall director and referring you for disciplinary action."

These two forms of assertive confrontation can be useful in your exchanges with students. They can also be useful in other interpersonal exchanges in which you feel that your personal rights have been infringed upon.

Broken Record Technique

A third assertive technique is called the *broken record technique*.[2] The repeated assertion of your belief, opinion, or request is all that is involved in this technique. Your response to any remark is the same until the person complies with your request. An example of this follows:

RA: John, I see that you have furniture in your room from the floor lounge. You know that this furniture should not be in your room. I would like you to take it back now, please.

JOHN: I need it in my room for studying.

RA: Unfortunately, there is not enough furniture for everyone, and the lounge furniture is to be in the lounge. Would you please take it back now?

JOHN: I am studying right now. I will do it later.

RA: I understand. I would like you to take it back now, if you would, please.

JOHN: But the furniture makes my room look so much better.

RA: Take it back now, please.

JOHN: I would really like to keep it.

RA: Take it back now, please. I will check with you later.

The exchange shows that the RA is requesting over and over that the same action be taken. Eventually, John will probably comply with the request, or the two will reach a compromise in which John may take the furniture back after he has completed studying. The RA could also try offering to help John take it back. The goal, after all, is to get the furniture returned to the lounge and to make John aware that the furniture did not belong in his room. The RA might accomplish this by offering to help John carry it.

HOW TO CONFRONT AN INTOXICATED PERSON

Almost every RA will be confronted at some point with a resident who is intoxicated. It is predictable on weekends: Intoxicated students often return to the residence hall and start trouble. The manner in which you confront an intoxicated person can make the difference between a quiet agreement and a brawl.

First, consider the intoxicated person. His or her judgment is impaired, physical coordination is diminished, and the person is more unpredictable, possibly more aggressive, and generally less inhibited. The person will probably resent interference and will question the authority or motive of any person who confronts him or her. If the person is with friends, he or she will probably be concerned that his friends view him or her in the most favorable light, which may mean that the person becomes defiant. If your past relationship with the student has been strained, the alcohol could bring to the surface any hostility harbored against you.

Confronting anyone is not easy. Confronting a person who is drunk is more difficult. So, when possible, avoid confrontations with people who are intoxicated. If a student returns to the residence hall after drinking, is a bit loud but presents no real problem, do not confront the student about the behavior. You only need to confront intoxi-

cated residents if (1) they disrupt the living environment, (2) they damage or destroy property, or (3) they physically injure or threaten to injure themselves or others. When one of these situations occurs, intervene.

Start by assessing your present emotional state. Are you angry, upset, or frightened of the other person? Any of these reactions is acceptable; you just need to be aware of your reaction before you make the confrontation. If you are angry, express your feelings to the other person, but do not demonstrate your anger through inflammatory remarks.

Once you have assessed your feelings, gather all the necessary information on what took place. If the person's stereo is too loud and other residents have asked him or her to turn it down, get the facts from these people before confronting the resident. If another student saw a student damage property, make certain you have the details of what the witness did and did not see.

If the gravity of the situation, your past relationship with the student, or your assessment of your feelings suggests that you should not handle the situation alone, do not hesitate to ask for assistance from your hall director, another RA, or possibly the campus police. However, these situations should not be escalated unless, in your judgment, failure to involve other people would be worse.

The last step before actual confrontation is to stop and consider exactly what specific behavior you wish the person to stop, change, or alter. What do you want the person to do at this particular time? Can the confrontation wait until a time when the person is not intoxicated? If the person is disrupting the environment, the goal of your encounter is obvious—to return the environment to its previous state. If the person is fighting or about to initiate a fight, again the goal is obvious. If, however, the person has damaged property or left beer bottles strewn throughout the corridors of the residence hall, you may accomplish very little by initiating a confrontation at this particular time.

The person will need to be held accountable for the behavior, but the best time may be the following day, after the person has sobered up. The student may be more reasonable and less confrontational when sober.

At this point, you have assessed your own feelings, have gathered the necessary facts, have decided whether or not to involve another staff person, know what behavior you wish the person to modify, and have decided whether to initiate the confrontation now or wait until the person is sober. Assuming that you believe a confrontation is needed immediately and that you will handle it alone, you must now confront the person.

Your first task in the confrontation is to make sure the person knows who you are. If the student is not one of your residents, you will need to identify yourself as an RA. Once this is accomplished, try to isolate him or her from friends or spectators. Ask the person to step into your room, or into his or her own room, if that is the most isolated place you can find. If at all possible, avoid discussing the situation in front of other people.

In approaching the person, do so in a non-threatening way. Remember, your goal is to return the environment to its previous state or to prevent some injury. It is not to moralize, lecture, condemn, evaluate, or in some other manner demean the person's behavior. Be sincere in your emotions and in what you are saying. Avoid accusations or inflammatory remarks. Use an approach that will elicit a feeling on the student's part that he or she is cooperating. Ask for the student's cooperation; do not demand it. Use assertiveness techniques and skills.

Caution—Never become physical, except to protect yourself, and then only to protect yourself—not to retaliate or demonstrate your force or anger. Grabbing, pushing, or restraining the person may lead to unnecessary problems.

If the student chooses to escalate the situation by failing to cooperate or if you are threatened in some manner, do not hesitate to involve other members of the residence hall staff or the campus police if appropriate. Whatever your college pays you, it is not enough for you to place yourself in a position of imminent physical harm. Though physical altercations between students and staff are rare, they do happen. Many of these could be avoided if people would exercise more discretion.

Confront only the specific behavior that the person has exhibited. Do not make value-judgment statements. You need only say that the disturbance is creating difficulty for others or that it is presenting some other problem. If you are disturbed by the situation or if you were awakened because of the disturbance, express your anger; however, you need not lecture. Use questions that require more than a simple yes or no answer to clarify the situation. Questions you might ask include, "Why are you yelling?" or "Why is your stereo that loud?" or "Why are you acting this way?" In any case, communicate clearly. Ask the person to explain or clarify behavior. Do not threaten; instead, clearly and calmly explain how the behavior is affecting others.

Remember always that your goal is to get the person to cease the behavior that is causing the disturbance. If you can do this by asking him or her in a friendly and cooperative tone to change the behavior, you will have a better chance of accomplishing the goal. Depending on your personal judgment, the degree to which the student has disrupted the environment, the student's history of similar behavior, and your institution's policy, an administrator may need to review the student's behavior to determine if formal disciplinary action is necessary. If, in your judgment, such a referral is necessary, it is appropriate that you indicate during your confrontation that a referral will be made. This referral should not be used as a threat. Rather, you should present your decision in such a way as to inform the student without it appearing as a punishment. You might say something like, "I will be discussing this incident with the hall director for possible disciplinary action. I would like to talk with you about it again tomorrow."

TIPS ON DISCIPLINARY COUNSELING

- Never openly discuss your objections to policies or regulations with students with whom you are expected to work in an enforcement capacity. You may have objections to certain policies; most people do. The appropriate forum for discussion of these objections is with staff and the people who can effect change. To share your personal concerns about policies with other students may make you seem hypocritical when you are obliged to enforce these policies.

- Never tell your residents that, as long as you do not see them, they may violate a policy. This often occurs in institutions where RAs are expected to enforce marijuana and alcohol policies. RAs will say that the residents can smoke or drink in their rooms as long as they, the RAs, do not know about it. This communicates to students that certain behavior is approved as long as they are not caught. You will find that this position will defeat your credibility in the unit when you are obliged to enforce the policy.

- Do not withhold information from supervisory staff. If you had information about certain events and promised not to release it, you could be removed from your position. Remember, you are not a student advocate whose function is to defend students against the college; you are an employee of the college whose function is to help implement its goals, policies, and philosophies. Dissension has it place, but it should not include leading your residents to disobey policies.

- Enforce policies and regulations consistently throughout the year. Do not, however, earn the reputation of being a "supersleuth." Be flexible and understanding, but clearly outline the boundaries for acceptable and unacceptable behavior. Remember that the immediate goal of a disciplinary encounter is to terminate the violation. If the goal is to end a fight, deal with ending the fight and move on from there. Every time you have an encounter with a student because of his or her behavior, you do not need to make a referral.

- Keep a personal log of your interactions with students who continually engage in disruptive and irritating behaviors that are not sufficient to merit a referral. When you talk with a student about a specific behavior (such as a loud stereo, smearing shaving cream on the floor, or other minor actions that do not merit a referral to a disciplinary officer), make a record of the time, date, event, and the fact that you spoke to him or her. If you need to make a referral later, this information will help establish for others that you have been performing your duty and that you are not referring the student for a single small infraction. Too often, RAs become so exasperated with a student's behavior that they make a referral in a mood of "I finally got you." They expect a disciplinary officer or a hearing committee to punish the student strongly, but if the student has had no other violations and you are not able to establish that you have had continual problems with him or her, chances are that only the current situation will be considered and not past events. Some committees refuse to examine past events that are not substantiated by a hearing; however, most committees and disciplinary officers will listen to your statement of specific and documented disciplinary encounters related to the student's behavior.

- Do not become ego-involved in making referrals and in the outcomes of those referrals. A referral is not a win-lose situation. It is not a contest between you and the student. It is not important that the student be found guilty or that he or she receive a harsh punishment for a violation. Your role is to provide information and to bring disruptive misconduct to the attention of officials who will help the student overcome the problem.

If you must make a referral in a threatening situation involving students who are intimidating, or in a situation that will probably result in a disciplinary hearing, enlist the assistance of another staff member or at least someone who is willing to support your statements. In a hearing, you will be given some degree of credibility; however, you too will need to substantiate or support your assessment of the situation and of how you conducted yourself.

If you are forced to confront students who are hostile and possibly violent, get help from your hall director or campus police. Avoid getting into a physical altercation. If this seems possible, get assistance before you get involved.

Finally, remember that behavioral limits in your living unit are set the first few weeks. If you allow students to be disruptive and violate college policies the first few weeks of the semester, you can expect to be confronting these problems all year. Put a stop to these problems early in the year, and you will save yourself and your residents time and aggravation throughout the year.

REVIEW

1. Identify the five types of regulations universities enforce.
2. Why is it not a good idea to accept information from students under the condition you not tell anyone else?
3. Give three typical responses a student might give when approached about a behavioral violation.
4. The text says that the RA should achieve a meaningful dialogue with the student. What is meant by a "meaningful dialogue" and what are some of the dos and don'ts for achieving it?
5. Define *rationalization* and *projection*.
6. Why is the follow-up step important in the disciplinary encounter?
7. How is assertive communication different from aggressive communication?
8. What are the only three reasons for confronting an intoxicated person?
9. In the case of confronting an intoxicated person with a disciplinary problem, what is the immediate goal?
10. Why are the first few weeks of the fall semester important in avoiding disciplinary problems in your living unit?

APPLICATIONS

THE VIKING

Howell is a second-semester freshman living on the fourteenth floor of North Tower. His RA is Franco. Howell came to State University to play football, but was not quite good enough to make the team. His nickname on the floor is "The Viking." He got this nickname as the result of his large size, table manners, temper, and ability to consume very large quantities of beer. Howell is not much of a student. This semester he is only enrolled for six hours, having dropped nine hours because he was not doing well academically.

Franco was on duty Friday night and went to sleep about 1:00 A.M., hoping that all would remain quiet on his floor. About 2:30 A.M., Franco was awakened by a loud noise coming from the hall bathroom next to his room. He got up and saw Howell walking down the hall away from the restroom toward his room. His right hand appeared to be bloody. When Franco entered the restroom, he observed that someone had broken the mirror and had thrown a trash can through the restroom window. There was blood in the sink and on the floor.

WHAT WOULD YOU DO?

1. If you were Franco, what would you do? Explain the steps you would follow.
2. Do you believe there is enough evidence to charge Howell with a violation of university policy? If you did, Howell might hold it against you and try to get even.
3. What, if anything, could be done to address the reputation Howell has developed on the floor, which is encouraged by the residents?
4. What are the advantages and disadvantages of approaching Howell about the damage the night it happened?

CATCH ME IF YOU CAN

Shirley and Laverne are first-semester freshmen. They went to an inner-city school and have not tried to make friends with any of the other women in the living unit. They keep to themselves and have expressed no interest in interacting with the other residents on the floor. Most of the other residents find them somewhat annoying. They have this habit of turning up their heavy-metal music so loud that it disturbs the whole floor. When the other residents try to ask them to turn it down, they refuse to answer the door and they hang up on anyone who calls their room to complain. Phyllis is their RA. She has spoken to them about their stereo on several occasions, and she has referred them to the hall judicial council on one occasion. This referral resulted in a fine and a warning. It also resulted in Laverne and Shirley threatening Phyllis.

Phyllis returned to her room late one evening after studying with friends. When she passed Shirley and Laverne's room, their stereo was blasting. She pounded on the door and identified herself, and after some period of time a man opened the door and asked what she wanted. Phyllis noticed the smell of what she believed was marijuana in the room, that a wet towel had been placed under the door, and that a fan was blowing air out of the room. Several scented candles and some incense were burning. There was another man in the room with Shirley and Laverne. Phyllis told the group that their stereo was too loud and that they would need to turn it down. Laverne got up and went to the door and closed it in Phyllis's face. Someone then turned the stereo down to an acceptable level.

WHAT WOULD YOU DO?

1. What would you do at this point if you were the RA?
2. Is there anything the RA might have done differently, either before this incident or during the incident?
3. Two of Phyllis's other residents were standing in the hallway during the incident and saw the whole thing. What do you think will happen if Phyllis decides to ignore the incident and talk to the students at some later time?
4. What is your institution's policy about entering students' rooms and searching for drugs when you have reason to believe that students are using marijuana?

Behavior Problems, Confrontation, and Discipline   157

CHAPTER NINE

MEDIATION

©1998 PHOTODISK, INC.

A s an RA, you will be confronted by many conflicts. Most will involve disagreements between a person and a policy or between two individuals. A conflict exists when two parties perceive that they have mutually exclusive goals—that is, the satisfaction of one goal is incompatible with the satisfaction of the other.

DEFINING CONFLICT SITUATIONS

Many people have misconceptions about conflicts. They believe conflicts are bad and should be eliminated. Conflict can be productive and can lead to increased understanding. A conflict can stimulate the examination and resolution of many problems. It stimulates curiosity, creativity, and an exploration of personal values. When conflict is viewed in a positive framework, it can offer an enjoyable exchange of ideas. People are required to use their capabilities to the fullest to defend their interests and to explore their own ideas. Through conflict, people can shape their values. A positive conflict situation can foster respect and can consolidate groups of individuals.

Conflicts are positive when all participants are satisfied with some part of the outcome. A constructive conflict situation is characterized by a constructive spirit and friendly attitude; trust; open, honest communication; sensitivity to similarities; a nonthreatening atmosphere; and some satisfaction for all parties.[1] A destructive conflict is characterized by distrust, defensiveness, hostility, lack of communication, maximized differences, and general competitiveness.

Conflicts are not usually the result of individuals misunderstanding each other. Usually, the parties understand the other's position but disagree with it. The most common causes of conflicts are value differences, lifestyle differences, and communication breakdowns. Of these, value differences probably create the greatest number of conflicts. One person may require a neat and orderly environment, whereas another person needs the freedom to be disorganized and sloppy. This difference can lay the foundation for a roommate conflict over the degree to which their room will be cluttered or kept clean.

Some of the fiercest conflicts come in discussions of politics, religion, sex, and other value-loaded subjects. These are areas in which conflict and discussion can be very positive and provide opportunities for students to express and explore their values and to deal with other people's views. Such a conflict assumes the context of a potentially positive encounter.

People are usually most comfortable with other people who are most like themselves and least comfortable with people who are most unlike themselves. When people from different back-grounds are placed together in a living unit, the foundation is laid for conflicts based on differences in lifestyles. For example, if a student who likes classical music is placed with a roommate who likes hard rock, often the result is a lifestyle conflict. Such a situation provides the opportunity for each to learn something about the other's background and lifestyle and, perhaps, to alter or at least reevaluate his or her own values. The outcome depends on how the people involved perceive the conflict. If they understand that different lifestyles exist and talk about the differences in their backgrounds, why they believe what they do, and how they were raised, chances are that many negative conflicts can be avoided.

A lack of appreciation for, or understanding of, other people's human needs lays the groundwork for other conflict situations. If people feel they are not being treated fairly, or if they believe that their ideas are discounted or devalued, they will feel rejected and may lash out at others. Such conflicts are created by poor interpersonal communication or by the inability of one person to accept the other without being judgmental or evaluative. Conflicts of this type are common, but they often require the attention of a skilled observer to discover the reason why one person is reacting negatively to another.

MANAGEMENT MODEL FOR ROOMMATE CONFLICTS

Most of the time roommates can resolve their problems without outside intervention. Roommate conflicts are a little like family feuds: Outsiders are not always welcome. Occasionally a roommate conflict may affect other residents in the unit. When this happens, you will be compelled to intervene. On other occasions, one or both of the roommates will come to you for advice, suggestions, or mediation in the conflict between them. When you enter into this type of situation, bear in mind that the student is not coming to you for a judgment about whose behavior is correct and whose is incorrect, but for assistance in working through the conflict.

Grant E. Miller and Steven D. Zoradi developed a simple behavioral approach for roommate conflict resolution based on a seven-point model often used for resolving marital conflicts.[2] The roommate model is as follows:

1. *Problem recognition.* RA meets with roommates X and Y in their room for a conference to urge a discussion of the conflict.

2. *Problem definition.* RA listens alternately to both roommates' stories, using frequent paraphrasing to achieve full understanding.

3. *Commitment.* RA asks both X and Y if they are willing to solve the problem.

4. *Highlighting pleasing and displeasing behaviors.* If both roommates agree to attempt to resolve their conflict, in X's presence, Y identifies specific pleasing and displeasing behaviors that X does. X then identifies Y's behaviors. Pleasing and displeasing behavior must be observable (that is, not statements such as "X is sloppy," but rather "X never washes his jeans").

5. *Negotiation.* Roommates trade and negotiate specific behaviors to satisfy the needs of each. For example, X will allow Y to smoke in the room if the window is open.

6. *Contracting.* A contract is made using the specific likes and dislikes of each roommate. After X and Y come to an agreement, they cosign a contract that will be posted conspicuously in their room.

7. *Follow-up.* New contracts are made weekly. Intervention by the RA is terminated as soon as possible.

Using this model, Miller and Zoradi conducted an experiment in two residence halls. In the experiment, half of the RAs were trained in the conflict-resolution model and half were not. In most of the conflicts in living units where the RAs were trained to use this model, the RAs used it to resolve conflicts. In the other living units, conflicts were handled by using whatever other resources were available to the RA, along with his or her individual skills. At the end of the semester, almost twice as many roommate changes had occurred in living units where the conflict-resolution model was not used.[3]

In using this model, the RA serves solely as a mediator. The goal of the model is to help students work through their own problem. The RA makes no attempt to resolve the conflict by a determination of right or wrong.

STEPS TO RESOLVE CONFLICT

1. Problem Recognition
2. Problem Definition
3. Commitment
4. Highlighting Behaviors
5. Negotiation
6. Contracting
7. Follow-up

ANALYZING CONFLICT SITUATIONS

The negative elements of conflicts—competition; mistrust; defensiveness; impaired communication; maximized differences; reduced alternative courses of action; and threats, coercion, and deception—are identified closely with nonconstructive conflicts between individuals. The conflict interaction between two individuals can be observed and analyzed. If you happen to be an agent in the exchange, you must stop and analyze the conflict situation.

The first thing to look for is *defensive communication.* People become defensive when they feel threatened and attempt to dominate, impress, or assert they are correct. Characteristics of such defensive communication are an almost total lack of listening or understanding, and attacking, aggressive, and hostile behavior. Defensive communication is not conducive to the resolution of the problem.

Hostile communication is characterized by direct verbal assaults. A person criticizes, ridicules, or makes fun of the other person. Hostile communication is often a prelude to overt action such as physical violence.

Manipulative communication often takes place in conflict situations. One person tries to interpret or reshape the circumstances of the conflict. That participant may try to misrepresent the facts, draw unfounded conclusions, or claim understandings not supported.

Avoidance is a way of changing the subject to avoid confronting a topic that is threatening. A person in a conflict may not respond to specific issues, or may change the subject to unrelated matters.

Evaluative responses of the other person's message is another approach that some people use when they attempt to discuss conflicts. One person makes a statement, and instead of responding directly to the statement, the other person evaluates or judges it. An example is saying, "That remark is childish."

People in a conflict situation often hear only what they wish to hear or expect to hear. This is called *selective perception.* They are not listening.

These communication exchanges are typical in conflicts. They are characterized by confrontation and by each person trying to win the support of the other person or of third-party nonparticipants. As a mediator or facilitator in the resolution of the information, you can employ two communication approaches to intervene in helping the disputing individuals resolve their differences.

Metacommunication

The first communication technique is called *metacommunication.* It means talking about what has been communicated. For example, you can make such statements as, "What I hear both of you saying is . . ." or "I don't believe you are actually hearing what *X* was saying," or "Could you paraphrase for us what you just heard *X* say?" In this way you are establishing a common understanding of what is actually being transmitted.

The real difficulty in communication is conveying one's thoughts and feelings through the

STRATEGIES FOR

Conflict Mediation

- Never take sides. Never become the decision maker. Never defend one person's point of view. When necessary, ask questions for clarification or feed back your perceptions, not to devalue one person's position but to bring to the attention of both parties what was said.

- When possible, employ a win-win strategy to resolve conflicts. It is almost always possible that each person can walk away feeling as though he or she has won at least part of the conflict.

- Ensure that each person's personal integrity is maintained. It is never acceptable to have one person feel debased or humiliated. This lays a foundation for greater hostility and is not an adequate resolution to any conflict.

- Get conflicts into the open. If people are arguing back and forth about a particular situation, you may be able to assist them in defining their conflict. It is better that they get a conflict in the open where it can be confronted rather than react negatively to each other without adequate explanation.

- Be aware of barriers to conflict resolution. Defensiveness, put-downs, judgmental reactions, gamesmanship, manipulation, discounting, and aggressive attacks are barriers to communication and are counterproductive.

- Do not escalate conflicts by involving more people than necessary. Resolve conflicts at the lowest possible level between the individuals who are directly involved. When too many people are involved, people become concerned with maintaining loyalties and saving face.

abstract symbols of words. Words do not always accurately convey what people are trying to say. Words and phrases have different meanings for different people. When lifestyles are in conflict, words and phrases frequently carry different cultural meanings.

When you discuss the differences between disputants, you should emphasize an understanding of what each person is saying. Metacommunication can help you do this. As a mediator you can comment on both what is said and the way it is said. Pay particular attention to nonverbal communication including posture, facial expressions, and gestures. Comment on what you observe. Ask the students to talk about the meaning of words and the meaning of their nonverbal communication. An example might be, "You looked sad when your roommate said she was angry with you. What are you sad about?"

Empathy

Empathy is the second skill that you can employ as a mediator. Although you should not take the side of one person against the other, you can empathize with each person's situation by showing concern. Be careful that the students do not focus on trying to win your support for their particular point of view. Your goal is to have the students exchange ideas about how they feel about one another, not to convince you that one is right and the other is wrong. So, although you show empathy for each person's problem, you must also remain objective. This means that you must be able to empathize with each student and show

compassion and caring for the resolution of the particular problem. You should try to feel what each student is feeling. Most importantly, you need to help each party understand what the other is feeling. Help each to empathize with the other person's view or perception of the situation.

To prevent threats, coercion, deceptions, and hostile types of conflict, attempt to maximize the similarities between the differing points of view. Concentrate not on their differences, but on their similarities. Define the differences and help each of the participants understand why the differences exist. Rather than condemn or judge the other person's behavior, which would be counterproductive, each participant should express personal feelings about the other person's behavior. Neither party should devalue or discount the other person's views; each participant should listen actively and ask questions for clarification and meaning

REVIEW

1. List three elements of a constructive conflict.

2. What are the most common causes of conflict?

3. What are the seven steps Miller and Zoradi identified to manage roommate conflicts?

4. List four types of nonconstructive communication behaviors and give an example of each?

5. What is *metacommunication?*

6. Give one technique for preventing threats, coercion, and deception, which sometimes accompany conflict situations.

APPLICATIONS

LIFESTYLES OF THE RICH AND FAMOUS

Gloria was a freshman at Jones College. She came from a wealthy family in East Texas and was the only child. There was hardly anything that money could buy that her parents did not provide for her. She attended Jones College because both her mother and father had attended there. Her mother was on the board of trustees and the family had been financially generous to the college.

Freshman housing was full, and Gloria was assigned a roommate named Amanda. Amanda was also a freshman. She came from a middle-class family. Her mother was a carpenter, and her father taught elementary school. Amanda was attending Jones College with some financial aid, a part-time job in the cafeteria, and help from her parents. She worked throughout high school and was one of four children.

Gloria was not accustomed to taking care of herself. She tended to leave her clothing lying about the room, never made her bed, and left food and other trash about the room. In short, she was a slob. She had never had to do these things for herself, and the clutter did not seem to bother her. Periodically, she would gather up her clothes and send them to the cleaners.

In high school Amanda shared a room with her younger sister and was accustomed to keeping her room orderly and to doing a variety of household chores. She was generally a neat person.

The lifestyle differences between the two women extended to other areas. Gloria liked country music; Amanda liked rock and roll. Amanda had to get up early in the morning to work in the cafeteria; Gloria liked to stay up late to watch television and sleep late in the morning.

Gloria did not like sharing a room with another person and was consumed with her own importance. Amanda was not thrilled about living with Gloria, hated how sloppy she was, and secretly wished Gloria would drop out of school. One night after an argument between the two women over Gloria's forgetting to give Amanda a telephone message, Amanda went to the RA and said that she could not stand living with Gloria one more minute. She said that Gloria was a spoiled brat and that if the RA didn't do something about her, she was going to take her softball bat and beat the girl senseless! Not wanting to explain to the president of the college why the daughter of a member of the board of trustees was beaten senseless by her roommate, the RA decided to intercede.

WHAT WOULD YOU DO?

1. If you were the RA, what steps would you take with Amanda and Gloria the night that Amanda came to complain?

2. If you were the RA and talked to Gloria and Amanda, what would you do if Gloria stated that she had no interest in resolving the problem and that she would talk with her parents and have Amanda moved to another room?

3. What are the major points of disagreement between the two women?

4. What is the likelihood of these two students resolving their lifestyle differences? Should the RA even try to get things worked out between them? Why or why not?

5. What is your institution's policy on roommate changes? What would happen if the women could not resolve their problems and neither wished to move?

6. If neither of the women wished to move, who do you think should move and why?

WHY ME?

Josh and Stuart are second-semester freshmen who were assigned as roommates in the fall semester and became good friends. At their college, fraternity rush is held in the spring. Stuart had always wanted to join a fraternity like his older brother and his father. Josh was not sure if he was interested. No one in his family had every been to college, and Josh was a little concerned whether he could afford the additional cost associated with joining a fraternity. Stuart talked Josh into going through rush with him.

Stuart was particularly interested in the fraternity which his father and brother joined, and was invited to pledge this fraternity. He gladly accepted. Both Stuart and Josh were upset when the same fraternity did not offer Josh the opportunity to pledge. A less prestigious fraternity offered Josh a bid, but he did not know anyone in that fraternity, and with the added cost, he just was not interested.

The relationship between the two boys changed after rush. Stuart spent all of his free time with his pledge brothers and never seemed to have enough time for Josh. Even when Stuart came back to the residence hall room, he usually came with one or two of his fraternity friends, and they would spend time in the room talking about the fraternity or people that Josh did not know.

One night about 2:00 A.M., the RA was awakened by loud noises in the hallway. When he opened the door, he saw Stuart and Josh wrestling on the ground while several of the residents watched. The RA managed to separate the two. He learned that the fight started when Stuart came back to the room and started to search for an item for a fraternity scavenger hunt. In the commotion of searching the room and turning on the lights, he awoke Josh. Words were exchanged, followed by pushing, and finally a fight began.

WHAT WOULD YOU DO

1. What should the RA have done that evening after he stopped the fight and what should he do to follow up?

2. What do you think Josh is feeling about Stuart's involvement in the fraternity? What do you believe Stuart is feeling about his involvement in the fraternity and his relationship with Josh?

3. Assuming that Stuart continues in the fraternity and Josh is not invited to pledge, what would you suggest that might help them continue their relationship?

4. What are the advantages and disadvantages of a room change for one or both of the students?

CHAPTER TEN

SUICIDE INTERVENTION

©1998 PHOTODISK, INC.

Following unintentional injury and homicide, suicide ranks third in the leading causes of death for young people 15 to 24 years of age. The Centers for Disease Control report that young White males are at least four times more likely to die from suicide than females, though females are more likely to attempt suicide. Although the risk is greatest for men who are both young and White, from 1980 to 1992 the rate of suicide among young Black males increased dramatically.[1] Compared to nonstudents of the same age, college students are more likely to employ the use of drugs in attempting suicide than firearms.[2] A comprehensive review of studies revealed that the presence of psychosis and previous contact with campus counseling services were significantly associated with suicide attempts among college students. Further evidence suggests that suicide among college students occurs more frequently in the months of September, January, and March.[3] During these periods, which are commonly associated with the beginning of terms, holidays, and breaks, many people feel alone and isolated and are more inclined to attempt to take their lives.

These statistics may represent only a portion of the actual number of people who kill themselves. Because of religious and social stigmas attached to the act, families are quick to cover up suicides. Many deaths attributed to automobile accidents, for example, may actually be suicides. Because of the poor reporting of suicides, researchers have estimated that the actual number of suicides in the United States may be three to four times higher than reported.

Few campuses have been spared the tragic occurrence of a student committing suicide. The pressures of college life and the difficult transition from adolescent to adult roles while balancing the pressures of academic work, parental demands, financial problems, and competition for grades all too frequently culminate in suicide. At institutions in which academic pressure and competition for grades are rigorous, the potential for suicide increases.

CAUSES OF SUICIDE

The causes of suicide are many. Binstock attributed many suicides to cultural pressures that prohibit individuals from freely expressing their aggressive feelings. In childrearing practices and other forms of interaction in our society, Binstock believes that natural feelings of aggression are regressed through an emphasis on guilt as a source of control. In support of her contention, Binstock pointed out that suicides are highest among people with better education, artistic and professional people, and generally people who fall into the upper middle class. Repressed feelings of anger among these individuals, she explained, encourage some to escape from this inner anger and pressure by suicide.[4]

Pretzel attributed suicide to the combination of increased stress beyond what an individual considers tolerable and the recognition of an in-ability to cope with this stress.[5] Coleman attributed the cause of suicide to an interplay of (1) interpersonal crisis, (2) failure in self-evaluation, and (3) loss of meaning and hope. These factors create a sense of despair beyond the individual's tolerance, and suicide becomes the means of escape, a final solution to the problem.[6]

Santrock suggested that suicide should be thought of as the result of long-term experiences and short-term circumstances. Family history, depression, self-esteem, and low impulse control are long-term experiences that lay the foundation for suicidal behavior. Highly stressful situations such as loss of a boyfriend or girlfriend, an unwanted pregnancy, or expulsion from college may be a proximal trigger for suicide. The combination of these two factors, long-term and short-term experiences, may lead to feelings of despair, depression, and worthlessness culminating in suicide.[7]

SYMPTOMS OF SUICIDAL BEHAVIOR

Most suicides are preventable. About 75 percent of suicidal students give some type of warning. Miller (1988) identifies four types of signals students give about suicide. Some characteristics are common in people under severe emotional strain that may culminate in suicide. Some of the more obvious symptoms are giving away prized possessions, living alone, a radical change in a person's lifestyle, and the loss of something very important (e.g., home, money, parent). Continual loss of sleep, stress, anxiety, depression, and the loss of a sense of identity indicate a person's dissatisfaction with the current state of affairs and may trigger suicidal thoughts.

Lee divided the signs and symptoms into three general categories which she identifies as (1) emotional, (2) behavioral, and (3) physical.

These are signs you should be able to observe through your daily interaction with the students in your living unit. Reports by a roommate or others in the unit can also be indications that a person is experiencing some problem. Most people indicate

"High Spirits" after suffering from one or more of the signs of depression could indicate that a student has made the decision to end her life.

that they plan to take their own life prior to the actual commission of the act. In essence, the person is asking for somebody to help. Through nonverbal signs, such as severe depression and anxiety, or by talking about the act of suicide itself, the person may be signaling for assistance.

The symptoms of suicidal behavior can also be grouped into two major categories: those that relate to depression and those that relate to ambivalence. These are the two major components or characteristics of the suicidal person.

Depression.   Although not all persons who are depressed are suicidal, almost all people who are suicidal are depressed. Depression is the psychopathology found most often in the suicide deaths of adolescents 15 to 19 years old.[9] As Lee pointed out, "Unrecognized and unrelated depressive illness all to often leads to suicide or at least attempted suicide. Anxiety, agitation, apprehensions, and a pervasive feeling of worthlessness are the components of a depressive state that could lead to suicide."[10]

Ambivalence.   The feeling of ambivalence is analogous to a feeling of hopelessness and a loss of caring about the future. It is characterized by no longer thinking in terms of the future. Once

SUICIDE SIGNS AND SYMPTOMS

- *Emotional* signs include dull, tired, empty, sad, numb feelings, with little or no pleasure derived from ordinarily enjoyable activities and people.

- *Behavioral* signs include irritability, excessive complaining about small annoyances, inability to concentrate, difficulty in making decisions, crying, and excessive guilt feelings.

- *Physical* signs include loss of appetite, insomnia or restless sleep, weight loss, headache, and indigestion.[8]

a person has reached the decision to end his or her life, the person may exhibit a feeling of elation. This occurrence of "good spirits" is often interpreted as an improvement. In reality, this improved sense of well-being may be a signal that the person has made the decision and is now relieved that finally the pressure and stress are lifted by the resolution to the problem. The attitude of not caring what happens is also typical and summarizes may of the symptoms discussed previously.

SUICIDE MYTHS

One of the main difficulties in understanding the suicidal person
is the amount of misinformation and myth that surround the subject.
Following are common myths about suicide.

Myth

People who talk about suicide do not follow through.

Once a person has tried to
commit suicide, he or she
will not try again.

People who commit suicide
have an intrinsic death wish.

Women are more likely to
commit suicide than men.

The decision to take one's
own life is a sudden decision
generally triggered by some
traumatic or immediate crisis.

Only mentally ill people commit suicide.

Fact

About 70 percent of all people who commit suicide
clearly announce their intentions within three months
prior to the act.

Approximately 12 percent of those who fail an attempted suicide try again within three years.[11]

Most suicidal people are actually gambling with suicide. Generally, suicidal people will leave themselves a
way out. On the one hand, they want to take their
own lives; on the other hand, they are still not sure
that they really want to die.

Although more women attempt suicide, approximately
four times as many men actually succeed in killing
themselves because they choose more lethal methods
than women do.

Most suicides are the result of a long period of stress,
crisis, depression, and poor self-image.

Though many who commit suicide are unhappy and
emotionally upset, most people are not mentally ill
when they commit suicide.

INTERVIEWING POTENTIALLY SUICIDAL STUDENTS

Whatever the causes of suicide, the key problems for you as an RA are how to deal with the
crisis when it occurs and, most importantly, how
to recognize a suicidal student. The possibility of
a suicide occurring within your living unit is real.
You need to know the signs of suicide and the ap-

propriate responses. Because of your close contact with students in your living unit, you are the
person with the greatest likelihood of recognizing
the symptoms of a suicidal student, and the one
most likely for the student to consult.

You must also be prepared to work with the
student who has attempted suicide and has returned to live in your unit. This person may continue to be suicidal. Your ability to recognize and
understand your own feelings about the subject

and to help the individual will influence your ability to be effective and nonjugmental.

Remember that the student is in charge of his or her life and is ultimately responsible for its course. Develop some objectivity and psychological distance when you work with suicidal students to protect yourself from feeling guilt about decisions the student may make regardless of how well you have done your job.

Counseling suicidal people is a difficult, complex task. No RA can be asked to master the necessary skills. Professional counselors spend years learning to understand and help people through the personal crises that precipitate suicide attempts. Your responsibility as an RA is to be a supportive guide to the individual in crisis, and your goal is to have the student seek professional assistance for his or her problems and to encourage continuing treatment.

Dos and Don'ts for Working with a Suicidal Student

The first rule in working with a suicidal student is to recognize your own skills and limitations. Remember, you are not in this alone. Your institution has professional staff to guide and support you. You must keep these people informed and involved in the ongoing discussions with the individual student throughout this time of crisis and stress. Your assistance in bringing about a realization on the part of the troubled student that he or she needs additional help is the greatest service that you can render. If you are confronted with a student who is discussing suicide or perhaps a student who has recently attempted suicide, the following are some things that you should and should not do.

Model for Suicide Intervention

One course of action for working with a potentially suicidal person is outlined below.

Step 1. Assess the immediacy or severity of a student's potential for committing suicide.

Step 2. Assess the availability of others to help.

Step 3. Discuss with the student some coping mechanisms available to deal with the problem.

Step 4. Help the student determine a course of positive action by helping him or her assess the problem, brainstorm alternatives, consider consequences of each, identify a specific alternative, and determine a timetable; then, schedule a second interview.

Step 5. Get the student to agree not to kill himself or herself for a stated period of time as a nonsuicide contract. If the student refuses, get immediate help.

This model is designed to help you in counseling a student who may be contemplating suicide. If you panic and run for the telephone to get a professional staff member to handle the situation whenever there is a mention of suicide, you may be overreacting. Many people contemplate suicide at some point in their lives, and it is all right to think and talk about it. This model is designed to help you assess the seriousness of the situation, as well as to help you in your discussions with the individual. Any attempt or discussion with a student about suicide should be taken seriously. Although the person may be asking only for support, or attention, you are not in a position to second-guess the motive. If a student is unable to get attention in this manner, he or she may take additional steps to get this needed attention.

Again, this model is intended to apply to a student who is contemplating suicide. It is not designed to be used with a person who may be in the process of attempting suicide which, obviously, would be an emergency situation that calls for the involvement of professional staff and medical personnel. If someone has taken an overdose of drugs or is in some way threatening to kill himself or

Dos

Take every suicide threat seriously. Sometimes a person who is only making a gesture to get attention may accidentally injure himself or herself seriously enough to cause death.

Be aware of information regarding drugs and how they may be lethal.

Use questions that force the student to concentrate on his or her positive resources and on contributions that he or she has made. Such questions as "I know that there have been many things that you have enjoyed about life; what are they?" or "You must have considered the reasons for living as well as dying. What reasons did you consider for living?"

Seek support and help in a crisis situation by sending others for assistance.

Stay with the person if he or she has attempted suicide.

Be willing to listen. Do be sensitive, empathetic, and attentive.

Be supportive and offer your continued help to the student in the future.

 ## Don'ts

Dismiss or discount any suicide threat.

Argue with the individual about whether he or she should live or die. This is not the time for a philosophical discussion about the pros and cons of living. The discussion should center only around living.

Make statements like, "Oh, go ahead and do it. I dare you." Such challenges and shock statements may be all the impetus the student needs to commit the act.

Be afraid to ask the person if he or she is considering suicide. This may be the opportunity the student is seeking to discuss the subject. Most people do not really want to commit suicide and are looking for people to help them find reasons to live.

Overreact or panic when a person begins to talk about suicide.

Argue with the person by making such statements as "This isn't going to make things better. Suicide is a mortal sin, and you will go to hell."

Try to cajole a person out of choosing suicide by changing the subject or trying to make light of it by being overly humorous. The person intends you to take this situation seriously.

Be overly cool about the crisis. Show concern and care about the person's crisis and stress.

Try to analyze or interpret the person's behavior. He or she does not need a psychoanalytic session with you. The student needs you to listen and to be supportive.

herself, send for help and continue talking with the individual in a calm, soothing voice about reasons for living.

Step 1: Assessment of Potential.

You can assess the lethality or potential for a student to commit suicide by reviewing the student's particular situation with regard to the following eight areas:

- *Sex.* The potential is higher if the person is male or a first-year female student.

- *Symptoms.* The potential is greater if the person cannot sleep or has dramatically altered sleeping or eating patterns within the past few weeks.

- *Stress.* The potential is greater if the person is under stress from exams, pressure from parents, competition for admittance to graduate school, and other such stresses.

- *Suicidal plan.* The potential is greater when the plan is detailed, where the victim has access to a means (e.g., guns, drugs), and where the method is highly lethal.

- *Family and friends.* The potential is greater if the person is a loner in the living unit and has no family or close friends.

- *Past history.* The potential is greater if the person has attempted suicide previously. It is particularly high if this attempt has occurred within the past year.

- *Communication.* The potential is greater if the person has few outlets for communicating with others about his or her problems. If the person tends to internalize his or her problems and seldom shares them with others, the potential is greater.

- *Medical problems.* The person suffering from a terminal illness has a greater likelihood of taking his or her own life.

You make these assessments by asking fairly direct questions, such as, "How are you planning to take your own life?" or "Have you ever attempted suicide before?"

Step 2: Determine Availability of Others to Help.

Once you get some basic information about the suicidal person's background, and how serious the person is, the next step is to assess the availability of others who can assist in preventing the suicide. These include the student's roommate, any friends he or she has, and members of professional staff at your institution. Discuss these options with the individual, expressing your availability and the availability of the professional staff to assist. Whenever you have a discussion like this with a student, you should discuss your observations with your hall director and follow up with the student.

Step 3: Determine Coping Mechanisms.

In your discussion with the student, focus on coping mechanisms the student has available to assist with the problem. One method of doing this is to begin by helping the student focus on what he or she sees as the problem. By doing that, you are helping the student clarify the problem.

Step 4: Determine a Positive Course of Action.

Ask the student the causes of the problem, what he or she has done about it, and what else can be done about it. Together with the student, brainstorm some alternatives and possible solutions. Most of these solutions should come from the student. Examine together the consequences of these alternatives and identify specific steps the student can take. Determine these steps within the framework of a timetable so that the student will have goals to accomplish and something to look forward to tomorrow and the day after. Schedule a follow-up meeting to check on the student's emotional well-being.

Step 5: Nonsuicide Contract.

In various discussions, where the student claims that he or she is seriously thinking about suicide, you may be able to get the student to agree to make a contract with you. In a contract of this type, a student agrees not to harm himself or herself for a specified period of time. This might be an hour, a day, or a week. In making such a contract, the student must clearly understand that you are concerned about him or her and that you expect the student to honor the contract. Ask the student directly if he or she intends to honor the contract and to repeat in detail the agreed-upon commitment, such as, "I agree not to harm myself in the next 48 hours, to talk with you at the end of the 48 hours, and not to break the contract for any reason." This gives you time to get the professional staff involved and to give the student time to rethink alternatives. This permits the student to retain the power that he or she needs and a reason to continue living—a personal commitment to you.

Nonsuicide contracts often work, but not always. If a person seriously wants to take his or her life, you can do very little about it. Your responsibility is to help the student with the crisis, help analyze the potential for suicide, keep senior staff members at your institution informed, recognize the signs of a person who is potentially suicidal, and lend emergency crisis intervention whenever and wherever possible. Perhaps most importantly, you need to encourage and assist a suicidal student to seek help from a mental health professional with the necessary therapeutic skills.

MAKING A REFERRAL

RAs do not have the skills or experience to work with another student who is contemplating suicide. The steps discussed thus far are designed to help you support a student during a time of personal crisis and assist the student in getting the attention he or she needs. Remember, you are not in this alone. Your university has people available with the expertise to help the student both in the immediate situation and long term.

First, always discuss the student's situation with your hall director. Only in a highly unusual situation, such as the hall director was somehow negatively involved, would you not share what you know with the hall director. At this point, your hall director will probably ask you a series of background questions about the student. He or she will be analyzing what your relationship is with the student and discover a way for him or her to constructively address the topic of suicide with the student. Very few hall directors have the training necessary to work with suicidal students, but they have the necessary training and experience to mobilize institutional resources needed to assist the student.

Most likely, the hall director will talk with the student and take steps to insure the student is seen by a mental health professional for an evaluation.

RAs need to remember that a suicide affects all students in the residence hall.

Based on the evaluation, the student may enter therapy, receive medication for depression, be hospitalized for treatment and protection, or be returned home for treatment by a mental health professional of the student's and his or her parents' choice. Whatever the resolution, you have done what your institution requires of you—identify a student in need and insure that the student gets help.

If the student remains in the university and in your living unit, you should offer continued support, but do not interject yourself unnecessarily. Likely, the student will be in therapy. You will not be given any information about the student's progress or status. At the most, you may—if necessary—be given instructions on who to call if the student experiences additional problems.

Remember, normal people in periods of stress or depression will occasionally contemplate suicide. This does not mean the person has a mental illness. With support, most people can get through these situations without any further difficulty.

REVIEW

1. Why do many suicides go unreported?
2. What are four theories or causes of suicide?
3. List four symptoms of suicide.
4. The symptoms of suicide can be divided into two major categories. Identify these two categories. *emotional, physical, behavioral*
5. What are your feelings about suicide as it relates to the counseling of students who may be considering it?
6. What is your goal as an RA in counseling a suicidal student?
7. What is the first rule in working with a suicidal student?
8. Many people consider suicide at some time in their lives. How do you know when they are serious about it and in danger of doing something about it, and when they are only expressing feelings of depression?
9. Name three factors that would increase the likelihood of an individual actually attempting suicide.
10. What is a nonsuicide contract and how does it work?

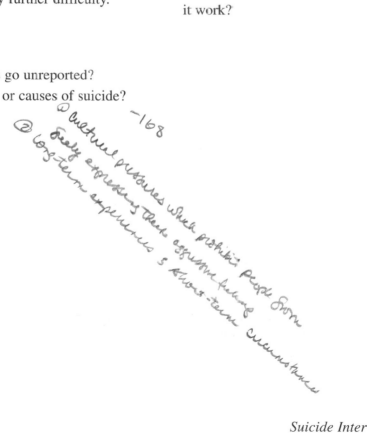

APPLICATIONS

ALL ALONE

Clark and Garrison came to Big East University from California. They had been friends since junior high and were living as roommates while in college. Garrison started his freshman year with a full load of classes but began dropping classes about a month into the first semester. By midterm examinations, he was down to one class. Garrison was a nice young man. He kept to himself and his only friend on the floor was Clark. Since coming to Big East, Garrison had started drinking. In high school Garrison would not drink at all; in fact, he was involved with a group that worked to keep students from drinking. Garrison's parents were divorced. His father was an alcoholic and had been in and out of treatment programs several times. Garrison was not close to his father. His mother was a high school guidance counselor.

Garrison was a very neat and organized person, but recently he had lost interest in keeping things in place. He gave some of his most valued possessions to Clark. In recent weeks his sleeping had become erratic. He frequently missed class and started drinking more frequently. Hardly a night went by when he didn't consume 8 to 10 beers.

There was one woman who Garrison liked, and they had gone out once or twice. She quickly lost interest and began dating someone else in what appeared to be a serious relationship. Garrison felt rejected and somewhat angry over losing out to this other student.

One night Clark returned from the library and found Garrison lying unconscious on the floor of the room. He did not appear to be breathing and could not be awakened. A suicide letter addressed to Clark was in his shirt pocket and a large, half-empty bottle of aspirin on the sink. A lot of empty beer cans were strewn about the room. Clark ran to get the RA.

WHAT WOULD YOU DO?

1. Explain your institution's medical emergency procedure for situations such as the one described above.
2. What signs did Garrison give that may have indicated he was suicidal?

3. What is your institution's policy for returning students to school who have attempted suicide?

4. Once the medical personnel arrive to attend to Garrison, what should the RA do to help Clark?

5. What information and assistance can the RA provide to help the medical personnel and the campus police?

6. Should the RA tell the other students living on the floor what happened? If yes, why? And how could this be used educationally? If no, why not? And how would you respond to the inquiries from those who observed all the activity on the floor?

QUIET DESPERATION

Shara had broken up with a young man after they had dated for about three months. The relationship was over, and she really did not want to see him anymore. It was a difficult relationship for her. She liked the young man but had difficulty with the fact that he was African American and she was White. They had unprotected intercourse several times during their relationship, but only during the times when she was not ovulating.

Shara missed a period but convinced herself that the stress of breaking up and her schoolwork were the cause. When she missed a second period, she became concerned. On the chance she was pregnant, she bought a home pregnancy test. When it was positive for pregnancy, she bought and took two more tests; each test was positive.

She did not want anyone to know about this, least of all her parents who were strong Catholics and had negative attitudes about African Americans. She thought about going to the student health center but ruled it out for fear that her parents might be informed or that they would keep some record of her medical condition. Abortion was an option she considered, but she did not have the money and, anyway, believed that abortion was murder.

Shara was depressed and often cried for no apparent reason. She stopped socializing with the other women on the floor, stopped eating, and slept at least 10 to 12 hours a day. Within the past two days, Shara's disposition seemed to improve. She cleaned her room, straightened all of her belongings, and was giving away her favorite pieces of jewelry and her favorite compact disks to her roommate and another woman on the floor. Her roommate went to the RA, concerned after discovering an empty home pregnancy test box in the room, which Shara said she had never seen before.

WHAT WOULD YOU DO?

1. What signs has Shara given that she might be considering suicide?
2. What action would you take if you were Shara's RA? How could the RA help Shara get counseling?
3. As the RA, what would you do if Shara denies everything and refuses to go for counseling?
4. What policy does your institution have regarding informing parents about their children's records in the student health center?

CHAPTER ELEVEN

CRIME IN RESIDENCE HALLS

©1998 PHOTODISK, INC.

R ape, burglary, assault, drug violations, and armed robbery happen on college campuses just like in the rest of society. In 1987, 698 campuses (approximately one-sixth of all colleges and universities in the United States) received reports of 285,932 crimes. Among the crimes disclosed were 653 rapes, 22,170 burglaries, 13,079 assaults, 3,366 drug violations, and 1,874 armed robberies. In total, this represented a 5.1 percent increase between 1986 and 1987. At the institutions surveyed:

- One in four students had been a victim of a crime.
- A violent crime (rape, robbery, assault) occurred on campus once for every 500 students.
- Eleven percent of surveyed students had been confronted by an assailant and 3 percent had been confronted more than once.

- Almost 30 percent of the surveyed students believed their campuses were not safe, and 42 percent of the women surveyed said they did not feel safe walking on campus alone at night.[1]

In 1993, the *Chronical of Higher Education* surveyed 2,400 schools in the United States regarding crime on campus and found that at these institutions 30 murders, 1,000 rapes, 1,800 robberies, 32,127 burglaries, and 8,981 motor vehicle thefts were reported. These figures—particularly those involving rape—may be too low.[2]

Crime is a problem on campus and in residence halls. This chapter focuses on three areas of crime. First is the issue of battered women. Increasingly, romantic relationships on college campuses include physical violence. You may be involved with a resident who has been assaulted or who has assaulted someone. A second issue on campus is rape, perpetrated both by strangers and by acquaintances. This chapter includes discussions of causes of these assaults, what to do when one of your residents is raped, and precautions which can be taken to prevent rape. In the final segment of the chapter, the issue of campus theft and security is discussed. This is a continuing problem in all residence halls and one you need to discuss with your residents.

BATTERED WOMEN

Between 22 and 35 percent of all women who go to emergency rooms are there because of domestic assaults. In 1991, police reports showed that more than 4 million women were beaten and approximately 1,320 women were murdered in domestic attacks. Between one-third and one-half of all women who are murdered in the United States are murdered by husbands or lovers.[3]

Men beat women for a number of reasons. Some men were abused as children and have internalized this abusive behavior. When they become angry, they express their anger through violence—the way they learned to as a child.

Other men believe they have the right to dominate women because they are men, and women are simply to do as they are told.

Young men in the stage of discovering their sexual identity may overreact to the need for power and control. When they encounter a problem with a girlfriend, some become possessive and act out their feelings by attempting to control or dominate her. This may involve physical abuse.

Part of the reason men physically abuse women may be due to low impulse control, low self-esteem, and the belief that their behavior is controlled by the actions of women. A typical response from a man who has beaten his girlfriend is, "She made me do it." The idea that someone else is responsible for one's behavior is a problem in locus of control. These people rationalize their behavior by attributing it to the control of others.

Why do women stay in relationships with men who abuse them? One reason is that some of these women have low self-esteem and come to believe they were responsible for getting hit. They believe they deserved it. Insecurity about the relationship and fear of losing a boyfriend who has offered them some kind of security are other reasons. Having a boyfriend who takes you places, involves you in the social life of college, and who makes you feel important presents a form of security. Women sometimes fear that if they break off these relationships they will be all alone and will lose access to the social life of college.

While dating, people sometimes develop a love-hate relationship. They love intently, and they fight intently. They are so emotionally caught up with one another that both lose good judgment. The script that they write for the relationship progresses to the point where outrageous physical behavior becomes acceptable.

After a woman has been battered, she may feel guilty or embarrassed about what has happened. She may not know with whom to share this information and may fear reporting it to campus authorities or to her parents. This fear may be associated with concern over her parents' reaction or fear that the boyfriend will seek revenge.

Factors that contribute to men physically abusing women are alcohol use, stress, immaturity of both students in the relationship, and a conspiracy of secrecy that surrounds a violent episode. These contributing factors make it difficult for you as an RA to intervene. You may notice one of your female residents returning from a date frightened and physically abused. A roommate may disclose to you in confidence that the woman she rooms with has been beaten by her boyfriend. Such incidents should be treated seriously. Assault is never acceptable, and it is not part of a normal relationship. If the violence is not confronted the first time it happens, the perpetrator has no reason to stop. Although it is unusual, there have been instances on college campuses where a man in a fit of rage, jealousy, or revenge has killed his girlfriend. Take each report of physical abuse seriously.

If you learn a student has been physically abused in a relationship, first assure the battered woman that she will be protected. If you have guest hours in your residence hall, generally the boyfriend can be kept out of the building. If you live in a coed residence hall or one without limited guest hours, this may be more difficult. In either case, you should report the incident to the hall director, and the hall director will consider what other steps need to be taken. Usually the man who assaulted the woman is either referred for disciplinary action or arrested. These may appear to be punitive measures, and the woman may not want her boyfriend to get into trouble; however, if the man is not confronted with the consequences of his behavior, he is unlikely to get the help he needs to control the unacceptable behavior.

Universities can and do have ways to compel men with these problems to get help. Mandatory counseling, a criminal trespass notice prohibiting the man from entering the woman's residence hall, and suspension or expulsion from the institution are options that the university has at its disposal to ensure the safety of a female resident. None of these steps can occur unless those people charged with managing these responsibilities at your university are informed about what is happening. Somewhere the conspiracy of silence must be broken.

Your role in working with a student who has been battered is to see that she talks to authorities at the institution about the incident. You should do what is necessary to help her feel secure, such as temporarily move her to another room or to another building. She may need medical treatment or counseling to overcome the trauma and to feel comfortable with men again.

Your residents need to know that violence can happen in dating relationships and that it is not normal. They need to know that the institution will protect them, help their boyfriend control his behavior, and ensure their safety. Students should feel comfortable coming to you to discuss their concerns in this area. At a floor meeting or through an educational program, you should introduce your residents to the topic of violence in dating relationships.

Men need to have this information just as much as women. Although most men understand that assaulting anyone is wrong, some men excuse their behavior by claiming they have a temper. This is not a valid excuse. The truth is that the man is unable to control his anger and goes into a violent rage, the result of which is that other people are injured. The consumption of alcohol is almost always associated with these episodes of violence. Because alcohol allows people to become less inhibited, they are more inclined to act impulsively. When they become angry or irritated, they disproportionately express their anger by destroying property or hurting others. Often their anger is not about anything another person has done. It just so happens that that person is a convenient and safe outlet for the accumulated anger.

Talking about these issues helps. Men who beat women need therapy. The behavior does not spontaneously disappear. Psychotherapy is effective in helping people change this behavior. Men who do not get help continue this violence until they are made to stop by police or university authorities. Unfortunately, the incident that finally triggers the intervention of authorities may leave a woman seriously injured, hospitalized, or even dead. Men who batter women have an emotional problem. If you know of men in your living unit who have this reputation or who have confided this problem, help them by getting them into counseling. It is not a problem they can work through by themselves; professional guidance is needed.

RAPE

Rape is a forced sexual encounter against a person's will. According to a survey of counseling centers during a six-month period, a total of 2,972 people reported that they had been raped; of these, 2,779 were female and 193 male.[4] The majority of rape victims are single women between the ages of 14 and 24, but it can happen to anyone regardless of age, personal appearance, or socioeconomic level. According to FBI crime reports, one out of every three women will be raped in her lifetime. In a survey of female college students,

MYTHS ABOUT RAPE

 Myth

 Fact

Myth	Fact
Victims cause rape.	Victims range from babies to women over 90 years old.
Rapists are mentally ill.	Most rapists are married men with families. They come from all educational backgrounds, occupations, and racial groups.
Assailants commit rape for sexual gratification.	Rape is an expression of aggression and dominance. Sexual gratification is not the primary concern.
Women secretly enjoy being raped.	Rape is a violent crime, and women do not enjoy rape any more than they enjoy a car accident or being beaten.
Women invite rape by dressing seductively.	Victims do not cause rape. Police believe that in stranger rape, the rapists tend to look for women who are frightened, easily intimidated, or daydreaming.
Rape is generally spontaneous.	Almost 71 percent of all reported rapes involve some planning by the rapists.
Men tend to rape women of a different race than their own.	Most rapes are perpetrated against a person of the same race or ethnic group.

Adapted from National Crime Prevention Council, "Sexual Assault: Reducing the Risk and Coping with an Attack (Washington, D.C.: Author n.d).

25 percent reported that they had been victims of either rape or attempted rape.[5] The vast majority of rapes involve men raping women. Reports of homosexual rapes have increased. The victims in these cases are usually children or adolescents. Although cases of homosexual rape have occurred on college campus, they are clearly the exception. The rapes discussed in this chapter concern women who have been raped by a stranger or by their dates or acquaintances.

Although a common image conjured up by the word *rape* involves a sexually frustrated stranger hiding in bushes at night waiting for an unsuspecting female to happen by, this image is almost completely unrepresentative of the actual crime. Rapes are not spontaneous and impulsive acts. They are usually elaborately planned by the rapist, and frequently the rapist is acquainted with the victim. Although most women are fearful of rapists in dark alleys or lurking behind bushes, most rapes occur in the victim's home or the assailant's home. This is particularly true of date rape.[6] More stranger rapes occur during the day than at night; however, most acquaintance rapes occur at night and on weekends. All statistics on rape show that acquaintance rapes are far more common than rapes by strangers. During the summer months rapes increase. Over 30 percent of all rapes occur outdoors, and approximately 25 percent involve more than one attacker. One-half of victims know their assailant at least casually.

Rapists can be any age, but most are between the ages of 20 and 30. Although rapes involve intercourse, sexual gratification is not the main goal of rapists. They have a need to dominate and degrade women. For them, the excitement of the rape is the sense of power and control. Most enjoy the violence more than the sexual experience. Forcing one's will over another, leaving the person helpless and at their mercy, is the emotional gratification for many rapists.

Many rapists were sexually abused as children. Some were also physically abused. Men who rape are out of control. They enjoy the vio-

lence and need it to assert their masculinity. Rape provides them with feelings of power and control, which often are missing in rapists' daily lives. Rapists are often contributing members of society, living normal family lives. A person who rapes once will likely rape again.

Reducing the Risks of Rape by a Stranger

College campuses sometimes give young women a false sense of safety. Because they see other students on campus their same age throughout the day, they assume they are safe to walk through the campus at night. Women need to be made aware that most college campuses are no safer than the streets of the communities in which they are located. Although security may be good in your particular residence hall or on your campus, it is not so good that it can prevent assailants from hiding in the parking lots or unlighted areas of the campus. Rapes occur in residence halls just as they occur in apartments off campus.

- When few people are on the floor, women should keep their doors locked.

- Women should not walk on campus late at night unless they are with another person. Many campuses provide night escort services; unfortunately, 84 percent of the women surveyed in one study did not use the escort services provided by their college.[7]

- While walking, women should be alert to their surroundings and the people they pass. They should remain in well-lit areas and areas where other people are. When walking alone on a street, women should walk close to the curb to avoid doorways, bushes, and alleys. They should respond carefully when people stop and ask for directions, not getting too close to the car. If a female student suspects she is being followed or is concerned about a particular area, she should walk to the nearest building and get help.

- Every women's residence hall should have a program about campus safety that includes a discussion about rape. It should include not only the issues related to rapes on campus, but also the issues of rape in the community or city in which the college is located.

- In choosing to fight, run, or submit when confronted by a rapist, a woman's first priority should be to stay alive. Fighting may be effective, but submission may be safer and wiser if the assailant has a weapon. Because men tend to have more upper body strength than women, a woman's goal in fighting back should not be to win but to distract the rapist long enough to permit her to get away. "The earlier [the] aggressive response, the more likely it will work. . . . Often the most effective action a woman can take is to make noise, cause a scene, and otherwise draw attention to her predicament. Yelling 'no,' or 'fire' has a greater chance of attracting attention than yelling 'help' or 'rape.'"[8]

Acquaintance Rape

A three-year study of 6,200 students at 35 colleges and universities throughout the United States revealed that 90 percent of women who had been raped knew their assailants and 47 percent of the rapes were by first dates or romantic acquaintances. More than 90 percent of the women did not report the rape. One out of 12 men admitted to having fulfilled the definition of rape or attempted rape, yet none identified themselves as a rapist.[9]

In another survey of 6,000 students at 32 colleges, one in six female students reported being the victim of a rape or an attempt. Most of those fell into the category of acquaintance rape.[10]

A survey of females at a large Midwestern university found that 45 percent indicated that they were the victim of some form of dating violence, ranging from intimidation to rape. Students in this survey also were asked the locations of these incidents; the most common response (30 percent) was that the act occurred in a residence hall. Women's residence halls accounted for 22 percent, and men's residence halls accounted for 8 percent. Fraternity houses were the next most likely location, with 25 percent of the respondents reporting this as the location for the act of dating violence.[11]

Estimates of the number of women who have been involved in acquaintance rape run as high as one in five.[12] One of the reasons acquaintance rapes are not reported is that women feel responsible for what happened. Many do not consider the incident technically to be rape. They usually describe the act using other terms such as "He forced himself on me," or "He forced me into

WHAT TO DO IF ATTACKED

There is no one correct answer to the question of what to do if you are attacked. The National Crime Prevention Council has recommended the following:

- Keep your head. Stay as calm as possible; think rationally and evaluate your resources and options.

- It may be more advisable to submit than to resist and risk injury or death. You will have to make the decision based on the circumstances. But don't resist if the attacker has a weapon.

- Keep assessing the situation as it is happening. If one strategy does not work, try another. Possible options in addition to nonresistance are negotiating, stalling for time, distracting the assailant and fleeing to a safe place, verbal assertiveness, screaming to attract attention, and physical resistance.

- You may be able to repulse the attacker with bizarre behavior such as throwing up, acting crazy, or picking your nose.

having sex with him." Most acquaintance rapes happen to young woman inexperienced in dating relationships. High school seniors and college freshmen are most often the victims, but it can happen to any woman. Usually the rape involves some type of physical restraint. Occasionally slapping or hitting is involved, but rarely is a weapon involved. Acquaintance rapes do happen on the first date and sometimes with blind dates, but most date rape situations occur on the second or third date after the initial discomfort of the first date is resolved.

Theories on Date Rape

Researchers have proposed several theories about what causes date rape. Some claim that it is motivated by the need to dominate, to express anger toward women, or simply to inflict pain. Another theory is that acquaintance rape is a result of misread social cues in the dating relationship. In some circumstances, men and women may misinterpret each other's signals. Some have argued that when a man hears a woman passively say no to a sexual encounter she may simply be acting coy by showing an appropriate degree of token resistance. Some research has shown that men who commit acquaintance rape may be more sexually active than other men and more likely to have a history of antisocial behavior.[13]

Smith believed that alcohol and sexual promiscuity are two of the major reasons for campus acquaintance rapes.[14] The limits of acceptable behavior are simply not as clear when the norm is sex on the first or second date. Alcohol is a compounding problem. It impairs judgment and in dating situations can lead to aggressive behavior, including acquaintance rape. O'Shaughnessy and Palmer found that when sexual assaults occurred, approximately 71 percent of the women and 81 percent of the men had been drinking.[15]

Whatever the causes of acquaintance rape, it is legally and morally wrong. Women should take precautions by not placing themselves in situations that might lead to unwanted sexual attention, and men need to know that *no* means "no." Acquaintance rape most often happens when both parties have been drinking alcohol and return to either party's residence hall room or apartment. What starts as an innocent kiss turns into heavy necking and petting and sometimes into forced intercourse.

RAs need to make their female residents aware of the following:

- Women have the right to set limits, and when they are not sure about a sexual involvement, they have the right to stop and discuss these limits.
- Women have an obligation to communicate these limits to their date. If their date begins touching them in intimate places, if only by accident, they need to say no and mean it.
- Women need to be assertive in what they say. A man might misinterpret a soft or passive no. The response should be direct, clear, and firm.
- Women need to be aware that their nonverbal actions send messages. If they flirt, touch men in intimate ways, and generally try to turn them on, they should be aware that they probably are communicating nonverbally the desire to have sex.
- Women need to be conscious of what is happening in the situation. A locked door, drinking, and heavy petting are signs of where this situation could be leading.
- Women should trust their intuition. If they think they are being pressured into having sex, they probably are.
- Women need to avoid excessive use of alcohol and drugs, and should avoid intimate social circumstances with men who have been using alcohol and drugs.[16]

Men must bear responsibility for their own behavior. Women may flirt, be seductive, or be in vulnerable situations, but when they say no they always mean "no." No matter how sexually aroused a man gets, he has no right to force his sexual desires on a woman. RAs need to make their male residents aware of the following:

- Men need to know their sexual desires and limits and communicate them clearly.

- Men need to understand that when a woman says no to sex it is not a rejection of them. It is simply an indication that the woman does not have the desire to have sex.

- Men must accept the woman's decision. Sex must be mutually agreeable.

- Men cannot assume that previous sexual encounters with a woman grants them permission to have sex with this person at will. Because a woman has said yes once does not indicate that she is going to have sex whenever the man wants to.

- Men need to avoid excessive use of alcohol and drugs when dating. It impairs good judgment and may lead to acting on emotions without thinking. They should be aware of their date's consumption as well.[17]

Reaction to Rape

Victims react to rape in two major stages. The first is the *acute* phase. This involves her initial emotional reaction. Women who have been raped are angry, afraid, and may feel guilty. They blame themselves, reasoning that they must have done something to bring this upon themselves. They are afraid of encountering the man again and ashamed of what has happened. Having been degraded and humiliated in this way, they may fear facing both family and friends. Victims of rape report feeling unclean and violated. A natural reaction that a woman has after being raped is to shower and clean her body.

The second phase of a reaction to rape is the *rape trauma syndrome*. Victims express a fear of being left alone and a fear of men. It may be months before they feel comfortable being around men and even longer before they feel comfortable engaging in sex. Because they have been so dominated by another person, victims of rape have a need to gain control of their lives. This control is sometimes equated with having power to protect themselves. A common reaction is for women to obtain a handgun or move into a building with increased security.

Depression, feelings of low self-esteem, spontaneous and uncontrolled crying, and a feeling of

ACQUAINTANCE RAPE: WAYS TO FIGHT BACK

Although each acquaintance rape situation is different, the National Crime Prevention Council has recommended the following ways for women to fight back:

1. Be assertive. Say no firmly, even if he tries to make you feel guilty or unpopular.
2. If no doesn't work, be rude!
3. Make noise. Talk loudly, scream, honk the car horn, or yell.
4. Repulse him by acting crazy, saying you have a venereal disease, or threatening to throw up.
5. Try to get away and call your parents or a friend to come and get you.
6. If all else fails, resort to physical resistance, a swift jab to the throat or eyes, or a solid kick between the legs.

being isolated are part of the psychological trauma that the victims of rape express. They fear what other people think of them, and may believe that others fault them for what happened. Victims repeatedly recall the rape scene in their mind. They will try to reason all of the things they could have done to prevent it or to have stopped it. Each time they discover what they consider to have been a viable alternative, they may condemn themselves for not having been smart enough or alert enough to apply that option.

Women who are in dating relationships or who are married often find it difficult to sustain their relationship after rape. The boyfriend or husband may also experience some trauma. Men often do not know how to respond. Some may even question whether or not the victim could have done more to prevent or stop the rape. People are possessive about relationships and care about what happens to a loved one. The husbands and significant others of women who have been raped feel anger about what happened, but they often have no way to channel their anger.

The rape trauma syndrome may last for a year or longer. Sometimes a rape so influences a person that she never totally recovers from the psychological trauma.

What to Do If One of Your Residents Is Raped

Rape is a traumatic experience both for the victim and for the other women on campus. It sends a shock wave of concern throughout an entire campus. Residents respond with heightened anxiety, and rumors of rapists circulate throughout the campus.

Your concern as the RA is to see that if a young woman on your floor is raped, she is seen by the police or campus authorities. If one of your residents has been raped, your hall director or other campus officials should immediately be notified. The police or a rape crisis center should also be contacted. If a person has been attacked, the first thing she needs to do is get to safety and make a report. Do not let the resident shower, brush her teeth, bathe, douche, or destroy any of the clothing she was wearing at the time of the attack. This is evidence and is needed by the police and/or campus officials. If the assault occurred in the student's room, do not disturb anything in the area until after an investigation has been completed. Police and other officials have been trained to preserve physical evidence for use in court.

The victim should be taken to a hospital emergency room for medical care. The doctor should be informed that this is a rape and that he or she should record the injuries. The doctor has been trained to handle these situations. He or she should also assess the risks of pregnancy and venereal disease. Bring a change of clothes for the student so that she may change at the hospital. The student should not be left alone. If a rape crisis counselor is not there, you should be. Either you or the student's roommate should stay with her at the hospital. A rape victim whose RA is male may prefer to have a female RA with her at this time.

As soon as feasible, the university's counseling center or a rape treatment or crisis center should be consulted. The student will need to have the support of someone who understands the experience of being raped and will need to begin therapy to deal with the anger, fear, and guilt that she will be feeling.

Police will interview the student and gather information about the assailant's description. If she relates any of this information to you, make note of it and share this information with the police or the campus authorities working with the police. Hospital personnel will use a special kit to gather evidence to be used in court. The physician will perform a gynecological examination, take a sperm specimen, take tissue samples from underneath the victim's nails, take pictures and notes to document injuries, and keep clothing and undergarments as evidence.

Some students do not want to report rape to the police. They are afraid of the reaction of their parents and friends. They are embarrassed by what happened and may feel responsible. In all cases you should take steps to see that the student does report it to the police. In all cases you should immediately contact your hall director and let him or her help the student make this decision. Even when the student chooses not to pursue prosecution, as an RA you must report the incident to your hall director or other residence hall staff members. The Crime Awareness and Campus Security Act provides definitions for forcible and nonforcible sex offenses and reporting procedures that colleges and universities must follow.

Counseling Students Who Have Been Raped

Your primary role is to help the student who has been raped enter therapy with a trained counselor. Even though the student may enter counseling, she will need your help. When you counsel a student who has been raped, supply warmth and support. She will usually want to talk with another woman and may feel more secure and protected when other women are present. Do not try to cross-examine or force her to relive the episode. Detailed descriptions of this sort may trigger other reactions that you are not prepared to confront. Thinking about or focusing on the issue will be an emotionally traumatic situation for the person and is best left to a professional counselor. Keep information about the rape confidential. The student should get support from persons whom she trusts, and she will determine in whom she wishes to confide.

If the victim does not drop out of school after having been raped and chooses to return to the residence hall, be sensitive to the crisis that she has experienced. Work on building her self-confidence and helping her reestablish personal relationships. She may feel awkward and as if everyone is star-ing at her. Anything you can do to dispel this feeling will help her. Some students cope better if they can return to the routine of studying as soon as possible while continuing their therapy.

OTHER CRIMES ON CAMPUS

Residents who observe unusual behavior around the residence hall, burglary, vandalism, or somebody creeping around automobiles in the parking lot should report it to you and to campus police. A survey of 698 U.S. colleges and universities found a 7.9 percent increase in burglary, a 6.1 percent increase in theft, a 2.8 percent increase in assault, and a 5.3 percent decrease in armed robbery. Twenty-four percent of the 2,470 students polled on 50 campuses across the nation reported that they had something stolen on campus at least once. And 12.8 percent reported that they had possessions stolen two to five times. Of respondents, 62.1 percent never had anything taken, and 1.1 percent had possessions taken five or more times. Most students (39.4 percent) in this survey believed that access to their residence hall was very easy, and that more campus lighting and better residence hall security would make their campus safer.[18] RAs are themselves sometimes the victims of violence, vandalism, and verbal harassment.

Theft

Theft has been a problem in college residence halls for years. Money, records, compact disks, and stereo equipment frequently come up missing. An unlocked room is an invitation to any dishonest person walking down the hall. One of the reasons that residence halls tend to make students so vulnerable is that they present a false sense of security. Students know the other students in their living units and often leave their door open or unlocked when they walk to the hall bathroom or when they visit a friend's room down the hall.

Although people are usually aware of strangers in the hallway, if they are college age, few people show much concern. A student can easily walk the corridors to find open doors and simply step in and take anything that looks valuable. Students who live on the ground floor of a residence hall can be particularly vulnerable. Frequently they leave their windows open, and a thief can easily cut the window screen and enter a room while the student is away.

As an RA you need to be particularly careful about any master keys you have been issued. If these keys are stolen or if you lose them, you jeopardize the security of every student whose room your master key will open. If an RA loses a set of master keys, generally the building or the living unit has to be rekeyed. This is usually a very expensive process and one that will make the residence hall staff quite angry with you.

You can take steps to help your residents take better care of their property. Tell them not to leave valuables such as wallets, checkbooks, and jewelry lying about their room. If they have a large amount of money in their room, they should put it in the bank. Items that can be easily stolen such as televisions, stereos, and computers should have the student's social security number etched someplace on the item. This identification helps the student recover property in the event that the item is stolen. The student should also make a list of any serial numbers, model numbers, and descriptions of his or her property. One way to do this is for the student to take a photograph of the item in question and record on the back of the photograph the serial and model number of the item.

Doors and windows should have working locks. If the locks are broken, the staff responsible for the campus physical plant should be contacted to repair them. If a student loses his or her room key, the door lock should be changed. Usually colleges have a procedure to bill the student for the cost of this lock change.

Broken windows, doors, and lights should be repaired. If students prop doors open that are to be secured at night, some type of buzzer or alarm system should be considered to alert people to the opening of this door. Talk with the students about the need to keep these doors secured to keep intruders out.

Bicycles.   Most residence halls are not designed to have bicycles inside the building. Although some students would like to put their bicycles in their rooms, most state fire codes prohibit this because they present an obstacle in the event of fire. If students bring bicycles to campus, they should record the serial numbers, photograph the bicycles, and put them in a secure location. Most importantly, they should purchase a heavy duty lock; inexpensive cable or chain locks are ineffective. It only takes a bolt cutter to cut most of the locks securing expensive bicycles. College campuses are known targets for bicycle thieves who often come on campus with a truck and simply load bicycles into the back and drive away. Bikes should be secured to a nonmovable item. Simply putting a lock on a bike and sitting it against the wall is an unsatisfactory solution to the problem of theft.

Alarm Systems.   Within recent years, inexpensive burglar alarm systems have been developed. These systems usually consist of a motion detector or an infrared detector and some type of sound device. Students with valuable property in their room might consider one of these systems. No matter what time of the day or night, residence halls usually have somebody in them. The alarm alerts people that something is going on and people will come to check. Usually, this is enough to discourage or frighten away any person who has entered the room illegally. Sometimes a parent's homeowners insurance policy will cover the theft of property from a residence hall room; often it does not. Many colleges and universities offer students an insurance policy through a commercial vendor to cover theft and damage to personal property in the residence halls.

Robberies. A 1993 survey found that approximately 1,800 armed robberies occur annually on college and university campuses.[19] A presentation by your campus police department about residence hall safety and personal safety on campus would be helpful. Your residents should know that, if someone tries to assault them on campus, they should think rationally and evaluate their resources. They should consider their options, including escape, use of self-defense techniques, negotiation, screaming to get attention, or acting disgusting or crazy. If the person is armed, the National Crime Prevention Council has suggested that it may be more advisable to submit than to risk injury or death. The student should try to get an accurate description of the assailant's appearance and the license number of any vehicles involved. This information should be given to campus police as soon as possible. If a person is robbed, threatened, or raped, campus police should be immediately notified. This notification may save someone else from becoming a victim.

Every resident has the responsibility to report suspicious happenings to the campus police.

You can set up a role play of a potentially dangerous situation with your residents and discuss the possible responses. A role-play issue such as what to do if you return to your residence hall room and find somebody stealing your property is useful preparation. You can also establish a sort of neighborhood watch in the residence hall. When strangers enter the hall, everyone should be observant of what the stranger is doing. It is not inappropriate to ask visitors if they need assistance. If they are there for the purpose of mischief, the direct contact may discourage it.

In your floor meeting and in your staff meeting with the other RAs, talk about the issue of residence hall security. Spend time thinking about ways in which the residence halls could be made more secure. When lights are burned out, see that they are replaced. If doors are broken, see that they are repaired. If bushes provide concealment for people to break into ground-floor windows or allow people to hide for the purpose of robbing passersby, have your hall director talk with physical plant personnel about trimming the bushes. If cars in the parking lot adjacent to your building are being vandalized or items are being stolen from them, see that these occurrences are reported to the police. Police have plainclothes stakeouts of high-crime areas. They will sometimes station police officers on top of buildings for the purpose of watching these areas. Some campuses have installed closed circuit television monitors to monitor these areas. When you see something suspicious, or whenever any of your residents sees something suspicious, it should be reported.

If you have a serious problem in your residence hall with security, have your hall director invite the director of housing/resident life, the director of physical plant, and the chief of your campus police to a meeting with the RA staff and with students. Some ways to improve security include removing shrubbery or replacing it with natural barriers such as holly or bramble bushes, installing better lighting, replacing poorly fitting doors, installing security screens on ground floor windows, and purchasing electronic locking systems for exterior doors at night.

Every resident in the building has a responsibility to every other resident to help keep the environment safe. As an RA you need to help convey this to the students living on your floor. The best possible security occurs when everyone looks out for one another. Everyone has a duty to make sure that doors are locked, that windows are secured, and that strangers are not left to wander the buildings unchallenged.

REVIEW

1. Give three explanations for why men beat women.

2. Give three reasons why women stay in relationships with men who beat them.

3. What are the two most important ways an RA can help a woman who has been beaten?

4. Although a rapist can be any age, what is the most likely age range?

5. What is a rapist's motivation?

6. What are the two major stages in reaction to rape? List two characteristics of each.

7. List three ways a woman can reduce the risk of rape from a stranger.

8. Briefly explain two of the theories about the causes of acquaintance rape.

9. List three ways a woman can reduce the risk of acquaintance rape.

10. What do men need to know about acquaintance rape?

11. What is your institution's procedure for responding to a victim of a rape?

12. What can the RA do to help a woman who has been raped and returns to the residence hall after seeing the police and appropriate medical personnel?

13. List four ways to improve the security in your residence hall.

14. According to the National Crime Prevention Council, what should people do if someone tries to rob them with a weapon?

15. Give four ways RAs can help to make their residence halls safer.

APPLICATIONS

LOVING AND FIGHTING

Louis is a senior and has been dating Robin for almost three years. They plan to get married when they graduate. One night the RA is called to Louis's room by several of the men on the floor. When the RA arrives, Louis is in a rage. He is throwing his belongings against the wall and pounding his fist against the wall.

The RA goes into Louis's room and closes the door behind him. He asks Louis what's wrong. Louis pauses, regains his composure and tells the RA that he and Robin are having problems. They had a big fight. He shows the RA where Robin scratched him on the arms and face. "You can't let women get away with that kind of thing. Give them an inch and they will take a mile. Unless you keep them in their place, they will walk all over you," Louis tells the RA.

The RA asks Louis if he hit Robin. Louis says, "Yes, but only to defend myself, and then only enough to teach her not to do it again."

The next afternoon the RA sees Louis and Robin together in the dining hall. He notices that she has a bruise on her face. That evening after a staff meeting, Louis's RA mentions to Robin's RA that their residents seemed to have gotten everything worked out. Robin's RA was not aware of any problem. She had seen the bruise on Robin's face and was told by Robin that it happened playing field hockey with some of her friends.

WHAT WOULD YOU DO?

1. Is there anything that Robin's RA could say or do to pursue this matter with Robin? If so, what?

2. Is there anything that Louis's RA could say or do to pursue this matter with Louis? If so, what?

3. Some people might argue that this is a problem between Robin and Louis and the RAs should not get involved. Do you agree? Why or why not?

4. Give three reasons why Robin may have chosen not to tell anyone about the physical fight she had with Louis.

5. Write two endings to this case study: the best case scenario and the worst case scenario. Which one do you think is most likely? Why?

WITHOUT PERMISSION

Helen met Patrick at a floor party. Her roommate, Cindy, introduced them. Patrick was a resident on the same floor where Cindy's boyfriend was the RA. Patrick and Helen had a nice time on their first date. Patrick was a perfect gentleman and asked permission to kiss her goodnight—she consented. On their second date, Patrick took her to dinner, then to a movie. They kissed a few times in his car.

On their third date, Patrick took Helen to an off-campus party where they both had plenty to drink. They went to Patrick's room to listen to music. They started kissing and had intercourse. Helen liked Patrick and did not object. The next morning she felt guilty about having had intercourse with Patrick. She decided that had she not been drinking, she probably would not have had sex with him.

During the week that followed, Helen and Patrick saw each other only once over dinner in the cafeteria. On Friday night, they went to a party at Patrick's fraternity. Patrick was drinking, but Helen chose not to. About 11:30 P.M., Patrick asked Helen if she wanted to go upstairs to see his friend's room. She agreed. When they got to the room, Patrick told her that his friend was gone for the weekend, and they could have the room all to themselves. He turned on some music and sat next to her on the bed. They started kissing, but when Patrick started to remove Helen's blouse, she said no. Patrick was persistent and managed to remove some of her clothing. When he continued, she said, "NO!" He wouldn't listen. She struggled, but he was much stronger. They had intercourse without her consent. When it was over she began to cry, and asked to be taken home. Patrick tried to calm her down, but Helen didn't want to talk. She just wanted to be taken home.

Patrick drove her to her residence hall. She got out of the car and, without saying another word, walked into her residence hall. She went to her room, changed clothes, and took a shower.

On Sunday night, Cindy returned from being gone all weekend. Helen was still upset. She started crying and told Cindy what happened. Her roommate went to their RA and had her come to the room. Helen told the RA what happened, but wouldn't give her Patrick's name and does not want the incident reported to anyone.

WHAT WOULD YOU DO?

1. Did Patrick have the right to expect that he and Helen would continue to have intercourse while they dated? Why or why not?

2. What situational variables in this case contributed to this act of nonconsensual intercourse?

3. Would you describe this act of nonconsensual intercourse as "rape"? Why or why not?

4. What are three reasons why Helen might be reluctant to report this assault? Do you think she should? Why or why not?

5. Do you think that Patrick should be criminally prosecuted and/or expelled permanently from the college for his actions as described in the case study? Why or why not?

6. What are Helen's RA's options at this point? What would you do if you were her RA?

7. Cindy knows that Patrick is the man Helen was with. She tells her boyfriend, Patrick's RA. With no official complaint from Helen, what could Patrick's RA do, if anything, to address Patrick's behavior?

8. If Helen had claimed that Patrick raped her on their third date (the first time they had intercourse) would you agree? Why or why not?

PART FOUR

SOCIAL ISSUES

Food Abuse

Alcohol Abuse

Drug Abuse

Sexuality

Sexual Orientation

Issues of Race and Gender

CHAPTER TWELVE

FOOD ABUSE

©1998 PHOTODISK, INC.

Substance abuse is not a problem exclusive to college students. It affects all of us in some form: personal experience, the experience of friends, or the effect it has on society. This chapter covers food abuse—perhaps the most common substance abuse. This discussion does not encompass diet and health care, but rather the problems of bulimia and anorexia nervosa. These two forms of food abuse primarily affect women and occur most often during the college years.

Although the two disorders are described separately here the behaviors or symptoms of people who abuse food usually include elements of both disorders.

BULIMIA

Bulimic is an eating disorder characterized by a cycle of consuming mass quantities of food and then purging, usually by vomiting and/or the use of strong laxatives followed by fasting. It is a form of obsessive-compulsive behavior that has been estimated to occur in somewhere between 5 and 25 percent of college-aged women.

A person with this form of eating disorder has usually come to associate eating with emotions, so that not only hunger, but also emotions, trigger the desire to consume food. The food is used to satisfy the emotion. This disease usually involves consuming foods used as desserts, like cookies and ice cream. The person feels guilty about the binging, usually for weight control reasons, and purges the food to alleviate the guilt.

Researchers have estimated that approximately 90 to 95 percent of all bulimics are women. Most are from White, middle-class and upper-middle-class families, with parents who are generally achievement oriented. Bulimic students usually express fears of not pleasing their parents. This is coupled with low self-esteem and the high need for achievement. They often feel that they are being dominated by others and that they have lost control of their lives.

Many of these young women place an emphasis on an idealized romantic relationship and in doing so emphasize their physical attractiveness and sexuality. American women have been socialized by magazines, movies, and television to believe that thin is beautiful and seductive. To enter this idealized romantic relationship—in other words, to be loved—these women believe that they must emulate the media-depicted sexual fantasy. They equate self-worth with how closely they approximate the slender ideal. People with this illness believe that if they can become thin enough, others will love them more.

Physical Damage Associated with Bulimia

The binging and purging of bulimia sets up a cycle triggered by emotions. As these women purge their digestive systems, usually by vomit-ing, their bodies change. Vomiting reduces the potassium in the body's system. It disrupts blood sugar and insulin levels, and influences the body's fluid and electrolyte balance. Continual vomiting removes the mucous membrane of the esophagus that acts as a protective layer in the throat and leaves the throat susceptible to infections and the body susceptible to illness. In some extreme cases, the person may develop a conditioned response to the consumption of food so that whenever she eats, her body automatically regurgitates the food. The nutritional problems inherent in this constant disruption of the system are evident. In extreme cases, people die.

Coping Mechanisms

One of the difficulties in confronting this disease is the embarrassment associated with the symptoms. People generally do not discuss vomiting or laxatives. Usually, the purging is done in private, and the person experiences guilt. Sometimes in residence halls, RAs become aware of this behavior as a result of discussions with residents, by observing a particular resident in the restroom, or by reports from the janitorial staff.

This problem should be treated like any other substance abuse problem. The goal in working with students with this illness is to get them to see a counselor who can begin a process of therapy that addresses their problem. As an RA, you are faced not only with the problem of identifying a bulimic person but also with the problem of confronting her with this disorder. Because these people are dealing with issues of low self-esteem, confronting them with the idea that something is wrong with their behavior will not be easy. Many college counseling centers and health centers have developed brochures about bulimia. The realization of the physical problems associated with this disorder and the desire to regain control of one's life may help a student make the decision to seek assistance.

Therapy for bulimic students focuses on increasing personal self-esteem. It is usually done in group-counseling environments to help the students gain positive feedback from peers and to help them understand that their problem is not unique. In addition to the therapy, sometimes they are referred to a nutritionist who helps them design a weight management program as one step in beginning to regain control of their lives. Antidepressant drugs are sometimes prescribed for people with eating disorders.

You may wish to consider doing some educational programming (e.g., speakers, displays) in this area. Pamphlets and other materials should be made available in conspicuous places. If you have suspicions about a person who exhibits symptoms of bulimia, talk to your hall director about it. Together the two of you may be able to design a strategy for helping this resident receive help from the counseling center.

ANOREXIA NERVOSA

Anorexia nervosa is an eating disorder that may include bulimic symptoms. Again, it is a problem that almost exclusively affects women. Like bulimia, anorexia nervosa stems from a need for love and a belief that being thin—sexually attractive, as defined by media—will result in being loved. Low self-esteem issues, with an emphasis on approval from others as the determinant of self-worth, characterizes this illness. One of the primary ways it differs from bulimia is that anorexia nervosa is a form of suicidal behavior. It shares with the disease of alcoholism the desire to die, the rejection of love, and a distorted sense of reality.

Anorexics actually develop a fear of food. They come to believe that if they eat any food at all they will put on weight. If they do eat anything, they are likely to force themselves to regurgitate. Anorexia nervosa is sometimes seen in women who have lost a considerable amount of weight through crash dieting, prolonged fasting, and other hazardous weight-reduction methods. Even when anorexics become so thin that they are emaciated, their perceptions of themselves are that they are still too heavy. Anorexics never believe they are thin enough. They believe that once they reach ideal thinness they will suddenly be loved by everyone. If this illness is left unattended, anorexics will die from malnutrition. They sometimes require hospitalization and force-feeding. Even this is not always enough to save their lives.

Again, the anorexic shares many of the same characteristics as the bulimic. Victims of this illness are usually White and from a middle- to upper-class family background. They have low self-esteem, high need for approval from others, an idealized concept of romance, and an intense desire to be loved, which they believe can be realized by becoming thin.

You can identify the anorexic in some of the same ways you identify the bulimic. In addition, you can also watch for fainting spells, nutritional disease problems, obsessive exercise habits, and continual illnesses. The anorexic person usually is extremely thin, has an unhealthy look, continues to say she is overweight, and turns down food or consumes minute portions of selected foods.

Anorexics require psychotherapy and medical health care. Because they want to die and their judgment is blurred, they are difficult to work with. They are unwilling, obstinate, uncooperative, and disbelieving. They reject help. For these reasons, victims of this illness often do not receive treatment until the disease is in its advanced stages. Sometimes the person has to be in a life-threatening situation, such as unconsciousness, to begin to get needed health care. A person who is anorexic should be viewed as suicidal and in immediate need of psychological care. However, a psychotherapist may have little or no effect on the person until the person is in an immediate life-threatening situation or is in a situation in which therapy is offered as the only alternative, as might be found in a court-ordered commitment.

REVIEW

1. What are three common characteristics of people with bulimia and anorexia nervosa?

2. What are three of the complications associated with bulimia?

3. Name one difference between anorexia and bulimia?

4. What are three signs that may identify someone with bulimia or anorexia?

5. What is the goal for RAs working with students with these disorders?

College aged female, white, middle class, low self-esteem, need to please parents

lowered potassium, disrupts blood sugar and insulin levels, removes mucus membranes from esophagus

to have the student see a counselor

APPLICATIONS

YOU CAN NEVER BE TOO THIN

Nina was a sophomore at Prestigious University. She studied hard in high school, determined to earn the high marks required for entrance to PU. Although her parents could afford to pay her way, she earned a full academic scholarship. Despite her achievements, Nina usually walked with her head down.

Nina's RA hardly ever saw Nina at the cafeteria, and when she invited Nina to join her for dinner, Nina always said, "Don't tempt me." On the rare occasions Nina's RA had seen her eat, it was only from the salad bar in the cafeteria. However, Nina and her RA often ran into each other at the campus fitness center. Nina was usually on a treadmill reading a fashion magazine, or riding a stationary bicycle reading a romance novel.

One day, Nina's roommate told their RA that Nina had fainted that morning and so was staying in bed for the day. The RA stopped by their room that afternoon to see how Nina was feeling and was surprised to see her doing leg exercises while she brushed her teeth. When the RA asked about it, Nina explained to her the number of calories that could be burned just by doing a few exercises throughout the day. Perplexed, Nina's RA asked why she was so concerned about calories, noting that under those loose clothes, Nina seemed to be fairly slender. The loose clothes, Nina told her, were to help disguise her weight problem.

WHAT WOULD YOU DO?

1. What are the indicators that Nina may be bulimic or anorexic?
2. What would you say to her if you were her RA?
3. Who should the RA speak to about this? Does she have enough information to contact her hall director?

ALCOHOL ABUSE

©1998 PHOTODISK, INC.

The consumption of alcohol has become as much a part of college life as football. It has been part of the collegiate experience since the 1800s, when whiskey and ale played such an important part in collegiate life that some institutions, such as Yale University, appointed a full-time faculty member as an ale tester. Drinking continued at most colleges and universities through World War II, even though most institutions had developed policies prohibiting its con-

sumption on campus. After World War II, most institutions still prohibited drinking on campus—which meant in the residence halls or at football games—but some authorities extended approval for students who were over 21 or granted some form of tacit approval for students who had seen military service. This approval, however, usually was more a lack of policy enforcement rather than a change in written regulations. Only after 18 was accepted as the age of majority by most states did colleges and universities begin to officially permit the use of alcohol on campuses.

In 1986 and 1987 all states changed their alcohol consumption laws to permit only people 21 years old or older to possess or consume alcohol. Because some states maintained a drinking age of 21 and others a drinking age of 18, young adults between 18 and 21 would often drive to neighboring states that had younger drinking ages. They would then drive home while intoxicated, created a danger for public safety. The U.S. Congress passed a law making the receipt of federal highway funds contingent on having a state drinking age of not less than 21. The millions of dollars states would lose prompted each state to change its drinking age to 21.

Although the law has changed, 76 to 92 percent of all college students drink alcohol, if only occasionally. It is the drug of choice among college students as well as the rest of the American population. In fact, it is the most heavily used drug in America today—even more so than aspirin.

SHORT-TERM EFFECTS OF ALCOHOL

Alcohol is such an integral part of American society that many people overlook that it is a drug, that its misuse can kill, and that it is the cause of a serious disease. Many people believe that alcohol is a stimulant, because its moderate use increases the heart rate, slightly dilates blood vessels, increases appetite, stimulates the output of urine, slightly lowers blood temperature, anesthetizes higher-order nerve centers in the brain, and provides energy. Part of this energy surge results from the calories in alcohol—approximately 100 per ounce.

Although the moderate use of alcohol appears to have a simulating effect on the body, alcohol is actually a depressant that affects some of the functions of the central nervous system. The degree of depression is related to the concentration

of alcohol in the blood. Because the liver continually oxidizes the alcohol, and because some alcohol is lost through perspiration, the actual concentration of alcohol in the body varies. The rate and type of alcohol ingested also affects the percentage of alcohol in the blood.

Alcohol is absorbed directly into the bloodstream through the stomach walls and the small intestine, so its effects are felt rapidly. If there are other substances in the stomach, the rate of absorption is slowed. Also, some alcoholic beverages, such as beer and wine, contain nonalcoholic substances that slow the absorption rate. As the concentration of alcohol increases, more of the central nervous system is anesthetized. Alcohol depresses brain functions in the following stages:

1. When the concentration of alcohol in the blood is less than 0.1 percent, a person feels relaxed, may have some difficulty solving complex problems, and may become talkative, very active, or aggressive. In some states, driving with a blood-alcohol level of 0.08 is illegal.

2. When the blood-alcohol level is between 0.1 and 0.2 percent, the person begins to lose motor-skill coordination. Reaction time is impaired, and judgment and coordination are lessened. Driving at this level of intoxication is very dangerous and illegal in all states (although no one should drive after drinking—even after only one drink).

3. When the blood-alcohol level is between 0.2 and 0.3 percent, the person experiences severe impairment of motor skills and general confusion and disorientation. Equilibrium is also affected. As the blood-alcohol level nears 0.3 percent, the drinker may accidentally injure himself or herself by falling down or stumbling about.

4. At 0.3 percent and above, people usually pass out.

5. If someone is able to consume enough alcohol to reach a blood-alcohol level of 0.4 percent

INFLUENCE OF ALCOHOL ON BEHAVIOR

The following chart shows the general relation between blood-alcohol levels and behavior for a 155-pound moderate drinker who rapidly consumes 90-proof whiskey on an empty stomach.

Quantity	Percent Blood-Alcohol Level	Effect
3 oz.	0.05	sedation and tranquility
6 oz.	0.1	lack of coordination
12 oz.	0.2	obvious intoxication
15 oz.	0.3	unconsciousness
30 oz.	0.5+	death likely

without passing out, coma or death is possible. Drinking games involving downing shots of alcohol one after another in a short period of time can produce this state.

A number of factors affect a person's responses to using alcohol. These can be divided into two major categories—psychological and physiological. The following factors affect the physiological reaction to alcohol:[1]

• **Speed of consumption.** Normally a person can consume one-half ounce of pure alcohol, or what might be considered one shot of whiskey, per hour with moderate effect. The liver can oxidize approximately this much alcohol per hour. Lingering over a drink or sipping a drink is a good way to minimize the concentration of alcohol in the bloodstream.

• **Body weight.** The greater a person's weight (muscle tissue, not fat), the faster his or her body can metabolize alcohol.

• **Type of beverage consumed.** Pure grain alcohol (e.g., vodka, whiskey, gin) has the most immediate and dramatic effect. Practically 20 percent of the alcohol is absorbed immediately by the stomach, and the other 80 percent is absorbed by the time it reaches the small intestine. Other

beverages such as beer and wine have the same effects; however, the rate at which the person becomes intoxicated is lessened because of other substances contained in the beverages.

• **Whether the stomach is full or empty.** If the person is eating and drinking or has recently eaten a large meal, the absorption of alcohol into the system is slowed. Drinking after a meal or drinking in conjunction with any type of food are ways to slow the absorption of alcohol into the system—and thus remain more sober.

Some psychological factors that influence a person's reaction to alcohol include:

• **Why a person is drinking.** Drinking for the purpose of getting drunk, depression, or a desire to celebrate will affect how alcohol influences the person.

• **Drinking history.** A person who drinks regularly develops a tolerance to alcohol. An experienced drinker reacts differently to the same amount of alcohol than an inexperienced drinker of the same weight and similar physiological condition. This tolerance means that the person must increase the amount of alcohol consumed to feel the same effect. Although some of this tolerance is physiological, for most people their impairment occurs at approximately the same blood-alcohol levels, but their perception of intoxication is decreased.

- **Body chemistry.** Each person has a unique body chemistry that in part determines how alcohol affects him or her. Body chemistry is related to the psychological mood or state of the individual. The effects of body chemistry are most apparent in what is known as the *dumping syndrome.* This refers to how rapidly the stomach empties into the small intestine. The rate at which the stomach empties can be slowed or increased by psychological conditions such as anger, fear, stress, euphoria, state of relaxation, and other factors. This is why a tired or upset person is more susceptible to the influence of alcohol.

- **Family history.** Children of alcoholics almost always have a higher tolerance for alcohol than people without this family history. They are also at greater risk for addiction. Family history and genetic predisposition for alcohol tolerance affect a person's reaction to alcohol and his or her ability to control its use.

- **Drinking environment.** Certain social situations encourage misuse of alcohol. If, for example, someone is comfortably sitting with a friend and alcohol is used as an adjunct to this activity, the impact of the alcohol will probably be less than if that person were drinking in a bar, at a party, or during a "happy hour" in what might be a stressful situation. Other people's expectations of how much a person has drunk or should drink, or how that person should act, also influence behavior.

Sobering Up

Once alcohol has been ingested, the body must metabolize it to enable the drinker to sober up. This process takes place primarily in the liver, although 2 to 5 percent of the alcohol ingested is excreted through the urine, breath, and perspiration. The liver turns the alcohol into acetaldehyde, then into acetate, and into a variety of other compounds. Finally the body oxidizes the alcohol completely into carbon dioxide and water. The rate of metabolism is affected by a variety of factors, including body chemistry, but generally the liver can oxidize approximately seven grams of pure alcohol per hour.

At this rate, it takes approximately one hour to sober up for each alcoholic drink ingested. Coffee, oxygen, cold showers, and other home remedies have little or no effect on the rate at which a person sobers up. A moderate amount of exercise, however, increases the metabolic rate and thus aids the sobering up process, although it has a minimal effect on behavior and can be dangerous if the person is very intoxicated.

Hangovers

Often the result of consuming too much alcohol is a hangover the next morning. Scientists are not certain what causes a hangover. Some researchers have hypothesized that it is caused by vitamin deficiencies, by oils in the alcoholic beverage, or by dehydration; however, no conclusive findings support these or other theories. The only known way to cure a hangover is time, bed rest, and solid food when possible. Aspirin can be used to ease the pain, but will not prevent or cure a hangover. Other home remedies, such as drinking a foul-tasting concoction of tomato juice, raw eggs, and hot peppers; consuming "a hair of the dog that bit you" (some of the same type of liquor that got you intoxicated in the first place); vitamins; tranquilizers; oxygen; or exercise do not work.

Alcohol Used with Other Drugs

Alcohol reacts with other drugs. One of the most dangerous effects of alcohol is when it is mixed with depressants or "downers." This combination causes a synergistic effect; in other words, if a person mixes one beer with a depressant drug, the combined effect will be greater than the individual effects of either drug when consumed alone. The effect could be the same as having consumed three or four beers. Combining alcohol with depressants can so rapidly intoxicate a person or shock the system that it can cause a coma or even death.

The second way that alcohol reacts with other drugs is that it *potentiates* them. This means that it can accelerate or change the effect of the drug. Such drugs as antihistamines, antihypertensive agents, anticoagulants, anticonvulsants, antidepressants, and diuretics, among others, are changed when a person ingests them with alcohol. Mixing alcohol with these drugs can cause negative side-effects or so interfere with the medicine that the person's life could be in danger.

PROBLEMS ASSOCIATED WITH ALCOHOL ABUSE

Between 53 and 84 percent of college students get drunk at least once a year, and between 26 and 48 percent get drunk at least once a month.[2] The negative consequences of alcohol misuse are considerable. A clear relationship exists between alcohol use and diminished academic performance. More frequent involvement with alcohol is accompanied by lower grades. In one study researchers found that students who consumed an average of 10.87 drinks per week had grade point averages in the D or F range. Students who drank an average of 6.77 drinks per week averaged a C grade. Students who drank 4.95 drinks per week averaged B grades, and those who averaged 3.45 or less drinks per week averaged A grades. These correlations do not necessarily indicate a causal relationship.[3]

Educators are concerned with the misuse of alcohol in part because of the behavior associated with it. The top 10 negative consequences of alcohol misuse that students reported over a one-year period were:

1. had a hangover (63 percent)
2. became nauseated or vomited (40.9 percent)
3. later regretted actions (39.3 percent)
4. drove while intoxicated (36 percent)
5. got into an argument or fight (33.2 percent)
6. missed a class (30.4 percent)
7. were criticized for drinking habits (29 percent)
8. experienced memory loss (28 percent)
9. performed poorly on a test (23.2 percent)
10. had a hangover six or more times (22 percent)[4]

It comes as no surprise to any RA that behavior which results in damage to residence halls, sexual assault, and other disruptions also accompanies the misuse of alcohol.

Nationally, approximately 27 percent of people between 18 and 20 experience some problem (frequent intoxication; psychological dependence; physical dependence; or problems with friends, relatives, and employers) as a result of drinking. The next highest frequency of problems related to drinking was for people 21 to 24 years of age, among whom approximately 18 percent experienced some problem related to drinking.[5]

Binge Drinking

One of the more serious issues associated with college drinking is the frequency with which students binge drink. This form of drinking is defined as four or more consecutive drinks at one sitting for women and five or more drinks for men. A recent study revealed that 50 percent of college men and 40 percent of college women binge drink. Some social organizations, such as fraternities, have a higher percentage of binge drinkers. Whether students who overconsume enter fraternities, the fraternity encourages behavior, or some combination of both, is unclear.[6]

Binge drinking is seen predominantly with American college students at institutions in the United States. Students in other countries, such as Germany and England, drink—sometimes to excess—but usually with a greater degree of moderation and they seldom binge for the purpose of getting drunk.

Deadly Drinking Games

Perhaps the most serious and frightening abuse of alcohol occurs when a person ingests enough alcohol to kill himself or herself. This has happened at a number of colleges. Other students have come near to death from ingesting too much alcohol or have developed acute alcohol toxicity. An untold number of injuries and near-fatal accidents have occurred that are attributable to the misuse of alcohol.

Drinking games that require a participant to consume large quantities of alcohol in a short period of time were the cause of most of these incidents. The body's natural way of ensuring that the person does not continue to drink is to pass out. Vomiting is another way the body attempts to expel alcohol as a person reaches a critical level of alcohol poisoning. In these drinking games, the body does not have time to employ these tactics before the alcohol in the system reaches a critical level.

CAUSES OF ALCOHOL ABUSE IN COLLEGE

People abuse alcohol for many reasons; depression, celebrations, and alcoholism are only a few. College, however, presents a special set of demands during a period in which the individual is struggling with the transition to adulthood. There are four major explanations, other than chronic alcoholism, why so many students are influenced to abuse alcohol in college.

Sex Roles

Drinking seems important for students during college because they are in the midst of struggling with their own identity, emulating behavior that confirms for themselves and others their appropriate sex role. The heavy use of alcohol is part of the traditional sex role assigned to men.[7] Men use alcohol more often than women and in greater quantities. Wilsnack and Wilsnack explained it this way: "Masculine roles may encourage boys to drink: by selectively exposing them to situations in which unrestricted drinking is normally expected, by making it useful to drink as a means of showing adult manliness, and by creating internal needs and conflicts which drinking can assuage. . . . It is important to note also that traditional masculinity not only encourages drinking, but in contrast to traditional femininity, apparently does not impose any specific inhibitions on drinking behavior."[8]

The traditional drinking role for women has been one of moderation or abstinence, but in recent years drinking among women has increased sharply.[9] A study of the drinking behavior of college women revealed that the heavier use of alcohol was related to a rejection of the traditional feminine role in favor of the more contemporary role of a "liberated woman."[10] As Wilsnack and Wilsnack summarized, "Traditional masculine and feminine roles may influence drinking behavior in four ways: by creating opportunities to drink, by creating normative obligations to drink (or not to drink), by creating needs and desires to drink, and by creating symbolic uses for drinking."[11]

Peer-Group Influences

The influence of peers is closely associated with the fulfillment of students' perceptions of appropriate sex roles. New freshmen who come to live in the residence hall, like most students, want to be accepted by the other members of the living unit. To do this, freshmen emulate behavior they believe can gain them the acceptance of others or that they believe is expected of them.

Take the traditional male sex role as an example. A young man may consume a large quantity of alcohol to demonstrate to his peers that he is manly. His peers will likely respond by reinforcing the excessive use of alcohol. As the student's peers continue this reinforcement through laughter, joking, and often nicknames that reflect a past drinking episode, the student may continue or even increase his abuse of alcohol. Once a certain kind of drinking behavior becomes associated with the student, his reputation within the group can depend on that behavior.

As people mature, they become less dependent on outside approval; the importance of peer-group recognition diminishes. Interests broaden and role expectations change as students grow older. Behavior that was once socially acceptable eventually draws social disapproval and is usually curtailed.

Unfortunately for the RA, this need for peer approval is strongest during the first year or two of college—the years when the average student is most likely to be drinking the heaviest and most likely to be living in a residence hall.

The Search for the College Experience

Movies, books, television, and stories from friends and relatives about the wild and crazy things they did in college all contribute to a new student's expectations about college. Many drinking behaviors are built on myths about the college experience. Students may enter college with the expectation that college is one of those unique experiences where freedom abounds. These students often involve themselves in dangerous or irresponsible acts for the assumed benefit of such experiences or for their storytelling value. Sit with a group of students telling stories about their college experiences and count how many times the stories include the phrases, "I was so drunk that . . ." or "I was so high that . . ." The experiences that many students relate fulfill their preconceived ideas about college life and help to perpetuate the myths about it.

Maturity

Freudian psychological theory proposes that three basic spheres govern the psychological composition of the individual: the *id,* which is the base of the primitive instincts of every individual; the *ego,* which constitutes the reasoning abilities of the individual; and the *superego,* which comprises the ethical and moral principles of people in society. When a person consumes alcohol, the higher-order nerve centers in the brain are anesthetized. In the Freudian model, this means that the superego and the ego are suppressed, and the more primitive instincts of the id begin to emerge. The longer a person has lived with social mores, expectations, and standards, the longer it takes to suppress these entrenched patterns of behavior. In short, a person's experience in life makes him or her somewhat more inhibited. Students who are 18 to 24 simply have not lived with these expectations as long as people who are older.

Alcohol affects younger people more profoundly because they have less experience with the superego and, consequently, less restraint. They are already less inhibited, and the excessive use of alcohol allows the id to emerge.

Other Reasons

Students may choose to drink to excess for other reasons as well. When students are asked why they consumed more alcohol than they should have, the most common response is, "I didn't realize I was drinking that much." Other common reasons that students give for drinking too much are that they like the taste, like the effect that it gives them, or like to get high occasionally.

Whatever the reason, the person who drinks bears the obligation to drink responsibly.

IDENTIFYING THE PROBLEM DRINKER

During the traditional college years (ages 18 to 24) a problem drinker is difficult to distinguish from other drinkers. Students this age are among the heaviest drinkers in the United States. During this period, they probably drink more than at any other time in their lives. Most of these people become moderate and reasonable drinkers. However, national statistics show that approximately 20 percent of people who graduate from college eventually become alcoholics. This rate is higher than the rate among noncollege graduates. The overwhelming majority of college students will admit to knowing someone currently in college who has a drinking problem.

During your time as an RA you will likely encounter one or more students who have a problem with alcohol. Some of these students may be alcoholics, meaning that they suffer from alcoholism. *Alcoholism* can be defined as "a chronic disease, or disorder of behavior, characterized by the repeated drinking of alcoholic beverages to an extent that exceeds customary dietary use or ordinary compliance with the social drinking customs of the community, and which interferes with the drinker's health, interpersonal relations, or economic functions."[12]

Another way of defining alcoholism is through the behavior of the alcoholic. Generally, an alcoholic (1) loses control of the amounts of alcohol consumed; (2) in some way damages himself or herself psychologically, emotionally, physically, economically, or in other ways; (3) comes to rely on alcohol as a panacea for all ills, turning to it during any time of stress or discomfort. Note that heavy drinking does not necessarily denote alcoholism.

As an RA, you can watch for these signs in students that may indicate a drinking problem:

- **Blackouts.** This is distinct from passing out in that the drinkers do not lose consciousness. Blackouts occur when people experience memory loss due to drinking. During the blackout period they appear drunk but otherwise normal, conscious, and functioning; however, conversations and events simply are not being recorded in their memory. Some alcoholics black out for several days. People in the first stages of alcoholism may experience these blackouts for shorter periods of time—like one evening.

- **A change in drinking behavior.** Students begin drinking more often or continually, drinking in the mornings or early afternoons, or on a regular basis. They may also find that each time they begin drinking, they drink until passing out. Either an increased frequency in the consumption of alcohol or the increased use of alcohol in a drinking episode is an indication of possible alcoholism.

- **Avoidance.** People who avoid talking about their drinking behavior or are ashamed of discussing it probably have a problem with drinking. Hiding liquor in their rooms, carrying liquor to classes, and drinking before or between classes are signs of a drinking problem.

- **Chronic hangovers.** People who find that they are sick almost every morning because of drinking have a drinking problem.

- **Other indicators of problem drinking.** These include frequent drinking to intoxication; frequent blackouts; high tolerance for alcohol; frequent hangovers; frequent vomiting and passing out; behavior problems (i.e., assaults, property damage, driving while intoxicated, getting hurt, and aggressive responses); Jekyll/Hyde personality change when intoxicated; missing classes or work; becoming socially withdrawn or isolated; drop in academic performance; self-concern about possible alcoholism; other people expressing concern; and relationship problems related to alcohol misuse.

ADDRESSING ALCOHOL PROBLEMS

If you believe someone has a drinking problem, confront the student with the behavior you have observed. Express care and concern in a nonjudgmental way. Do not accuse the person of having a drinking problem or of being an alcoholic. He or she will be defensive, deny your evaluation, and possibly react negatively. You are not in a position to make this type of diagnosis. What you can and should do is discuss what you have observed with the person in a one-to-one dialogue.

If you have noticed the person staying in his or her room and drinking instead of attending classes, this behavior could be pointed out. You might say something like, "I have noticed that for the past few days you have not been attending class and have been drinking all day. Do you find this is creating a problem for you?" Questions like this can promote a helping relationship.

Very possibly, the first time you bring this behavior to the person's attention, he or she will not respond. At this point, if you are not willing to help, then you may need to discuss alternatives with your hall director. If you are willing to help, do not give up. When you notice other or similar behavior, bring it to the person's attention again.

In this type of encounter with a student who has a serious drinking problem, your objective is to help the student seek assistance from a professional counselor. This is not an easy task. Students may not recognize that they need assistance and are likely to be in a stage of denial. Talk with someone in your college counseling center or with a residence life staff person who can give you some assistance in making a referral. Working with a person who has a problem with alcohol requires specialized training that should be available through your college counseling center. In addition, many colleges have support groups for students who have problems with alcohol. Often, chapters of Alcoholics Anonymous meet on college campuses and offer an alternative to students who prefer to work with an association not directly connected with their college or university.

LOW-RISK DRINKING

Low-risk drinking does not harm the individual, other persons, or their property. This level of alcohol intake is appropriate to the social situation and is used to enhance the social experience. You can provide guidelines and support students' efforts at low-risk drinking behavior that will help them avoid the harmful effects of overindulgence.

Party-Planning Suggestions

Floor parties and similar gatherings are important for socializing. New students coming to the institution need to share some common experiences, and planning and attending a party together can be one of these experiences. These gatherings aid students in developing social and organizational skills and in gaining a better understanding of themselves in social situations. Of course, parties also provide an acceptable vehicle for meeting new people and establishing social relationships.

Institutions enforce alcohol consumption policies in various ways. Some institutions prohibit the possession or consumption of alcohol at all institutional social events, including parties in the residence halls. Other institutions permit the consumption of alcohol by those 21 years old or older, either by students bringing their own beverages to parties or by a system of students showing their student ID card to prove they are of legal age to drink. Unless you can be reasonably certain that the people who will attend a party are of legal age—and you can verify this—it is best not to include alcohol at a party in the residence halls.

Whatever policy your institution has adopted, parties where alcohol is served—whether in apartments off campus, fraternity houses, or in rented

GUIDELINES FOR LOW-RISK DRINKING

- Use alcohol as an adjunct to other activities and not as the primary focus of any particular activity.
- View alcohol as a beverage and not as a means to achieve a desired mood state.
- Avoid drinking games and other contests involving the rapid consumption of alcohol.
- Pace drinks to consume approximately one per hour.
- Do not use alcohol to impair social relationships or to degrade or humiliate a person.
- Never use alcohol in conjunction with other drugs.
- Know your limits.
- Plan ahead of time how many drinks you intend to have.
- Never consume more than three alcoholic drinks in any one evening.
- Have a drink only when you truly want one.
- Eat something while you are drinking.
- Be careful if you consume unfamiliar drinks.
- Use mixers with your drinks.
- While you drink, occasionally switch to a nonalcoholic beverage, like plain soda or tonic water.

party facilities off campus—are part of the normal social experience of most college students. Students need to have some information on how to host parties where alcohol is served.

ALCOHOL EDUCATION PROGRAMMING

Most universities have programs to help students learn about the issues and problems surrounding drinking. These programs have resulted from an increased concern for the behavior of abusive drinkers, the increased awareness of alcoholism, and the blatant abuses of alcohol visible on college campuses. Although most students decide prior to college whether or not they will drink alcohol, drinking patterns are established during the college years. Some successful programs have focused on identifying problem drinkers early and offering support and information to students with

alcoholic parents. The most successful programs have focused on helping students of legal age who choose to drink to do so in a manner that does not harm themselves, other people, or property.

Simply providing students with information about drinking does little to encourage them to change their attitudes about drinking or change the drinking behavior itself. A variety of approaches are required to help students change these attitudes. Although having only one alcohol education program is better than not having any at all, one program alone will not be effective. You should develop a continuing program of information, value-oriented discussions, role modeling, and opportunities for students to experience the controlled use of alcohol.

The potent peer environment in the residence hall plays a critical role in determining the standards of drinking behavior. If that standard encourages the overconsumption of alcohol, chances are, as the RA, you will spend a disproportionate

Ensuring that Alcohol Remains an Adjunct to and Not the Focus of a Party

- **Serve an alternative beverage.** Students not drinking alcohol should be made to feel comfortable at the gathering. An alternative beverage gives everyone a choice, such as nonalcoholic punches kept in closed containers. Sometimes inconsiderate people spike the nonalcoholic punch, thinking such a trick is funny or cute. Some people choose not to drink because they have a problem with alcohol, either medical or personal, and their rights must be protected. Alcohol added to a supposedly nonalcoholic punch may produce an unforeseen drug reaction that could result in convulsions or shock. Giving alcohol to someone who doesn't want it should be viewed with the same disdain as slipping somebody any other drug.

- **Serve snacks.** A party is more than drinking. Small amounts of alcohol stimulate the appetite, and people will be hungry when they begin drinking. Simple, inexpensive snacks will satisfy this hunger and slow the absorption rate of alcohol. However, salty foods may increase alcohol consumption.

- **Use a bartender at large parties.** A bartender can control the flow of alcohol. He or she will also help prevent drinking contests and other disruptions that may occur at the party.

- **Set a cut-off time for the party.** Make sure that you actually stop the party at that time. This allows people to plan ahead and discourages people from staying around, drinking into the early hours of the morning.

- **Avoid using kegs.** The use of kegs of beer encourages high-risk drinking behavior. Too often people feel they must empty a keg once it is tapped, claiming that they hate to see the beer go to waste. In some ways, it becomes a contest to empty the flowing fountain of beer. The best way to avoid this whole situation is to not use kegs; have people bring their own beverages.

- **Discourage people from forcing drinks on others.** Talk to the residents on your floor and help them understand that this practice is immature and often obnoxious.

- **Provide some form of entertainment.** If the party is small, conversation may be sufficient entertainment. If, however, it is to be a large gathering, dancing or some other form of party entertainment should be planned. If the main focus of the party is on dancing, people will be less inclined to focus on the consumption of alcohol.

- **Use a guest list for large parties.** Appoint one or two people who are capable of making sensible decisions to monitor the flow of guests into the party. These persons should inform uninvited guests that they are not welcome at the party. You can have some control over situations arising between people you know, but outsiders whom you do not know and with whom you have no personal relationship can present difficulties. If the party becomes an open public gathering, you put yourself in the difficult position of dealing with irresponsible behavior by strangers. This situation can lead to very negative and embarrassing confrontations. It is easier to prevent such problems than to confront them. A sign at the door saying "Invited Guests Only" helps to discourage roving bands of social marauders who search out parties—sometimes for the purpose of creating trouble.

amount of your time confronting behavioral problems created by alcohol abuse. However, if you can discourage drinking in the residence halls by the enforcement of college policy, and provide information about low-risk drinking to those who drink at parties off campus, you are likely to spare yourself a host of behavior problems that accompany the misuse of alcohol.

REVIEW

Indicate whether each of the following statements is true or false.

1. A cold shower and a cup of black coffee will help a person sober up faster.

2. One beer contains as much alcohol as a jigger (1 = 4 oz.) of 80-proof whiskey.

3. The use of alcohol increases sexual ability.

4. A person will get intoxicated faster by switching drinks rather than by taking the same amount of alcohol in only one form, such as scotch.

5. About 80 percent of college students use alcohol regularly.

6. There is a higher percentage of students using alcohol today than there was ten years ago.

7. The best way to handle someone who is drunk is to be assertive and understanding.

8. The majority of serious behavioral infractions in residence halls are related to behavior resulting from an excessive use of alcohol.

9. A student with a drinking problem should be held accountable for his or her actions and made to suffer any consequences.

10. Most students, by the time they reach college, have made a decision about whether or not to drink.

11. Eating some butter or drinking a glass of milk will coat your stomach and enable you to drink more.

12. Having several good drinks before you go to sleep will insure a deep restful sleep.

13. Vitamins and/or "the hair of the dog" (small quantity of the alcoholic beverage that was used to become intoxicated) will help a hangover.

14. Drinking alcohol will kill brain cells.

15. Approximately one-third of the students on your floor will have some problems associated with drinking during the coming academic year.

16. You can die from drinking too much alcohol.

17. Drinking alcohol in moderate amounts, for most people, does the body little permanent harm.

18. Blackouts are common after a few drinks.

APPLICATIONS

LET THE GOOD TIMES ROLL

Stacy is 21 years old and is the oldest woman on the floor. She is a sophomore and has a single room. Recently she joined a "little sister" group affiliated with one of the campus fraternities. Since then her social life has become much more active. At least four nights a week she is out at one of the college bars or at some party off campus. Several times the RA has seen her come in late at night staggering drunk. One night the RA found her in the restroom vomiting and drunk, and another night the RA on duty called to ask her to help Stacy to her room because she was too drunk to get there herself. Other residence have told the RA that Stacy often spends the night away from the residence hall.

The hall director received a call from the dean of students office reporting that Stacy has been missing classes. The hall director asked the RA to talk with Stacy about missing classes. The RA found Stacy in her room watching television and drinking something the RA suspected was alcohol. She asked Stacy about her classes and told Stacy that she was concerned about her drinking and her very active social life. Stacy's reaction was unexpected. She became angry and told the RA to mind her own business. She told the RA she would drink as much as she wanted when she wanted, and she would sleep with whomever she wanted and when she wanted. She told the RA to leave her alone and get out of her room.

WHAT WOULD YOU DO?

1. What, if anything, can be done to help Stacy?
2. What is your institution's policy about the possession and consumption of alcohol in the residence hall? Do you agree with it? Why or why not? If you do not agree with it, what justification would you give to your residents for enforcing the policy?
3. Stacy believes she has the right to live her life the way she wants, and no one has the right to interfere with her. Do you agree or disagree with Stacy? Why or why not?
4. What signs has Stacy given which indicate that she is experiencing a problem with alcohol?
5. Speculate on some of the reasons for Stacy getting so angry when the RA expressed concern about her behavior.

CHAPTER FOURTEEN

DRUG ABUSE

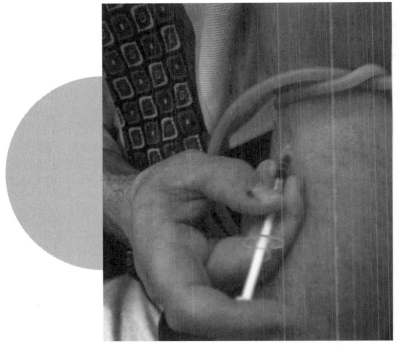

©1998 PHOTODISK, INC.

Drug abuse has a long history in the United States, dating back to morphine addiction among soldiers in the Civil War, the use of codeine in patent medicines throughout the 1800s, and the use of amphetamines (speed) by American and Japanese pilots during World War II. Opium and heroin addiction in the United States was not uncommon in the early 1990s. During the 1960s, many students tried illegal drugs. This was a period of social change that gave rise to a countercultural youth movement, and experimentation with drugs was viewed as a way of expanding one's mind and enhancing one's abilities. Drugs became identified with a process of self-discovery and as a way of making a statement in opposition to the established social/governmental system that supported the war in Vietnam.

DRUG ENFORCEMENT

As more people began experimenting with drugs in the hope of expanding their minds or identifying with the countercultural movement of that decade, the federal government moved to restrict the use of these new substances through increased drug enforcement and more stringent laws. When popular drugs became more difficult to obtain, street varieties or substitutes were developed to take their place. The result of this has been a variety of different substances sold on the streets as something that they are not. Suppliers of these drugs unscrupulously "cut" or dilute the original drug with other substances, creating street varieties that in many cases are very dangerous. As the drug supply in the 1960s increased to meet the demand, possession and use of certain drugs became socially acceptable in some young-adult communities and, within certain groups, was a status symbol. People who were able to supply their friends with certain drugs were "cool." It became acceptable to use drugs at parties with almost the same freedom that one used alcohol. Drugs became readily available among college students, and soon thereafter, in the high schools and grade schools. The alarm that people felt over the visible sign of change within the American culture helped foster the emphasis on more closely monitored distribution of drugs, enforcement of drug laws, and research into drugs.

The predominant use of drugs among college students falls into four major categories: cannabis (marijuana and related substances), stimulants, depressants, and psychedelics. Narcotics, such as heroin and morphine, though experimentally used by some college students in the 1960s, never gained popularity. Evidence suggests that more students are now experimenting with heroin. Apparently, some people in the fashion industry have popularized the strung-out druggy look—very strange! Some musicians popular among older adolescents and young adults are also using this drug, which may contribute to the current interest. The greatest change has been the increase in the use of cocaine and LSD among college students. Marijuana, amphetamines, and barbiturates are still in use by college students.

From a purely physiological perspective, it is inadvisable for a person to ingest substances that alter the body chemistry without a clear understanding of the ramifications of using such substances. Evidence clearly indicates that the introduction of any drug, unless prescribed for a specific medical purpose by a qualified medical expert, creates an effect that may be harmful to the body. Drugs are not only physically harmful, but they also may present social adjustment problems. Students who are experimenting with drugs or who use drugs for recreational purposes inhibit their ability to perform at their optimum level of achievement. All drugs have negative side effects.

REFERENCE SECTION ON DRUGS

This section contains information about drugs that are being or have been used among college students. It includes a brief discussion about each but is not intended to be definitive nor to include all drugs that may be available. Pharmacological desk reference guides are available to give more in-depth descriptions than are provided here.

Cannabis

Marijuana. Marijuana is generally classified as a mind-altering drug with a low potential for overdose. Although marijuana is generally believed to have no physical addictive potential, it clearly has addicting properties and is habituating—meaning that it becomes emotionally or psychologically addictive. Marijuana is consumed by either smoking it or ingesting it, usually through some food substance. A person under the influence of marijuana generally exhibits dilated pupils, impaired coordination, inappropriate laughter and rambling speech, increased appetite, and distorted sense of time or space. If the drug is used heavily over a prolonged period, fatigue and psychosis may result.

More has been written about marijuana than any other drug in the past 20 years. The country has moved from long prison terms for possession of marijuana during the early 1960s, to laws in the late 1970s that made possession a misdemeanor with fines as low as five dollars. Most of the marijuana now sold in the United States is of relatively high potency. It is as much as 600 percent more potent than that available in the 1960s and 1970s.

Marijuana is used primarily among people ages 18 to 25, with a clear trend toward use in the younger ages. In this age group, approximately 60 percent of college students report having used marijuana at least once. There is no significant evidence of any mental injuries from the moderate use of this drug, and there is no correlation between the use of marijuana and the need to advance to drugs of stronger potency. Some researchers have described it as a gateway drug—meaning that once students choose to use any drug, it becomes easier for them to justify use of and experimentation with other drugs.

Marijuana is not harmless. Tetrahydrocannabinol (THC) is the active chemical in marijuana, and it accumulates in body fat. Substances stored in body fat are not eliminated quickly. Continued use of marijuana increases the level of this substance in the body fat.

Marijuana use is also associated with increased lung and breast cancer. Smokers of marijuana are about seven times more likely to develop cancer than nonmarijuana smokers. Part of this has to do with how marijuana is smoked—inhaled and held in the lungs. Some sources have estimated that 1 year of heavy marijuana smoking can be as damaging as 20 years of heavy cigarette smoking. Use of marijuana also has been linked to damage to the immune system, increased male impotence, reduction in sperm-count levels, and reduction in motivation. Long-term use of marijuana may result in increased tolerance and

psychological or possibly physical dependence. Symptoms of withdrawal include agitation and stomach cramps. Driving while under the influence of marijuana is dangerous. Because marijuana distorts time and distance and slows reaction time, it is at least as dangerous as drinking prior to driving.

Other dangers associated with the use of marijuana are that it is illegal in all states, and its frequent use may impair normal social developmental experiences needed for growth to maturity. Research with adolescents and college students who use marijuana frequently shows that they often do not have the same type, frequency, or intensity of normal socializing experiences as those young adults who do not regularly use the drug. These socializing experiences help people grow and develop toward maturity. If much of one's life centers on the use of a particular drug that clouds perception and distorts reality, that person has difficulty internalizing socially learned developmental skills that prepare him or her psychologically and emotionally for adulthood.

Some of the marijuana available "on the streets" is treated with PCP (sernyl or phencyclidine), also known as angel dust. This animal tranquilizer is a controlled substance. Derivatives or imitations of PCP are sometimes used to "enhance" the marijuana. Marijuana that has been mixed with these or other substances tastes and smells like a strong chemical and is dangerous.

Hashish.   Hashish is an hallucinogen with low overdose potential, is habituating, and has some addicting properties. Generally it is either smoked or ingested in some food substance. Hashish is sold in grams or by the ounce. It is cut or broken into small bits and smoked. Like marijuana, it is sometimes mixed with liquid PCP or other fillers. Hashish is made from the resin of cannabis plants. Its effects are different from those of marijuana. Hashish is more hallucinogenic and less calming. A person using this drug acts very much the same as someone who has been smoking marijuana;

however, the person usually becomes more irritable, more agitated, and may become somewhat paranoid. Historically this drug was used as an anesthetic for pain, but because it was slower than some modern anesthetics it was abandoned.

THC. THC is the active chemical of marijuana, pharmacologically known as tetrahydrocannabinol. At one time, drug dealers claimed to sell THC, and occasionally people claim that a substance they are distributing is actually the chemical derivative of marijuana, thus giving the same effects without having to smoke the drug. Despite this claim, in reality THC has never been available except to clinical government researchers. The synthetic processing is time-consuming, very costly, and requires that a substance be kept at a very low temperature. Because of its highly unstable condition and its high cost, it has never been available on the street. Therefore, the substance drug dealers are selling is some other substance represented as THC.

Psychedelic Drugs

LSD. Lysergic acid diethylamide (LSD) is probably the best known of the psychedelic drugs. It has a high potential for overdose, although no physically addicting properties. It is consumed in a variety of ways, including tablets, capsules, or in liquid form that has been put on sugar cubes or pieces of blotter paper. An LSD experience varies with the individual, the environment, and the amount of drug that has been ingested. People under the influence of LSD hallucinate and have wide and varied mood swings, ranging from excitement and hyperactivity to lethargy. They can become anxious, panicky, confused, and out of control. Constricted pupils, glazed eyes, and a complete disorientation of space and time are some of the physical signs of a person using LSD. The long-term effects of the use of this drug involve convulsions, unconsciousness, psychotic

episodes, increased delusions, and panic psychosis.

LSD or "acid" was popular in the late 1960s as a consciousness-expanding drug that promised to increase the user's activity and intelligence. The drug was originally developed by the U.S. Department of Defense to create disorientation and confusion in an enemy. LSD is the most potent of all psychedelic drugs with which students experiment. A small amount can produce dramatic changes in the brain chemistry and its functions.

Most of the LSD available today is produced in illegal laboratories. Because it is odorless and tasteless, it is difficult to detect. Like other illegally produced street drugs, LSD is often diluted with other substances, such as speed, to produce a high. Two of the greatest harms associated with the use of this drug are having an acute psychotic episode, which is a bad emotional hallucinogenic experience, while taking the drug and having flashback experiences when not taking the drug. While having an acute psychotic episode, people have been known to attempt to hurt themselves or others. Some users who are psychologically unable to deal with the experience can remain in a permanent psychotic state.

PCP or Angel Dust. PCP is a tranquilizer-hallucinogen that has a high risk for overdose and a potential for physical addiction. A person who is under the influence of this drug will act drowsy, euphoric, panicky, confused, uncoordinated, and dizzy. PCP was originally developed as a horse tranquilizer, and pharmacologically is known as sernyl or phencyclidine. This substance is sometimes sprayed on marijuana or parsley and either smoked or ingested. The repeated use of this drug causes severe paranoia and damage to the central nervous system. The drug causes hallucinations, and users usually have bad experiences while hallucinating. One of the side effects of the drug is either temporary or permanent paralysis. The user also may panic and become violent when using the drug. This panic reaction may have lingering psychological effects, even when the chemical effects of the drug have worn off. PCP is distinguishable if used in marijuana or other substances by its heavy chemical odor and heavy chemical taste. This substance presents a serious risk to the person's life and other people's safety.

Psilocybin and Mescaline. Psilocybin is a chemical found in various mushrooms. This drug is sometimes distilled by boiling the mushrooms and making a type of tea. In laboratories the chemical can be extracted from the mushrooms. The substance is ingested orally. A person under the influence of this drug acts excited, restless, anxious; the user also hallucinates. The person may become irrational, have rambling speech, increased perspiration, dilated pupils, and periods of insomnia. The effects of the drug, depending on the amount taken, lasts for approximately six hours. If the drug is taken over a prolonged period of time, the person may begin to have increased delusions and eventually exhibit a type of panic psychosis.

Mescaline, a drug developed by Plains Indians for use in ritual ceremonies, has similar effects.

Ecstasy and Designer Drugs. From time to time "designer" drugs are developed. These are synthetic drugs that alter the molecular structure of a federally controlled substance to avoid the technical definitions of the controlled substance. It usually takes law enforcement authorities several months to get the new drug on the register of controlled substances.

Ecstasy is one such drug. It is an hallucinogenic amphetamine and can be dangerous. One of the major problems of the so-called designer drugs is that no one can be sure what effect altering the chemical composition of these drugs will have on people. A related problem for all street drugs is that users and treatment staff never can be sure of exactly what someone who is only interested in profit has put into the drug. A user's health and mental well-being are at significant risk when the person ingests substances that alter the body's chemistry without knowing what effect the drug will have. Physicians are often reluctant to prescribe medication, even when they know the effects of the drug, because any drug alters the system and most have some side effects.

Stimulants

Amphetamines or Speed. Amphetamines, commonly referred to collectively as speed, are stimulants whose users have a very high potential for overdose and high potential for physical addiction. Amphetamines include drugs such as dexedrine, benzedrine, and methedrine. In many ways these drugs give a reaction similar to adrenaline (a hormone from the adrenal gland that stimulates the central nervous system). Amphetamines are usually distributed in capsule or tablet form and marketed among college students as "black beauties," "white cross," "reds," and "uppers." Because they reduce the appetite in people taking them, amphetamines were once used as diet aids. The use of amphetamines as diet pills is no longer an acceptable medical practice. Other effects of this drug includes hyperactivity, irritability, restlessness, anxiousness, euphoria, and irrationality. The speed user also tends to be much more talkative, somewhat paranoid, uncoordinated, dizzy, and poor in reflexes. Users' eyes have constricted pupils. The long-term effects of amphetamines include insomnia, skin disorders, excitability, and malnutrition. One of the real dangers to the users of this drug is that speed increases the heart rate and blood pressure, increasing the possibility that the user will experience a stroke.

Speed is popular on college campuses during exam times. It creates a state of total stimulation. Wide-awake alertness is characteristic of this drug, and it was this property that caused its use during World War II and the Korean War by pilots on long bombing missions. Prolonged use of the drug significantly damages the body. Because of

CONTROLLED SUBSTANCES: USES AND EFFECTS

	Drugs	Often Prescribed Brand Names	Medical Uses	Dependence Potential	
				Physical	Psychological
Narcotics	Opium	Paregoric	Analgesic, antidiarrheal	High	High
	Morphine	Morphine	Analgesic	High	High
	Codeine	Codeine	Analgesic, antitussive	Moderate	Moderate
	Heroin	None	None	High	High
	Meperidine (Pethidine)	Demerol	Analgesic	High	High
	Methadone	Dolophine, Methadone	Analgesic, heroin substitute	High	High
	Other Narcotics	Dilaudid, Numorphan, Percodan	Analgesic, antidiarrheal, antitussive	High	High
Depressants	Chloral Hydrate	Noctec	Hypnotic	Moderate	Moderate
	Barbiturates	Amytal, Bulisol, Nembutal, Phenobarbital, Seconal, Tuinal	Anesthetic, anticonvulsant, sedation, sleep	High	High
	Glutethimide	None	Sedation, sleep	High	High
	Methaqualone	None	Sedation, sleep	High	High
	Tranquilizers	Equanil, Librium, Miltown Serax, Tranxene, Valium	Antianxiety, muscle relaxant, sedation	Moderate	Moderate
	Other Depressants	Clonopin, Dalmane, Noludar, Placydil, Valmid	Antianxiety, sedation, sleep	Possible	Possible

Tolerance	Duration of Effects (in hours)	Usual Methods of Administration	Possible Effects	Effects of Overdose	Withdrawal Syndrome
Yes	3 to 6	Oral, smoked	Euphoria, drowsiness, respiratory depression, constricted pupils, nausea	Slow and shallow breathing, clammy skin, convulsions, coma, possible death	Watery eyes, runny nose, yawning, loss of appetite, irritability, tremors, panic, chills and sweating, cramps, nausea
Yes	3 to 6	Injected, smoked			
Yes	3 to 6	Oral, injected			
Yes	3 to 6	Injected, sniffed			
Yes	3 to 6	Oral, injected			
Yes	12 to 24	Oral, injected			
Yes	3 to 6	Oral, injected			
Probable	5 to 8	Oral	Slurred speech, disorientation, drunken behavior without odor of alcohol	Shallow respiration, cold and clammy skin, dilated pupils, weak and rapid pulse, coma, possible death	Anxiety, insomnia, tremors, delirium, convulsions, possible death
Yes	1 to 16	Oral, injected			
Yes	4 to 8	Oral			
Yes	4 to 8	Oral			
Yes	4 to 8	Oral			
Yes	4 to 8	Oral			

(continued)

CONTROLLED SUBSTANCES: USES AND EFFECTS

	Drugs	Often Prescribed Brand Names	Medical Uses	Dependence Potential:	
				Physical	Psychological
Stimulants	Cocaine†	Cocaine	Local anesthetic	Possible	High
	Amphetamines	Desoxyn, Dexedrine	Hyperkinesis, narcolepsy, weight control	Possible	High
	Phenmetrazine	Prelu-2	Weight control	Possible	High
	Methyl-phenidate	Ritalin	Hyperkinesis	Possible	High
	Other Stimulants	Cylert, Didrex, Ionamin, Plegine, Sanorex	Weight control	Possible	Possible
Hallucinogens	LSD	None	None	None	Degree unknown
	Mescaline	None	None	None	Degree unknown
	Psilocybin	None	None	None	Degree unkrown
	MDA MDNA	None	None	None	Degree unknown
	PCP‡	Sernylan	Veterinary anesthetic	None	Degree unknown
Cannabis	Marijuana Hashish Hashish Oil	None	Treatment of side-effects from chemotherapy n some cancer patients	Degree unknown	Moderate

Source: United States Department of Justice Drug Enforcement Administration (N.D.)
†Designated a narcotic under the Controlled Substances Act.
‡Designated a depressant under the Controlled Substances Act.

Tolerance	Duration of Effects (in hours)	Usual Methods of Administration	Possible Effects	Effects of Overdose	Withdrawal Syndrome
Yes	2	Injected, sniffed, smoked	Increased alertness, excitation, euphoria, dilated pupils, increased pulse rate and blood pressure, insomnia, loss of appetite	Agitation, increase in body temperature, hallucinations, convulsions, possible death	Apathy, long periods of sleep, irritability, depression, disorientation
Yes	2 to 4	Oral, injected			
Yes	2 to 4	Oral			
Yes	2 to 4	Oral			
Yes	2 to 4	Oral			
Yes	Variable	Oral	Illusions and hallucinations (with exception of MDA); poor perception of time and distance	Longer, more intense "trip" episodes, psychosis, possible death	Withdrawal syndrome not reported
Yes	Variable	Oral, injected			
Yes	Variable	Oral			
Yes	Variable	Oral, injected, sniffed			
Yes	Variable	Oral, injected, smoked			
Yes	2 to 4	Oral, smoked	Euphoria, relaxed inhibitions, increased appetite, disoriented behavior	Fatigue, paranoia, possible psychosis	Insomnia, hyperactivity, and decreased appetite reported in a limited number of individuals

the acceleration of the user's metabolism, the liver and kidneys cannot filter the impurities fast enough and are forced to overwork. In a short time, they begin to disintegrate. The accelerated blood pressure, coupled with decreased food intake and erratic sleep, push the effects of many years of living into a short period of time. Irreparable brain damage, speech impairment, and other negative side effects have accompanied the prolonged use of amphetamines. A person who has been using the drug regularly for a period of time may have difficulty withdrawing from it. Though the withdrawal itself does not generally require hospitalization, the immediate "come down" after withdrawing from the drug can create significant psychological disturbance.

Methamphetamines. Methamphetamine is a stimulant chemically similar to amphetamines. The major difference is that methamphetamines have less effect on blood pressure and heart rate, but more effect on the central nervous system than do amphetamines. The slang terms for this drug include "speed," "crystal," "ice," and "meth." "Crystal meth" is one form of methamphetamine being sold on the street. It is usually smoked, but it can be melted and injected. Its relatively low cost and high overdose potential make crystal meth particularly dangerous.

Acute toxic effects of methamphetamines are similar to amphetamines and include irritability, confusion, aggression, deliriums, and depression. Long-term use may result in toxic psychosis. Long-term physical damage to the liver, the heart, and the brain may result from chronic use or overdose; stroke or cerebral hemorrhage and death are also possible.

Imitation Drugs. Imitation or "legal drugs" have been produced and marketed to college students. These are usually capsules that use many of the traditional names assigned to actual amphetamines, such as black beauties, yellow jackets, and white cross, but the imitations usually contain caffeine or some other legal substance. One of the dangers associated with the use of these imitation drugs is that they are sometimes confused with the real drug, and they set the precedent for the use of substances to meet certain demands of the individual. Although the use of caffeine or other moderately stimulating substances in low amounts may not present a serious risk, concentrated or excessive dosages of the substances may. A person needing to study may decide to take a handful of the imitation speed drug and physiologically create some of the short-term effects of amphetamines.

Cocaine. Within recent years cocaine has enjoyed a popularity among more affluent college students. It has been known as the "rich person's drug." Cocaine is a narcotic stimulant. Users have a high potential for overdose, and cocaine is addictive in a way similar to the type of addiction found in those who use amphetamines. Cocaine is most often consumed by sniffing or snorting; however, it can be injected. When using this drug, a person is hyperactive, somewhat irritable, a little anxious, generally euphoric, talkative, and shows a distorted sense of time and space. If this drug is used for a prolonged period of time by snorting or sniffing, it begins to destroy the mucous membrane tissues of the nose. Some of the signs of someone who has been using the drug for a period of time are a red and runny nose, dilated pupils, and a rather hyperactive or anxious state of being.

Cocaine is an odorless, white fluffy powder. It is a stimulant that activates the central nervous system, producing constricted blood vessels and other physiological effects similar to those of amphetamines. The potential for overdose of cocaine is increased when it is injected. An overdose of this drug may cause convulsions and death. The drug, originally developed as an anesthetic, causes an effect similar to that found in speed, but for a shorter duration. It is costly, and its regular use can amount to thousands of dollars per week.

Crack.   Crack is a hard, rock-like version of cocaine. It is smoked in a pipe. It gives a short intense elevation in awareness and is highly addictive. One or two uses of crack may be enough to cause an addiction. The feelings of being high are followed by depression. Those addicted to the substance use it to alleviate this depressed feeling. The more often the drug is used, the shorter the length of time associated with the elevated euphoric feeling.

Depressants

Barbiturates are a category of depressant drugs commonly referred to as "downers." Their users have a high potential for overdose, particularly when barbiturates are mixed with alcohol. Physical addiction is possible with the use of this drug, as was seen with the rather liberal prescription of tranquilizers by some physicians in the past. Barbiturates may be injected; however, the most common form of consumption is by ingestion in tablet or capsule form.

People under the influence of this drug are drowsy, belligerent, depressed, irrational, and often confused; they slur their speech. Users may begin laughing for no reason, and they have impaired coordination, dizziness, increased sweating, and constricted or dilated pupils. People who continue to take barbiturates over a prolonged period of time become excessively sleepy, confused, and irrational, and they experience severe withdrawal symptoms when they cease taking this drug. These symptoms include vomiting, tremors, hallucinations, hypertension, and seizures. Barbiturates are particularly dangerous for people who suffer from low blood pressure, heart defects, or depression.

The overdose of barbiturates in the form of tranquilizers and sleeping pills is often seen in suicide attempts. The overdose produces respiratory failure and cardiac arrest. If a person survives an overdose of barbiturates, he or she often experiences permanent brain damage.

One of the more foolish methods of abusing barbiturates is to consume them in combination with alcohol. This combination heightens the effect of each drug beyond the effect that the alcohol and barbiturates would create independently. This combination of taking barbiturates and alcohol is sometimes referred to as "loading." The combination of these two chemicals results in a multiplier effect. It causes increased risk of overdose, brain damage, psychological damage, and related physical problems.

Quaaludes, pharmacologically known as methaqualone, are barbiturates that also possess some of the depressant characteristics of alcohol. One of the popular myths surrounding this drug is that it increases sexual pleasure. Because it is a depressant, it probably lowers one's inhibitions, making a person more relaxed. The drug may also produce a sense of euphoria.

Frequent use of this drug causes psychological dependency. If consumed in excess, like other barbiturates, quaaludes will result in coma, convulsions, delusions, and death. Withdrawal from this drug is very unpleasant and may cause severe nausea, liver damage, and temporary paralysis. When combined with alcohol, the effects can be lethal.

Narcotics: Heroin and Other Opiate Drugs

Heroin and other opiate derivatives, such as morphine, codeine, and opium, have a high potential for overdose and a strong physical addiction. Although these drugs are sometimes taken by inhalation or by sprinkling them on marijuana and then smoking it, the most common method of consumption is through injection. A person under the influence of heroin or other opiate derivatives appears drowsy, euphoric, and uncoordinated. He or she has depressed reflexes, constrictive pupils, and loss of appetite. If these drugs are used over a prolonged period of time, the user will show dramatic weight loss, lethargy, and temporary sterility and impotency. Withdrawal symptoms include cramps, nausea, and vomiting. Because a person develops a tolerance to the drug, increased dosages are required to maintain the euphoric effect.

Much has been written about opiate drugs. They are highly addictive and very dangerous. Despite sporadic experimentation with these drugs on college campuses, their daily use so impairs users' ability to cope with college life that they drop out. Narcotics are usually difficult to obtain on most college campuses, although, like other drugs, a person searching hard enough usually finds them.

Opiates are expensive and often dangerous to obtain. The sale of this category of drug is scrutinized carefully by federal and state police agencies. Although some police officers may be willing to overlook the use of a small amount of marijuana, they seldom overlook the use or distribution of narcotics. Narcotics are not considered to be drugs consumed by the casual user. Possessing even small amounts of these drugs can result in serious legal repercussions.

EDUCATIONAL INSTITUTIONS AND DRUG USE

The use or possession of drugs is inconsistent with the goals of an educational environment and cannot be permitted to exist unchecked by the educational institution. The use of drugs in the residence hall presents major problems for the institution and students. Where drugs exist unchecked, use and distribution increases. No one is more vulnerable to violence than somebody who is dealing with drugs. Students dealing in drugs have been beaten, robbed, and, in several situa-

tions, killed for their money and their drug supply. This kind of violence does not belong in any community, whether it be a residence hall or a city. Administrators have an obligation to create a safe living environment in residence halls. No environment where drug use is open and drug selling continues is safe.

As mentioned many times throughout this book, the college years of late adolescence and early adulthood are a period in which men and women are subject to considerable peer pressure. The desire to conform is enhanced by a living environment such as a residence hall. In this environment where peer groups play such an important role in the development of students, the widespread use of drugs can establish a peer standard that encourages drug use. Students who under other circumstances may not consider trying drugs may be encouraged to do so. In an effort to gain the approval of their peers, students can easily be caught in a cycle of drug abuse that inhibits them from attaining their educational goals.

Drug use clouds a person's perception and retards his or her ability to obtain socially learned skills that are important for maturation. Residence halls provide the opportunity to grow and mature in an enriched educational environment with other intelligent people pursuing academic goals. Students learn new social skills from interacting with their environment and their peers, by handling crises, and understanding their emotions. When people are under the influence of drugs, their perception is clouded and their emotions are artificially controlled; their social development is never fully realized, and they cannot obtain the full benefits of the educational experience the institution has to offer.

Because one of the goals of higher education is to help people realize their full academic and personal potential, students who have made the decision not to pursue this goal by choosing to impair their development through the use of drugs probably do not belong in college. Such students are wasting their time and money, and the resources and interest of the institution, when they decide to inhibit their development through the use of drugs.

Educational institutions have a broad constituency. Their reputations affect not only enrolled students but also the faculty, the alumni, the community, and future students. Because these institutions enjoy the benefit of the laws of the communities in which they thrive, they have an obligation to uphold these laws. Institutions for higher learning also have a social responsibility to develop an educated and law-abiding citizenry through the students they graduate. No institution of higher education can, in all good conscience, refuse to uphold the laws of the state that supports it.

RAs: COUNSELORS OR ENFORCERS?

Having said that colleges and universities should prohibit drug use in residence halls, confronting the problem of drugs on campus—through enforcement by RAs, the campus police department, or through drug counseling—is a separate issue. The educators at some institutions see RAs strictly as counselors. These educators believe that enforcement of drug policies interferes with this counseling role and is the responsibility of law enforcement agencies. They see RAs as friends, confidants, and counselors, and believe that drug enforcement inhibits students from sharing concerns about drugs or other issues.

Other institutions require their RAs to call the campus police whenever they suspect a violation of drug policies has occurred or is occurring. The police then arrest any students in possession of drugs. The role of the RAs in this case is clearly one of enforcement, which the residents of the floor understand to be an expectation of that RA at that institution. Most institutions fall somewhere in the middle. The issue of enforcement of drug policies is usually handled internally within the institution's disciplinary system.

Detectable and Undetectable Drugs

Detectable drugs, such as marijuana and hashish, are detectable outside the room by the odor. What can be classified as the undetectable variety of drugs must be physically observed in the room or must be observed in the student as he or she experiences the effects. Most institutions have established procedures for handling detectable drugs in the residence halls. According to such procedures, the first incident for a student often results in a warning and an explanation that any future violation may result in referral to college disciplinary authorities. Any second violation of the policy involves a referral to the university's disciplinary authority. Each institution establishes its own set of policies for handling these confrontations.

One frequently used approach is when an RA suspects the use of marijuana, the RA, accompanied by another staff member, knocks on the door and identifies himself or herself to the resident of the room, asking permission to enter. If the person does not respond within a reasonable period of time, the RA is usually authorized to use a master key to enter the room to determine the cause of the smoke odor for fire safety purposes. Upon entering the room the RA is able to stand and observe but not to conduct a search. Things that are observable include towels stuck under the door, the odor of marijuana or hashish, smoking pipes and related paraphernalia, fans drawing smoke to an open window, and any drugs in plain view. Depending on institutional policies, sometimes drugs are confiscated by a senior staff member or campus police are called. The students are generally informed that they will be referred to the institution's disciplinary authorities.

To reiterate, each institution has its own set of policies. Some have selected a less confrontational method, which may or may not involve entering a student's room. Confronting students who use drugs can be dangerous. In 1996, an RA at Purdue University discovered drugs in a student's room. The student became so distraught about the notification of campus authorities that he shot and killed the RA. Although this incident is not typical, it illustrates the irrational and unpredictable behavior of students using drugs and the potential danger for RAs.

The discovery of students using other drugs, such as amphetamines, LSD, or cocaine, happens less often. Occasionally an RA is informed that a resident is using drugs, the RA may observe a resident who may be using drugs, or an RA may enter a student's room and accidentally see certain drugs in plain view. RAs are really not in a position to be detectives or supersleuths in the discovery of drugs.

Although you will need to address this topic with residents and to confront the problem when it becomes apparent, you are not in the residence hall for the primary purpose of enforcing drug policies. It is realistically an element of your job, and it should be performed with the same efficiency as other elements of the job. When you believe there is a problem with the use of drugs by a resident or a group of your residents, discuss it with your hall director or senior residence hall staff. These individuals have training, experience, and skills in handling these situations. They may have information about the student that has not been shared with you, or there may be special ways of treating these situations within your institution.

Counseling Students About Drugs

From time to time students may raise the topic of drug use. Sometimes it will be in the context of what they did in high school, some experimentation they are currently doing, or the context of what friends of theirs have done with drugs. These discussions on the legitimacy of drug laws and the effects of certain substances can be as informative to a student as a college lecture. You should have some facts about drugs and be able to relate them to students. You can also provide students with referrals to campus counseling services if they are interested. If such a discussion occurs, and possibly at some point it will, it should provide a good opportunity to invite a speaker on the topic of drugs, their legality, and their effects. Many city- or state-run detoxification programs have a public service program available on the topic, and many colleges have substance abuse educators.

You may learn that someone in your living unit is using drugs. This information may come from another resident, or the person with the problem may come to discuss it with you. Your role in these counseling situations is to support the person's desire to get assistance with the problem; at such times, put aside the issue of drug enforcement and policies for the more important goal of assisting the student with his or her personal problem. Although these occasions will arise, you and other staff will be in positions of enforcement of college drug policies. Enforcement is one of the ways that people are confronted with their behavior and forced to change it. For many substance abusers, only when they have no other options are they willing to confront their substance abuse. Never make excuses for someone's behavior who was under the influence of drugs or alcohol. Students must be held accountable for their conduct, including their decision to use alcohol or drugs. When people make excuses for others who misuse drugs or alcohol, they actually help enable those people to continue the abuse. As long as people who are abusing drugs or alcohol can find others who will excuse or explain away behavior, they have no reason to change their pattern of substance abuse.

Confronting a student who is using drugs or is misusing alcohol will create a crisis. Out of crises come change. When a student is confronted by the possibility of serious disciplinary action by the college, including suspension, expulsion, or possible arrest, the consequences may be so great that the student is compelled to address his or her substance abuse program. Until the student is confronted by this alternative, he or she may not have the motivation or personal courage to make this needed change in his or her life.

People who have been abusing drugs for a period of time will need the assistance of a professionally trained counselor. They need to attend a detoxification program to handle some of the psychological and physical withdrawals. These individuals also need to build their own concepts of self-worth and discover new ways of coping with the stress of everyday life in college. This therapeutic change can be accomplished by working with a trained professional over time in the right environment. You can be of greatest assistance by helping students locate a professional to help with their problem and then reassuring them that these matters will be handled confidentially, without police involvement, reports to institutional disciplinary records, or any breach of confidence to parents, employers, or others outside the institution. Only in rare circumstances will the parents of a student need to be notified, and this decision should be made by members of the professional staff in consultation with the student.

DRUG OVERDOSES

Drug overdose occurs whenever the body is called on to react to a substance beyond its ability to do so. The body reacts to substances up to a particular point, and then either damages itself or begins shutting off systems. This may be life threatening. If a person ingests too many amphetamines, the body begins pumping blood and increases respiration to the point that it begins breaking down by causing hemorrhages in small blood vessels, which may cause death. Sometimes the body attempts to expel substances that have been ingested by vomiting, or at other times the body may simply shut down or become only partially functional, as when a person becomes unconscious.

Many substances ingested in excess can be toxic to the body. Too much alcohol, too many aspirins, or a handful or two of salt can have a toxic or fatal effect on a person. With the exception of cannabis, the overdose potential is particularly high among the drugs discussed in this chapter. As a staff member you need to be familiar with the emergency procedures at your institution so that, should you encounter a drug overdose, you will know what to do.

Generally, if you confront a situation in which someone is unconscious and difficult to rouse, your first responsibility is to stay with the person and send someone else for assistance.

In cases in which a person has ingested some psychedelic drug and is not unconscious, but is simply experiencing the drug and is in a trance-like state, two options exist. First, you or someone else may stay with the person to help ensure that the person does not injure himself or herself or others. In this event, keep a tranquil atmosphere in the room and have at least two people who know the student stay in the room with him or her.

The second and preferred option is to contact medical personnel who can take custody of the person and assist him or her in the event of a violent outburst or a negative physical reaction. Unless you are highly skilled in dealing with people who are on drugs and familiar with the behavioral effects associated with drugs, you run the risk of being injured by the student or bearing some responsibility for the student's possible injury. This is particularly true if a student has taken PCP. The adrenaline surge is so strong in people using the drug that they may become disproportionately strong for their size. Because users are reacting to the drug and not thinking, they may unintentionally injure themselves or someone else.

Early assistance from medical personnel trained in handling these situations is preferable to finding yourself in the midst of a crisis and having to send for medical assistance at the last minute.

STRATEGIES FOR

Handling Unconscious Persons

- Have someone else call for an ambulance, the campus police, or the health center, whichever is the procedure at your institution; have them notify your hall director as well.

- If the victim is unconscious, check him or her for signs of breathing. If he or she is not breathing, first check to see if there is an obstruction in the throat.

- If there is, clear the obstruction and administer rescue breathing.

- Check for evidence of an accident, such as falling from a chair or being shocked by an electrical appliance. If the victim has fallen, do not move him or her.

- If the victim has received an electrical shock, immediately initiate rescue breathing.

- Check the pulse by locating the carotid artery in the neck directly to the right or left of the larynx (Adam's apple).

- In the absence of any evidence of injury, convulsion, or accident, and the appearance of drugs or any evidence that the victim may have injected something, try to rouse him or her. Try calling the victim by name, placing a cold washcloth on his or her face, or shaking the victim.

- If the victim is conscious and has taken a large dose of some drug (not a caustic or corrosive poisonous substance, such as Drano), attempt to help the victim vomit by having the person put his or her fingers down the back of their own throat or having the victim drink a glass of warm salt water or a mixture of mustard and water.

- Look around for any drugs in plain view. If drugs are present, give them to the medical personnel when they arrive. This will assist in determining an antidote for the drug.

- If you are unable to see any drugs in the room, question the victim's associates to determine what he or she may have taken.

REVIEW

1. What are three dangers associated with the use of marijuana?
2. How do the effects of marijuana and hashish differ?
3. What is THC?
4. What are two of the harms associated with the use of LSD?
5. What is the greatest danger a person faces when he or she buys drugs off the street?
6. What are two of the problems associated with imitation drugs?
7. What are two of the problems associated with having drugs in the residence halls?
8. What types of drugs are least likely to be detected by RAs and why?
9. What is your institution's procedure for the RA detecting and enforcing campus drug policies?
10. If you encounter someone who has used an hallucinogenic drug (e.g., LSD), and is "tripping" what is your institution's policy regarding how you should proceed?

APPLICATIONS

WINNING THROUGH FEAR AND INTIMIDATION

Dewey's new roommate was not what he expected. He was assigned to live with Allen, a 20-year-old sophomore from a large urban area near the university. Dewey came to the RA about the third week of school frightened. He told the RA that he needed to tell him something, but he made the RA swear that he wouldn't tell another person.

Dewey believed that Allen was dealing drugs. He had seen some blotter paper cut into squares and some kind of pills which Allen keep hidden inside a broken clock radio next to his bed. Several times Dewey took telephone messages for Allen which sounded suspicious, and people he had never seen before were coming by the room at odd hours of the day and night.

When Dewey asked Allen what was going on, Allen told him that if he knew what was good for him he would mind his own business and keep his mouth shut. Allen then told Dewey a story about a fellow from Allen's neighborhood who got too nosy and had a terrible accident from which he died. The message Dewey got was clear. He was frightened and believed that Allen had both the means and the disposition to hurt him or anyone else who interfered with his activities.

Dewey told the RA that he thinks Allen uses some of the drugs regularly himself and is a violent person. Allen has already indicated that he does not like the RA and has suggested that he might have someone teach the RA a lesson.

WHAT WOULD YOU DO?

1. Having given his word not to tell anyone, what should the RA do with the information be has received?

2. What dangers does Allen present to himself and to the other residents of the building?

3. Assuming that Dewey refuses to tell anyone else about this and refuses to talk with the police for fear of reprisal from Allen, what steps can the RA take to help Dewey?

4. What signs, if any, can the RA look for which might give him enough evidence to pursue this problem independent of the information he has received from Dewey?

5. Write two endings to the above case. One should describe the best outcome for Dewey and Allen, and one should describe, based on your experience, what you think is the most likely outcome.

CHAPTER FIFTEEN

SEXUALITY

© 1998 PHOTODISK, INC.

In the 1980s, college students became increasingly aware of a host of sexual issues: acquired immunodeficiency syndrome (AIDS), codoms, teenage pregnancy, date rape, abortion, right to life, adoption, chlamydia, homosexuality, drugs, alcohol, and caring or uncaring relationships. These issues and controversies did not go away as the population of our country increased and became more diverse.

Sexuality is one part of the total person and involves the sense of being male or female. It includes and is influenced by sex roles, self-esteem, family structure, education, dating, and a multitude of other complex, intertwining factors. There are probably as many perceptions of what constitutes "normal" sexuality as there are people on the earth.

RAs need information about sexuality among college students. Many students, living away from home for the first time, usually date more, drink more, and become more intimate with others. Each student is confronted by social and sexual issues. Students must ask themselves questions such as: How far will I go? What are my values? What risks will I take? What should I do if I have problems?

As an RA you must become a knowledgeable resource person about sexuality. To do this, you must first look within and assess your own attitudes, feelings, and values regarding various aspects of sexuality. Did you take a sex education class in high school or college? Have you attended seminars on sexual issues? Have you examined your feelings and attitudes about homosexuality, abortions, human immunodeficiency virus (HIV) and AIDS, premarital sex, and teenage pregnancy? You need to be aware of your attitudes and values about sexual issues.

This chapter focuses on topics such as contraceptives, pregnancy, abortion, AIDS and a few other sexually transmitted diseases (STDs), and quality relationships. Sexual orientation is addressed in the next chapter.

As an RA you need to be aware of resources on campus and in the community. You should be able to answer the following questions about your campus.

Ask Yourself...

- Does your campus have a student health center and/or student counseling center? What do students say about these services? What services are available?

- Are the health practitioners and counselors sensitive to the sexual problems of young adults?

- Can students get contraceptives and sexual health information at the student health center?

- What family planning clinics are nearby? Do the facilities perform anonymous HIV testing?

CONTRACEPTIVES

Sexual urges and sexual activity are normal. If a man and woman are engaging in sex, they should expect pregnancy to occur if nothing is done to avoid conception. Some students believe they can be sexually active and not take precautions to avoid pregnancy and STDs. Anyone who is sexually active and does not intend to initiate a pregnancy should plan and prepare for contraception. Both the man and the woman have a responsibility to prevent unwanted pregnancies and transmission of STDs. An unwanted pregnancy causes emotional and physical anguish. Once conception happens, serious decisions must be made. Preplanning, learning about contraceptives, and talking about sex and contraceptives with a sexual partner can prevent a lot of pain.

Over 20 percent of women become pregnant during their college careers.[1] Frequent intercourse (three times or more per week) and age less than 30 years are two characteristics associated with a higher-than-average risk of unwanted pregnancy.[2] Planned Parenthood reports that the average couple has been sexually active for nine months before requesting contraceptive information. Even though the woman has the most adjustments and decisions to make if pregnancy does occur, both individuals need to consider their contraceptive options and the risks of the various methods. Even if the male partner is not willing to assume his part of the responsibility, the woman must.

Abstinence from sexual activity with others has become more important due to concern about AIDS. Abstinence is the only sure way to prevent pregnancy and STDs, including AIDS. However, many college students choose not to be abstinent.

Every contraceptive method has advantages and disadvantages. RAs cannot be totally knowledgeable about all the methods; however, they should be aware of the basic information regarding the methods discussed here. Students are usually interested in this topic, regardless of their sexual activity. Most students are aware that no contraceptive is 100 percent effective. The selection of the best contraceptive is a matter of individual choice, with consideration of the person's health history. Some college health centers require that female students view a videotape on the various contraceptive choices before discussing the best choice for the individual at specific times in her life. Women should be prepared and comfortable with more than one type of contraceptive.

Birth Control Pills

The birth control pill is the number one choice of college women who are sexually active and wish to avoid an unplanned pregnancy. More than 20 different kinds and strengths of pills are available, although all use hormones to fool the body to prevent ovulation. Beginning users, especially, should consult with their health practitioner regarding any concerns or problems. Because birth control pills have low dosages of estrogen and progesterone, the pills must be taken at the same time every day and as directed. The pills are effective for pregnancy prevention after seven days. Many physicians recommend a second form of contraception be used during the first month, however, in case the dosage is not strong enough and must be adjusted.

Depo-Provera

The contraceptive injection Depo-Provera is a highly effective method of contraception.[3] Studies have shown that only one of every 300 to 400 women becomes pregnant during its use. This estrogen-free contraceptive is administered every 90 days, and protection from pregnancy begins within two weeks of the first injection. The most common side effect associated with this method of birth control is bleeding irregularity. Weight gain as well as changes in bone mineral density have also been linked with Depo-Provera.

The Morning-after Pill

Prescription medication can be taken following intercourse to prevent pregnancy. The most common morning-after pill is called Ovral. The first dose must be taken within 72 hours of the encounter, followed by a second dose 12 hours later. For this regimen to be most effective, the pills need to be ingested as soon as possible following unprotected intercourse.[4] One-third of women choosing this option are affected by severe nausea following the treatment.[5]

Norplant

Use of the Norplant implant system requires the surgical insertion of six small tubes into the woman's upper inner arm. The tubes begin preventing pregnancy within 24 hours of insertion and are effective for up to five years. Because the implants release progesterone slowly into the bloodstream and are free of estrogen, complications due to the medication are rare, with the exception of minor side effects such as irregular bleeding. The tubes do not dissolve and must be removed and replaced to continue contraception; some women experience complications from the removal of these tubes. Although the Norplant system initially costs more than most methods of contraception, studies have concluded that 85 percent of women who use this system continue its use after one year.[6]

Condoms

Condoms are the second most popular reversible contraceptive in the United States (the pill is first).[7] RAs should know about the availability of condoms on their campus. Condoms are frequently sold in the health center, the bookstore, the student union, and through vending machines in the residence halls. Millions of condoms are sold through mail-order companies each year. Many people find this a convenient way to purchase them. Spermicidal latex condoms for men, with a reservoir tip, offer the best protection against many STDs. Condoms for women, although somewhat less effective, are also available. Many nurse practitioners and family planners recommend the use of condoms and spermicidal foam together.

Diaphragm

As with other barrier methods of birth control, the efficacy of the diaphragm is dependent on its consistent and correct usage.[8] The woman must see a doctor to obtain the diaphragm.

This method of birth control also lowers the risk of contracting some sexually transmitted diseases.[9]

Contraceptives Summary

Students who have infrequent or unexpected sexual relations may prefer using a nonprescription method of contraceptive. The most effective is the condom plus a spermicidal agent, preferably the foam. The foam is more evenly distributed in the vagina. If used properly, the effectiveness of this combination is slightly less than the pill.

Many excellent references provide specific information about various contraceptives. All students who wish to avoid an unwanted pregnancy and take precautions against AIDS and other STDs should know all that they can about the various methods.

WHICH CONDOMS WORK BEST?

Several types of condoms are now on the market:

- The male latex condom is the most effective at preventing pregnancy and STDs. It is inexpensive and may prolong erections.

- The female condom also helps prevent pregnancy and STDs. The woman puts the female condom in her vagina, so she can initiate condom use. She can put it in up to eight hours before sex.

- The male plastic condom is still under study for HIV and STD prevention. The primary benefit is for people who are allergic to latex.

- Natural membrane ("animal skin") condoms are not recommended for STD/HIV prevention.

Whichever type of condom people choose, the most important factor is that they use it from start to finish every time they have vaginal, oral, or anal sex. Not using a condom at all is the leading cause of condom "failure." Even used correctly, condoms may not protect users from herpes transmission because the lesions may be in a place that the condom does not cover.

Adapted from American Social Health Association, "Condoms, contraceptives, and STDs" brochure, 1997.

PREGNANCY

The most common sign of pregnancy is a missed menstrual period. Nausea and vomiting, breast tenderness, frequent urination, and fatigue can all be early signs of pregnancy. However, none of these signs always signifies pregnancy. Uncertainty and wondering are so agonizing that any woman who suspects she may be pregnant should purchase a kit at a drugstore or go to a clinic, health center, nurse practitioner, or physician to have a pregnancy test. Confirming a pregnancy as soon as possible not only relieves a woman of uncertainty but allows the health provider to discover any health problems that may endanger the life of the mother or the unborn child. The RA can serve a vital function if he or she understands the importance of having the pregnancy test done, and can properly advise the possibly pregnant student or her boyfriend.

Women miss menstrual periods for all sorts of reasons, and a missed period does not necessarily indicate a pregnancy. Verifying pregnancy involves two procedures: a laboratory test that checks the urine for human chorionic gonadotropin (HCG), a hormone produced by the developing embryo, and a pelvic examination by a health professional to check for relevant changes in the cervix and uterus.

The most common pregnancy urine test is the two-minute slide test, which is accurate within 12 days after conception. If it is absolutely critical that the person have the diagnosis of pregnancy confirmed, a more expensive blood test for HCG can be done.

The laboratory tests can be positive, negative, or inconclusive. "False positive" means that the test is positive for pregnancy, even though the woman is not pregnant. This is rare, but it can occur, even with experienced laboratory personnel performing the test. False positives can be caused by drugs such as marijuana, methadone, large amounts of aspirin, birth control pills, and some tranquilizers. "False negative" means that

the test shows that the woman is not pregnant, when in actuality she is. False negatives are fairly common. In other words, the woman is pregnant, but the test results do not confirm the pregnancy. A false negative could be a result of urine that got too warm on its way to the lab; urine that was not concentrated enough; or contamination of the urine by soap, aspirin, or other substances in the specimen container. If the specimen is taken too early in the pregnancy, there may be an insufficient amount of the hormone to cause a positive lab test. If it is too late in the pregnancy, after about three months, the test may be falsely negative.

If the woman has a negative pregnancy test and her period does not start, she should return for another test in a week and continue using contraception, because if she is not pregnant and continues to be sexually active, she could get pregnant. After two or three negative tests, she should be advised to schedule a pelvic examination, as some pregnancies never get positive test results.

Given the effects of various drugs on a variety of laboratory tests, women students should not get upset when a health professional asks them about drug use. The professional needs to have factual information to make these important health diagnoses.

Home pregnancy test kits claim accuracy as early as nine days after a missed period. As one might expect, the accuracy of the test varies from person to person, depending on the woman's skill in performing the test and on individual hormone variations. Experts on pregnancy caution that women should be careful in depending on the home tests, which may delay seeking professional medical care during the crucial early weeks of pregnancy. The usual cost of a home test is about the amount one would pay to have the test done at a clinic.

If a student is pregnant, it is important to determine how far along she is in the pregnancy. Medical professionals calculate the weeks of pregnancy from the first day of the last normal menstrual period and not from the day conception may have occurred.

Choices

Early in the pregnancy the student has some time—not a lot—to make her choice about what to do. She can (1) continue the pregnancy and keep the baby; (2) continue the pregnancy and give the baby up for adoption; or (3) terminate the pregnancy by having a legal abortion at a medical facility. Usually this is a very difficult and personal decision for a woman to make. The important point is that she should be aware of all of the options available and not be pressured to do something she does not want to do, whether it be to have an abortion or to continue the pregnancy. You should be aware of agencies where the woman can receive proper counseling. Some of these agencies are the college health center, the college counseling center, the community mental health center, a local women's center, Planned Parenthood clinics, child and family services agency offices, or a religiously affiliated person or group. Antiabortion groups will provide information but will also try to persuade the student not to terminate the pregnancy.

The decision of whether or not to share the information with the woman's sexual partner is sometimes difficult. If she does not share the pain of the unplanned pregnancy, then she either allows her partner to avoid his responsibility or else prevents him from assuming it.

If the student is single and considers keeping the child, it would be advisable for her to talk with other single mothers about their experiences. Some of the groups mentioned above can help her realistically prepare for single parenthood. Antiabortion groups are more invested in women delivering their babies and so may have more services to offer students who choose this option. If the student is considering terminating the pregnancy, it is important for her to know that the earlier an abortion is done, the safer it is.

Abortion is a controversial political, religious, and ethical issue. Women choose abortion for various reasons. Proper use of contraceptive methods cannot absolutely prevent unwanted pregnancies. Whether or not a woman believes she has the right to terminate a pregnancy, she definitely has the right to know the details of an abortion procedure.

ABORTION

Nobody really believes that abortion is good. Abortion may be an answer for some women in certain situations given the complex social issues of our multicultural world.

Many Americans believe in freedom of choice, but there is still disagreement about the issue of when life begins. People have argued for years about whether human life begins at conception, at the age of viability (considered to be approximately 20 weeks), or at the actual birth. Medical personnel know that many spontaneous abortions or miscarriages occur during the first three months of pregnancies. It is estimated that 40 percent to 60 percent of all fertilized eggs are never implanted and are sloughed off naturally in menstrual blood.

Since the late 1980s, the ratio of abortion to live births has declined. In 1985, 35 legal abortions were performed per 100 live births; by 1994, the ratio of legal abortions to live births was 32 : 100.[10] Despite this decline, abortion is still the "most commonly performed surgical procedure in the United States."[11] Studies confirm that women choosing abortion are typically young, White, and unmarried.[12]

Many articles and books describe in detail the recommended methods, procedures, risks, and possible complications of abortion. You should familiarize yourself with basic information about how and when abortions are performed. However, actual counseling and assistance in decision making should be done by a professional counselor, nurse practitioner, or physician.

Legalization does not guarantee decent abortion services, which ideally should provide quality care, counseling, good health education, and birth control services in an atmosphere that is accepting of the individual's sexuality. For all women, abortion involves health issues of vital importance. Abortion is an operation involving the risks of blood loss and infection. Like other surgical procedures, it should be avoided if possible.

You must be especially careful not to be judgmental of the pregnant student's final decision. A woman who has chosen to undergo an abortion needs emotional support and acceptance during this difficult time. In addition to expressing concern and availability, you should be aware of the support services available on campus and in the local community to help the woman and her partner deal with any emotional problem resulting from the abortion. Usually, it is a great relief for a woman to end an unwanted pregnancy. However, she may have mixed or confused feelings after the operation. The RA needs to understand that some sadness and a sense of loss may occur. The person who has often been left out of the abortion issue is the woman's partner. If the man is thought of, it is usually with hostility and blame. You might lend a sympathetic ear if a male student wants to talk about what a personal experience with abortion has meant to him.

In 1988, an antiprogesterone steroid called RU486 was in use in five countries by over 20,000 women who ended pregnancies up to three weeks after a missed menstrual period. This drug has been approved for use in France, China, Sweden, the Netherlands, and Great Britain. In 1996, it was approved for testing in the United States. The RU486 pill is taken orally under a doctor's supervision. When coupled with another drug called *prostaglandin,* RU486 is reported to be over 90 percent effective.

HIV AND AIDS

As an RA you should assess the available resources on your campus about HIV and AIDS. Evaluate the educational response of your institution to this issue; remember that the problem crosses many disciplines and various departments. The American College Health Association provides HIV and AIDS resources specific for the college-age population. The American Red Cross and state health departments have pamphlets and educators available to address various groups.

On many campuses the current health issues have stimulated changes in student health centers. Many centers now employ health educators, nurse practitioners, physicians, and nurses who are wellness oriented. The emphasis is not only on treating illnesses and injuries but on helping students to be more knowledgeable and responsible for making healthy lifestyle choices. As an RA you should know the resources and services provided by your student health center.

AIDS is a disease in which the body's immune system breaks down. When the system fails, a person with AIDS can develop a variety of life-threatening illnesses. AIDS is caused by human immunodeficiency virus (HIV). About half of the people infected with HIV develop AIDS within 10 years, but the time between infection with HIV and the onset of AIDS can vary greatly. The severity of HIV-related illness or illnesses will differ from person to person. Today, promising medical treatments can postpone many of the illnesses associated with AIDS.

The two main ways of becoming infected with AIDS are (1) having unprotected sexual intercourse—anal, vaginal, or oral—with an infected person and (2) sharing needles or syringes with an infected person. Some people have become infected through blood transfusions. Since 1985, however, when careful screening and laboratory testing of all blood donations began, this possibility has been greatly reduced. You cannot be infected by donating blood.

HIV can be spread through sexual intercourse, from male to male, male to female, female to male, and from female to female. HIV and other STDs, such as gonorrhea, syphilis, herpes, and chlamydia, can be contracted through anal, vaginal, and oral intercourse. A person who has one of these STDs and engages in sexual behaviors that can transmit HIV is at a higher risk for HIV infection.

Sharing needles or syringes with an infected person, even once, is very risky. HIV from an infected person can remain in a needle or syringe and then be injected directly into the body of the next person who uses it. These needles include those used to inject steroids or vitamins and those used for tattooing or for ear or body piercing. People planning to have their ears or bodies pierced or to get a tattoo should go to a qualified person who uses brand-new or sterile equipment.

HIV Testing

The HIV-antibody test is *not* a test for AIDS. It tests for antibodies produced by the body in response to being exposed to the HIV virus that

PRECAUTIONS AGAINST HIV AND STDS

The only sure ways to avoid infection through sex are to abstain from sexual intercourse or to engage in a monogamous relationship for life. Following are ways to reduce the risk of contracting HIV and STDs. Each person must take responsibility for his or her own protection.

- Do not feel pressured to have sex.
- Practice "outercourse." In general, using hands to give pleasure is safe.
- Be prepared. Both men and women should have condoms on hand.
- Avoid direct contact between the penis, vagina, mouth, and anus to prevent the exchange of body fluids, including semen, vaginal secretions, and blood. One STD, hepatitis B, can also be transmitted through saliva.
- When engaging in intercourse, always use a condom. If another form of contraceptive is being used, it should be in addition to, not in place of, condoms.
- For extra protection against some STDs, women can use spermicidal foam gel, or suppositories. Researchers do not yet know the effect of spermicides on HIV risk.
- Do not use lotions, creams, or Vaseline with latex condoms. The oil in these products can weaken the condom. Use water-based lubricants such as K-Y Jelly or glycerin.
- Limit sex partners and choose partners carefully.
- Do not mix alcohol and other drugs with sexual activity; this behavior impairs judgment and may contribute to engaging in risky behavior.
- Never share a needle—for drugs, steroids, vitamins, tattoos, or ear or body piercing—with anyone.
- Do not share razors or toothbrushes (they could have small amounts of blood on them).

causes AIDS. HIV testing is a very serious matter, especially if the test results are positive. Supportive counseling during this stressful time is essential.

If a student requests information from you, refer him or her to the student health center, Planned Parenthood clinic, or an agency such as a state health department. You have a key part to play in not disclosing personal information and not contributing to rumors.

If someone living on your floor is HIV positive, remember that the virus is not spread by casual contact. AIDS is a devastating disease that can lead to many serious emotional and physical problems.

The threat of AIDS has challenged many people to assess their priorities and to be more responsible for sexual decisions. It is better for people to think more about preventing something than to cope with the consequences. As an RA you can help students become more knowledgeable and encourage behaviors that promote long, healthy lives.

OTHER STDs

Initially, it may appear that the RA would not need to know about sexually transmitted diseases. However, these diseases do involve the college population.

The STD problem is epidemic. Despite the seriousness and increased incidence of these diseases, the majority of sexually active people have little awareness of the risks and dangers involved. Table 15.1 presents the facts on major STDs.

STDs always involve at least two people, and any person who has an STD should assume the responsibility for informing partners with whom he or she has had sexual contact. Obviously, some people are embarrassed about discussing it or fear the effects on a particular relationship. However, the consequences of undetected infection are so harmful that they have no excuse for not telling their partners. If students are afraid to tell their partners directly, the local public health services or college student health centers will do it for them, preserving anonymity.

Free diagnosis and treatment for STDs are available at public health centers and college health centers throughout the country. However, infected people must take the initiative by reporting the earliest symptoms. Ignoring the symptoms in hopes that they will disappear is very risky. Sometimes symptoms do disappear or seem to subside, but this does not mean that the disease is gone. With some infections, such as syphilis, it merely means that the infection may be entering a new stage.

At either the college health center or a public health center, the individual will be asked to describe the symptoms and to recall if he or she has had sexual contact with someone who may have had an STD. Patients will then be examined and laboratory tests done to determine if a disease is actually present.

Once the specific disease has been diagnosed, the recommended treatment will be instituted. Sometimes antibiotics are effective, and other times specific medications or treatments are prescribed. The examinations, tests, and treatments vary with the disease. However, reexamination is important to make sure the disease has been arrested.

Following diagnosis and treatment in a clinic, patients are asked who may have infected them and whom they may have infected. This information is confidential, and contacts will not be informed of the source of identification unless permission is given to do so. Usually the contacts are notified by means of a letter informing them that they have been exposed to an STD and that they are required to go to a doctor or clinic within 48 hours. These people must be examined and possibly treated so they will not spread the disease to others.

SEXUALLY TRANSMITTED DISEASES

● Disease	● Transmission	● Symptoms	● Diagnosis	● Treatment	● Comments
Bacterial Vaginosis (Nonspecific vaginitis, Hemophilis vaginalis, Gardnerella vaginitis)	Mucus membrane contact with bacteria; may naturally occur within vagina without transmission.	Gray, white, watery, foamy, and/or foul-smelling vaginal discharge; painful urination; vaginal itching; painful intercourse.	Culture by health practitioner.	Oral antibiotics or other prescribed medications. Partners must be treated at the same time to avoid reinfection.	Use condoms when having sex until all partners have completed treatment.
Chlamydia	Mucus membrane contact with bacteria (vagina or male urethra).	Burning during urination; vaginal discharge; painful intercourse; lower abdominal pain; bleeding between periods.	Urinalysis or culture by health practitioner; not Pap smear.	Oral antibiotics. Partners must be treated at the same time to avoid reinfection.	Avoid sex during treatment. Infection could affect woman's fertility.
Gonorrhea (the clap, drip)	Mucus membrane contact.	Throat—usually asymptomatic; sore throat. Anus—usually asymptomatic; rectal itching, painful defecation. Vagina—usually asymptomatic; pus-like vaginal discharge, frequent and painful urination, bleeding between periods.	Bacterial smear and culture of throat, anus, vagina, or male urethra by health practitioner.	Antibiotic shots or pills. Partners must be treated.	Abstain from oral, anal, and vaginal sex until follow-up evaluation shows that all partners are cured. Can cause inflammation, pain, and sterility in males and females. Frequent cause of PID. Early treatment is very important. Damage prior to treat-

(continued)

SEXUALLY TRANSMITTED DISEASES

● Disease	● Transmission	● Symptoms	● Diagnosis	● Treatment	● Comments
Gonorrhea —cont'd		Penis—cloudy, pus-like discharge from the penis, frequent and painful urination; may be asymptomatic.			ment is irreversible. Can cause infant blindness during delivery through infected birth canal.
Hepatitis B	Contact between body fluids (saliva, semen, vaginal secretions, blood) and mucus membrane or open wound.	Jaundice (yellowing of skin and eyes), nausea, fatigue, dark urine; may be asymptomatic.	Blood test by health practitioner.	No known cure. Treatment includes rest, high-protein diet to repair damaged cells, high carbohydrate diet to protect liver.	Inform partners of infection, avoid contact between saliva and partners' mucus membrane, use condoms. Can lead to cirrhosis or liver cancer. One hundred times more infectious than HIV. Vaccination available (three shots in the arm);
Herpes Simplex	Contact between virus (nearly always through sores, but may be present on the skin with no symptoms) and mucus membrane, thin skin (e.g., eye area, geni-	Blister-like sores in or around the genital area including penis, vulva, thigh, anus, and/or buttocks.	Pap smear of lesions and culture by health practitioner. This method is the most accurate method to determine the type (I or II) and may not be conclusive	No known cure. Oral or topical medications can decrease symptoms through episodic or suppressive therapy.	Abstain from sex when lesions are present. Researchers estimate about one in four adults in the United States has latent genital herpes infection.

(continued)

● Disease	● Transmission	● Symptoms	● Diagnosis	● Treatment	● Comments
Herpes Simplex —cont'd	tals), or open wound. Can be transmitted to infant during birth and from cold sores on the mouth to genitals during oral sex. Spermicides may provide some protection.	No specific pattern of symptoms; persistent (for months) or recurring illnesses.	if sores have been present for more than a few days. Physical examination of sores.		About one-third of victims experience recurring lesions.
HIV/AIDS	Contact between body fluids (preseminal fluids, semen, vaginal secretions, breast milk, blood) and mucus membrane or open wound or sore. From mother to unborn children.		Blood test for HIV; positive HIV test and white blood cell count of 200 or less indicates AIDS.	No known cure. Currently, 11 medications are used in various combinations to help prolong life of AIDS patients; more drugs are being developed.	About half the people with HIV develop AIDS within 10 years; time between HIV infection and onset of AIDS can vary widely.

(continued)

SEXUALLY TRANSMITTED DISEASES

Disease	Transmission	Symptoms	Diagnosis	Treatment	Comments
HPV (Human papilloma virus, venereal warts, condylomata)	Mucus membrane contact with the virus (warts may not be present). Very rarely, mothers to infants during birth.	Growths, bumps, or skin changes in, on, or near penis, vagina, vulva, or anus. May be asymptomatic. Rarely—itching, pain, or bleeding in the genital area.	Visual exam, sometimes using magnification by health practitioner. Women—Pap smear to detect precancerous cervical changes.	No effective cure. Treatment to remove visible warts and eliminate symptoms includes cryotherapy (freezing), chemical compounds, electrocautery (electric current), laser, and injected interferon (antiviral drug). Over-the-counter wart removal preparations should not be used in the genital area.	Condoms can help prevent transmission, if they cover all areas where the virus is present (not just the warts). Generally, warts on other parts of the body, such as the hands, cannot be transmitted to the genital area.

(continued)

SEXUALLY TRANSMITTED DISEASES

Disease	Transmission	Symptoms	Diagnosis	Treatment	Comments
Nongonococcal urethritis (NGU)	Contact between bacteria and male urethra. Can be contracted through sexual or nonsexual exposure.	Discharge from penis, burning upon urination, burning or itching around anus.	Culture, stain by health practitioner to rule out gonorrhea as cause of infection of the urethra.	Oral antibiotics. Partners must be treated. Abstain from sex during treatment.	Bacteria can cause infection in women, but usually infects vagina rather than urethra. Can cause permanent damage to male and female reproductive organs. Can cause pregnancy complications and eye, ear, and lung infections in newborns.
Pelvic Inflammatory Disease (PID), salpingitis (inflammation of fallopian tubes), endometritis (inflammation of uterus lining)	Most commonly caused by gonorrhea or chlamydia.	Lower abdominal pain, fever, chills, vomiting, painful intercourse, increased or changed vaginal discharge, bleeding between periods.	Gram stain, culture, exam, and medical history by health practitioner	Oral antibiotics as prescribed. Treatment of all partners is essential.	Only women develop this disease. Can cause sterility, chronic pain, and infections. Avoid sex or use condoms until all partners are completely cured.

(continued)

Disease	Transmission	Symptoms	Diagnosis	Treatment	Comments
Pubic Lice (crabs, Phthirus pubis), tiny creatures not larger than a pinhead that when magnified look like crabs	Sexual or non-sexual direct skin contact with parasite, which can survive 24 hours apart from host.	Itching, lice in pubic hair.	Lice or eggs in pubic hair (self-diagnosis or by health practitioner.)	Prescription (Kwell) or over-the-counter shampoos (RID, Nix, A200) specifically designed to treat lice; follow directions carefully. Treatment of partners only if they are infected. To prevent reinfection, wash infected clothing, bed linens, sleeping bags, and other items in hot water and dry on high heat; non-washable items can be sealed in plastic bags for two weeks to kill the parasite.	Avoid intercourse during treatment. Special prevention measures: Do not sleep in others' beds, wear their clothes, or use their towels.

(continued)

SEXUALLY TRANSMITTED DISEASES

● Disease	● Transmission	● Symptoms	● Diagnosis	● Treatment	● Comments
Syphilis	Mucus membrane contact with chancres, rash, warts, lesions, or sores. Not transmitted through blood or body fluids. From mother to unborn infant.	Primary (onset three weeks postexposure, lasting for average of three weeks): chancre (painless sore) on penis, vagina, rectum, anus, cervix, mouth, or throat. Secondary (onset six weeks postexposure, lasting for average of three months): rash on soles of feet, palms, chest, and back; appetite loss; fever; sore throat; nausea; painful joints; and/or headaches. Symptoms go away after six months, even without treatment. Tertiary (2 to 30 years postexposure): Evidence of damage to brain, heart, and spinal cord may be detected.	Blood test by health practitioner three months postexposure (to allow antibodies to reach detectable level).	Penicillin shot. Must complete treatment, and retest to verify cure. Partners must be treated. Abstain from sex until treatment is completed.	Damage prior to treatment is irreversible.

(continued)

SEXUALLY TRANSMITTED DISEASES

● Disease	● Transmission	● Symptoms	● Diagnosis	● Treatment	● Comments
Trichomoniasis (Trich)	Mucus membrane contact with parasite during heterosexual vaginal intercourse. Cannot be contracted through urethra, anus, or mouth.	Green, yellow, gray, and/or foul-smelling vaginal discharge; vaginal and vulvar itching; painful urination; painful intercourse; irritation and inflammation of urethra; may be asymptomatic in women; usually asymptomatic in men.	Wet mount, culture, and Pap smear by health practicner.	Oral medication. Partners must be treated. Abstain from sex until treatment is completed.	

HEALTHY RELATIONSHIPS

College students confront all types of relationships with family, friends, girlfriends, boyfriends, fellow students, teachers, and other adults. Some people are good at building satisfying and healthy relationships, whereas other young adults have difficulty. Good relationships do not just happen. They take time, patience, and communication. This is true for all relationships, but particularly true of intimate relationships.

The ingredients of a healthy relationship include open and honest communications on each side. Both people are comfortable with exchanges that are assertive, accurate, and clear. This level of communication requires trust and the ability to listen.

Couples who have a healthy relationship have friends outside this relationship. These other friends are important. Being isolated and feeling dependent on another person is not healthy. When one person in the relationship becomes jealous of these other friends, he or she is becoming possessive and is signaling that he or she is insecure in the relationship.

Healthy relationships provide opportunities for growth and mutual support. Because each person grows in a relationship, relationships change; like people, they mature. Healthy relationships allow people to fulfill their potential. One person does not try to hold the other back or try to compete with the other.

Another characteristic of healthy relationships is that the people depend on one another when things are good and when things are not good. There is commitment. There is support. There is a sense of being a team; work and play are shared. Both share the responsibility for the relationship, the maintenance of the household if the two are living together, and the fun activities.

In healthy relationships there is freedom—freedom to be honest without the fear of hurting the other person, to express one's emotions openly, and to talk to the other person about feelings and needs.

People learn from all relationships. Those that are not constructive help people develop a perspective on what they need in relationships and to gain insight into their own ability to function supportively in an intimate relationship with another person. Nobody needs to remain in an unhealthy relationship. As an RA you will talk with students about their relationships. You can offer perspective and help students assess the health of their relationships.

Sharing experiences helps develop healthy relationships.

REVIEW

1. Is there a student health center on your campus? If so, what services are offered through it?
2. Can students obtain contraceptives at the health center and/or get counseling about STDs?

3. Is there a family planning or Planned Parenthood clinic near the campus? If so, do they do anonymous HIV testing? If not, where can a student go to get an anonymous HIV test?

4. What telephone number can students call to receive information anonymously about AIDS? About STDs? About abortions?

5. Over 20 percent of college women become pregnant during their college career. Most college couples are sexually active for nine months before they begin using contraceptives. Why is this, and what can be done to get sexually active students who do not want to have children to use birth control?

6. How long should a woman wait after beginning to use birth control pills before she relies on them for contraception?

7. What is the most common sign of pregnancy?

8. How can an RA help a student after she has had an abortion?

9. What is the difference between AIDS and HIV?

10. List four ways a sexually active person can limit his or her exposure to STDs.

11. What is your health center's policy about confidentiality of student medical problems?

12. What is your institution's policy about students who have AIDS and who wish to live in the residence halls?

APPLICATIONS

THE MOST DIFFICULT DECISION OF THEIR LIVES

Brenda and Robert have been dating since high school and have talked about getting married when they graduate. Both are sophomores in college. They have been having intercourse throughout most of their relationship but have not regularly used birth control. Brenda does not want anyone to know that she and Robert are having intercourse and will not go to the health center to talk with a physician about birth control pills, a diaphragm, or any other method. Brenda has suggested that Robert use condoms, but he prefers not to. He claims using a condom is too artificial and isn't how "real men" have sex. Most of the time, they use a combination of the rhythm method and withdrawal.

Brenda occasionally missed a period and was not overly concerned when her period was a week late. She told Robert. He got nervous and insisted that she take a home pregnancy test. Both were relieved when the test was negative. When she was five weeks late, she got the courage to go to the student health center. The pregnancy test and the gynecological examination showed that she was approximately two months pregnant.

Brenda returned to her residence hall room and, in a state of near hysteria, told everything to her roommate, who went to get the RA. When the RA came into the room, Brenda was sobbing uncontrollably. She does not want the child. She wants to finish college and go to medical school. If she has a baby, she believes this will not be possible. She does not want either Robert or her parents to know that she is pregnant. If Robert finds out, Brenda fears that he will insist on getting married and keeping the child. She does not want this. Brenda is not sure how her parents would act if they found out, but she is not interested in knowing. She has enough money saved to get an abortion, and that is what she wants to do.

WHAT WOULD YOU DO?

1. If you were Brenda's RA how would you assist Brenda during this crisis?
2. What are your personal opinions about abortion?
3. Do you think that Robert should be told? Why or why not?
4. Do you think Brenda should tell her parents? Why or why not?

5. If Brenda elects not to tell Robert or her parents, should the university inform her parents and/or Robert? Why or why not?

6. Brenda's roommate does not want Brenda to have an abortion and secretly tells Robert. One of Robert's best friends is his RA, whom he talks to about the issue. If you were Robert's RA, how would you help Robert deal with this situation?

SEXUAL RESPONSIBILITY

Tony transferred to Farm State University from a community college in New York City. He was a couple of years older than most of the other men in the living unit and was much more worldly. He was very at ease with women and frequently had women in his room for the evening. Tony did not believe in dating just one woman at a time; instead he was interested in "playing the field." He took pride in the number of sexual conquests he made.

The RA was somewhat befuddled by all of Tony's activity, even though it did not violate any of the university's policies. The RA talked with Tony generally about his activity, particularly about the issue of sexually transmitted diseases. Tony assured him that he knew all about those issues and the RA need not worry.

In time, Tony and the RA became friends. Occasionally the RA dated a woman Tony had dated and had intercourse with her. During the second semester, Tony suddenly came down with severe pneumonia and went to the student health center. Tony tested positive for HIV. When he learned of this, he went to the RA and told him about the test results. He cried and said he was afraid of dying.

When Tony's physical symptoms subsided, he started dating again. He told the RA that he would be "safe" but was not about to give up sex. He would continue to have sex with whomever he wished and figured that, if someone else contracted the disease, that was fate. He got it from someone and, if he gave it to someone, well that was just their tough luck.

WHAT WOULD YOU DO?

1. What could the RA do, if anything, to help protect other students from Tony?

2. Should the RA tell his hall director or other university official about Tony? Why or why not?

3. If you were Tony's RA, would you go and have an HIV test? Why or why not?

4. Does the RA have a duty to inform Tony's roommate and the other students in the living unit about Tony testing positive for HIV? Why or why not?

5. Tony is not having sex with the other people in his living unit. Are they at risk for contracting HIV by Tony's presence? Why or why not?

6. Can Tony conduct his sex life in such a way that he will not put other people at risk? Why or why not?

7. Does Tony have a legal, moral, or ethical duty to give health center officials the names of students with whom he has had intercourse so they can be tested for HIV? If Tony refuses to cooperate, should he be removed from the university? Why or why not?

CHAPTER SIXTEEN

SEXUAL ORIENTATION

©1998 PHOTODISK, INC.

People are sexual. Some are heterosexual, some are bisexual, and some are homosexual. A few people are asexual, meaning that they are not sexually involved with either gender. Heterosexuality is the accepted sexual orientation in most areas of the world. This has not always been the case. In ancient Greece and Rome, and during much of the Middle Ages, homosexuality and bisexuality were viewed as simply other forms of sexual expression. For religious and social reasons, attitudes towards sexuality changed and monogamous, heterosexual relationships were considered the norm. Laws were passed to punish individuals for behavior that fell outside of traditional heterosexual relationships. Social sanctions included mocking, ostracism, and physical attacks directed at homosexuals. Throughout much of America's history, homosexuals have been discriminated against in employment, in social contacts, in the military, and in other ways. The media and the movies, which help shape public opinions, have portrayed homosexuals as child molesters, poor parents, effeminate (males), and indiscriminate in their choice of sexual partners.

In the 1980s and 1990s awareness and acceptance of homosexuality increased. Some cities

257

passed laws that prohibit discrimination on the basis of sexual orientation. Despite a growing acceptance of homosexuality, homosexuals continue to suffer discrimination and social sanctions because of their sexual orientation. "Gay bashing" and other violent acts against homosexuals have always been present in society. In recent years, violence against homosexuals has increased as they publicly pressed for laws to prohibit discrimination against them and allow them to serve openly in the military.

When HIV and AIDS first became an issue of public concern in the mid-1980s, the disease was particularly prevalent among the homosexual community, which led to a strong backlash against homosexuals. Some fundamentalist religious groups and groups with very conservative ideologies advocated extreme measures against homosexuals. Homosexuals have been attacked and beaten merely because of their sexual orientation. The federal courts have not protected individuals from state laws that regulate private sexual conduct between consenting adults, making sodomy and similar sexual conduct illegal.

The number of homosexuals in the United States is difficult to determine. Kinsey's early studies suggested that approximately one-third of all men had had some homosexual contact. Most of this contact occurred during adolescence and young adulthood. In Kinsey's studies approximately 10 percent of all males were exclusively gay for a three-year period in their adult life, whereas less than 4 percent of homosexual males were exclusively gay throughout their whole life. The most common pattern was varying degrees of bisexuality.[1] A 1993 survey found that 2 percent of men had had a homosexual experience in the past decade. Only 1 percent identified themselves as exclusively gay.[2]

Apparently, gay men greatly outnumber lesbian women. Kinsey estimated about two to three times as many men as women had had some

MYTHS ABOUT HOMOSEXUALS

Myths

Homosexuals look different than other people.

Homosexual males are effeminate and weak; lesbian females are masculine and physically strong.

Homosexuals sexually molest children.

Homosexuals choose a gay or lesbian orientation.

Facts

Most gay men and lesbian women look and act publicly like everyone else.

Sexual preference has nothing to do with body type. Also, no relationship has been demonstrated between occupational choice and sexual preference.

Children (including boys) are more likely to be molested by heterosexual men than by women or homosexual men.

Gay men or lesbian women do not choose to be subjects of rejection, ridicule, and persecution. Many researchers believe that a person's sexuality is not a matter of choice.

homosexual contact. He estimated that 19 percent of all women had had some type of homosexual experience before the age of 40, but less than 3 percent remained exclusively lesbian for their whole lives, having had no heterosexual experiences.[3]

Genetic factors may determine a person's sexual orientation. In 1952, Kallman found a significantly high percentage of identical twins who were homosexual. In virtually every case that Kallman studied, if one twin was homosexual, so was the other.[4] More recent research on homosexuality also has suggested that it may have some biological basis. In 1993, researchers examined the chromosomes of openly gay men and their close relatives. They found a predominant number of gay men among the maternal relatives of the study's participants. The researchers suspected that if a genetic link existed, it was transmitted by the mother to the son. Because mothers donate the son's X chromosome (fathers donate the Y chromosome), scientists looked at detailed maps of the X chromosomes for the link. They studied brothers who were gay and found that of 40 pairs studied, 33 pairs had identical patterns in a particular region of the X chromosome.[5] This was the first study to show a possible genetic link to a particular behavior. However, the presence of this particular DNA pattern on the X chromosome does not necessarily indicate homosexuality. It may merely be an influencing factor. Further research in this area is needed.

A number of factors contribute to a person's sexual orientation. Close friendships, genetic or biological factors, opportunity, learned experiences, curiosity, social acceptability, and early childhood experiences all shape a person's sexual orientation. Sexual orientation is not an indication of intelligence, trustworthiness, loyalty, or any other factors that might influence how people participate in our communities. Many males have had some homosexual contact in preadolescence or during adolescence. Sexual orientation tends to emerge as people become sexually active. This begins with puberty, and the process continues throughout adolescence and young adulthood. Usually this is the time when people experiment. Most homosexuals have had a number of heterosexual experiences. A person who has one or two homosexual experiences is not necessarily homosexual or bisexual. One homosexual experience does not a homosexual make, just as one heterosexual experience does not a heterosexual make.

Identity Development

Evans and Levine identified four steps shown in most models of gay identity development: (1) an increasing acceptance of the homosexual label as applied to oneself, (2) a shift from negative to positive feelings about this self-identity, (3) an increasing desire to inform both gay and nongay individuals of one's gay identity, and (4) more frequent and closer involvement with the gay community. These various models show a movement from self-acknowledgment to self-disclosure to greater degrees of involvement and association in the gay community.[5]

Most of the theories on gay identity development treat the sexual identity of men and women similarly. However, Evans and Levine noted that women tend to develop a lesbian identity later than men develop a gay identity; they also found that women tend to develop that identity prior to becoming sexually active. In lesbian relationships, emotional attachment tends to be more important than sexual activity, and homosexuality appears to be less threatening to other women than homosexuality is to men.[6]

Cass identified six stages in the sexual identity formation of homosexuals. These stages are as follows:

Stage 1. Identity Confusion. The person experiences sexual identity conflict in sexual attractiveness to the same gender and attempts to resolve the dissonance this creates.

Stage 2. Identity Comparison. In this stage the person attempts to bring greater congruence between self-perceptions and behavior. This causes additional conflicts with the person's other self-perceptions which are resolved, or not, through this process.

Stage 3. Identity Tolerance. In this stage the person begins to accept a homosexual identity. At this stage the person may have increased contact with the gay community and attempts to redefine himself or herself in this context.

Stage 4. Identity Acceptance. Increased contact with the gay or lesbian community develops friendships and helps the individual validate his or her homosexual identity. At this stage the person may begin limited disclosure of sexual orientation to others.

Stage 5. Identity Pride. Feelings of anger and disdain for the heterosexual community's treatment of homosexuals increase and increasingly shape the individual's attitudes toward the heterosexual community pressing him or her into greater solidarity with the gay or lesbian community. In this stage, there is a tendency to dichotomize issues into (good) gay community and (bad) heterosexual world view.

Stage 6. Identity Synthesis. As the person synthesizes his or her feelings and recognizes that many of the views expressed in the heterosexual community are extremist, the person becomes less frustrated and less overwhelmed with his or her identity. The person's sexual identity is integrated into his or her personal identity, and the person has by this time usually established a place for himself or herself in a support network that allows for the person to proceed with other elements of his or her life.[7]

There are alternative theories to this process and the explanation above is simplified. The most important element is that the sexual identity formation takes on increased importance in the overall identity development because it deviates from the normative views of the heterosexual community. This deviation means that the person must redefine himself or herself as different from the majority culture, thus creating additional conflicts that need to be resolved in the process of identity formation.

SELF-DISCLOSURE

Because of the social stigma surrounding homosexuality, people choose varying degrees of disclosure. There are at least four general categories of homosexual disclosure. The first is being openly gay. The person does not attempt to hide his or her homosexuality and lives openly in the community as a homosexual male or female. The opposite of this is referred to as being "closeted." A closeted gay person may or may not be sexually active. He or she may be married or unmarried. The closeted gay's sexual orientation is to members of the same sex, but for reasons of social stigma, he or she is unwilling to admit this publicly. People in the third category are privately gay, meaning that they are open about being gay to selected close friends, but do not disclose this to others. A fourth category includes those people who are openly gay and who are married. Some people in married heterosexual relationships also openly engage in some homosexual conduct outside the marriage with their husband or wife's knowledge and acceptance.

Coming Out

Coming out is a term used to describe the act of a person who has decided to publicly acknowledge his or her homosexuality. This often happens in young adulthood. At this age people are in the process of discovering their sexual identity and separating from their family. This disclosure produces a more open and honest relationship but carries with it the threat of rejection. Accepting oneself as homosexual is an important element of self-concept and identity. Lifestyle and life-direction issues must be considered in being open about one's homosexuality.

Robert Rhoads identified four themes in the coming out experience: (1) coming out as a process, (2) personal changes related to coming out, (3) negative experiences of coming out, and (4) ongoing experiences of harassment and discrimination. The process of coming out starts with self-acknowledgment, one admitting to oneself that he or she is gay. The next step is to share this information with another person, usually a close friend.

Self-declaration of being gay, or the coming out process, changes a person's self-image. Most have tended to view this experience as positive because it allows for an increased sense of openness and self-confidence. Although a greater sense of self-respect may result, there are negative consequences that frequently accompany the process of self-disclosure. Students who came out in college reported that close friends sometimes withdrew and that people whom they knew acted differently toward them. In the more extreme cases, students who have come out have been the subject of violence, various forms of discrimination, and frequent verbal assaults. They become increasingly aware of the prejudice against them because of their sexual orientation.

Rhoads explained that coming out is an ongoing process that helps define a student's identity. He argues against defining various stages of gay identity for fear that this will develop a normative view similar to the sexual identity formation in heterosexuals.

HOMOSEXUAL LIFESTYLE

There is not a specific homosexual lifestyle. Gays and lesbians, just like heterosexuals, conduct quite diverse relationships, ranging from permanent, monogamous, intimate relationships to sexual contact with many different partners. Most gays and lesbians are indistinguishable in their behavior and mannerisms from heterosexuals. Some gay men have acquired certain effeminate mannerisms; most have not. Effeminate mannerisms are not characteristic of being gay. Some lesbians have masculine mannerisms; most do not. Transvestism is present in the gay community as well as the heterosexual community; it is not a behavior that is specifically linked to homosexuality. Every career and profession has members who are gay or lesbian. Homosexuals may be football players, fraternity members, construction workers, clergy, college administrators or faculty, or physicians. Sexual orientation has little to do with vocation, productivity, or intelligence. It is only one dimension of a person's identity.

Bars have been the traditional meeting places for gays and lesbians due to the social stigma of being homosexual and the need for places where homosexuals could feel comfortable. Gay bars are still a frequent meeting place for gay men and lesbian women.

Particularly in large cities, homosexuals have developed communities of support that include support groups, social clubs, religious organizations that support gay and lesbian concerns, and all other other social structures found in any other community. College campuses often have a student group of gay men and lesbian women who offer information and support to students who are wrestling with their sexual identity or who are gay or lesbian.

Most gay men and women are productive members of society, and most live in monogamous relationships and have the same relationship problems that married couples do in heterosexual relationships. They are no less loving and no less caring for each other.

HOMOSEXUALITY AND THE RESIDENCE HALLS

Undergraduate men and women who are in the process of discovering their own sexual identity often feel threatened by homosexuality. Heterosexual men seem to have the most difficulty accepting gay men. Young heterosexual males are often insecure about their own sexual identity and believe that by ridiculing or abusing homosexuals they affirm their heterosexuality for their male peers. This fear of homosexuality is referred to as *homophobia*. The issue of homosexuality is complex for young males because it is tied to the issue of power and dominance.

A gay or lesbian student living in your resident unit can create concern on the part of the other residents. He or she may become the object of ridicule, practical jokes, and abuse. Other students may feel uncomfortable using the same restroom as the gay or lesbian student and may have unfounded fears of contracting HIV or AIDS merely by living on the same floor with these residents. Often other males believe that they are the object of attention and desire of the homosexual student simply because they are male. This is one of the great myths surrounding homosexuality. Just as heterosexual women do not perceive all males as potential sex partners or are interested in developing some type of intimate relationship with all of them, homosexual males do not view all other males as potential sex partners or wish to enter into an intimate relationship with them.

Sometimes heterosexual males who have certain effeminate traits or females who have certain traditionally masculine traits are labeled by other students as homosexual. No matter what they might say or do to deny these allegations, they may suffer the same ostracism, social stigma, and harassment that homosexual students suffer who are open about being gay.

If handled correctly, with education and support, an openly gay student in your residence living unit can be accepted by the other students. This coexistence is rare in traditional all-male residence halls, but this level of maturity is possible. In apartment-style living situations, or in living units that provide isolation and single rooms, gay and lesbian students—individually or as roommates—sometimes coexist with residents in the living unit with little difficulty.

COUNSELING GAY AND LESBIAN STUDENTS

During college, people are coming to better understand their sexual identity. It is a period in which one discovers or acknowledges his or her sexual orientation. It may be a time in which a student may experiment with homosexuality. This sexual experimentation should not be misconstrued as having adopted a homosexual lifestyle.

Homosexual students may have some difficulty with some aspects of their orientation and may be interested in discussing counseling options. Whatever the situation, you must assess your own knowledge, attitudes, and beliefs about homosexuality. You must be able to talk with a person who is homosexual and see the many aspects of his or her personality without focusing on sexual orientation. You must be overtly and covertly nonjudgmental when you see certain people who portray the stereotype of male or female homosexuals.

As an RA you must honestly examine your feelings and attitudes regarding homosexuality. If you are prejudiced about homosexuality, you would be wise to read about the subject and work at being more tolerant.

A student may talk to you about issues of his or her sexual identity. A student who is wrestling with this may not discuss an issue as intimate as his or her sexuality with you because of fear of rejection and ostracism. If by chance a student does trust you enough to share such an intimate concern, talk with the student about the basis of his or her concern. Focus on the student's knowledge about the issue and the extent of his or her experience. A surprising number of students who think they might be gay or lesbian have never had a homosexual experience. This is not an opportunity for the student to graphically describe sexual conduct to you, but an opportunity for the student to think about how he or she has come to think of himself or herself as homosexual. Remember that this issue is about the student learning or discovering his or her own sexual identity. It is not about you advocating a particular lifestyle or being judgmental about homosexuality.

You should recommend that the student speak with a counselor in your counseling center. This may help the student gain perspective and give him or her more information. Therapy does not change a person's sexual orientation and most therapists will not try to do so. For students who are still in the stage of shaping or who are uncertain about their sexual identity, counseling may help them resolve some issues. But if students are truly homosexual, they will know, and therapy will be directed at helping them accept themselves and getting the support they need.

Some students who are gay or lesbian may talk with you about whether or not they should tell their parents. This is an individual decision each person must reach for himself or herself. The advantage of being openly gay is an honest and open relationship with parents and others; the disadvantage is possible rejection. Whatever the outcome, the student needs your support and probably the support of a counselor to reason and reach the decision that is best for him or her.

Sometime during the academic year it would be helpful to sponsor a speaker on homosexuality as part of your residence hall program. Such a speaker can provide some information to the general student population, dispel some myths regarding homosexuality, and give some students the courage to discuss their own homosexual feelings. In the best case it may help to develop among the residents a more mature and accepting attitude toward people who are homosexual.

Acceptance and support of a gay lifestyle by parents makes possible honest and open communication and high self-esteem for gay students.

REVIEW

1. List the six stages of sexual identity formation identified by Cass.

2. What is *homophobia* and why are men more likely to be homophobic than women.

3. Identify two problems a homosexual male is likely to experience in a men's residence hall and two ways his RA could help.

4. If the hall director or other university official has knowledge that a student is homosexual, do you think that this information should be shared with the RA? Why or why not?

5. What is your institution's policy for making roommate changes when the request is based on dissatisfaction with the other person's sexual orientation?

APPLICATIONS

CLOSE FRIENDS

Seymour was starting his second year at State University. He was a good student. He studied hard and wanted to get into a good medical school when he finished. This was also his second year in the same residence hall on the same floor. He returned to live in the hall because it was simpler than finding a new place, and he knew most of the men with whom he would be living.

Seymour had requested a single room, but none were available. The roommate assigned to live with him was a freshman named Mike. Seymour had a roommate much like himself last year: a person who studied, kept somewhat to himself, but had a number of friends on the floor. Two things were very noticeable about Mike. First, he was very good looking. He lifted weights regularly and had been a high school varsity athlete. The second noticeable thing about Mike was that he spent a lot of time talking about sex and girls. Seymour was not accustomed to all of this talk about sex and had had only one sexual experience with a girl he dated in high school.

Seymour liked and admired Mike. He found that the more time he spent with Mike the closer they became. Seymour began having sexual fantasies about Mike. The more he thought about it, the more appealing the idea of having sex with another man became. One night he got the courage to go to a local gay bar. There he met another college student who was gay, and Seymour went to this student's apartment; he had sex with another man for the first time in his life. Seymour had really mixed feelings about what had happened. One night when Seymour and Mike were drinking and talking late into the evening, Seymour, who trusted Mike and still harbored sexual feelings for him, told Mike about his one homosexual experience and that he really liked Mike.

Mike was shocked and a little frightened. The conversation ended when Mike changed the subject. About an hour after Seymour went to sleep, Mike left the room and went to the RA's room and awoke him. He told the RA that he had to tell him something in strictest confidence. Mike related everything that Seymour had told him that evening. He also said that, although he liked Seymour, he wasn't about to live with any queer and that he was afraid Seymour might try to rape him or something. He was also afraid that Seymour might now have AIDS and that he was going to be contaminated. Mike demanded that the RA get rid of Seymour, but he did not want Seymour to know that he told the RA this information, or that he was the one requesting that Seymour be moved. All Mike knew for sure was that he was scared of living with a gay student.

WHAT WOULD YOU DO?

1. If you were the RA, what would you say to Mike?
2. If you were the RA, what action, if any, would you take with Mike?
3. What action, if any, would you take with Seymour?
4. What developmental crisis is Seymour facing?
5. What developmental crisis is Mike facing?
6. Do you think Seymour is gay? Why or why not?
7. What would you do if you were Mike? Would you have responded similarly?

THE CASE OF THE GAY ROOMMATES

As Tom and Scott left their room, they were not sure what to expect when they returned. For the past two months, they had endured catcalls, death threats, abusive language, and a daily barrage of laughter and ridicule from the other residents on their floor. Tom and Scott were openly gay.

Tom was an English major, and Scott was majoring in engineering. Both students were good athletes, and both were involved in the university's community service efforts. Tom and Scott met during their freshman year, became friends, and chose to room together in their sophomore year. Both dated other gay students; they chose to room together, not because they were romantically involved with each other, but because they felt more comfortable living with another gay person.

Tom's parents accepted his sexual orientation. He had a brother who also was openly gay, and his parents were not surprised when Tom announced that he was gay. Scott told his parents that he was gay just before returning to college in his sophomore year. His parents were shocked and angry.

Tom and Scott were sensitive to how the other residents on the floor would react when they found out they were gay; but they believed that it would be too stressful to hide it from others and that they had nothing to be ashamed of.

Bubba was a resident on the same floor with Tom and Scott. One afternoon when he was reading the student newspaper, he read an article written by Scott about gay rights. In the article, it encouraged students who had questions about their sexual orientation to come to a meeting of the gay student alliance. It gave Tom's name as the president of the organization and listed their telephone number to call for more information. Bubba walked across the hall and showed the article to three other male residents of the hall. The conversation went like this:

BUBBA: Hey, guys, read this. The two guys at the end of the hall, Tom and Scott, are both fags. I hate fags.

NORMAN: You've got to be kidding. God, I was taking a shower the other day and one was in the bathroom. I'll never let that happen again.

FRANK: I'll bet those two are having sex in their room every night. They probably have AIDS and we're all going to catch it.

PAUL: I'll bet the university doesn't know this is going on. They'll put a stop to it once they learn these two are gay and are messing around with each other in the residence halls.

The four men went to the RA, Joe, and informed him of this situation. Joe did not know that Tom and Scott were gay, but he wasn't surprised. He explained that the university prohibited discrimination on the basis of sexual orientation, and that during RA training they had a session on gay and lesbian issues. He explained that these students had a right to be in the residence halls and the university did not consider sexual orientation in the assignment of roommates, just like they did not consider race when assigning roommates. Joe told the students, "I don't like queers any more than you do, but the university's philosophy is live and let live."

That night someone scrawled on the outside of Tom and Scott's door: "We don't want any queers on our floor. MOVE OR DIE!" Tom and Scott showed the note to Joe and asked him to do something. He took it to the hall director, who called the director of residence life. It was decided that the RA should talk with the residents of the floor and determine if anybody knew anything about who did it. No one would say. The next few weeks involved more of the same kinds of behavior. If Tom or Scott went to the restroom on the floor, the other students would immediately leave. They could hear students laughing at them behind their backs and calling them names. Some would yell sexually explicit remarks.

Joe's efforts to discover who was responsible for the constant harassment of water, shaving cream, fireworks, and urine left under their door on almost a nightly basis was unsuccessful. It reached the point that Tom and Scott feared for their lives. They couldn't study, and they could no longer tolerate the harassment. Together they went to see the dean of students and explained to him in detail what had transpired. Accompanying them to this meeting was the university's affirmative action officer, part of whose responsibility included insuring that the university's nondiscrimination policies were enforced. The dean of students listened carefully and assured the young men that he would do everything in his power to see that this behavior stopped. The dean called a meeting with the director of residence life, the hall director, and Joe. Joe informed the group that he had tried hard to locate the people responsible for the harassment and the threats but was unsuccessful. Even an investigation by police officers and the hall director was negative in linking specific individuals to specific events. Joe's best guess was that everybody on the floor was involved to some degree.

WHAT WOULD YOU DO?

1. Select four people and assign to them the following four roles: dean of students, hall director, resident assistant, and affirmative action officer. Role play the meeting to resolve the problems on Tom and Scott's floor.

2. Design a strategy to stop the harassment of Tom and Scott, keeping in mind that the university has a policy which prohibits discrimination on the basis of sexual orientation and that Tom and Scott are aware of their legal rights if the university fails to take appropriate action.

3. Tom's parents call the president of the university and tell her about what transpired. They ask her why she is unable to provide a satisfactory educational environment for their son and suggest that if she can't insure the safety of their son and his right to an education, they will hire an attorney, sue the university, and bring as much public attention through the media and through gay and lesbian organizations as possible to punish the university for its failure to act. If you were the president of the university, how would you respond to Tom's parents and what action, if any, would you take?

CHAPTER SEVENTEEN

ISSUES OF RACE AND GENDER

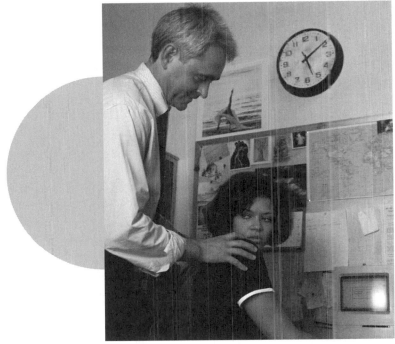

Most colleges and universities are heterogeneous environments in which students from wide and varied racial groups, nationalities, and social classes study together. This has not always been the case. Prior to World War II, most college campuses could be described as homogeneous environments, composed principally of White, upper-middle-class males. A number of important social movements and federal intervention programs changed the scope of higher education. Programs such as the GI Bill, which provided educational benefits to men and women in the military, and a number of financial aid programs greatly changed the demographic profile of American higher education.

College provides students an opportunity to establish friendships with people of other cultures.

PSYCHOSOCIAL DEVELOPMENT AND THE INFLUENCE OF GENDER AND RACE

One problem with much psychosocial development research is that it tends to reduce students' experiences to the lowest common denominator. Although this process helps identify trends, themes, or vectors in development, it hides some of the distinctive characteristics about the individual experience of development. Gender and race are two of these distinctive characteristics that influence development.

Cross identified four stages in the development of people of color. These four stages are: (1) pre-encounter, (2) encounter, (3) immersion, and (4) internalization.[1] During the pre-encounter stage, students have only a limited awareness of how they are different from the majority culture. They develop a dependency on the majority and use it to define their own self-worth and to shape their attitudes about the world. The majority culture provides feedback about who they are and helps to shape their self-concept.

During the encounter stage, students become more aware of differences between the majority and minority culture. The focus is on how the minority culture differs from the majority culture. Usually the transition into this stage is triggered by some type of event (crisis) that forces students to reexamine how they have been defining themselves and the emotional dependency they have had on the majority culture. In this stage, students often begin to examine group history and events in their own life from their racial group's perspective, and develop a heightened awareness and sensitivity to issues of discrimination.

In the immersion stage, people of color discard the values, stereotypes, and beliefs of the majority culture and adopt those represented by their racial group. Some develop animosity toward the majority culture and become active in address-ing issues through political activism, confrontation, and other forms of expression. During this stage, attachment to their particular racial group is heightened as they immerse themselves more fully in the culture of that group.

The internalization stage is the last stage in the development process leading toward acceptance of one's race by people of color. During this stage, they vacate the old identity structure and adopt one that redefines themselves in the context of their racial heritage. Acceptance brings with it an enhanced sense of inner security and understanding. They develop compassion for other people of color and other minorities and redefine their relationship with the majority culture. Through this redefinition, they commit to human rights principles and an active participation in making needed social changes.

O'Neil and Roberts-Carrolls identified five phases of gender role identity. These five phases are: (1) acceptance of traditional gender roles, (2) ambivalence about gender roles, (3) anger, (4) activism, (5) celebration and integration of gender roles.[2]

In the first phase—acceptance of traditional gender roles—students integrate the stereotypic male and female roles. Men usually are viewed as strong, powerful, controlling, and achievement oriented. Women usually are viewed as nurturing, passive, verbal, and secondary to men.

Ambivalence about gender roles occurs in the second phase. It is initiated by general dissatisfaction with stereotypes and discovery that the stereotypes are inaccurate. Exposure to a variety of men and women in various roles and discussions of expanded roles for both men and women enhance the identity roles associated with gender. Because of the new ideas and the questioning of stereotypes, students become interested in the possibilities of expanding gender roles and changing traditional concepts surrounding gender identity.

As one becomes more aware of the restrictiveness of traditional gender roles presented by the normative environments, anger emerges and creates a third phase in this process. Anger is expressed towards individuals, institutions, and groups that perpetuate traditional gender role stereotypes. Because outlets for this anger are not easily identifiable, some people in this stage become anxious, conflicted, and depressed.

Social activism is the fourth phase. People who enter this stage become involved in groups that advocate change in traditonal sex roles and pursue political and social change. Students may become involved in awareness-raising groups, may support politcal legislation, or may advocate that universities implement new policies regarding the use of certain language or expression on campus.

In the final phase there is a celebration and integration of gender roles. In this phase people develop a new awareness of their gender and its role in society. A new satisfaction with themselves and their place in society is enhanced. They develop greater comfort and a less restricted stereotypic way of viewing their own lives and the lives of others.

In both of these theories—people can stop at any of the stages and remain there. Not everyone achieves the last stage in the developmental process. Some people may remain ambivalent about gender roles or remain locked in the encounter stage where they are concerned about differences between majority culture and minority group members but do nothing about it.

RACE AND ETHNOCENTRISM

Today's complex world forces each of us to categorize elements of our world. We define these categories based on what we have been told and what we have experienced. The more remote our experience, the more we rely on the perception of others and on cultural myths. This process of creating general classifications and attributing generalizations to them is called *stereotyping*. Stereotypes are a first element in differentiating our immediate social group from other social groups. It is one of the methods by which we define our social position and normative environment.

Unfortunately, broad generalizations often associated with stereotypes are factually inaccurate. Not all African American people are lazy; not all Chinese are industrious; White people are not smarter than other racial groups; not all Hispanics in the United States are migrant farm workers. Although stereotypes help us deal with abstracts, they presume that all members of a group operate similarly. These broad generalizations enable us to ignore human qualities that do not conform to the cultural stereotype.

Stereotypes prejudge people based on their race, social status, gender, sexual orientation, hair length, or lifestyle. Prejudice is negative prejudgment. When one acts on this negative prejudgment by treating a group or a person unequally, this action is discrimination.

People can hold prejudices without discriminating. They can harbor negative feelings and attitudes without acting on these feelings while believing in equal treatment for all people. People can also be prejudiced and actively discriminate or not be prejudiced and not discriminate. In many cases, people cognitively discount stereotypes as irrational but emotionally harbor some negative feelings about a particular group. One example of this might be a person who recognizes that racial discrimination has no rational basis, but disapproves of interracial dating and marriage. This person may not discriminate in employment, performance evaluations, or social acquaintances but may choose not to date or befriend somebody from a different racial group.

Sources of Prejudice

Three general sources of prejudice are psychological, social, and historical. Some people feel a need to discriminate against other groups. The basis of this need may be feelings of personal inadequacy or inferiority. These people believe that their self-worth is enhanced when the worth of others is diminished.

Another source of psychological prejudice is using underrepresented groups as a "scapegoat" for frustration and aggressive feelings. If something happens that is inconsistent with someone's preconceived idea of how it should have happened, he or she needs to explain why his or her perceptions did not reflect reality. One way to resolve this cognitive dissonance, created by the gap between perception and fact, is to attribute the reason to a particular group, making that group a scapegoat. A person passed over for a promotion which is given to a member of an underrepresented group might easily channel his or her frustration and aggressive feelings toward the minority group. Racial or ethnic groups also may become scapegoats in a broader sense when people are angry and frustrated and vent their anger and frustration on a group even though that group

is not the cause of the problem or the source of the anger. The group might simply be a convenient and safe outlet for negative emotions. For example, a poor White man may join the Ku Klux Klan, blaming African Americans for the ills of society, when the true source of his frustration may be the economic policies of powerful, wealthy White men.

Yet another type of psychological source of prejudice is found in people who have authoritarian personalities. These people are rigid, inflexible, intolerant of others, and have a need for others to submit to their will. Authoritarian personalities need for society to be well ordered and consistent with their view of how the world should function. They are likely to be very conventional and fundamentalistic. People with authoritarian personalities often view racial and ethnic groups other than their own as unconventional, and therefore disruptive of their ordering of the world. As such they are likely to hold a low opinion of members in these groups, discriminate against them, and generally consider the groups to have inferior qualities and characteristics.

Some feelings of prejudice are the result of socialization. Prejudice is learned from generation to generation by being a member of a particular group. Some of these prejudices may be ingrained into the group and thus become part of its members' view of reality. As children, people learn these myths and stereotypes about racial and ethnic groups. The family environment and the peer environment in which they live reinforce and validate these beliefs. This form of prejudice is developed in the same way as feelings of nationalism, patriotism, and religion. The process is the same, although the feelings are markedly different.

Society also promotes prejudice through competition in the workplace. For many years some groups have had control in certain industries or civil service positions. A classic example of this has been the Irish immigrants and their influence in the New York City Police Department. At one time in New York City, Irish people were predominant in civil service positions. When Italians and people from other ethnic groups began to vie for the same positions, they encountered animosity and discrimination. The same competition for jobs and resulting animosity occurred when African Americans were hired at the same wages as Whites in construction work, civil service positions, and in the military. Competition for jobs and the idea that a person thought of as less skilled, less intelligent, and less capable was now employed in an equal position was threatening. It threatened people's economic survival and challenged them to reexamine their identities. If a racial or ethnic group member regarded as less qualified was placed in an equal position, then a person was forced to either upgrade his or her view of that group, of that individual, or to diminish his or her own self-worth. This process of social adjustment was another source of prejudice.

The clearest example of historical prejudice is African Americans who were held as slaves until the conclusion of the Civil War. For many years after the war, African Americans were held in economic bondage and still remain the subject of prejudice and discrimination. At one time, similar feelings were directed toward Native Americans, whose culture was viewed as inferior to that of Whites. Hispanics and other groups have suffered from similar historic sources of prejudice and discrimination.

Students and Cultural Differences

On balance, if one looks at all of higher education—two-year institutions through research institutions—there are significant changes in the student population. In 1980, 81 percent of the more than 12 million American students enrolled in higher education were White; in 1990, 78 percent of the almost 14 million students were White; in 1995, 74 percent of the 14 million students were White. Remaining students during these years were comprised of African American, Asian American, and Hispanic students.[1] Between 1976 and 1988, the proportion of African American students enrolled in four-year colleges declined from 33 percent to 28 percent. The proportion of Hispanics declined from 36 percent to 31 percent. The number of Asian American students increased by 128 percent.[2] In 1997, non-White students made up 23 percent of the total enrollment at public four-year institutions.[3]

Large research universities often provide inhospitable environments for all but the best-prepared students. Often students from underrepresented groups attending large, predominately White institutions feel culturally isolated. They have, or at least feel they have, a marginal status. Many of these students, who have not shared the same cultural and social background as White students, find it difficult to operate in a predominately White institution while maintaining asso-ciations with members of their own racial or ethnic group.

In the educational community, members of many races find that they are at a collective disadvantage. Some claim that standardized tests such as the SAT and the ACT—the scores of which are commonly used as criteria for enrollment at universities—do not accurately measure the potential of some members of underrepresented groups because of cultural differences.[4] Once admission does occur, the needs of these students frequently are not met, either academically or socially. Professors are usually White. Only a few ethnic studies courses are available. Programs abroad may take students to European countries, but very few students have the option of studying in Africa, Latin America, or Asia. Often even the performing arts and other opportunities for participation in the surrounding community target majority students when they target students at all.[5] As a result of these disadvantages, students from underrepresented groups—especially non-Asians—attending predominately White universities, "are less likely to graduate within five years, have lower grade point averages, experience higher attrition rates, and matriculate into graduate programs at lower rates than White students and their counterparts at predominately Black or minority institutions."[6]

African American Students.   African American students who persevere through initial disadvantages and make the decision to apply to a college may face a new set of struggles in the admission process. African American student enrollment in higher education, particularly for males, has steadily declined in recent years despite the increasing number of African American high school graduates. There are several reasons for this. First, while tuition has risen, there have been cutbacks in federal aid grants. Although federal money to support student loans has increased, grants have not. The financial burden of assuming so much debt is a deterrent to many students. When financial aid is not forthcoming, the absence of funds tends to affect African American families' prospective education more than the same lack would affect White families, on a national average, because of the relative income disparity between these two groups.

Although attrition occurs among college students of all races, it happens more frequently among African American students. Five out of every 10 college students leave without completing degree requirements. However, for African American students, the rate of attrition increases to 7 out of every 10.[7]

Most studies on the roots of this problem have concentrated on the disadvantage of African Americans stemming from preenrollment situations. While the educational and financial backgrounds of many African American students justifiably cause concern, attrition relates more directly to existing campus conditions. Attrition does not always indicate that a student has discontinued his or her college education permanently. Students drop out of college for many reasons. Sometimes students leave school long enough to earn the money necessary to continue their education at a later date. These students are counted among the attrition rate, but they often complete their degrees.[8] Because finances are a problem for many African American students, they often find themselves in such a predicament.

This financial problem accounts for some of the discrepancy between general attrition rates and the attrition rates of African Americans.

Finances alone, however, are not the only cause for African Americans leaving White universities. The general campus environment contributes greatly to an African American's college experience and his or her decision whether or not to remain in school. Perhaps the most crucial lack of university support for underrepresented groups comes in the form of professors. All people of color are relatively underrepresented among faculties at universities across the country. The ratio of African American students to African American professors illustrates an imbalance. This imbalance has negative results on the college experience of students. The lack of African American professors creates a lack of African American role models and can contribute to students' feelings of loneliness and isolation on White campuses. The absence of professors with whom African American students can easily identify sometimes creates problems in students' feelings of strength and self-sufficiency. Students often look to professors for a reference point as to how they are managing compared to other students. If a professor feels uncomfortable with a student because of the student's race, the student may perceive that he or she is unwelcome.

For African Americans, the need for a sense of community manifests itself in frequent transfers from White universities, where African American students may feel isolated, to historically African American universities, where students may experience a more nurturing environment. "Predominantly White universities are perceived by Black students as environments that are predominantly [intellectual]-oriented, independence-oriented, achievement-oriented, and competition-oriented. Such orientations are least likely to produce the best environment for Black students, for whom socially oriented climates are crucial for learning and growth."[9] In other words, African Americans place a greater importance on the support of their community, and environments in which the sense of community flourishes provide the ideal background for both socialization and education.

The educational gains of African American students appear to be greater when the students attend predominantly Black universities. Many of the students whose experiences support this finding explain that they had the feeling in White colleges of "institutional abandonment, isolation, and bias in the classroom."[10] This link between community and success becomes clear when one realizes that in a supportive educational community, students have reasonable access to leaders with whom they feel comfortable, they study issues that relate to their life, and they have a strong support network of friends, counseling services, and trusted mentors. These aspects of university life form a feeling of belonging and community in which the students may study at ease. Many White students take these feelings for granted. Unfortunately, this supportive feeling often eludes African American students in White universities where minority needs are not considered or understood.

African American men appear to suffer more from the pressures of White universities than African American women, perhaps due to the men's traditional, rigidly masculine roles. The men may perceive that it is their role to confront racism, and so external stimuli may be more likely to distract them. Their emotional strength may be drained by these real and imagined battles and, consequently, they may find themselves unable to fulfill the stressful academic requirements of a university.[11] African American women, on the other hand, tend not to perceive the external environment as a controlling factor. They do not deny the presence of racism and discrimination, but "Black women report the belief that they are tougher, more callused, and more resistant to negative stimuli in their environment than are Black men. . . . They, too, seek support . . . but they seem not to depend on it for survival in college."[12]

Regardless of gender, African Americans often have difficulty facing the stressful and foreign environment of White universities. The specific changes needed are, among other things, improved financial assistance, more African American faculty, better minority support services, and appropriate matching of universities with students who are equal to their academic challenges.

Asian American Students. The problems of African Americans at predominately White universities parallel the problems of other ethnic and racial groups. However, each ethnic or racial group has its own share of unique difficulties. Asian American students, in particular, face increasing prejudices and discriminatory practices. With the growing heterogeneity of the population in the United States, a sense of competition between members of different underrepresented groups is growing also.[13] Competition in higher education reflects this trend. Universities admit limited numbers of students each year. Consequently, students must compete with one another for the available openings. If universities admit students solely on the basis of high school grades and test scores—which may or may not be accurate measures of the qualification of some underrepresented groups—Asian Americans tend to be quite successful. However, if universities establish quotas, and admit individuals according to race, Asian Americans may lose well-deserved positions simply because they are already well represented at many universities.[14] Admissions offices seem to be the victims of a no-win situation. But so are Asian Americans.

The educational process breeds many stresses for Asian Americans. They feel the pressures of being expected to perform well in math and the sciences. Their culture is different from the culture of a predominately White university. Priorities, styles of living, and methods of learning all vary from culture to culture. In a university setting, Asian Americans may experience particular isolation because they are not accustomed to the kinds of support services offered to them. When they feel pressure and need to talk to someone, Asian Americans frequently prefer to go to a family member, a friend, or an elderly member of the community whose advice they respect. The prospect of speaking to counselors and strangers is foreign, and often does not fit their needs.[15]

Language Issues.   Language presents a problem for some students. Hispanic students are usually bilingual: They are able to converse in both Spanish and English. Many White students who have had only one language throughout their life must adjust in college to a more sophisticated style of communicating. Books, lectures by faculty members, and discussions with members of the academic community generally demand a greater degree of linguistic sophistication. All students must adjust to this demand for a more elaborated linguistic code, but students for whom English is a second language must contend with this new elaborated linguistic code while maintaining sophistication in their native language.

Some students are bilingual, having two separate languages and being able to switch between the two; some African American students are bidialectal, having access to two separate, distinct dialects. What has been called "Black English" is a dialect with its own grammar and lexicon. Students who come from social backgrounds where "Black English" is a primary means of communicating must enrich their language skills, as White students do, by improving their standard English. However, African Americans usually are expected to retain linguistic sophistication in Black English to communicate with other African American students in certain social situations. Black English might be used with close friends at a party or to discuss music or just as a way to show common bonds and a sense of linkage or community with one's heritage.

Cajun students may experience a similar problem. In rural communities in Louisiana, Cajun French is the language used in the family and in many social circumstances. In school, standard English is taught, but some students retain a heavy Cajun French accent in the use of standard English. To be part of their culture, students must be able to speak Cajun French; they must also develop language sophistication for verbal and written communication with faculty in college-level standard English.

These examples highlight the special demands placed on students from some ethnic or racial groups when they function in predominately White, middleclass institutions. They are forced to develop not one, but two language systems, and be fluent in both. This fluency requires extra effort. It can contribute to students in these groups feeling marginal and apprehensive about the college culture.

Cultural Separateness

Each culture has qualities and traditions unique to its heritage. Members of ethnic groups such as the Irish, Italians, Greeks, or Chinese have a common heritage that links them together and links them with their past. Membership in an ethnic group affects one's identity. It influences a person's self-concept and models for the person's gender and occupational roles.

Tradition and ritual are also defined by ethnic group membership. These play an important part in how one lives and in the associations one makes. They help to reinforce one's ethnic heritage and to promote a sense of collective identity among members of the group.

Membership in an ethnic group might also define who one marries, the age at which one marries, and the marriage ceremony. Although it is not the custom in the United States for marriages to be arranged, arranged marriages are common in some ethnic communities. Symbols of ethnic identity may include the way one dresses, distinctive accents in the use of English, choice of food, and religion. A language other than English may be spoken in the home and used with other members of the community.

Isolation is an important element in maintaining ethnic separateness. To the extent that the group can develop a community separate from that of the majority culture, that group can maintain its traditions and heritage. In large cities such as San Francisco, Chicago, and New York, ethnic neighborhoods (such as Chinatown and Little Italy) maintain distinct identities from the majority culture.

Forms of Racial and Ethnic Interrelationship

Racial or ethnic interrelationship occurs in three forms. The first is *conformity* or *amelioration*. This is where the culture of the ethnic group is supplanted by the majority culture. Members of the ethnic or racial group are integrated into the majority culture, and the distinction or heritage that linked the group together is abandoned in favor of conformity to the normative social environment of the dominant group.

The second form of interrelationship is a merging of cultures, what has been referred to as a *melting-pot* approach. In this form of relationship, cultures are merged and the dominant culture adopts some of the characteristics of the minority culture and the minority culture adopts some of the cultural characteristics of the majority. The adoption of certain food or dress is an example of a superficial melding and appreciation of different cultures. Non-Irish wearing green on St. Patrick's Day is one sign of adoption of and appreciation for different cultures.

Cultural pluralism is the acceptance of separate enclaves for different cultures, with a common respect for different customs and a general pride in one's cultural heritage. Cultural pluralism is common in urban environments, where a multitude of ethnic communities thrive.

In the campus environment different cultures merge; on some campuses, students feel pressed to conform to the dominant Anglo culture. Some students maintain associations with students of the same ethnic or racial background through student clubs and organizations such as the Black Student Association, the Jewish Student Association, the Asian American Student Association, or the Hispanic Student Association. These groups provide an opportunity for students to reaffirm their ethnic, cultural, and racial heritage and provide a forum for these students to advance their political and social beliefs.

All people need to associate with those with whom they share a common heritage, perhaps by participating in a certain fraternity or sorority, joining a particular type of political organization, or forming linkages with an ethnic or racial heritage. These associations can become the intermediate peer environments through which students relate to the larger normative social environment. They offer security, acceptance, and, most importantly, a collective sense of identity or security.

Cross-Cultural Communication

As enrollment in higher education has grown over the years and become more egalitarian, institutions have moved from a homogeneous group to a more diverse student population. Many institutions have rigorously recruited students from underrepresented groups. Large campuses often have a wealth of students from different cultural backgrounds. This variety of cultural backgrounds and experiences increases the complexity of human relationships in a group living situation. This is one of the important opportunities students have to learn from people of various backgrounds and experiences.

Studying about a culture or learning its language is one step in developing an understanding and appreciation for that culture. Establishing true communication with somebody from another culture requires a conscious effort at understanding the person's background and experiences. Developing an understanding and appreciation for another culture is very valuable. It not only enables a person to enter into what might be a rewarding relationship, it also helps provide him or her with the skills to work with people from varied backgrounds and learn about those cultures.

Language is an integral part of both self-concept and psychological processes. One's view of the world and relationships with other people rest within language and one's ability to use it to control one's environment. The development of identity, one of the primary issues in the college years, is tied closely to the ability to use language to control one's environment. Success in controlling the environment through language begets more self-confidence. Through language, students get feedback about themselves and are able to communicate their innermost feelings to others. If students must communicate in a second language or dialect to receive feedback and to control their environment, they bear an additional burden that can inhibit success.

Language is one of the most evident signs of cultural difference. Cultures also have varied values, habits, hygiene, food preferences, social customs, and a host of other factors associated with culture. Americans are often judgmental toward other cultures, using their culture as the standard. Americans tend to ignore people who are different or to ostracize them because they do not share the same experiences. This attitude stems from a need to be in homogeneous groups, to be close to other people, and to develop relationships with others. It is more difficult to establish these relationships with people whose cultural experiences are different. However, such relationships are not impossible, and, if achieved, can provide some of the most rewarding friendships a person can have.

You can improve cross-cultural communication on your floor by spending time with people from different backgrounds. This enables you to develop an understanding of each ethnic group's unique experience. With international students, you may wish to treat yourself to spending time learning about their countries, where they went to school, some social differences between their country and yours, and aspects in their culture that you value. Often an international student will be interested in sharing his or her cultural experiences with other students in the living unit. Holding a floor program on that particular country or inviting the international student to participate in late-night discussions can encourage that person's participation in the living unit and diffuse cultural prejudices and biases that may be building.

When a student from another country exhibits some behavior you find questionable or seems particularly distraught, take the time to inquire. Males from Middle Eastern countries, as one example, are not reluctant to hold hands in public. In the American culture, two men holding hands may suggest that they are homosexual. In the cultures of the Mideast, it may only suggest that they are acquaintances. If you wonder about some type of behavior, religious practice, or other cultural aspect, take the time to ask and understand. If the particular behavior is disruptive and causes conflicts or resentment in the living unit, this is a reason to talk with the student about the behavior. The student will likely appreciate your inquiry and be interested in how the behavior is viewed in the American culture.

Never judge another person's experiences or culture. Cultures are different; one is not better than another. Be sensitive to how you would feel if the situation were reversed; try placing yourself in the other person's situation. You might feel alone in a different culture, using a language that you can speak but with which you still may have difficulty. Students can be very uncaring, overly involved in themselves, and searching for their own identity.

This same cultural sensitivity applies not just to people from other countries, but also to people from underrepresented groups within this country. Some experiences are unique to the African American community. They are not better or worse than the White middle-class cultural experience of most campuses. RAs unfamiliar with African American culture should take time to understand this experience. Also understand that students may feel more comfortable in relationships with people from their own racial or ethnic background. In the African American community, sometimes students experience sanctions for participation or emulation of the dominant White culture of the university. This is also true for Native American, Chinese, and Hispanic students.

Understanding cultural differences and getting to know more about individuals will assist you in breaking down the cultural barriers and stereotypes identified with these groups. By diffusing these racial and cultural stereotypes, you may be able to avoid some of the bigotry and cultural conflicts that occur when people live together without taking the time to know one another. Part of a student's education in the institution should include developing an appreciation for other cultures. Each has something to offer.

Counseling Minority Group Members

As an RA you will work with students from a variety of cultures. When students from different ethnic and racial heritages are asked to live together, one can anticipate some conflicts that arise as the cultural norms and expectations of one group come into conflict with those of another group. Common bases of conflict include taste in music, loudness of music, styles of conflict resolution, hygiene habits, frequency and type of alcohol use, and styles of holding parties. If you are a member of a majority group, be sensitive to some issues that may be unique to members of underrepresented groups. Know as much as you can about their culture and show respect for it. Be available and treat members of these groups as you do other students in the living group. Estab-

lish an accepting peer relationship. At all times, be yourself.

Don't assume that you have the right answers to the conflicts that occur. Don't assume that you know what it is like to be a member of a different racial or ethnic group, that you have an appreciation for their feelings of marginal status, or that you represent a culture they need to emulate. Do not try to convince them to violate their cultural norms.

By working with students and encouraging appreciation of the diversity of cultures, you help students develop tolerance for other lifestyles and acceptance of the heterogeneous, culturally diverse environment in which they live. If college is to prepare students to live in today's society, students must understand that society is becoming increasingly pluralistic, Living and working together in the residence halls is a microcosm of what living and working in American society is becoming. Acceptance, understanding, and appreciation now will help students develop the social and cultural sensitivity they will need to work and function cooperatively after college.

GENDER AND SEXISM

Historically, women were regarded as chattel —the possessions of their husbands—and were given limited freedoms. Their role in society was to bear children and maintain the home while the husband protected the family and provided its financial support. These traditional roles for men and women have promoted certain gender stereotypes, influenced how children are socialized, and impacted what students consider in developing their own self-concept.

Men and women behave differently. Whether these differences are innate or environmental is unclear. Most likely, a combination of biological and social influences result in certain behavior patterns identified with men and women. Research shows that boys are more aggressive than girls, children tend to prefer same-sex toys, and as children, boys and girls prefer to play with same-sex peers.[16] Studies also show that girls are allowed more freedom in their gender behavior than boys and that children are inclined to imitate behaviors associated with their same-sex parent. During adolescence, the normative social environment of the peer group tends to socialize men and women toward accentuating certain kinds of behaviors. Socialization includes boys being discouraged from crying and girls being discouraged from being aggressive. Boys are encouraged to pursue competitive activities—like aggressive athletic sports, whereas girls historically were encouraged to pursue cooperative activities, like dance and music.

The effect of this socialization process has been offered as an explanation for why in later adulthood men view masculinity in terms of success and power and women view femininity in terms of grace and beauty.[17] The socialization process for women also allows greater intensity in relationships and greater freedom in disclosing personal feelings. Consequently, women in college usually have a more in-depth and complex understanding of friendships and tend to be less demanding and more understanding in resolving conflicts than men.

The advantage women have in knowing how to work in groups can have mixed results in the workplace. For example, female supervisors may focus their concerns on their subordinates' expectations of them, as opposed to the expectations of their supervisor. Women managers tend to act more as counselors and confidants and thus sometimes find themselves in conflict between the interest of their supervisors and that of their subordinates.[18]

In male-dominated positions, women frequently are not accepted by their male peers. This results in a lack of cooperation and strained personal relationships, which tend to produce greater stress for women who place greater value on close peer relationships than do most of their male counterparts.[19]

Discrimination against Women

Despite the increasing access women have to higher education, they still are overrepresented in what have been considered historically women's occupations. Women make up more than 80 percent of all hairdressers, maids, social workers, RNs, librarians, telephone operators, and secretaries. They make up less than 20 percent of engineers, dentists, clergy, architects, lawyers, judges, police officers, pilots, detectives, firefighters, and mechanics.[20]

More than 50 percent of the students attending college today are women, yet more men than women are enrolled in graduate programs. However, enrollment trends indicate movement toward parity. Women attending college are also more likely to be part-time students and have family commitments, including the need for day care, special lifestyle and vocational counseling, and the need for more flexible schedules.

Sexual Harassment

Sexual harassment involves some form of sexual submission as a condition of employment or education as a way to affect employment, job evaluations, or letters of recommendation. Such harassment almost always involves some form of power relationship, usually with males in a supervisory position. Sexual harassment includes men harassing other men, women harassing men, women harassing other women, and, most commonly, men harassing women.

Sexual harassment may range from sexual innuendos made at inappropriate times, perhaps in the guise of humor, to coerced sexual relations. Harassment at its extreme occurs when someone in a position to control, influence, or affect another person's job, career, or grades, uses his or her authority and power to coerce the other person into sexual relations, or to punish him or her for refusing. It may include:

- verbal harassment or abuse
- subtle pressure for sexual activity
- sexist remarks about a person's clothing, body, or sexual activities
- unnecessary touching, patting, or pinching
- leering or ogling of a person's body
- constant brushing against a person's body
- demanding sexual favors accompanied by implied or overt threats concerning a person's job, grades, or letter of recommendation
- physical assault

The most direct kind of sexual harassment involves an employer who solicits sexual favors from an employee under the threat of terminating his or her employment. On college campuses, a faculty member who suggests awarding grades for sexual favors is clearly guilty of sexual harassment. Many less-clear circumstances may constitute sexual harassment. Under certain circumstances, sexist language, sexist jokes, suggestive comments, and other demeaning gestures or comments by a faculty member in the classroom or by an employer, may constitute sexual harassment. These and other actions may create a "hostile environment" in which a person is made to feel so uncomfortable that he or she is unable or unwilling to continue in that environment.

Sexual harassment is prohibited by Title VII of the Civil Rights Act, Title IX of the Education Amendment, and by the Equal Employment Opportunity Act, which expanded the authority of the Equal Employment Opportunity Commission. This commission and the federal courts have the authority to enforce these laws in the workplace and on college campuses. Most colleges and universities have developed their own sexual harassment policy. If you or one of your residents has been sexually harassed, you should approach your hall director, the dean of students, or a counselor in your counseling center to learn the correct steps to pursue the matter. Chances are that if a faculty member or an employer has harassed one student, he or she has possibly harassed others. Institutions as well as companies have an interest in stopping this behavior. Such conduct is detrimental to the teaching and educational process.

In making a claim of sexual harassment, the rights of the person being accused must also be respected. The accused person should be presumed innocent unless proven otherwise, and he or she is entitled to due process in the investigation and disposition of the accusation. Allegations of sexual harassment are often difficult to prove. One of the factors an administrator will consider is how often these claims have previously been made against this same faculty member or employer. Whatever procedure the institution uses, you or the resident who may have been sexually harassed need to report it to someone in authority. A staffperson can explain the process and advise you or your resident about how to proceed. Be careful to offer no promises or guarantees about the outcome of such a report. Although you may be tempted to offer reassurances that an accused harasser will be disciplined, the truth is that these situations are complex and the outcomes are often unpredictable.

Although sexual harassment is generally thought of as harassment against females, males also may be sexually harassed. These sexual advances may be homosexual or heterosexual. They may involve a female faculty member or employer harassing a male or female student or a male faculty member or employer harassing a male or female student. Under some circumstances, sexual harassment may also include a student harassing another student if a supervisory or power relationship has been established. All students should be aware of what constitutes sexual harassment to help ensure that they neither perpetrate nor tolerate this behavior.

SEXUAL HARASSMENT

● Myths

Sexual harassment is rare.

The seriousness of sexual harassment has been exaggerated; most so-called harassment is really trivial and harmless flirtation.

Many women make up and report stories of sexual harassment to get back at their employers or others who have angered them.

Women who are sexually harassed generally provoke harassment by the way they look, dress, and behave.

If you ignore harassment, it will go away.

● Facts

Sexual harassment is extremely widespread. It touches the lives of 40 to 60 percent of working women, and similar proportions of female students in colleges and universities.

Sexual harassment can be devastating. Studies indicate that most harassment has nothing to do with "flirtation" or sincere sexual or social interest. Rather, it is offensive, often frightening, and insulting to women; many experience serious psychological and health-related problems.

Research shows that less than 1 percent of complaints are false. Women rarely file complaints when they are not justified in doing so.

Harassment does not occur because women dress provocatively or initiate sexual activity in the hope of getting promoted and advancing their careers. Studies have found that victims of sexual harassment vary in physical appearance, type of dress, age, and behavior. The only thing they have in common is that the overwhelming majority are women.

It will not. Research has shown that simply ignoring the behavior is ineffective; harassers generally will not stop on their own. Ignoring such behavior may even be seen as agreement or encouragement.

Types of Sexual Harassment

Gender Harassment.   Generalized sexist statements and behavior that convey insulting or degrading attitudes about women. Examples include insulting remarks, offensive graffiti, obscene jokes, or humor about sex or women in general.

Seductive Behavior.   Unwanted, inappropriate and offensive sexual advances. Examples include repeated unwanted sexual invitations, insistent requests for dinner, drinks, or dates, persistent letters, phone calls, and other invitations.

Sexual Bribery.   Solicitation of sexual activity or other sex-linked behavior by promise of reward; the proposition may be either overt or subtle.

Sexual Coercion.   Coercion of sexual activity or other sex-linked behavior by threat of punishment; examples include negative performance evaluations, withholding of promotions, threat of termination.

Sexual Imposition. Gross sexual imposition (such as forceful touching, feeling, grabbing) or sexual assault.

Of these five types of behavior, gender harassment is by far the most common, followed by seductive behavior. The "classic" form of sexual harassment (bribery and coercion) are in fact relatively uncommon, while other forms of sexual imposition happen more frequently than most people think. Recent court decisions have also found that certain types of offensive visual displays in the workplace, such as pornography, can be considered sexual harassment.

The defining characteristic of sexual harassment is that it is unwanted. It is important to clearly let an offender know that certain actions are unwelcome.[21]

How to Respond to Harassment. Every situation is different and only the victim can evaluate the problem and decide on the best response. Friends, affirmative action officers, human resource professionals, and women's groups can offer information, advice, and support but only the victim can decide the best course of action. Only one thing is absolutely certain—ignoring the situation will not cause it to go away.

Above all the victim should **not blame himself or herself for the harassment.** The victim is not at fault. Place the blame where it belongs—on the harasser. Self-blame can cause depression and will not help the victim or the situation.

STRATEGIES FOR

Dealing with Harassment . . .

- Say **NO** to the harasser! Be direct.

- Write a letter to the harasser. Describe the incident and how it made you feel. State that you would like the harassment to stop. Send the letter by certified mail. Keep a copy.

- Keep a record of what happened and when. Include dates, times, places, names of persons involved and witnesses, and who said what to whom.

- Tell someone; do not keep it to yourself. By being quiet about the harassment, you do not help stop it. Chances are extremely good that you are not the only victim of your harasser. Speaking up can be helpful in finding support and in protecting others from being victims.

- Find out who is responsible for dealing with harassment in your organization and whether you can talk in confidence with that person. Almost all organizations have sexual harassment policies, procedures, and individuals or counselors who administer them. Find out what the procedure is at your workplace or school; it is the organization's responsibility to provide you with advice, help, and support. Not only can your company offer you support, but such meetings at the workplace can provide an important record if legal action is ever advisable.

- If you are experiencing severe psychological distress, you may want to consult a psychologist or other mental health professional who understands the problems caused by sexual harassment.

REVIEW

1. What are stereotypes, and how do they help us in perceiving the world around us?

2. What is the difference between prejudice and discrimination?

3. Briefly describe three sources of prejudice.

4. Give three reasons why people of color often feel unwelcome at predominantly White universities?

5. What is *cross-cultural communication,* and how can the RA improve it among the residents in his or her living unit?

6. How does the socialization process for women influence the nature and complexity of their relationships with others?

7. Define *sexual harassment.*

8. Does your institution have a policy on sexual harassment? If so, briefly explain the policy.

9. What is your institution's policy for making roommate changes when the request is based on dissatisfaction with the other person's race?

APPLICATIONS

CROSS-CULTURAL MISCOMMUNICATION

Scott had always wanted to attend Big Sky University and was thrilled when he was granted admission. He moved in the first day the residence halls opened and was primed for what he envisioned would be the ultimate college experience. His roommate had not arrived, but he was eager to meet the person who he hoped would become one of his closest friends.

The day after he moved in, Scott returned to his room and discovered a young man who introduced himself as Mohammed. The man proceeded to tell Scott that he was 21 and a citizen of Iran. He came to the United States on a scholarship from his government to study engineering. He had been married since he was 18. He planned to study alone in the United States for a year, then bring his wife to live with him while he finished his studies.

Mohammed was a strict Muslim. He prayed five times a day, observed all of the Islamic holidays, and read the Koran each day. His English was understandable to the careful listener but he often had difficulty.

This was not the roommate Scott had envisioned he would have. He was from a small town and didn't know any international students. All he knew about Iran was from the television news. Much of what they reported about the political climate of the country was unfavorable. Mohammed had made friends with some other Iranian students and, when Scott returned to his room the next day, his roommate had three other Arab students in the room, speaking Arabic. Scott didn't know what to do, where to sit, or how to fit in with these other men.

By the time classes started, Scott just couldn't deal with his disappointment and frustration any longer. He didn't want to cause trouble, but he wanted a roommate who was like himself and who had the same interests. He went to the RA and asked him to help him get a room change. The residence halls at Big Sky University were full, and no roommate changes were allowed for four weeks, after which time room change requests would be honored on a class priority system beginning with seniors. There were always more requests than could be accommodated. The one exception to the four-week waiting period and priority system was a "special situation petition" supported by the RA and the hall director.

Scott asked to be granted a "special situation petition." He wrote the following:

Dear Director of Residence Life:
   I need a room change. My roommate is not what I expected. He doesn't speak English and he is married. He is always bringing his friends into the room, and they talk in Arabic. I can't understand them.
   Once I walked in on all of them praying together on the floor. I didn't know what to do, and they got angry when I came in and got my books.
   I need to get out of this room. This isn't what I thought Big Sky University would be like. I want a roommate that I can do stuff with. I talked this over with my Mom and Dad, and they want me to move too. If you want, you can call them.
Very truly yours,
Scott
P.S. If I don't get moved, I might have to drop out of college.

WHAT WOULD YOU DO?

1. If you were Scott's RA, would you support his "special situation petition"? If not, would you support his request for special consideration after the four-week period? Explain your answer.
2. How might the RA ease Scott's concerns?
3. If Mohammed was an African American student, born and raised in the United States, and his friends were African American students, would you feel differently about Scott (a White student) requesting special consideration for a room change? Explain your answer.
4. What are the three largest racial groups on your campus? When a student from another group does not want to live with a member of one of these groups, what complaints do they make?
5. Some institutions have adopted a policy that forbids roommate changes on the basis of race, creed, color, national origin, disability, or sexual orientation. What is your opinion of such a policy?

HARASSMENT

Cranston was a Ph.D. candidate, and as part of his assistantship he agreed to live in the university's living-and-learning residence hall. He and his wife lived in a special apartment in the hall and he taught a philosophy course in the residence hall. Students in this class lived in the residence hall, which was coed. Cranston's class of 20 had 10 women in it.

Cranston liked to start each class with a joke. Most had sexual overtones and generally were degrading to women. Cranston flirted with all the women in his class, but showed particular attention to Shawn. She liked the attention and encouraged it. She would come to class in very seductive clothing and flirt shamelessly with Cranston whenever she had the opportunity. Time and time again she would invite Cranston to her room to see something, and he would go willingly.

Shawn bragged to her roommate that she wanted to have an affair with Cranston. She was carrying a heavy course load this semester and could not afford to put as much effort into the philosophy class as Cranston was requiring. She also thought he was cute. She decided she might be able to get him to give her a break if she were particularly nice to him.

Before long, Cranston and Shawn were sexually involved by mutual consent. About half the time Shawn would go to Cranston's apartment after his wife went to work. Other times, they used Shawn's room while her roommate was in class.

Most of the women on Shawn's floor knew or suspected what was going on. At the end of the semester, Shawn found out that she had earned a C in the course. She was angry because she had expected an A. Cranston and Shawn had a big fight over the grade, and Shawn went to her RA.

Shawn told her RA that Cranston had slept with her and that she wanted to file sexual harassment charges against him.

WHAT WOULD YOU DO?

1. Given that Shawn was a willing and consenting participant in the affair, does she have grounds for filing charges of sexual harassment against Cranston? Why or why not?
2. Do the students in Cranston's class have grounds for filing charges of sexual harassment against him? If so, what are the grounds?

3. If you were Shawn's RA, how would you advise her?

4. If Cranston were a bachelor and he had an affair with Shawn, would it make any difference in your feelings about what happened? Explain your answer.

5. If Shawn were a homosexual man and Cranston was bisexual, do you think Shawn would have grounds for filing sexual harassment charges? Why or why not?

6. Do you see anything wrong with a faculty member having an affair with a student who is not in his or her class and is not likely to be at any time in the future? Why or why not? How does your institution's policy address this issue?

7. If you were the president of the university and this situation came to your attention, what action, if any, would you take against Cranston? What action, if any, would you take against Shawn?

PART FIVE

EDUCATIONAL OUTREACH

Educational Programming

Community Development

CHAPTER EIGHTEEN

EDUCATIONAL PROGRAMMING

©1998 PHOTODISK, INC.

Programming may not be as easy as the professional staff in the office of residence life may tell you it is, but it is not nearly as difficult as some of your fellow RAs make it out to be. It does take time, it does take planning, and it is not always successful. The hardest thing about programming in the residence halls is getting your residents involved. Often, expecting students to sit through another lecture or to learn one more thing after spending a long day attending classes is just too much. Some days, all a student wants to do is vegetate in front of a television and escape. As the semester proceeds, stress increases, and it becomes increasingly difficult to stimulate interest in educational programs.

You might ask, Why bother? It would save time for everyone if you weren't expected to do programming. And, in some ways you might be right. However, programming is one of the major vehicles available to you to make the experience of living in a residence hall part of the educational experience of college. Education is most effective when it is a total experience and not just the 12 to 18 hours a week students spend in class and the 10 to 20 hours a week they must spend studying. As a total experience, all aspects of the environment should contribute to students' education. Woodrow Wilson expressed it this way: "So long as instruction and life do not merge in our colleges, so long as what the undergraduates do and what they are taught occupy two separate, airtight compartments in their consciousness, so long will the college be ineffectual."[1]

In the residence hall, instruction and leisure time can be blended to support common interests and promote shared experiences leading to self-discovery. Programming is a means of engaging students in active learning. It is the forum that you and your residents use to organize activities that make a positive contribution to the learning environment and the students' education. Programming is a tool that you can use to change an impersonal atmosphere into a supportive community environment.

As students in the residence halls share programs, they are drawn closer together. The interface of these common educational experiences creates opportunities for discovery, creativity, and self-exploration. Programs can inform, give people tools for development, and bind people to one another in community.

The parameters of programming have been defined as narrowly as the interaction between two people and as broadly as the assembly of a theater audience. For the purposes of this chapter, *programming* is defined as "any organized activity designed to advance student learning or develop community."

GOALS OF PROGRAMMING

Residence hall programs are designed to meet one of the following programming goals:

1. To help students improve interpersonal and social skills

2. To develop a sense of community on a residence hall floor or in a residence hall

3. To educate and inform students

4. To engage students in their own learning

5. To provide an outlet for the release of emotions or to maintain or develop physical fitness

6. To provide opportunities for students to expand their social acquaintances and friendships

7. To promote self-discovery

The development of community in a residence hall is enhanced when people have mutual respect for one another, respect one another's rights, trust one another, and have a commitment to the group as a whole. Programming that creates interaction related to common interests helps build understanding and acceptance within the group. As the group becomes mutually supportive and understanding of one another through personal experiences, respect for the other person's positions and rights is gained.

Programming also serves the goal of educating. Through programming, people can learn new hobbies, develop new leisure activities, and explore new interests. A program on mountain climbing may foster a sense of community and at the same time provide information to students interested in exploring this aspect of their potential. Skill-development programs for personal growth in areas such as assertiveness, time management, and value clarification also serve to educate students. Parties, social exchanges, and dinners teach social and interpersonal skills that contribute to students' general education and may aid in the release of emotions.

Students who participate in residence hall government or arrange programs are involving themselves in their own learning. People who spend time in a group discussion on values or develop a workable study schedule are also involving themselves in their own learning. Programming brings about the opportunities for this involvement.

A friendly game of pool with other students may provide a much needed break from studying.

Programming also assists students in the release of emotions. Intramural athletics, aerobics, any form of physical competition, canoe trips, overnight camping trips, and survival-training programs are examples of programs that can aid in achieving this particular goal. Participation in these programs helps students release aggressions, tensions, stress, anxiety, and similar emotions. The fun and excitement of the activity help students escape from the pressures of college and provide a legitimate time for students to revive themselves.

Educational programming provides students with the opportunity to work with other students for the accomplishment of a common goal. This working relationship often opens avenues for better understanding of others and leads to improved interpersonal relationships among students. Sometimes conflicts arise when groups attempt to accomplish an educational program. Resolving these conflicts, and learning to work through the dynamics of the group, is part of enhancing one's interpersonal skills. Educational programming provides this opportunity as well.

Social development also can be provided through educational programming in the residence halls. Social interaction with members of the same sex and the opposite sex requires skills that are developed through experience and through watching others in social situations. Parties, dances, and similar social functions provide students with the opportunity to experience these situations and to develop the skills associated with casual conversation, meeting new people, and common social courtesies. These social circumstances allow students to see themselves in new roles and help them understand and expand dimensions of their personality.

Self-discovery is another goal of programming. Taking students on a high ropes course or a similar field trip may help students learn self-confidence, teamwork, trust, and situational leadership.

TRADITIONAL PROGRAMMING MODEL

One traditional model for programming identifies topics or categories. Each category concerns an activity that, when combined with other activities, should develop a balanced programming effort for students. This might also be called a cocurricular model for programming. It presumes that students should gain information or knowledge in certain areas or categories through their experience in residence halls. The categories or curricula are as follows.

Educational

Educational programs are generally information oriented. Speakers, documentary movies, and group discussions centering on a particular current affairs topic are often categorized in this area of educational programming. Programs that help students explore career opportunities or give them information about a campus service (e.g., the student health center, study skills program, academic advising program) are other examples of educational programs.

Recreational

Recreational programs are entertainment oriented. Movies, field trips, canoe trips, hiking, mountain climbing, parachuting, and similar types of activities generally fall into this category.

Cultural

Cultural programs include exhibits and performances of various types. Theater productions, opera, and similar activities are included in this category.

Athletic

Athletic programming includes intramural sports, interresidence hall athletics, and other athletic competitions.

Wellness

Some of these activities might be athletic or educational or a combination of the two.

Programs that help students design a personal exercise program or teach them about nutrition are typical examples of wellness activities. A regular jogging program for members of your living unit or some type of aerobics program are other examples.

Crafts and Hobbies

Programs that teach students a craft such as knitting or pottery fall into this category. Hobbies include a diverse number of activities, from collecting baseball cards to gardening. Programs on these topics enable students to explore new areas of interests and to acquire new skills. Some of these may lead to a job after college or to the continuation and refinement of knowledge in the area for personal enjoyment.

Developmental

Developmental programming is considered skill development. It includes such programs as assertiveness and time-management training workshops on overcoming self-defeating behavior, and career- and life-planning workshops. These programs help people develop important personal skills that assist them in their growth toward maturity. Participation in group counseling, some form of encounter group, or biofeedback training are also developmental.

Social

Social programs are those activities that join people together to teach social skills, to have fun, and to release tension, anxiety, and frustration. Parties, dinners, and most gatherings for the purpose of socializing are classified as social programs.

Encounter

Programs that are located in places where students are likely to happen upon the program and participate are sometimes referred to as encounter programs. Examples might include a climbing wall assembled in the lobby, a band in a public place without admission, or a public debate. Such programs allow students to use uncommitted blocks of time and invite students to make spontaneous decisions based on exposure to the program.

Passive Programs

A bulletin board or display that conveys meaningful information on topics such as drugs, alcohol, or studying placed near the elevator where students are waiting might have a greater influence on students than a dozen speakers on these subjects. Use of passive programs is a way for students to use otherwise wasted time in productive ways

WELLNESS PROGRAMMING MODEL

Another frequently used model for residence hall programming is the wellness model. The *wellness model* is based on a unitary theory that educational programming in residence halls should help students fulfill their full human potential. To accomplish this, students need to grow in each dimension of their life. In many ways the wellness model is a reflection of student development theory, which proposes that people have different but interrelated dimensions of their lives in which they need to grow and learn. Many different wellness models exist. Some have four dimensions, some five, six, seven, or eight. They are all based on the early Greek model of human development that says a person needs to be sound in (1) mind, (2) body, (3) heart, and (4) soul. Figure 18.1 presents a wellness model in the form of a wheel. It has six sections, each comprised of two subsections.

Intellectual

Intellectual development includes efforts at mastering information and increasing one's cognitive complexity. It is composed of two subsections which involve the person's readiness to develop cognitively and the person's ability and desire to master information.

Spiritual

Spiritual development concerns the maturity of an individual's beliefs concerning creation, existence, and death. For most students it is comprised of some information about formal religious practices and an internal, personal awareness or understanding of beliefs concerning topics such as the existence of God and life after death. These internal beliefs may or may not be consistent with any formal religion.

Emotional

Emotional development refers to the ability of a person to recognize and develop appropriate adult responses to feelings that they have. One's reactions to feelings such as anger, jealousy, grief, and love are a combination of learning how to respond and the maturity and depth of ability to express those emotions. The first subsection is one's emotional maturity based on certain developmental experiences, and the second is how one has learned to express emotions based on social expectations and past experience.

Programming can help students in each of these six dimensions. A program concerning self might include a lecture on how students grow and develop in college or having students complete a

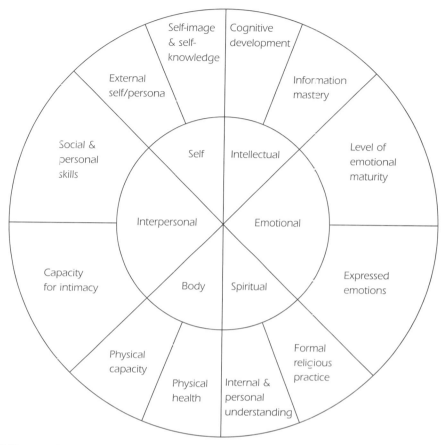

Figure 18.1. *Wellness wheel.*

personality test. This information would then be scored and interpreted in group sessions by a person trained in the interpretation of these tests. Programming can be designed for each of these six dimensions and for each of the twelve subdimensions.

HOW TO PROGRAM

Programs presented early in the fall term help establish the expectation for more programs. Students quickly come to accept programs as part of the natural order of life in residence halls. Some RAs with programming requirements wait until the last minute to plan their programs. Their motivation often is to meet job requirements. RAs in-

terested in the development of their residents set the expectation of education in the halls by having programs in the first month of the school term when habits are set. Last-minute programs are easy to recognize: speakers on information- or education-oriented topics brought in during the last part of the year. When this is the first attempt at programming, it is usually doomed to fail. If a good foundation for programming is laid early in the year, students will anticipate attending programs.

Programs can be arranged the spontaneous way or the organized way. The spontaneous approach is not the same as a last-minute program. Spontaneity is important in programming and is a legitimate programming effort. The spontaneous program capitalizes on the creative use of available resources. A spontaneous program may happen when you discover that in two days a well-known speaker will be on campus. You might try to arrange for that person to eat a meal in the residence hall with your residents or to have the person come to the floor for an informal reception and discussion. Another spontaneous program might concern a campus issue. You might respond by inviting somebody from the institution to come to discuss the issue, or arrange for your residents to attend a program on the topic.

The organized approach is the one that is most often successful and provides the greatest latitude for programming. You should not attempt to plan a canoe trip a hundred miles from your campus 48 hours before you want to leave.

Ten Steps to a Successful Program—Traditional Method

The 10 steps given here describe an organized way to plan programming. This is the way most good programs are accomplished, but it is not the only way. This planned approach pulls in different resources and enables you to move clearly to a successful program.

Step 1: Assess the Residents' Needs.
All too often people attempt to arrange programs without assessing the needs of the group. Needs assessment can be handled in several ways. Many educational programming teams in residence halls begin the year by administering an interest survey, which lists a number of possible programs for students to evaluate based on their interest. You can generate your own list of ideas for an interest survey.

Interest surveys can be particularly helpful for gaining an understanding of the common interests of your residents. They can give you an idea of the scope of programming and how you should direct it. People respond on surveys according to the options you provide. If you use surveys, try assessing programming needs through the survey at the beginning of the year, and then, intermittently throughout the year, review the surveys with groups of your residents. The ensuing discussions will help you discover new program ideas.

Brainstorming at a floor meeting is another way to generate ideas for programs. *Brainstorming* is a very simple technique that requires a person to ask questions and facilitate the flow of conversation and ideas. The key to using this technique in a small group is to allow a free flow of ideas, no matter how bizarre, without any limitations on their feasibility. It is an idea-generating time. You may use the following brainstorming format:

1. A small group of people is called together and the topic of programming is introduced. This is usually done best on a newsprint pad at the front of the room or on a large sheet of butcher paper.

2. The facilitator chooses an assistant to write down all the ideas that are generated. Generally a time limit is placed on the length of this brainstorming activity. The facilitator may wish to extend the time limit or alter the time limit depending on the interests and ideas being generated by the group.

3. The group is instructed to imagine any possible program in which they or others might be interested.

4. The facilitator asks the basic question, "What programs, activities, or interests would you like to see us undertake this year?"

5. The facilitator may offer a few ideas but should encourage the group to generate most of the ideas. The facilitator should reinforce people who offer ideas with comments like "That's a good idea; let's get that one down," or "Great idea!"

6. When the time limit is reached or the group has run out of ideas, the facilitator brings the brainstorming session to a close.

7. The group is then asked to rank those programs in which they would like most to participate.

8. Feasibility of the programs may be discussed at this time, relative to the rank order.

9. The top three or four programs are discussed and selected consistent with the group's rankings.

Another version of this brainstorming approach is to take a number of items (e.g., a fountain pen, a ball, a book, and a tennis shoe) and place them in a box or paper bag. Ask the group to divide into smaller groups; then ask each small group to suggest programs they could arrange with each one of the objects in the box or bag. The small groups then share their programming ideas with the larger group. This can be conducted as a contest among the small groups. These ideas can eventually be built into a series of programs.

Both brainstorming and interest surveys are formal techniques for determining programming needs within the hall. Informal contacts and discussions with students also can help determine needs. In your discussions with the residents of your living unit, certain needs may become apparent. For example, if a number of students mention some difficulties about meeting class assignment deadlines and are frustrated in their studies, perhaps they are expressing a need for a study-skills program or a program about procrastination. You may then wish to approach individuals in the living unit with such an idea to gauge their interest. Or, you may be sitting in on a late-night discussion with your residents during which the group begins to discuss their values related to sexuality. This might provide you with the opportunity to invite a speaker to discuss human sexuality and to answer some of the questions raised in the informal discussions.

Step 2: Set Objectives for the Program. An *objective* is a statement that describes the process by which a goal should be attained. It describes the expected performance and the conditions under which the performance is expected to occur. Objectives are useful in defining exactly

what you intend to do. They are particularly helpful in communicating to others what you are attempting to achieve and why. You can use the following five-step plan to state what is commonly referred to as a performance objective:

1. Identify who is to engage in a particular behavior (who will be affected).

2. Describe the behavior that is to be done in behavioral terms (what will be done).

3. Describe conditions under which behavior is expected to occur (how performance is to be manifested).

4. Specify standards of acceptable performance (how well behavior should be performed).

5. Specify criteria on which performance will be judged (how to judge behavior).

Examples of performance objectives are:

• Eighty percent of the students in my unit will have participated in at least one floor and one hall program before the end of the winter term, as measured by an informal poll of the residents on the floor during a floor meeting the week before winter term finals week in the winter term.

• On June 4, at least 25 percent of the residents of my floor will participate in a program on human sexuality in the floor lounge and will rate it as "interesting" or "very interesting" on an evaluation form that I will distribute at the end of the program.

Objectives are important because they state for you and others exactly who is to be affected, what specifically will be done, how it will be done, and how you will know that it has been accomplished.

Step 3: Involve Others. One of the most important elements of learning takes place through direct involvement in programs. It is the most efficient way to arrange programs, as well as the most educational way to accomplish them. As an RA, you are in a position of responsibility requiring organizational and coordinating skills.

However, you should not feel compelled to do all of the work in designing and implementing programs yourself; if you do, the programs then become your programs. Ideally, programs should be collective efforts. People are more likely to participate in programs to which they have contributed. If people design a program together, they become ego-involved in its success. On the other hand, if the program is your program, you must elicit the loyalty and faith of others for the program to succeed.

Two leadership styles which can be used to work with students are the autocratic style and the democratic style. The former is highly rigid and centralized. One person makes all the decisions and gives all the orders. This leadership style might be appropriate for combat or a police crisis, but is not useful for programming. The preferred leadership style is democratic. This style allows everyone to have input into the decision making, and to share responsibility for what is and is not accomplished. The democratic, or team-management approach, is the advisable way to work with students in programming. Although the autocratic approach may have limited success, it will not accomplish the goal of helping people involve themselves in their own education, nor is it the best way to achieve the programs that you will want.

The pragmatic part of educational programming is that sometimes no one wants to help. This occasionally happens, and the responsibility falls on you to insure that the program takes place.

STRATEGIES FOR

Involving Others

- **Delegate.** Delegation is essential to successful programming. Always ask a specific person to assume responsibility for a specific task. This is preferable to asking for volunteers, which communicates that the responsibility is not very important and that anyone could do the job. When you select a student, you communicate that he or she has a special talent which the group needs. This reinforces the student's self-esteem.

- **Coordinate.** The responsibility of a person organizing a program is to coordinate the program. This means attention to detail and continual follow-up with people who have responsibility for various parts of the program. As the program coordinator, you may have asked others to assist with the program, but the success of the program is still your responsibility. Programming is a process, and students learn from that process. Coordinate the skills of others, keeping in mind that your ultimate goal is eventually to move to the next step.

- **Abdicate.** Abdicate your involvement when possible. Try to put someone else in charge of designing, organizing, and coordinating the program. Become a true advisor. Advise your residents on how they can accomplish what they need to do, but do not do it for them. The one exception to this rule will perhaps occur at the beginning of the year, when you must role model good organizational and programming skills to give your residents the opportunity to learn from you. One of your personal goals should be to turn over much of the programming responsibility to a group of students in your living unit. Ideally, these students should come up with the ideas, arrange the programs, evaluate them, and gain the reinforcement or glory from the success of those programs.

- **Motivate.** Encourage, support, and reward those in the group who are helping with a program. Mention in front of others the accomplishments of these students and tell them how much you appreciate their contribution.

Programming may be easier to do yourself, but doing so deprives others of the opportunity to learn important skills associated with this activity. When you are unsuccessful at involving others, do the programs yourself. Try to get one or two students to help you if possible. Remember, it is better that you do the programming yourself than not to have any educational programming on your floor.

Step 4: Preprogram Planning.
By this stage, you have discussed the needs of the group, determined your specific objectives, and hopefully involved others in the formation of the ideas and the organization of the program. You and your residents are now ready to plan the program's general format. Essentially, you examine the feasibility of your proposed program. In this stage of the planning, you find answers to the following questions.

Ask Yourself...

Are facilities available?

What resources will we need to accomplish this program?

What tentative dates would be possible for this program? Are there any conflicts?

What monetary support is necessary for the success of this program?

What special equipment or facility (sound equipment and so on) is needed for the completion of this program?

Who on the programming staff should be contacted to get approval for the program or to get additional information?

Does this program comply with university policies regulating residence hall activities?

Who will attend the program (coed group, people from other living units)?

Draw up a tentative plan. Does the plan meet the needs of the group? If it does not, revise the objective or revise the plan. You are now ready to plan the actual event.

Step 5: Plan the Program.
Every good program needs a good title, one that will motivate, excite, and encourage people to attend. If the audience that you have defined in the preprogram plan is the residents of your living unit, your title may be different from one for a program intended for the entire residence hall or campus. If your audience will consist of the residents of your living unit, you may wish to choose a title like "The Art of Keeping the Group in the South Wing Quiet," "Study Skills for Stereo Buffs," or "Bluffing Your Way through College." If the audience is to be the entire residence hall, you may wish to title the program something like "Academic Success Through the Art of Studying."

Good programmers keep accurate records. If you are writing to companies for promotional items or contacting speakers, you should keep good records of these contacts. Try setting up a file for each program that you are planning. Although getting too meticulous about paperwork can inhibit programming and make it overly complicated, it is better to be slightly too organized than not organized enough to complete the program. You will find that good organization saves time.

Step 6: Publicity.
If you have done everything correctly up to this point, you probably have the design of a reasonably good program, but the program will not achieve your objective unless people actually attend. No matter how much deemphasis is put on evaluating programs solely on the basis of attendance, attendance is important. Spending $100 on a program that only one student attends is not a good allocation of money—even if the student really enjoys the program. Poor attendance can be attributed to poor needs

assessment, poor planning and organization, or poor publicity.

Publicity is a key element in the success of a program. Good publicity that motivates and encourages people to attend helps bring people in contact with what your program has to offer. Poor publicity turns people off (or doesn't reach them in the first place) and limits the success of your program. Preparing and distributing the publicity is not easy; it is hard work, and it takes a lot of time. This is one reason why sharing responsibilities is key. Publicity is one of the items that people most often do not like to do. If you find somebody who is interested in doing publicity, especially an artist, cherish that person dearly. He or she can help ensure the success of many of your programs.

Elaborate publicity is not generally necessary in a residence hall. The element of creativity is more important. Some publicity ideas that have been used successfully are:

- a note about a program placed in a bottle hung in the shower
- logos or buttons worn by residents carrying the time, date, and place of the program
- a telephone or E-mail campaign within the residence hall
- notes on the cafeteria line
- flyers in the floor restrooms, on the back of urinals, and on the mirrors

Do not forget the importance of a positive attitude and word-of-mouth. A group of people who communicate excitedly about having a program can often be the most effective publicity. People want to go to programs that other people are attending. If a group of your friends were planning to attend a program, you would be much more inclined to go whether or not you were interested in the specific topic. Talk positively and excitedly about the program. Ask specific people in your living unit to attend the program. When you go to a program, gather several other people to go with you. Ask several of the residents in the

STRATEGIES FOR

Designing a Program . . .

- Determine program title.
- Set specific date.
- Set specific location.
- Delegate responsibilities.
- Reserve facilities, equipment, an speaker(s)
- Determine budget (if applicable).
- Do publicity.
- Set time for program.
- Review policies related to program (if applicable).
- Review program with hall director.
- Set deadlines for each project and delegated assignment.
- Confirm dates, time, place, topic, telephone numbers, and money in writing.

living unit to do the same. If you have five or six people who agree to bring four friends each, you now have a group of 25 to 30 people. That could be a reasonably good showing and will allow more people to be introduced to the program.

Step 7: Final Checklist. Simply check what you have done. Go through every step and make sure that you have accomplished what you need to accomplish The checklist should be a review of your program plan. This is the time for you to check with everyone who has agreed to do something for the program to confirm that he or she has done it or will do it.

Step 8: The Day of the Program. On the day of the program, check your speaker, program material, transportation, or other resources to see that everything is ready. Make sure facilities to be used are clean, neat, and usable. If you are having refreshments, confirm that they will be delivered or that somebody will pick them up. Have special publicity prepared for the day of the program and the day before the program. People usually notice new items on the bulletin board, so this is a good publicity technique to encourage attendance.

Be at the site of the program at least a half hour before the program is to start. This will enable you to fix any unexpected problems or to answer any last-minute questions. Make sure that somebody meets the speaker, if there is one, or brings the material necessary for the program.

Step 9: At the Program.   If the program has a speaker, somebody needs to introduce him or her. This could be you, but preferably someone else who has worked with the program should do it. Make sure that the speaker is introduced to any administration representatives who may be at the program and make sure that the speaker has the opportunity to meet as many students as possible before the program begins.

TEN STEPS TO A SUCCESSFUL PROGRAM

1. Assess Needs
2. Set Objectives
3. Involve Others
4. Pre Plan
5. Plan
6. Publicity
7. Final Checklist
8. Double Check
9. Execute
10. Evaluate

Before the program, think of some questions that will help stimulate discussion. You may wish to provide a few members of the audience with questions ahead of time. People ask questions when they see others doing it. You can start the discussion by asking some general questions and having your friends do the same.

Remember, nothing succeeds like success. A successful program, well executed, will mean better attendance, more support, more involvement, and better attainment of your program goals. Poor programs produce opposite results. If a program is boring, too long, or does not meet the needs of the students, people will be unlikely to come to the next program.

Step 10: After the Program.   Once a program has concluded, evaluate the degree to which it met your goals. You can do this in several ways. A survey is probably most common, although people often do not like to fill out surveys at the end of a program. Surveys are useful in that they give you a collective reaction. However, they are somewhat formal, and they may not be appropriate for all the programs.

Another form of evaluation is an informal discussion that occurs later that evening or directly after the program. Make a point of asking people what they thought of the program—what they liked and what they did not like. Ask how they think the program could have been improved and if they would recommend it to other people. Whether or not you hand out formal evaluations to a number of residents or talk informally with a group, you should make some summary comments on every program presented. After all, you cannot determine if your program objective has been accomplished until you evaluate it.

Be sure to reinforce those students who helped with the program. This is best done publicly. Call them by name and say something like, "John found the speaker for this topic, and I think he has done a very good job. Let's give him a round of applause." Publicly congratulate and praise people who helped. This, after all, is the only payment they will receive. Recognition and reinforcement are two key ways of communicating your thanks for their help. There is nothing worse than leaving a program to which you have devoted your time without some expression of thanks. If your program planners did not do well, reinforce what they did do well and privately make some suggestions to them on what could have been done better.

Thank-you notes to speakers or people who helped with the program are always appropriate. Never invite a speaker to your living unit without sending a formal thank-you letter. If it was a large program presented to the entire residence hall, it may be appropriate to send a formal thank-you letter to the speaker and a copy to his or her supervisor. You should check this idea with your hall director to determine when it is appropriate.

Do not count on many rewards for yourself. Although you may feel a sense of accomplishment for what took place, people may not congratulate you. Your rewards will come later in knowing that you have presented a successful program and that people are interested and motivated to go to your programs. Other RAs in the building, as well as your hall director, will recognize your programming contribution.

Programming is one way for people to share a common educational experience that facilitates student learning. However, other methods and approaches might work just as well—or better. Spending a weekend on a community service project or taking a field trip to the museum or a baseball game might achieve the same results—a common educational experience shared among your residents. Outdoor education programs, such as challenge courses, group interaction courses, high ropes courses, or nature hikes might better meet the interests and needs of your residents and are programs at least equal in value to the traditional 10-step approach discussed earlier.

CONCLUSION

The only limits to programming are those set by your institution or by your own creativity. Individual living units within residence halls have joined together to plan such programs as ski trips, field trips off campus, organization and promotion of a commercial carnival on campus, and speakers on almost any conceivable topic. Programming should be seen as an opportunity for your residents to share a common experience.

Although some educational programming may take funds, it does not need to. When funds are

EIGHT STEPS FOR PLANNING AN UNSUCCESSFUL PROGRAM

1. Guess at what you think others want to do.
2. Don't plan anything. Don't have any goals.
3. Wait until the last minute to prepare the program.
4. Don't involve anyone else—after all, you can do it better yourself.
5. Tell as few people as possible and make sure you wait until they have made other plans.
6. When you do tell people about the program, tell them how wonderful you are to have planned such a great program. Be sure to take all the credit and don't involve anyone else. (People will especially like this.)
7. Don't meet any outside contributors to the program or the speaker. Let them try to track you down in the best way they can. This will give them an opportunity to show resourcefulness.
8. Don't evaluate. Don't thank anyone. You won't want to see the evaluations, and you will get all the thanks you deserve.

Easier Programming

Chances are that your hall director or other people on your residence life staff also have special tips that will help you:

- **Approval.** Get approval from superiors for all programs.

- **Transportation.** Do not use your vehicle to transport people to a program unless your insurance covers such transportation or unless a special clause in your contract covers transportation related to your position as an RA.

- **Financial Transactions.** Do not use your personal checking or savings account for any financial transactions.

- **Publicity.** Publicity should be heaviest the day before a program and on the day of the program.

- **Speaker.** A speaker should be informed beforehand of the conditions under which he or she will speak and of the possibility that the group may be small.

- **Location.** Central lounge locations with a heavy flow of traffic will attract a number of people. These locations are generally good for programs designed to accommodate the entire residence hall.

- **Room Setup.** Do not trap students in the program by putting a speaker or a movie screen in front of the door. Keep a free flow of traffic for people to enter and exit easily if they choose.

- **Length of Program.** Determine with the programming committee an approximate length for the program. People's interest spans vary, but generally an hour to a maximum of two hours is considered a good length. The topic and interest of the participants should ideally determine length. Make sure before the program starts that you know how long it is to last. This makes a difference to the person conducting the program. If a speaker knows he or she is responsible for a 30-minute lecture with 30 minutes of questions, that takes one type of preparation. If he or she is expected to present a longer program, he or she may be able to incorporate other activities into the program.

- **Time.** The best programming time varies from campus to campus. Generally, Sunday to Thursday evenings prove to be the best time for programs. Most schools find that immediately after dinner—between 5 P.M. and 7 P.M. is a good time for programs. Part of this depends on assessing the habits and interests of the people in your living unit. Groups that are already formed and have a particular interest, such as a club or hobby group, will set their own times. Weekend programs involving hiking, trips, and evening programs are also possible.

- **Theme Programs.** Theme programs or a series of programs on the same topic can be effective. These should be held, when possible, at the same time, place, and location each week. Movie theme programs are often popular, but expensive.

- **Refreshments.** If refreshments are to be provided, this should be mentioned in the publicity. Some people may come to have refreshments and listen to the speaker. Every program need not have refreshments. Work with the food service to determine the quantity needed. Be aware of what packaged items can be returned to the food service for credit and which items cannot be returned. Compare the prices offered through the food service with the price of similar packaged goods at the grocery. Some items may be less expensive from the grocery.

required, the residence hall council or the housing administration often can support your program. Many programs involve little or no expense. Some of the most creative programs take the least amount of money. Programs that permit people to interact and to learn organizational or leadership skills are always worthwhile.

REVIEW

1. What are four goals of programming?
2. What are four categories of the traditional programming model?
3. Why should programming be established early in the academic year?
4. How do spontaneous programs differ from last-minute programs?
5. Identify three ways to do a needs assessment for programming in your living unit.
6. Write one performance objective for programming on your floor for next semester.
7. What is the best time to do programming on your floor and why?
8. List two of the best programs you attended in the residence halls and explain what made them good programs.
9. Identify a theme for a series of programs (other than movies) which you believe would be of interest to your residents, and identify at least three programs, each in a different category of the traditional model, which would fit within the theme you identified.
10. What programming model, if any, is used in the residence halls at your institution?

APPLICATIONS

TRYING TO GET BY IN PROGRAMMING

Carlo was in his third year as an RA. He had lost much of his enthusiasm for the job and had become somewhat cynical in his last year of school. He did not see any reason to inconvenience himself by organizing educational programs on his floor. The problem was that he was required to do at least two programs on his floor each semester. If he failed, the university's policy was to terminate his employment. All RAs clearly understood this, and it was given to them in writing as part of their contract.

When midterm examinations were past and he still had not done his first program, the hall director called Carlo into his office for a discussion about the importance of programming. Carlo called a friend of his who was a representative of the student government association (SGA) to come to his floor and speak. He announced a required floor meeting for all of the students on his floor, and Carlo's speaker came and talked for ten minutes about SGA, what it does for students, and how students could get involved. The speaker then offered to answer questions. No one had any questions, and the meeting was adjourned after a few comments from Carlo about noise on the floor.

As the semester drew to a close, Carlo had not done his second program, and he knew he needed to have one. He wrote a programming report that said that members of the floor were organized to attend a sporting event to be followed by a discussion about the relationship of college sports to the education of students.

Upon reading this programming report, the hall director approached one of the students on Carlo's floor to inquire about the program. The student had no idea what the hall director was talking about. When the hall director quizzed Carlo, he puffed up his explanation but finally admitted that the program was nothing more than seven of the men who lived on the floor going to a home football game together and talking about it afterwards. Anyone from the floor who had tickets was welcome to attend.

WHAT WOULD YOU DO?

1. If you were Carlo's hall director, would you terminate him for failure to complete two programs as required by his contract? Why or why not?

2. Identify five things that Carlo did not do in his first program, which, had he done, would have made it better.

3. If you were Carlo's hall director, and you decided to let Carlo remain an RA, what guidelines would you give him to make sure he did a better job in programming the second semester?

4. If you were Carlo's hall director and wanted to convince Carlo of the need to do educational programs on his floor, what would you tell him?

PROGRAM PROBLEM SOLVER

Dixie was a new RA in an all-freshmen residence hall. It was an older building with long, double-loaded, single hallways which housed about 60 women; two women were assigned to each room. Dixie wanted to do a good job in her first semester and decided to schedule twice as many programs as was expected. She was well organized and planned all of her programs before the semester started. The six programs she scheduled were (1) a speaker on the student health center services, (2) a movie about birth control, (3) a speaker about the university's honor program, (4) a speaker from the university police office to discuss campus safety, (5) a movie on the history of the university and some of the tourist attractions in the community in which the university was located, and (6) a speaker from the public health department to talk about HIV and AIDS.

At the end of the first semester, the Office of Residence Life administers a survey which assesses the social climate of each floor and the social climate of the building. The surveys from Dixie's floor showed that her residents rated the social climate of the living unit low. They felt isolated, were dissatisfied with the experience in the hall, and had no sense of belonging or community.

WHAT WOULD YOU DO?

1. Give two reasons why students on Dixie's floor may have rated the social climate low.

2. Give two strengths and three weaknesses in Dixie's programming.

3. If you were Dixie's hall director, what approach to programming would you suggest that Dixie use to build community on her floor?

4. List three programs that were held on your floor or in your building which you believe helped students develop a sense of community.

COMMUNITY DEVELOPMENT

Perhaps one of the greatest tragedies of the latter half of the twentieth century has been the breakdown of community and the rise of individualism. *Community* is both a sense of attachment to a group and a set of values that are commonly shared within a group.

In considering some 94 different definitions of *community,* Hillery discovered many similarities among them. From these definitions he developed a single definition of *community:* "A group of individuals engaged in social interaction, possessing common interests and goals, who show concern for and are sensitive to the needs of other members, and are primarily interested in furthering the group's goals over all others."[1]

For students in residence halls, *community* is the sense of belonging with other members of the group and a set of shared experiences that bind them together and make them a mutually identifiable group. For the student, the attachment to the other people in the living unit forms an all-important sense of belonging. In many ways, it is like a substitute family.

Why is this important to you as an RA? Very simply, the behavioral setting and the influence of peers within that setting are connected. The behavior of students in the living unit is shaped by interaction with the other students who compose their group. Both the formal structure of the facilities and the informal structure of the peer subculture have an influence. If the peer subculture can be developed in such a way as to promote concepts consistent with a supportive community feeling, it follows that students will internalize these values, assist one another in the accomplishment of their goals, and in general learn to function as members of a mutually supportive and sharing group. The far-reaching effects of having grown in such an environment, both in terms of one's self-image and the residual effects through community involvement in later adult years, are evident.

Specifically, a community transmits common goals and values. It fosters the ability to achieve deeper, more intimate relationships with people, frees interpersonal relationships, and increases self-acceptance and acceptance of others. It aids in shaping and developing a sense of personal integrity and ethics, shapes attitudes and values, and can modify human behavior in a positive direction.

The community also acts as a reference point for the individual. It is an identifiable group to which the person may point and claim allegiance. It provides specific social ties for the individual, encourages the development of adult social skills, and helps identify social contacts. One of its most important functions is as a mirror to assist the individual in developing a more accurate picture of himself or herself. Peers are used as a way of gauging one's behavior relative to group standards. A supportive community not only reflects positive values, but can assist an individual in gaining a better perspective of his or her own behavior. Of more intrinsic value, the availability of a community, in which the student trusts others, aids the student in times of crisis, need, and emotional stress.

ELEMENTS OF A COMMUNITY

Two issues to ponder about a community are what is necessary to establish it and how you, as the RA, can help foster a supportive community that will aid students in the accomplishment of their goals.

The establishment of a community is complex. For community to exist, people must have social contact. Physical proximity is necessary to allow people to interact with one another. The closer people are, the more likely they are to have frequent, informal, casual contact. People who see each other infrequently or who live at opposite ends of a residence hall floor are unlikely to establish the same feelings of community.

Shared values and a common primary group are another element of community. The group must have an identifiable set of shared goals and values in which it believes. For college students, this often means that they share many of the same attitudes and common peer-cultural values. These tend to be generational issues and often transcend the campus to a national level of peer culture. Examples of this include some fashions or trends, popular television shows, and favorite types of music. Although these are the most superficial forms of attitudes and opinions, they do form a common association among students of the same generation.

For community to exist on the floor, students need to consider the other residents of the floor as their primary group of friends and acquaintances. Students who join fraternities or sororities or who are involved in varsity athletic teams and some clubs and organizations often identify one of these groups as their primary group of friends and associates. However, many new students who move into a residence hall floor will come to identify their roommate and those students who live closest to them as their primary group of friends. As an RA, you can easily identify the cliques of students on your floor. They tend to be grouped at the ends of the corridors or around the use of the same shower facilities and stairwells.

For students to identify with a community, they must recognize that the group has the power or authority to act in some way. This may involve the power to grant rewards or status within the group or the collective authority to achieve some goal.

Members of a community must make a commitment to it. This is usually accomplished through a sense of self-sacrifice or personal transcendence. Community members need to recognize that the group is more important than any individual in it; and, by virtue of this belief, they must be willing to surrender some degree of individuality for the sake of the group. If the community decides that everyone will attend a football game together, this might mean that an individual not interested in football surrenders his or her individual wants to the community and attends the football game. If community exists, members likely will want to participate in the activities of the community. Because a strong sense of member identification develops communion with the group, it is an important element of how one defines oneself as an individual and as a member of the group.

All groups have a sense of informal or formal process by which they operate. This may be a parliamentary type of meeting or it may be an information interaction process. Fraternities and sororities have a formal process by which they operate and also an informal process by which things are accomplished within the organization. Residence hall floors function on the basis of an informal process. Usually they have a recognized leader and a process of dialogue or discussion that leads to a decision for the group to do something. Intramural teams often form a different community and have both an informal and formal structure. When the intramural team is comprised of a group of students from the same residence hall floor, dif-

ferent types of allegiances and a subgroup may form within the larger community.

Some elements of community are difficult to establish in a residence hall. One of these is a sense of mutual dependence, sometimes referred to as a survival need. In Israel, kibbutzes are communities in which people depend on one another for mutual survival. Food, security, entertainment, and the general welfare of the community depend on how each member of the community can contribute and share responsibility. This is usually not the case on a residence hall floor. This is more likely to exist in residence halls that operate as cooperatives.

Community members need to be able to distinguish the boundaries of the group. Solitude or some degree of isolation helps in defining the physical space controlled by the community. This is sometimes referred to as the *territorial imperative,* which is defined as "the need for individuals and groups to define and control a particular space." You will notice on residence hall floors that the territory is usually defined by the structural design of the living unit. If it has small interlocking corridors, for example, each one of these small corridors would probably be considered a separate territory. Physical properties of a residence hall floor tend to define the space (examples include doors, walls, or other segmentation of a larger unit). These physical boundaries help identify space and define who is and is not physically part of the community.

A sense of community on a residence hall floor also depends in part on individuals having enough time to contribute to the community. Interaction, informal meetings, and common shared experiences are necessary to sustain the individual within the community.

Finally, a community must have some type of formal or informal standard of normative behavior. Individuals who operate outside of the community standard receive some form of sanction. On residence hall floors, this sanctioning is usually informal. It may involve ridiculing the individual who violates the normative standard, open hostility and anger toward the individual, some form of ostracism, or a gradual devaluing of that person's contributions and suggestions to the community.

TYPES OF COMMUNITIES

The literature about residence hall living speaks of different types of communities. One type is a formal structured community, which often involves a special cooperative housing program, the support of the residence life staff, and a set of structured experiences that promote a sense of community. These communities may take the form of living-and-learning centers in which students may do many of the same things together by design of the program. Generally, these programs are characterized by a contract the student signs, faculty involvement, a set of goals to be accomplished during the committed experience, evaluation of the progress of the community, work as part of the students' contribution to the community, and similar activities designed to elicit a communal environment.

This is one way of approaching the development of a community environment, and it proves successful in many institutions. However, sense of community can also be established on a floor within a residence hall and—depending upon the size of the building—perhaps in a residential building as well.

HOW TO ESTABLISH A COMMUNITY

At this point you know what a community is, what it tries to achieve, and some of the factors necessary for a community to exist. How can you, as an RA, stimulate a sense of community within the group?

- The first thing you need is an appropriate physical setting that allows people to be in close proximity. Residence halls are ideal for this purpose, although large residence halls are less ideal than smaller living units. Groups of 10 to 20 individuals offer the best hope of establishing community involvement in a living unit; however, larger groups can be structured to develop community by breaking the groups into subgroups.

The physical structure of the living unit plays a major role in helping establish the community. If your living unit is somewhat isolated from other living units, through physical barriers such as walls and doors, or if the building that you occupy is small enough and isolated from other buildings, these physical divisions help define the boundaries or territory of the community. The group needs to define its territory in some fashion. Many residence life programs permit students to mark their territory, defining it as their own by decorating foyers, hallways, and lounges. Wall murals or signs with an agreed-upon name are examples of this marking behavior.

- The second component in the establishment of a community is a set of mutually shared experiences. This is where programming and general group activities such as intramural sports play an important role. The more opportunities the students have to interact in the same experience and with the same goals, the greater the chance for a community to exist. Intramural sports serve this function. If students participate on a football team in competition with a group outside of the residence hall, they enjoy a mutually shared experience with a common goal—winning the game.

This experience helps build a sense of team accomplishment and requires that individuals commit to one another, share skills with one another, and depend on one another for the accomplishment of their mutual goal. Building something together is another way of helping to establish a mutually shared experience that will promote a sense of community. This experience might be sewing a quilt, building some cabinets in the lounge, or painting murals on the walls of the corridor. Student projects give students a shared experience with a common goal.

- Communications and trust are intermingled to form the next element necessary for the development of a community. Communication is more than superficial talking. It involves an exchange of values and a sharing of personal emotions that one shares with trusted friends. Communication and trust are dependent on one another. These bonds can be enhanced by structured human relations experiences, such as may be found in the interpersonal training and self-awareness workshops conducted by campus counseling centers, and by talks about values and beliefs that occur in informal discussions. RAs can act as facilitators for the development of these discussions and can assist in further exploring the reasoning behind values.

Through communication and trust building, students can establish a sense that the group offers support for their individual accomplishments. This interpersonal support becomes self-perpetuating. It both enhances the community and maintains the importance of the community to the individual and to the group. For community to exist, people must feel free to share with one another at a level of personal intimacy and to feel that what they share will not be used to their disadvantage by others.

Community seems to crystallize when a group is faced with a task to accomplish, is threatened in some way, or experiences a crisis. When these situations exist, the group can readily identify a goal, a reason to work together, a reason for mutual support. Through the crisis or conflict, the group comes to recognize a common purpose in sharing and mutual dependence. Whether the crisis is contrived or real, the result is the same. A sense of external threat helps to stimulate a sense of community. Examples of this include the community support and effort to help flood or hurricane victims. People who have never worked together join and support each other as they work to rebuild structures and lives.

Your residence hall likely will never be threatened with attack from outside nor will you need to band together for mutual protection or support. Other ways of developing a sense of community exist. One way is through the establishment of a common goal at a general meeting of your residents. An identifiable common goal, something the group really wants to accomplish—winning a football trophy or remodeling the floor lounge—is one way to inspire the commitment necessary for the development of a feeling of community. People must have a reason to band together. This reason must be recognized as important by the group as a whole and must be considered attainable. Competition with other living units, intramural contests, or game tournaments also help in the formation of community by defining teams or membership boundaries—who is and is not a member of the community.

Whatever the group identifies as its goal or common purpose, it must be reaffirmed through a sense of communion within the group. The communion is a way of maintaining an inner group identity. It reaffirms the recognition of the community by the individual. Just seeing the entire living unit assembled is a visible sign of one's position within the community. But the members of the community need to feel involved in the community's accomplishments and its failures as well as its rewards. Every person must be solicited for involvement. This contact serves to maintain the group. In a more tangible way, the involvement may take the form of social interactions, recognized group accomplishment, rewards given to individual members, mutual recognition of individual members by the group, and shared authority within the community group. Whether these group-maintenance activities are parties, football games, concerts, construction projects, decorations, policy or program revisions, or new projects, they are important because they encourage the group to recognize and accept such activities as part of their identification with the group.

Students find it difficult to focus on others and to surrender part of their individuality to the community. One reason for this is that, during the developmental years of college, young people are focused on themselves. They are trying to establish a sense of who they are—an identity. Part of identity development is the process of differentiation. This makes the establishment of community in a residence hall more difficult. Other issues that interfere with the establishment of community include competing interests, other groups to which students belong, narcissistic self-interest, lack of relationship-building skills, and immaturity.

CONCLUSION

The French Revolution was predicated on liberty, equality, and fraternity. The United States has done much to help ensure liberty and has come a long way in trying to establish a policy of equality. Fraternity, or a sense of group community, has not been achieved, primarily because there are fewer opportunities for people to learn the skills of sharing with one another and to place allegiance to the group above commitment to self. Apathy on college campuses across the nation is no less obvious than apathy in the voting booth. Community membership is not something that simply exists; it is a commitment that one must learn and experience. As an RA you can give students the opportunity to experience a sense of community and to learn the skills of contributing as a group member.

REVIEW

1. What is your definition of *community?*

2. How can you tell when there is or is not a sense of community on a floor?

3. Why is a sense of community on a residence hall floor important? Give at least three reasons.

4. What are three important elements to establishing a community?

5. Given an example of a program or activity on your floor that helped make the residents more of a community, and explain why.

6. What role do intramural and other competitive sports play in the establishment of community on a residence hall floor?

7. What are the barriers hall directors face in establishing a sense of community within an entire residence hall?

8. Identify two groups on your campus that you believe have a strong sense of community, and explain why.

9. Do you believe students on your campus have a strong sense of identification (or feeling of community) with your institution? Why or why not?

10. How does the experience of living in a residence hall help or hinder the process of developing a sense of community with your institution?

11. What role, if any, do rituals and ceremonies play in the establishment of community on your residence hall floor and at your institution?

APPLICATIONS

ALTOGETHER

Rita was having a difficult time getting the students on her floor to interact with each other. About 40 women lived on her floor; half were residents last year and half were new freshmen. The returning students were grouped together in three clusters near the hall bathrooms. The new students were scattered about the hall and formed separate little pockets. By the end of the fall semester, Rita had five groups of eight women each on her floor. All the women seemed reasonably satisfied. There was occasionally some tension between one group of returning students at one end of the hall and some of the new students at the other end of the hall, but it was usually nothing serious.

None of the women on the floor knew all of the other students on the floor. Even Rita had a hard time remembering the names of all of her residents. At the two floor meetings she held in the fall semester, the students were not interested in having any social functions. Most of the returning women were involved with activities and jobs outside the residence hall, and most of the new students were pledging sororities and did not have time for any floor functions.

Rita met her programming requirement with two programs: one on sex education and one on drug education. Both were good programs, but poorly attended.

WHAT WOULD YOU DO?

1. Given the circumstances cited above, how important is it that Rita establish a sense of community among all 40 of her residents?
2. Do all 40 of the students in a living unit need to feel close to one another for a sense of community to exist? Explain your answer.
3. Could Rita have increased the communication and trust between the new students and the returning students? Explain how she could accomplish this or why it could not be accomplished.
4. What are the advantages and disadvantages to the development of community when mixing freshmen and upperclass students together in a residence hall?
5. When Rita is evaluated by her hall director, should she receive a low performance rating because she was unable to establish a sense of community among all of her residents?

THE WAR BETWEEN THE CORRIDORS

Oumar was the RA on the 12th floor of a 16-story high-rise residence hall. His 40 residents were all freshmen or transfer students. The building was constructed like a V. He had 20 residents down each corridor, and his room was located at the junction of the two corridors. The two flag football teams from his floor called themselves 12 North (composed of students from the north corridor) and 12 South (students from the south corridor).

The teams were in the same intramural league, and one evening after dinner they played a game of flag football. A fight broke out at the game, and both teams were suspended from participation in intramural football for that semester. By the time the students returned to the residence hall, tempers were running high.

Oumar found several students standing in front of the elevator yelling at one another and making threats. During the week that followed, students on 12 South had water dumped under their doors twice, had glue put in the locks of two of the doors, and the restroom at their end of the hall was trashed with paper and broken beer bottles.

Students on 12 North were not spared destruction. For every act of vandalism that occurred in the south corridor, there was retaliation. If two door locks were filled with glue in the south corridor, the students from 12 South saw to it that at least three were filled with glue in the north corridor. The fire alarm pull station had been pulled on several occasions at both ends of the floor.

The students from 12 South took to wearing T-shirts that showed a rebel flag inscribed with "12 South." Not to be outdone, the students on 12 North had their own T-shirt designed showing the American flag and bearing the inscription "12 North."

Oumar tried to catch the students responsible for the vandalism by sitting up all night, but was not successful. Apparently the whole thing had become a game, and each corridor was out to defeat the other by acts of vandalism. On two occasions, someone jammed Oumar's door shut, and on several occasions water was dumped under his door. Oumar tried to find out who was responsible, but no one would tell him. The only information he would receive was allegations about how one group or the other did this or that. Students on each corridor were very close with the men from their corridor, but the two groups of students disliked each other, and neither group like Oumar or the hall director.

WHAT WOULD YOU DO?

1. If you were Oumar, what would you do to end the conflict and floor vandalism?

2. Identify the elements of community (observable behavior) existing on Oumar's floor?

3. What could Oumar have done when the conflict first arose to diffuse the hostility between the two groups? If so, what?

4. The dean of students was consulted about the problems on the 12th floor, and she gave the students until the end of the semester to resolve their differences or she would instruct the Director of Residence Life to disband the entire floor and send each student to a different living unit on campus. What are the advantages and disadvantages of this solution?

5. List at least four programs or activities that Oumar might have done in the first few weeks of school to build community on the floor as a whole.

6. What are the possible negative repercussions to students from living on a floor characterized by this ongoing conflict?

PART SIX

RA SURVIVAL SKILLS

Time Management

Study Skills

CHAPTER TWENTY

TIME MANAGEMENT

©1993 PHOTODISK, INC.

Time management is a system of determining priorities and planning the allocation of units of time to accomplish what is important. How well you learn to use the 24 hours that make up each day, the 168 hours of each week, and the 720 hours of each month is the degree to which you practice time management. People who organize and plan their time usually make better use of it.

Learning to manage your time is learning to manage yourself. Time management involves planning, self-discipline, maintaining a schedule, knowing your own habits, and learning to set priorities. The average college student taking a full academic course load and sleeping approximately 8 hours a night still has at least 80 hours of uncommitted or plannable time each week. How effectively students use this time for study, social activities, and recreation may have a major influence on what they accomplish in their college experience.

Making a schedule will help you get started. It is a way to prevent yourself from avoiding those subjects or duties you dislike. More important, it is a way to discover more time for enjoyable activities. By planning your schedule, you can eliminate last-minute cramming for exams and still have recreational time for yourself. Planning can make studying more enjoyable (less painful) and will open new blocks of time that you can devote to other interests and better relationships with students in your living unit.

OVERPLANNING

The most common mistake people make in planning their schedules is to overplan. Many people believe that they must schedule every minute of every day. Schedules need to be realistic. Every person needs time each day for some type of recreation and relaxation. Your psychological health is a key element in your ability to concentrate and in your motivation to study. The remedy for study problems is generally not more studying but more efficient and better use of the time used for studying—in other words, quality studying time as opposed to quantity studying time.

As you begin to use time management, remember that schedules are products of your own invention. They should be used to assist you in allocating your time and using it effectively. Do not be a slave to your schedule. Let your lifestyle determine your schedule, rather than allowing your schedule to determine your lifestyle.

TIME

Time can be categorized into three general types. The first type is that over which you have

little or no control. This can be thought of as *predictable time.* Such activities as classes, organization meetings, team practice, RA staff meetings, eating in the cafeteria, and sleeping are predictable times. If you know that the cafeteria is open between 4:30 P.M. and 6:00 P.M., you probably plan to eat during some portion of that block of time. The same applies to sleeping. You can predict that you will spend between six and nine hours each day sleeping. Depending on your lifestyle, you can predict that this will occur sometime between 10 P.M. and 9 A.M. each day. The only decision you exercise over this type of time is whether or not you choose to attend a particular class, to eat, to sleep, and so on.

Studying, recreation, social activities, and most hobbies are plannable. These activities fall into the second type of time, called *discretionary time.* This is uncommitted time that should be planned in a manner consistent with your lifestyle and to accomplish the priorities in your life.

The third type of time is *other-imposed time.* It is unpredictable time. Activities include emergencies, individual student crises, telephone calls, people dropping by to visit, and job- or school-related assignments.

Time management is a system of (1) learning to assign priorities to the tasks you wish to accomplish, (2) maximizing discretionary time by minimizing predictable time and other-imposed time, (3) planning the use of discretionary time, and (4) learning to be more efficient. The key to being an efficient time manager is learning to maximize discretionary time and use it efficiently.

Predictable Time

Although you may choose whether you wish to perform a particular task or attend a particular meeting, you have no real control over when you will do it. Students who are involved in many campus activities find that the number of meetings and classes they must attend substantially increase their predictable time. When a manager in industry has a disproportionate amount of predictable time, business experts say that the person is letting the job run him or her, as opposed to him or her running the job. This can also apply to the RA position.

Assume that an RA is enrolled for 15 semester hours (15 hours per week of class attendance). The RA sleeps approximately eight hours a night, spends at least one and a half hours a day eating, at least one and a half hours a day for personal hygiene, and a minimum of one hour a day for traveling to and from classes. This amounts to 93 hours per week of predictable time. In addition, say the RA has a daily exercise program of jogging that accounts for approximately one hour per day. This moves the RA's predictable time up to 100 hours a week, leaving 68 hours of discretionary time each week.

When managing your time, you are really considering how to use those 68 remaining hours. Remember, this example considers a good amount of discretionary time. RAs may have less. Most residence hall programs require that the RA take duty at least once a week, and many halls require that the RA work at the information desk a specified number of hours per week. These two responsibilities may account for another 10 hours of predictable, job-related time each week. Don't forget about weekly RA staff meetings. These vary, but they generally take at least two hours. Already the RA has another 12 hours of committed time per week. This does not include time that may be unique but predictable in any one week, such as an intramural event that the RA has helped to organize, a program that the RA will hold that week, or a special committee or organization with which the RA is working.

On average, RAs devote at least two to three hours per week to miscellaneous meetings and programs associated with their job. With these, the predictable hours for the RA mounts to about 115, leaving only 53 hours of discretionary time.

On a piece of paper, list how much predictable time you have during a given week. Remember to include the items that are predictable for you. If you spend an hour every night watching television, you can count that as predictable time. If you have a regular exercise routine, you can count that time as predictable time. If you belong to a fraternity or sorority and attend a weekly chapter meeting, you can count that as predictable time. Add up the number of hours and subtract it from 168. The remaining time is discretionary. You probably have between 50 and 60 hours of discretionary time per week. If you have more than this, you are doing better than most. If you have less than 50 hours, chances are that you have a tight schedule.

Discretionary Time

The 50 to 60 hours you have left per week is plannable. You may start to plan this time by following four steps: assessment, organization, preparation of a to-do list, and scheduling time.

Step 1: Assess Your Own Situation. The first step in determining a schedule is to know yourself. People function differently. Some people are very active in the early morning and can accomplish much at that time. Others find that their peak intellectual time is later in the day. Make some assessments about yourself.

This information is used in planning your schedule, as described later. Set it aside for now.

Step 2: Get Organized. Purchase or make some type of scheduling notebook. This may seem rather simple, but you would be surprised how many people do not use this necessary instrument. Many people who do have notebooks use the wrong type. A good scheduling notebook should list times when you do things. If you rise with space allocated for every 30 minutes, is generally a good choice. You should be able to see an entire week's schedule at a time (sometimes known as Week-at-a-Glance). This basic scheduling tool is an important part of time management.

Step 3: Prepare the To-Do List. Consider all that you wish to accomplish and make a list. Put the list on one sheet of paper, preferably in the notebook that you bought. Do not put every item on a separate sheet of paper. You will find that this becomes very cumbersome and that shuffling papers will distract you.

This is a to-do list. You should make a to-do list every day, listing every task that you wish to accomplish during that day. Try to make your to-do list at the same time every day to ensure that it will get done, and allow some time each day (predictable time) to plan the next day. Though you will need to plan more than just from one day to the next, a day-to-day planning list is important to refresh your memory and set priorities for each day.

Once you have your list, prioritize the items on it, using the following three criteria:

1. Fist, rate tasks that are directly related to the accomplishment of the most important goal you have set for yourself. Give these items an A rating. Other items that rate an A are those directly related to the accomplishment of a goal that has some urgency.

2. Next, rate items related to a less important goal or that do not have immediate urgency with a B.

3. Finally, give all other items a C.

Each day work on As first until they are completed. When you finish the As, begin working on B items. If you finish all the As and all the Bs, then do the Cs. Do C items only when everything else is finished. For example, suppose you have the following things to accomplish during the day:

- Read a chapter for history.

- Write a short essay for English class tomorrow.

at 7 A.M. and work until 11 P.M., your scheduling notebook should list those hours for scheduling. Several good scheduling notebooks are available that include this time span. An appointment notebook similar to those found in doctor's offices,

- Buy some posters for your room.
- Do your laundry.
- Return a telephone call from a friend.
- Read the *Wall Street Journal* for your economics class.
- Find 10 new resources for your term paper in economics.
- Talk with your hall director about an upcoming program.

Having listed these eight tasks, you now must identify the ones you consider most important. Depending on your individual priorities, probably writing an essay for English class tomorrow would rate an immediate A. But equally important might be reading the chapter for history and looking up the resource items for the term paper. The rest of the items could be rated as B, except buying posters and doing laundry, which would probably rank as Cs.

The most important thing that this system of ranking does is help you decide what you must accomplish and what can wait. You may find that some C items never get done. That is okay. Sometimes a C item becomes an A. If you are out of underwear or other clothing, doing your laundry might jump from a C to an A priority. When it does, do it. But until it does, do it only after you have finished all of your A and B priority tasks.

Step 4: Schedule Your Time. Use the appointment calendar and questions you answered in Step 1 to schedule your time as follows:

1. Using a pencil, write in all of your predictable time for the week or as far in advance as you wish to plan.
2. Block out time for sleep. Be realistic. You probably need eight hours a night to rest properly. If your class schedule or lifestyle is such that you sleep until noon each day, that is fine. Start your schedule at noon.
3. Write in times when you usually eat. If you skip breakfast but have a late-night snack, then don't schedule breakfast but do schedule the snack.
4. Select some recreational time each day. For most college students, 4 P.M. to 7 P.M. tends to be a good time to plan some recreation. Include some type of physical exercise, if possible. This not only helps keep you healthy but gives you an opportunity to escape some of the pressures of the day.
5. Using your to-do list, starting with the As, schedule the things you would like to accomplish for the day. If you just have a list of study assignments, all of relatively equal value, some of these study scheduling hints may help you:

- Plan roughly two hours of study time for each hour of class time. This varies with the difficulty and demands of the course, the demands of the individual professor, and your skill in the subject area.
- Adapt the length of time you spend studying to the type of material being studied. For most subjects, studying in 20- to 30-minute blocks, with 5- to 10-minute breaks, for approximately one hour per subject works well. This is only an approximation. Drill work involving rote memorization differs from reading a novel.
- Eliminate dead hours from your schedule. If you have an hour between classes, do not waste it. Schedule that hour to review your lecture notes from the previous class or to prepare for the next one.
- For most people, one hour of studying during the day can be worth as much as one and a half hours of studying at night. Use daylight hours for studying whenever possible.

Other-Imposed Time

Three types of other-imposed time are: (1) necessary, (2) unnecessary, and (3) unavoidable.

Necessary Other-Imposed Time.   Necessary other-imposed time involves legitimate crises or important issues that need your attention. Because you are an RA, you will have many of these contacts. A student undergoing a significant emotional crisis has a right to interrupt you to discuss a problem. A fire drill, a fight in the residence hall, a student who is experiencing a major problem, or a program that you must attend is other-imposed time that is necessary for your job. Many times you will be in a situation in which only you have the information or authority to make a needed decision. This also is necessary other-imposed time. The last form of necessary other-imposed time is employer-imposed time related to legitimate job functions. If the residence hall director calls a staff meeting on a particular day or needs your assistance, this is related to a legitimate job function and, therefore, falls into the category of necessary other-imposed time. These are situations for which you must learn to adjust your schedule. You can minimize them only to the extent that you can ask that some of them be handled at a later time.

Unnecessary Other-Imposed Time.   Unnecessary other-imposed time is a serious problem for RAs. Items that fall into this category are telephone calls from people who wish only to chat, visitors for which you had not planned, regular meetings in which very little or nothing is accomplished, junk mail, junk E-mail, poor communication that needs further clarification from your superiors, disorganized meetings, campus red tape, unavailability of people you need to contact, questionnaires, and writing reports that nobody ever reads. You can minimize unnecessary other-imposed time in creative ways. Try some of the techniques that others have found successful. They take some self-discipline, but they may help increase your discretionary time.

Unavoidable Other-Imposed Time.   Unavoidable other-imposed time is wasted time over which you have no control. Everyone finds himself or herself wasting time for one reason or another. One unavoidable other-imposed waste of time is traffic jams. There is no excuse for them, yet they occur and little can be done about them.

Waiting for an appointment in a doctor's office or a dentist's office is another kind of unavoidable other-imposed time. Being stopped in the hallway by a faculty member or stopped by a friend to talk is unavoidable other-imposed time. The important thing is to minimize these situations (perhaps by bringing a textbook with you to the doctor's office) and not let them destroy your schedule.

CONCLUSION

Time is precious. You must learn to use it efficiently. Time wasted is lost forever. You can use time well and gain maximum benefits by setting goals, organizing yourself, assigning priorities to your daily tasks, and scheduling your time. You will find that the better organized you become, the more time you will discover that you have.

REVIEW

1. What is time management?
2. What is the most common mistake people make in managing their time?
3. Time can be categorized into three general categories. What are they?
4. Give two examples or necessary other-imposed time and two examples of unnecessary other-imposed time.
5. Identify two ways to control unnecessary other-imposed time.
6. Using a page from a planning calendar, identify all of your predictable time for the current week.
7. Make a to-do list for the week. (Note: a to-do list should be done each day. A week-long list helps with overall planning, but is subject to change.)
8. On your to-do list, assign an A to the most important or urgent tasks, a B to those which are of secondary importance or urgency, and a C to those of least importance.
9. Schedule your discretionary time on the planning calendar page.
10. How much unscheduled time do you have and how much time have you allowed for recreation and relaxation?
11. What can you do to increase your unscheduled time?

APPLICATIONS

HURRY, SCURRY

Hope was one of the most meticulous people you could meet. She was a master of efficiency and scheduling. She awoke every morning to an alarm clock and checked her schedule for the day. She would then make a to-do list outlining everything that she needed to do for the day. Time was precious, and she was a miser. She allotted herself exactly 20 minutes in the restroom each morning, 12 minutes to get dressed, 10 minutes to get to breakfast, 20 minutes to eat, and 15 minutes to get to her first class. Her every minute of every day was scheduled with the same meticulous care. Her efficiency was the marvel of everyone.

Hope was an RA and needed to control the time commitments imposed on her by others. To do this, she scheduled one and a half hours each night when she would talk with her residents. Students with a problem could make an appointment to see her for a 15-minute block of time. When the student's time had elapsed, and if another student was scheduled to see her, she would politely tell the student that her time had expired and she would need to make another appointment if more needed to be said.

Surprisingly, Hope always seemed to be in a rush. She compulsively looked at her wristwatch, and when someone talked with her they would get the feeling they were keeping her from someplace she needed to be.

Hope met all of the requirements of the residence life office and did not have any more problems on her floor than any of the other RAs in her building.

WHAT WOULD YOU DO?

1. What are some of the good and bad time management techniques Hope employs?
2. Would you like to be a student on Hope's floor? Why or why not?
3. If you were Hope's hall director, what suggestions would you give her to overcome her compulsion about scheduling?

HAPPENSTANCE

Albert was a free spirit. He loved the RA job and everything about it. He loved life and lived a carefree, easygoing lifestyle. He laughed at people who were slaves to schedules and liked to let life unfold for him. One of the things that gave Albert joy was playing cards; he was very good at it. He and three other residents played pinochle daily.

Albert was a great guy. All the men on his floor liked him, and he would always make time for them. He had a few problems. One was that he was always late to meetings. It was a joke among the staff that their meetings would start on "AT," which stood for "Albert Time." Albert was a pretty good student and did not see any reason to bother attending classes. He had the exam schedule and knew someone in each of his classes who could supply him with class notes.

The new freshmen looked up to Albert. They all admired his great personality, free lifestyle, and his ability not to let little things like other people's schedules and time commitments get in the way of what made him feel good.

WHAT WOULD YOU DO?

1. Is Albert a good role model for other students on the floor? Why or why not?
2. What do you see as the long-range implications of Albert's lack of concern about time management?
3. How do you feel when other people keep you waiting, are repeatedly late, or forget commitments?
4. If you were Albert's hall director, how would you address the issue of Albert being late for staff meetings?
5. If you were Albert's hall director, would you take some action to get Albert to attend class and manage his time better?
6. How could the hall director help Albert get control of his time without writing a schedule for him?

CHAPTER TWENTY-ONE

STUDY SKILLS

©1998 PHOTODISK, INC.

The last chapter covered one of the critical elements of developing good study skills—time management. The solution to most study problems is not spending more time studying but learning how to study better in the time allotted. Some simple techniques about studying will help you in your academic pursuits.

The need to achieve high grades is a reality. Students feel this pressure both in meeting their own personal goals and the expectations of parents. Often students' misbehavior in the living unit is a release of stress that has accumulated due to anxiety over not studying enough or not achieving a satisfactory academic return for the time invested in studying. These are major stress producers for students. Students seldom take the time to learn how to study.

This chapter is divided into four areas: preparation, basic skills, learning process, and test taking. Overall, studying can be viewed as getting ready to study, hearing or reading information, learning the information, and giving the information back to professors through tests and research papers.

PREPARING TO STUDY

Students often overlook preparing themselves to study. Most people need to get "psyched up" to concentrate on learning information. Preparing oneself to study follows the old adage, "Plan your work and work your plan." The first element of planning your work is learning to use a study schedule. The previous chapter on time management addresses how to create a workable schedule to allow time for studying as well as other activities. If you have not already developed a study schedule, employ time-management techniques to do so.

Creating a Study Environment

Residence halls are the location most often used by students to study. Libraries are generally ranked as the second location. Because residence

Libraries provide a quiet atmosphere for studying.

halls are an important place to study, this environment must be conducive to study. Interestingly, many residence halls present myriad distractions. If you walk down the corridor of your residence hall, you can observe students attempting to study with their doors open and playing their stereos. Their desks are lined with pictures of girlfriends, boyfriends, their automobile, or other mementos, and different items may be dangling from strings overhead. In the corridor, a group of people may be talking, while in the room next door a group of people may be cheering over a Monday night football game.

This hardly presents a conducive study environment. True, students can learn to adapt to a noisy and distracting environment; however, studying in such an environment requires greater concentration. If the noise is background noise, having little or no associative value, the distracting quality is diminished. A good example of this is a student who is studying and listening to the radio at the same time. If the background music is music with which the student has little association, chances are that it will present only a mild distraction. If, on the other hand, a song is played with which the student identifies, his or her thoughts will be inclined to drift toward the song.

Many students claim they can study better when their stereo is playing. This may be true for some students. Some research indicated that background music of a nonassociative value tends to help some males focus their concentration. For females this was not true. In some situations, playing music of little associative value may help muffle or drown other distracting noises in the environment. Part of this preference and the degree to which it influences one's ability to concentrate may be related to whether the person's primary way of perceiving the world is visual or aural. People whose primary means of sensing is aural may be more influenced by extraneous sound in the environment. Whatever your situation, the general principle for most people is that less noise is preferable when you are attempting to concentrate.

Pictures, memorabilia, and items that students use to clutter their desks can also be distracting. A student looking up for a moment catches a glance of a picture pinned to the bulletin board in front of his or her desk and spends a few minutes recalling some past experiences. This break in concentration can be as distracting as an auditory disturbance.

In arranging your room for studying, you should attempt to place your study table or desk against a wall. Do not pin, paste, or post anything against this wall that may distract you. Do not place your desk in front of a window; the activity on the outside could be a distraction. Pay special attention to removing anything that will compete with your concentration. Proper lighting in your study area is important. Glaring fluorescent or overly bright lights can be distracting, and they are more tiring to the eyes. If your desk has a plastic laminated top, light may reflect off the glossy surface into your eyes. This is easily solved by placing a cover or blotter over the top of the desk.

One key to using a study environment successfully is to develop positive study habits in that environment. If possible, try to use your study area only for study. Try not to play cards, make telephone calls, or do anything else unrelated to studying in this area. This establishes a positive, reinforcing atmosphere for study in this location. Soon the area will become associated with concentration and study. The fewer distractions and the more prepared your environment is for study, the quicker you will be able to start studying. You will be able to spend less time studying because the time you spend will be of greater quality.

Staying Healthy

People who are healthy can study better. If you are tired, anxious, and irritable, you will have difficulty concentrating and therefore difficulty studying. Drugs, alcohol, caffeine, and foods high in sugar tend to detract from your ability to study. Sugary foods and alcohol make you drowsy. You should approach studying in college as you would approach a job. Unless your body is functioning well, studying will be difficult.

Many students have a regular exercise routine. Exercise reduces stress, which is a major inhibitor to effective studying. Relaxation techniques such as meditation, biofeedback, and a host of other procedures may also be of assistance to individuals in reducing stress. If you are well in mind, body, and spirit, you have a better chance of performing at your optimum level.

STRATEGIES FOR

Establishing A Positive Study Environment

- Use your study area only for studying.
- Have all materials available and within easy reach.
- Keep the area free from all distractions.
- Study at the same time and in the same location whenever possible.
- Spend your study time in this area wisely. If you cannot concentrate, do not spend time there; go to another area until you are ready to resume your studying.
- Keep the room moderately cool rather than moderately warm.
- Assume a posture conducive to work and not one suggestive of relaxation. Lying on the bed with your feet propped against the wall is not conducive to most types of studying.
- Study when you are most alert and best able to concentrate. For most people, this is during the day.

Practical Realities of Studying

Before engaging in serious study, you must recognize some realities about the process. You will not automatically learn material by reading it. You may have to read some chapters in a textbook several times to understand it. In writing an essay or term paper, you will make more than one draft. The first draft is a general expression of ideas. Subsequent drafts are where you refine this information for presentation to others.

Waiting until the last minute to undertake term papers or study for tests increases one's anxiety. Starting early allows you greater freedom to plan your time, review your work, and fine-tune your knowledge. Try finishing an essay or paper two weeks before the deadline date—whenever possible. Let the paper sit for several days, and then reread it. You will find areas that you may want to improve.

Sometimes students need to escape their residence halls in order to be alone.

The more you are pressured in study situations, the more stress you experience and the less you can produce. Some people claim they work best under pressure. This is usually not true. What is true is that some people are able to motivate themselves only when they are under great pressure. This does not mean they do their best work; only that when left with no alternative but to do the work, they finally do the work.

Remember that studying is a gradual process. It involves learning bits of information and stringing the facts together over time. Studying a little each day, doing your reading as required throughout the course, and reviewing the material as you go, is the process of studying. Putting everything off until the last minute and hoping to cram all the information the night before an examination is the last act of a desperate student. It seldom offers the reward that the student is seeking.

Getting Started

Set a goal for yourself for each study period. If your goal is to read one chapter in that scheduled period, then read the chapter, and then do something else. Perhaps all you want to do is scan the chapter, or scan the chapter and take notes. Whatever you choose, make a conscious choice to do it. Plan it ahead of time.

If you just don't feel like studying, try easing yourself into the process by doing something mechanical such as surveying the chapter headings or clarifying some of your class notes. As you move through these tasks, spend time concentrating, examining, and questioning the material. This should begin to increase your concentration.

One deterrent to studying is the tendency to look at major projects as overwhelming. Thinking about the material that must be located, analyzed, and written in a term paper is so overwhelming for some students that they constantly put it off. If everyone approached their work in this way, very little would get accomplished. The best way to approach large projects, such as term papers or books, is to break the project into small segments. Try to think about writing a 50-page term paper as writing 10 segments of 5 pages each, and it will not seem nearly so difficult. If you need to read a book that has 50 chapters, you really only need to read 2 chapters a day for 25 days.

Procrastination

Procrastination is another word for avoidance or displacement. The energies that you should devote to studying are sometimes channeled into other areas. The more students delay studying, the more anxious they become. Procrastination may serve another function. Some people procrastinate because they subconsciously prefer not to succeed. Others are not willing to surrender the freedoms or the time that is required for studying.

People procrastinate by replacing something that they don't want to do with an alternative. This way they avoid the task that they don't want to do. When students procrastinate to the extent that they can no longer function in school or place themselves in situations that create great anxiety, then they probably need to discuss this procrastination with a trained counselor.

Everyone probably procrastinates to some extent and a little procrastination is acceptable. However, when somebody avoids and delays a project to the extent that it causes great emotional stress, this is an issue worth exploring with a counselor. You may be able to help other students who are experiencing this problem by having them talk about the reasons they are procrastinating. You can offer them some encouragement and perhaps review some of their study techniques. If their studying has been very unrewarding, this may be part of the reason for their procrastination. Students are more likely to undertake academic projects in areas in which they have succeeded than in areas where they have failed.

Types of Procrastinators

The Perfectionist. Perfectionists believe that everything they do must be perfect. One of their favorite expressions is, "If it is worth doing, it is worth doing right." They often get bogged down in the minutia of a project, labor for hours over insignificant details, and construct all kinds of roadblocks to the accomplishment of a project. Soon, each small assignment begins to look larger than life. All projects become major projects, and the weight of all this work causes the avoidance behavior.

The truth of the old adage about doing things right is that some things that are worth doing are worth doing even when they are not done right. The degree of care or precision should be in proportion to the task to be accomplished. So what if you spot a mistake and cross out a word in a term paper just before you turn it in? It hardly seems to justify turning it in late so you can reprint it. If you are cutting the grass and you happen to miss a few blades of grass here or there, it really does not matter. This is not to say that students should approach all of their work in a less-demanding way, only that varying degrees of precision are required.

The Self-Downer. Self-downers have something invested in failing. They believe they are not any good at some things, so they don't bother to try. Mathematics, for some students, is a good illustration. If in high school students did not like math and barely got by, when they get to required math courses in college, they avoid doing the homework or studying for the exams. These students believe they will fail. To avoid confronting the failure, they fill their time with things they do well or prefer doing and use these as excuses to avoid the tasks that need to get done.

Of course, their deep belief that they will fail is realized. One of the interesting facets about this approach is that students can avoid owning the failure because they can explain the failure by not having studied, by not trying, or by filling the time with other things that support the rationalization of not having the time to do what was needed.

The Angry Pacifist.

Angry pacifists spend all of their energy being angry at the person or events that created the need for the project to be completed. Instead of acknowledging the anger or confronting the cause, they avoid or delay doing the project as a way to get even.

The Excitement Junkie.

Excitement junkies are hooked on being entertained. They believe their life should be filled with variety and excitement. When they get bogged down with anything less than exciting, they seek escape by finding more exciting things to do. In filling their time with all the exciting things, they procrastinate getting necessary schoolwork done. For an excitement junkie, reading a novel is not nearly as exciting as watching TV or playing a video game.

The Whiner.

Whiners spend their time complaining about what they need to do but not doing it. They avoid the task by talking about how hard it is or how unfair it is. The result is that they keep complaining and not doing what needs to get done.

The Grasshopper.

Grasshoppers like to jump around from project to project without making any progress on the project. They have low impulse control, meaning that they are quick to act on their impulses. They may start on a project but can only stay with it for a few minutes before they act on an impulse to do something else. Typical of a grasshopper is having a dozen different things going at the same time, hopping from one project to another without much progress on anything.

The Miner.

Miners like to stockpile work. They are great organizers and great believers in that popular myth of procrastination, "The mood will strike someday." When the stockpile of work gets large enough, they get into digging into it, but slowly, so as not to disturb their elaborate structure of organization. Often what happens is that after the miner spends all of his or her time stockpiling and organizing, he or she looks one day at the huge pile of tasks that need to be accomplished and becomes too overwhelmed to dig in.

The Myths of Procrastination

Mañana Myth.

"I'll do it tomorrow" is probably the most widely used excuse for not doing something that needs to get done. It is the favorite myth of dieters and last-minute Christmas shoppers. The myth is, of course, that tomorrow you will be more motivated, have more time, feel more like doing it, be in a better mood, and so on. The problem is that tomorrow you feel the same as you did today.

Pressure Cooker Myth.

"I work better under pressure" is one of the favorite excuses of every student who has ever crammed for a test. Such students finally reach their threshold of tolerance for not doing something, and in desperation, they finish something they should have been working on for some time. They believe that this shows that they work better under pressure. What is probably true is that when they are against a deadline with no room to procrastinate, they finally focus their attention on the project. One reason they believe that they work better this way is that when they finally get the project finished, their sense of relief and feeling of accomplishment reinforce the behavior. It is difficult to believe a person can do as good a job on a paper that he or she spent two desperate hours on as a paper he or she spent two weeks on. Although greater effort spent is not always related to better work produced, expediency surely does not cause high quality.

The Inspiration Myth.

"I need to be inspired" is the myth that suddenly a person will become inspired to achieve what needs to get done. They believe a bolt of inspiration will strike them, and they will be embodied with the creative inspiration to undertake the assignment they have been delaying. These people believe that their life is controlled by others and that somehow they are not responsible for their own actions. Unfortunately, many times the bolt of inspiration misses them, and they either do not get their work done or delay it until the last minute and do the project poorly.

Life Is Always Fair Myth.

"Life should be fair" is the myth reflected in a need to be rewarded when we do well and to have others empathize with us. We sometimes translate these beliefs, or wants, into a belief that life is fair. Cognitively, most people understand that life is not always fair, but many people often find it difficult to accept situations when it is not. Unfair situations take the form of a professor not recognizing all the work done on a project, not asking the questions you thought should be asked on a test, or falling one point below the grade you would like to have gotten. It is easy to invest considerable energy into anger about the unfairness and let it get in the way of what needs to get done. People who buy into this system of believing life is always fair find people to blame when life is not fair.

The Entitlement Myth.

Some people believe that they are entitled to a certain amount of free time and that others should adjust to their needs. Wrong. No one promised that college would be easy, classes would adjust to everyone's schedule, or that faculty, administration, or anyone owes special accommodation. This entitlement approach does not exist in the world of work and need not exist in college.

Overcoming procrastination is not easy. You must honestly assess your ways of procrastinating and gain control of them. Once you have identified the problems, you can begin to address these behaviors directly. If procrastination is a serious problem for you and you have not been successful addressing it by yourself, do not be afraid to consult a counselor. This trained professional may help you uncover some of the hidden reasons for procrastinating.

BASIC SKILLS FOR ACQUIRING INFORMATION

A person acquires information in one of four ways—reading, listening, experimenting/applying, and discussing.

Textbook Reading

Textbooks are outlined to help students obtain an overview of the material. The outline for each chapter is determined by the headings and subheadings throughout the book. When you look at a chapter in a textbook, first become familiar with what that chapter covers. One successful method for reading a textbook employs a five-step process. First, survey the chapter to determine what the chapter will cover. Second, while you survey the chapter, ask yourself some questions about the material to be covered. Third, read the chapter, looking for answers to the questions you have asked. Fourth, review the outline of the chapter again, and fifth, recite your answers to the questions and other pertinent information that you have discovered.

Other methods for reading a textbook work just as well. Reading to answer questions and thinking about how certain material applies to specific situations will help you make the material meaningful. If you can associate the material in the textbook with an experience or in some way make it meaningful to you, your memory of the material is facilitated. Underlining or highlighting sections can aid retention of the material. Highlight only the most important material. Highlighting large segments does little good. A similar technique is to write comments or questions in the margins of the book. This reinforces what you've read and helps you summarize. It will be particularly helpful to you in reviewing the material later.

Many students believe that they can read a textbook as quickly as they read a novel. Textbooks are not meant to be read with great speed. They are meant to be read, studied, and reviewed. It is often necessary to reread sections of a text to get the full meaning.

Classroom Behavior and Lectures

The purpose of a lecture is to provide you with information not covered in the textbook or to explain textbook material in greater detail. In many courses the lecture is the focus of the course, and the textbook or other reading is used to augment the information covered in the lecture. Whatever the case, attending a lecture involves the process of active listening. Active listening does not just mean taking a voluminous series of notes. It does mean listening carefully to what is said, understanding the relationship provided by the lecturer, taking meaningful notes in an outline form that will aid in remembering the material covered in the lecture, and asking any relevant questions. Many students believe that taking good notes means they must take down every word that the lecturer says. This is simply not true. Notes of this detail become awkward and cumbersome. Often a student is so absorbed in transcribing words that the important concepts are missed.

In taking notes, use single sheets of paper that may be placed in a loose-leaf notebook. This en-

ables you to add, rewrite, or modify your notes. Use only one side of the paper. Save the back side to add material later or to clarify examples that have been given.

Your notes should be an outline. You should use abbreviations where possible, include examples the professor gives, and make sure that you include statements that the lecturer has emphasized or stressed. Focus first on concepts and then on details. After the lecture it is helpful to review and expand class notes. Although this takes additional time, it helps in later review of the information and in the accuracy of the notes.

Students who record lectures usually do not get as much from the lecture as a person who is actively listening and taking notes. Having to relisten to lectures becomes cumbersome and time-consuming. It is like having to do all the work again. To refer back to information requires spinning through tapes and relistening. Using a tape recorder is only helpful if the material is very complex, and you use it immediately following the lecture to supplement your notes. Remember, your notes do not need to be in such great detail that you catch every word. Your notes should be an outline of concepts, ideas, and important facts covered by the lecture.

Professors who lecture have the responsibility to teach. This means that as a student you paid for the right to ask questions and to talk with instructors during their office hours. They should be available to help explain material that you do not understand or have graduate assistants who can. Know the course instructor and do not be afraid to consult with him or her when you have questions. Generally, you will find that faculty members are available for these conversations and are willing to explain material that you do not understand.

Experimenting and Applying

The third way students learn is through experimenting or applying information. Labs associated with chemistry, physics, and similar fields are examples of learning through experience. Art, music, and the area of rhetoric and public address are other areas in which students acquire information by experimentation and application.

Students often believe their academic work is impractical because they are not able to see how this information will benefit them in later years. Information is easier to learn if you can see how it is to be applied. Doing research for an intercollegiate debate is a good example. Debaters usually do voluminous amounts of research on a topic, becoming experts in that topic. They research both sides of the question so that they can argue on either side in a tournament. Debaters who seriously invest themselves in the activity are usually voracious researchers. They read to gather information, constantly thinking how that information might be put to use in a debate or in formulating their presentation of the issue. They have learned to read for specific information. This increases retention. By using the information in a debate, the debaters come to know the information better. They not only understand its application but have experimented with it.

Discussion

Because discussion involves the exchange of information through inquiry, debate, and rebuttal, students are forced to think about what is being said to formulate an intelligent response. Forced to defend a point of view, students employ their best reasoning skills. They will evaluate information presented and analyze the consistency of the other person's argument. Discussion is an effective learning style and one preferred by many students.

Unfortunately, large classroom lectures do not always lend themselves to open class discussion. Students who attempt to engage in protracted discussions with the instructor are sometimes pressured by peers to stop. People hear in different ways. Some people learn best through discussions, while others learn best by reading, viewing visual representations of ideas, or listening to lectures. All are useful, and each has its place in college.

THE STUDYING PROCESS

Studying is a process of reading, organizing or outlining, reciting, and reviewing. Studying should be done on a regular basis and not just for exams.

In reviewing chapters of a textbook, focus on the outline presented, noting particularly the notes that you have made in the margin and facts that you have highlighted. The idea in reviewing the textbook is to digest concepts and the major facts presented. You may want to make an outline of the chapter with accompanying facts and details that you need to remember.

Review your notes in a similar fashion. First, read through the notes and then condense the material into a shorter outline. Review the condensed notes, and perhaps condense them again until you can remember or understand the material without having to look at it.

Review your text, outline, and the notes again and try to recite what is covered. Try to visualize the outline of the text and the outline of the notes that you have made. Think about how one supports or relates to the other. Focus particularly on examples that will help trigger the information you need.

Memorizing is required when you will be given objective examinations or need to access certain dates or formulas. Science courses tend to require more memory work than the humanities. Music requires more memory work for pianists and vocalists than for most other musicians. Memorize only the material you need to memorize.

Professors are usually interested in your understanding of the concepts and information presented. You may need to demonstrate this by remembering certain facts about a particular battle or theoretical approaches that are attributed to a particular psychologist. However, it is generally more important to be able to discuss the psychologists' theories and what they mean, or describe and explain the causes and what happened during a battle than to present dates, facts, and figures.

Generalizations in this area are hard to make. Much depends on what individual faculty members are expecting. The best way to find out what faculty members think is important and what type of information they will require of you is to ask. Most instructors will answer candidly.

For memory work, first write the facts you wish to memorize on a sheet of paper, or on a series of four-by-six-inch index cards. Break down large sections of information into smaller sections. Memorize the smaller sections and link them together. Visualizing the material can help. Either visualize what actually happened or visualize the actual words on the page. If you can associate facts that you need to remember with examples, your ability to remember those facts should be increased. One technique people use to remember other people's names, for example, is to associate the person's name with a physical feature of that individual. So if the person's name is Eileen, you may think of Eileen as a person who wears a certain type of eyeglasses. You can adapt this same technique to studying.

Memorization is done by reviewing and reciting. Some techniques that help are to review and recite the information before you go to bed at night. At night you may dream about some of this information. First thing in the morning, try to recite the information. Review and recite again. Do this over a two- or three-day period, and the information will become yours. Some researchers say that the information must be recited verbatim at least seven times before you can retain it. The more times you use, review, and recite information, the more and the longer you will remember the information.

Anagrams can also help. If you need to know a seven-stage process or the bones of the leg, try making an anagram (a word) from the first letter for each component. The U.S. government uses anagrams for many government programs. For example, HUD is the anagram for the Office of Housing and Urban Development. If you can remember the word, you will have the outline—the letters of the word—to help you recall the components.

Cramming

Cramming for a test is better than not studying at all, but it is not a substitute for studying the material over a period of time and learning it throughout the course of the semester. If you are in a position where you must cram, set aside a block of time and begin by condensing the material you have into an outline from which you can work. Try to get some help from another person in the class to determine what areas are particularly important in the course. Review the outline and the information the fellow student believes will be on the exam and disregard trying to read the entire textbook again or trying to copiously review someone else's notes.

If you must cram, do so systematically and from outlines that summarize the material covered. Use the outline to explore specific areas you believe are likely to be on the examination. Don't try to review everything in the course; it will overwhelm you and will squander your limited study time.

TEST TAKING

Professors do not always ask the questions you would like them to ask. You do not always have an opportunity to show them everything that you know about a given topic. Instead, they tend to test students to determine the varying degrees of information they have about a topic. Every test may include some questions you cannot answer or find very difficult to answer. Testing does not test how much knowledge you have about a subject; it tests what information you have about the questions asked in a given format and your ability to take the type of test being administered.

To prepare for a test, you first must know what type of test you will be asked to take. There are basically three types of tests: objective, multiple choice, and essay. Some tests are a combination of the three. A professor usually tells you beforehand what type of test is to be administered. If he or she does not, ask.

Objective Exams

An objective exam requires total recall. It is the most difficult type of exam to take. Fill-in-the-blank and short-answer questions are objective tests. You either know the information being sought, or you do not. If you do not know the information, write what you think is the right answer unless the professor indicates that he or she will deduct points from your total score for incorrect answers. Go through the exam and answer those questions you know; then go back and answer the questions that you are less sure of, leaving the most difficult questions until last.

As with all examination questions, read thoroughly to make sure you understand exactly what the question is asking.

Multiple-Choice Questions

Multiple-choice or multiple-guess questions come in many forms. The most common is where you are given a question and four or five alternative answers. Versions of this exam type include being given a question in which more than one of the alternatives may be correct and you are asked to pick *the best* answer; sometimes such a test asks for *all* the correct answers. Read multiple-choice questions carefully. The directions vary. Know particularly if there is more than one right answer to each question.

First, look through the questions and answer those you know. Next, go back and examine each remaining question. Eliminate the obviously incorrective alternatives. You should be able to narrow the options to two or three, thus giving you a better chance of determining the correct answer. Among these two or three, look for global statements such as *always, in every case, never,* and *absolutely.* You can usually eliminate these alternatives. An authority would rarely make such a global statement.

Finally, if you still cannot decide which answer is correct, and the professor is not deducting from your total score for answering incorrectly, take your best guess. You have a chance of guessing right.

True and false questions are a form of multiple choice. If you don't know the correct answer in a true-false test, take your best guess (unless the professor deducts for wrong answers). Never leave a yes-or-no question unanswered. You always have a 50-50 chance of choosing the correct answer.

Essay Exams

Essay exams call for you to organize your thoughts and present them in a coherent way that speaks directly to the question asked. This is your opportunity to express in your own words your understanding of the question raised. Pace your time on essay exams. Do not spend all of your time writing an elaborate answer to one question, only to find that you do not have enough time to answer the remaining questions on the test. Start by outlining in the margin of your paper or in your head what you want to say. Each essay question addresses certain facts the professor wants you to communicate. Think what those key elements must be and organize your essay around them. If the professor has asked you to explain a theory that has three parts, start your essay by introducing and explaining the three parts.

The purpose of an essay is for you to explain what you know, not for you to create a great literary masterpiece. This does not mean that you should be careless with your grammar and spelling. Quite the opposite is true. If you express yourself clearly, using correct English, it will add to the credibility of your response.

Include only necessary information in the essay. Do not waste your time and the instructor's time by adding extraneous material to pad the essay. If you believe you must pad the answers, do so in moderation. Remember that college professors are experienced students and experienced readers of essays. It is surprisingly simple to differentiate between students who have an understanding of the topic on an essay question and those students who are simply padding questions with extraneous information.

If you absolutely have no idea how to answer a particular essay question, and again the professor will not deduct for wrong answers, write something. Even if it is extraneous material, the professor may, out of pity, give you one or two points for your attempt.

Test Anxiety

Some students get so anxious about a test that they block (become unable to remember information they have studied). You might call this a type of stage fright. Students can feel nervous, have a headache, feel dizzy, and develop a fear reaction. In other words, they panic. There is more than one way to combat test anxiety. One approach that always helps is to have confidence in your ability to do well. If you have studied and know the information, this will help provide you with the confidence to do well. Success on other tests also tends to help build confidence in test taking. The more confident students feel about the information they have covered, the more confident they should be about taking the examination.

Even though some students are confident that they have studied enough, they nevertheless panic when beginning the examination. Relaxing before the examination is one way to help reduce anxiety. Another way is to take several deep breaths and look through the examination to find the easiest questions first. Sometimes by answering a few easy questions, the student builds enough confidence to answer some of the more difficult ones. Students should have a realistic perspective on any examination; few are make-or-break situations. If you experience some text anxiety, think about positive test experiences that you have had. Admit to yourself that you are not going to be able to answer all the questions right. Remember that a test examines the depth of one's information, and people normally miss answers to some questions. If you cram just before a test, your anxiety may be heightened.

Biofeedback Relaxation.   One technique used by professional counselors to reduce test anxiety is biofeedback relaxation. They have the student explain each segment of taking an examination, starting with the student getting up in the morning and proceeding step-by-step through to the student actually sitting down to take the examination. As a student relates each segment of his or her behavior, counselors have the student relax. This process takes place in a safe and secure environment. The student learns to associate the relaxation response with the experiences leading to the test. This process is usually coupled with some therapy that focuses on issues of self-esteem and fear of failure.

If you or some of your residents experience test anxiety to the extent where you cannot function during the exam, you should talk with a counselor about the problem. Some anxiety before a test is normal. It is not normal, however, to be so anxious and disturbed that you cannot remember or produce the information that you know you have learned.

One final word about taking examinations. Most exams are given in a specified amount of time, usually one class period. You need to be conscious of how much time you are allotting to questions and the value of those questions. In a 60-minute class period, you would be unwise to spend 30 minutes responding to a 10-point essay, leaving the remaining 30 minutes to answer questions for the remaining 90 points on the exam. A few professors will let students write as much as they wish with no time constraints. Find out before the exam how long you will be given to complete it. If it will be one class period, use your time wisely, apportioning appropriate amounts of time based on the value assigned to individual questions. If no specific value is assigned to each question, inquire as to the value of the questions or if all will receive equal weight.

ACADEMIC HONESTY AND DISHONESTY

A surprising number of students choose to cheat on examinations or plagiarize term papers. This reprehensible conduct seriously jeopardizes the academic integrity of the institution and raises the question as to whether or not that student should be permitted to continue at the institution. One of the reasons the institution exists is for the purpose of helping students master information. If a student chooses to represent to the faculty that he or she has mastered information that he or she has truly not mastered, it calls into question that person's purpose in attending the institution. Academic dishonesty is inexcusable, despite the pressures to get good grades or whatever personal problems may exist. Academic dishonesty demonstrates a lack of integrity and a breach of trust.

Some students experience personal problems that prevent them from studying. The solution is not for them to press on with their course work but to explain the situation to the appropriate college authorities and seek their advice and help in resolving the problem. Most schools allow students to take incomplete grades when they have a legitimate reason. Students should be aware of the dates when they can withdraw from courses and when that is no longer possible. In cases of serious mental, emotional, or physical health problems, the college counseling or health center will be able to assist students in securing an extension for courses or perhaps a withdrawal. Whatever the institutional policies, alternatives usually exist. There are always alternatives if a student acts early enough. Help students on your floor understand their options. The stigma of being expelled or suspended from a college for academic dishonesty is much greater than receiving a failing mark in a course.

Spend some time talking with the residents of your living unit about the issue of academic honesty. Help them understand that "everybody" does not cheat and that academic dishonesty will not get them through college. Make sure they understand the institution's position on academic dishonesty.

A college education trains not only the mind but also the character of the individual. The student's character is questioned when he or she cheats in a course. If you know of academic dishonesty, you should confront the students involved. It is appropriate for you to consult with your hall director on how your particular institution handles these situations and what is expected of you.

REVIEW

1. For each of the following rationalizations, identify the false assumption(s) and give a rebuttal to the rationalization.

   EXAMPLE:

   Rationalization: I find it easier to study when I am under pressure. So I will not do any studying until it gets time for a test.

   False Assumption: The greater the pressure the easier it is to study.

   False Assumption: Quality of academic work is related to the degree of pressure to get it done.

   False Assumption: The amount of studying needed to pass a test is proportional to the time between the date of the test and the moment at which the pressure builds to the point that causes the person to study.

   Rebuttal: Studying may seem easier under pressure, but if you wait until the last minute, you may not assemble all of the material you need, you will not have time to rewrite or review some material that you know less well, you may not be able to get all of the materials or notes that you need to study, there may be something unexpected that happens that prevents you from studying, etc.

   a. The world won't come to an end if I put this project off, so it does not really matter if I delay.

   b. I'll put the project off until I am in the mood to do it.

   c. I waited until the last minute to do the term paper the last time and it worked, so why not do it the same way again?

   d. If I wait until the last minute to do this term paper, I won't need to spend too much time on it and will save myself time and effort.

   e. If I do the project now, instead of putting if off until next week, I may never get the same opportunity to enjoy what I am doing right now.

   f. I would have gotten around to doing the project sooner, but there were circumstances beyond my control that prevented me from doing it.

   g. No one really cares if I finish the term paper or not. The professor probably won't even read it.

   h. I should not have to do this homework. It is unfair for the professor to expect me to do all of this work. He or she has unrealistic expectations.

   i. College is supposed to be more than just studying.

   j. I have been working hard all quarter and I deserve a break, so I'll work on the project some other time.

2. How does the place where one studies influence the process of studying?

3. Describe the ideal study environment for you, and explain why.

4. What are five steps that can be used to study a textbook?

5. How would you define "good note taking" in class?

6. Why is tape recording a class lecture a less effective study method than note taking?

7. Identify the four principal ways people master information?

8. Give two suggestions for taking an essay exam.

9. What is test anxiety, and what are some ways it can be controlled?

10. What is your institution's policy on academic dishonesty, and what is the most likely penalty a student would receive for academic dishonesty at your institution?

APPLICATIONS

ELROY

Elroy is a first-quarter freshman. He was an average student in high school partially because he seldom studied. When he arrived at the university, he moved into a residence hall. He and his roommate both went through fraternity rush and both pledged the prestigious XX fraternity. Elroy is very excited about becoming part of the fraternity and has devoted much of his time to making sure he knows all the actives and attends all the social functions and intramural athletic events in which the fraternity is involved. When Elroy pledged the fraternity, he was told that the national fraternity regulations require a pledge to have a minimum grade point average of at least a 2.0 and to be a full-time student carrying not less than 15 quarter hours in the quarter prior to initiation. By the 5th week of the 10-week quarter, Elroy realized that he was not doing very well in his five three-hour classes.

Elroy was not the only one to notice that he is not studying. The RA also noticed that Elroy was not studying and went to talk with him. The conversation went like this:

RA: Elroy, what classes are you taking this quarter? How are you doing in them?

Elroy: All right—not great. I'm taking English 101, Math 101, Speech 101, History 101, Journalism 101. I really haven't gotten many grades yet.

RA: You mean you haven't had any assignments or tests?

Elroy: No, there were some tests and assignments; I just haven't had a chance to turn in my stuff, or I wasn't in class when the tests were given.

RA: Why haven't you been going to class?

Elroy: I've had other things to do. I have been working extra hard around the fraternity. Joining XX is a once-in-a-lifetime opportunity. I wanted to make sure that I got everything just right. I did talk to some of my teachers. My English teacher doesn't like me. She keeps giving all kinds of stupid assignments that aren't worth my time to do. Last night I was up late doing things for my fraternity; I decided it would be better for me to sleep in and get a good night's rest. That is why I missed the quiz in history. I forgot about it. I had some other things to do and didn't go to class the last few times—the professor is real boring. I went to him and asked him if I could do a make-up because I didn't know about the quiz, and he said no. He really doesn't care if I get the information or not. He is being unfair about it.

RA: Is there any chance that you can still salvage this semester based on the assignments you have left to do?

Elroy: Sure, I still have at least 60 percent of my grade in each of the classes resting on how I do in the next three weeks. I really plan to get down to studying soon. I do my best work when I am under pressure, and I didn't see any reason why I should devote the whole quarter worrying about assignments that aren't due until the end of the quarter. You know college is more than just going to classes.

The RA asks Elroy to make a list of the final exams and papers he has due prior to the end of the quarter. What he has left to complete this semester is the following:

- Math—two problem solution tests
- Speech—one speech and one multiple choice test
- English—one essay exam
- History—one 20-page term paper on George Washington
- Journalism—two stories of approximately three pages each

After analyzing the assignments, Elroy starts to feel a little panicked. He has so much to do and does not know how or where to begin. Elroy asks his RA to help him organize the last three weeks of the quarter.

WHAT WOULD YOU DO?

1. Identify the rationalizations Elroy has used to avoid studying.

2. Identify the steps that Elroy needs to undertake to begin the process of studying.

3. To complete the 20-page history paper, the RA suggests that Elroy divide the research and writing of the paper into segments, and do some work on the paper each day. Divide the paper into logical segments and estimate the number of days within the three-week period you would devote to each segment.

4. What suggestions would you make for how Elroy should complete the two assignments he has yet to complete in Speech (one speech and one multiple-choice test)?

5. What suggestions would you make for how Elroy should study for his English assignment (one essay test)?

6. What suggestions would you make for how Elroy should study for his math tests (two problem-solving math tests)?

A TWO-WEEK VACATION

Leona is a very busy RA. She is busy helping everyone with their problems, developing programs for her residents, helping at the main desk, and spending time with the other RAs in the building. She is a very nice person. All the women on her floor like her, and she is one of the most energetic and fun people on the RA staff. She thinks she might want to go to graduate school in student personnel administration.

She has one problem; she is not a good student. Each semester the hall director reminds her that she must have at least a 2.0 grade average each semester to remain an RA. So far, she has made it, but just barely. In truth, she can do the academic work. She just likes being an RA so much more than being a student that she spends all of her time helping others and doing "RA stuff" that she puts her studying off and then tries to cram at the last minute.

Two weeks before final exams, Leona begins to study. First, she tries to study in her room, but because she is so popular, there is a steady stream of visitors. Not wanting to be rude, she sits and chats with her friends as they come into her room. After three days of this, she decides to go to the library to study. She sets aside each evening from 7:00 P.M. to midnight to study. She finds a place she likes in the library and starts to study but is soon interrupted by people at the next table talking. She wanders the library trying to find the best place to study, but can't seem to get comfortable anywhere.

Eventually, she goes to a friend's apartment off campus and more or less moves in for the last two weeks of the semester. She figures that she has given the students on her floor all her time up to this point, and from now through finals week they will just have to fend for themselves. She believes that she has more than met her RA obligations in the amount of time she has devoted to the job, and the university owes her the time off at the end of the semester to complete her academic work.

WHAT WOULD YOU DO?

1. Is Leona justified in leaving her residents to fend for themselves in the last two weeks of the semester? Why or why not?

2. If you were Leona's hall director, what advice would you give her for studying in her room and still being available for the residents on her floor?

3. If you were Leona's hall director, how would you evaluate her overall performance as an RA? Explain your answer.

4. What adjectives would you use to explain Leona's reasoning for delaying studying until the end of the semester and then spending all of her time off campus studying?

REFERENCES

Chapter 2: The History of Residence Halls

1. Cowley, W. H. (1934). The history of student residential housing. *School and Society, 40,* 705-712; (continued) *40,* 758-764.

2. Thompson, S. E. (1946, April 18-20). *The program of student housing.* Paper presented at the conference on the National Association of Deans and Advisers of Men, Lafayette, IN, 95.

3. James, E. (1917). College residence halls. *The Journal of Home Economics, 9* (3), 101.

4. Cowley (1934).

5. Thwing, C. F. (1909). Dormitory life for college men. *Religious Education, 4* (1), 34.

6. Cowley (1934), 708.

7. Cowley (1934).

8. Ibid.

9. Cowley (1934), 709.

10. Rudolph, F. (1962). *The American college and university: A history.* New York: Vintage Books, 97.

11. Shay, J. E., Jr. (1964). The evolution of the campus residence hall. Part I: The decline. *Journal of the National Association of Women Deans, Administrators, and Counselors, 27,* 181.

12. Cowley, W. H. (1949). Some history and a venture in prophecy. In E. G. Williamson (Ed.), *Trends in student personnel work.* Minneapolis: The University of Minnesota Press, 19-20.

13. Kolbe, P. R. (1936, April 30-May 2). *Address of welcome.* Speech presented at the annual conference of the National Association of Dean and Advisers of Men, Philadelphia, PA, 11.

14. Cowley (1949).

15. Ibid.

16. Leonard, E. (1956). *Origins of personnel services in American higher education.* Minneapolis: University of Minnesota Press.

17. Thwing, 34.

18. Cowley (1949), 21.

19. Shay, J. E., Jr. (1964). The evolution of the campus residence hall. Part II: The resurgence. *Journal of the National Association of Women Deans, Administrators, and Counselors, 28,* 29.

20. Cowley (1934).

21. Hughes, R. C. (1909). Factors in the dormitory problem. *Religious Education, 4* (1), 47.

22. James

23. Cowley (1934).

24. James, 105-106.

25. Talbot, M. (1909). Moral and religious influences as related to environment of student life; dormitory life for college women. *Religious Education, 4* (1), 43.

26. Ibid., 5.

27. Findlay, J. F. (1937, April 3). *The origin and development of the work of the Dean of Men.* Paper presented at the annual conference of the National Association of Deans and Advisers of Men, Austin, TX, 105.

28. Cowley (1934), 761.

29. Findlay (1937), 115.

30. Eliot, C. W. (1909). The private dormitory. *Religious Education, 4* (1), 58.

31. Birdseye, C. F. (1906). The college home life as a means for securing a right moral atmosphere for students. *Religious Education, 3* (6), 221.

32. Cowley (1934).

33. Shay (1964). "Part II," 29.

34. Funds for dormitories in Virginia institutions of higher learning. (1926, September 4). *School and Society, 24,* 294-295.

35. Dormitory system at the University of Minnesota. (1926, July 2). *School and Society, 24,* 103.

36. Proposed residential colleges at the University of Michigan. (1927, January 1). *School and Society, 35,* 10-11.

37. Lowell, A. L. (1929). Residential houses at Harvard University. *School and Society, 24,* 262-263.

38. Ibid., 263.

39. Ibid., 264.

40. Residential colleges at Harvard and Yale. (1929, January 26). *School and Society, 24,* 124-125.

41. Student housing facilities at land-grant colleges. (1931, April 18). *School and Society, 33,* 522-523.

42. Young, D. P., & Gehring, D. D. (1977). The college student and the courts. *College Administration Publications,* 1-13.

43. *L.S.U. Student Handbook.* (1934/1935). Baton Rouge, LA: Student Y.M.C.A., 41-44.

44. American Council on Education. (1937). *The student personnel point of view* (American Council on Education Series 1, Vol. 1, No. 3). Washington, DC: Author, 3.

45. Sorenson, G. P. (1985). Indoctrination and the purpose of American education: A 1930s debate. *Issues in Education, 3* (2), 80.

46. Cowley, W. H., & Waller, W. (1935). A study of student life: The appraisal of student traditions as a field of research. *Journal of Higher Education, 50,* 385. (Original reprinted in 1979)

47. Low cost housing for students at the University of Wisconsin. (1938, November 12). *School and Society, 48,* 623.

48. Cooperative dormitories. (1938, September 10). *School and Society, 48,* 344.

49. Stewart, R. B. (1941, April 17-19). *Institutional housing policies.* Paper presented at the annual conference of the National Association of Deans and Advisers of Men, Cincinnati, OH, 110.

50. Findlay, J. F. (1936, April 30-May 2). *The independent men's association: An effort to integrate the nonfraternity man.* Paper presented at the annual conference of the National Association of Deans and Advisers of Men, Philadelphia, PA, 156.

51. Brown, F. J. (1951, March 30). *Higher education and the national emergency.* Paper presented at the conference of the National Association of Deans and Advisers of Men, St. Louis, MO.

52. Thompson, 100.

53. Ferris, W. B. (1946, April 18-20). *Comments made in response to S. Earl Thompson's paper entitled "The program of student housing."* Presented at the conference of the National Association of Deans and Advisors of Men, Lafayette, IN.

54. Association of College and University Housing Officers-International. (1985). *The purpose and history of the Association.* Columbus, OH.

55. Mayhew L. B. (1977). *Legacy of the seventies.* San Francisco: Jossey-Bass.

56. Brown, 108.

57. National Center for Education Statistics. (1981). *Digest of Education Statistics, 1981* (NCES No. 81-400). Washington, DC: U.S. Government Printing Office.

58. Shay, J. E., Jr. (1969). Freedom and privacy in student residences. *NASPA Journal, 7* (2), 77.

59. Unseem, R. H. (1966). A sociologist views learning in college residence halls. *Journal of the National Association of Women Deans and Counselors, 29* (3), 118-119.

60. Shay (1969), 77.

61. Cowley, W. H. (1957). Student personnel services in retrospect and prospect. In G. Saddlemire & A. Rentz (Eds.), *Student affairs: A profession's heritage. Significant articles, authors, issues, and documents.* Carbondale, IL: American College Personnel Association, 174. (Original work reprinted in 1983)

62. Ibid., 175.

63. Lind, M. (1946, December). The college dormitory as an emerging force in new education. *Association of American Colleges Bulletin,* 32, 529-538; Orme, R. (1950). *Counseling in residence halls.* New York: Columbia University, Teachers College, Bureau of Publications; Strang, R. (1949). *Counseling techniques in college and secondary school.* New York: Harper and Brothers.

64. Pierson, I. (1962). *Campus cues* (3rd ed.). Danville, IL: Interstate Printers and Publishers.

65. Ibid., 88.

66. Ibid., 52.

67. Moynihan, D. P. (1975, Winter). The politics of higher education. *Daedalus,* 128-147.

68. Gladieus, L. E., & Wolamin, T. R. (1976). *Congress and the colleges.* Lexington, MA: Lexington Books.

69. National Center for Education Statistics, 92.

70. Carnegie Foundation for the Advancement of Teaching. (1976). *The states and higher education: A proud past and a vital future.* San Francisco: Jossey-Bass.

71. Bess, J. L. (1973). More than room and board: Linking residence and classroom. In J. Katz (Ed.), *Services for students* (New Directions for Higher Education Series No. 3). San Francisco: Jossey-Bass, 37-38.

72. Greenleaf, E. A. (1969). Residence halls 1970s. *NASPA Journal, 7* (2), 65-71.

73. Van der Ryn, S., & Silverstein, M. (1967). *Dorms at Berkeley: An environmental analysis.* New York: Educational Facilities Laboratories, Center for Planning and Development Research, 28.

74. Dixon v. Alabama State Board of Education, 294 F. 2d 150. (US Court of Appeals, Fifth Circuit, 1961).

75. Prostrollo v. University of South Dakota, 507 F.2d. 775 (US Court of Appeals, Eighth Circuit, 1974).

76. Mayhew, 298.

77. Levine, A. (1981). Going first class on the Titanic. *Change, 13* (2), 16-23.

78. Astin, A. W., Green, K. C., & Korn, W. S. (1987). *The American freshman: Twenty year trends.* Los Angeles: University of California, The Higher Education Research Institute.

79. Sax, L. J., Astin, A. W., Korn, W. S., & Mahoney, K. M. (1996). *The American freshman: National norms for Fall 1996.* Los Angeles: University of California, the Higher Education Research Institute.

80. Shea, C. (1995, July 14). Dorms for the 90s: Students want residence halls to provide the comforts of home. *Chronicle of Higher Education,* pp. A29-A30.

81. Schroeder, C. C., & Mable, P. (1994). Residence halls and the college experience: Past and present. In C. C. Schroeder & P. Mable (Eds.), *Realizing the educational potential of residence halls* (pp. 3-21). San Francisco: Jossey-Bass.

82. Blimling, G. S. (1993). New challenges and goals for residential life programs. In R. B. Winston, Jr. & S. Anchors (Ed.), *Student housing and residential life* (pp. 1-20). San Francisco: Jossey-Bass.

Chapter 3: Educational Philosophies for Residence Halls

1 American College Personnel Association. (1994). *The student learning imperative: Implications for student affairs.* Washington, DC: Author.

2. Council for the Advancement of Standards in Higher Education. (1997). *The book of professional standards for higher education.* Washington, DC: Author.

Chapter 4: The Influence of Residence Halls on the Development of Students

1. Blimling, G. (1989). A meta-analysis of the influence of college residence halls on academic performance. *Journal of College Student Development, 30,* 298-308.

2. Chickering, A. (1974). *Commuting versus resident students.* San Francisco: Jossey-Bass.

3. Blimling, G. S. (1993). The influence of college residence halls on students. In J. Smart (Ed.), *Higher education: Handbook of theory and research* (Vol. 9, pp. 248-307). New York: Agathon Press.

4. Blimling, G. (1988). *The influence of college residence halls on students: A meta-analysis of the empirical research, 1966-1985.* Unpublished doctoral dissertation, The Ohio State University, Columbus; Heilweil, M. (1973). The influence of dormitory architecture on resident behavior. *Environment and Behavior, 5,* 377-412.

5. Newcomb, T. (1960). Exploiting student resources. In Sprague (Ed.), *Research on College Students.* Boulder, CO: The Western Interstate Commission for Higher Education.

6. Ibid.

7. Ecklund, C. et al. (1972). *The effects of proximity, willingness to engage in social interaction, and sorority membership on the initial formation of friendship patterns among previously unacquainted college freshmen.* Paper presented at Southeastern Psychological Association, Atlanta, GA; Martin R. (1974). Friendship choices and resident hall proximity among freshmen. *Psychological Reports, 34;* Menne, J., & Sinnett, E. (1971). Proximity and social interaction in residence halls. *Journal of College Student Personnel;* Priest, R., & Sawyer, J. (1967). Proximity and peership: Bases of balance in interpersonal attraction. *American Journal of Sociology, 72,* 633-649.

8. Whittaker, D. (1969). Student subcultures reviewed and revisited. *NASPA Journal, 7,* 23-34.

9. Heath, D. (1968). *Growing up in college.* San Francisco: Jossey-Bass.

10. Vreeland, R. (1970). The effects of houses on students' attitudes and values. In Whitley & Sprandel (Eds.), *The growth and development of college students.* Washington, DC: American College Personnel Association.

11. Murray, M. (1961). The effects of roommates on the scholastic achievement of college students. *Dissertation Abstracts.*

12. Sommer, R. (1969). Study conditions in student residences. *Journal of College Student Personnel, 9,* 232-237.

13. Blai, B., Jr. (1972). Roommate impact upon academic performance. *Psychology, 9* (3), 47-48.

14. Ainsworth, C., & Maynard, D. (1976). The impact of roommate personality on achievement: An exploratory study and model of analysis. *Research in Higher Education, 4,* 291-301.

15. Lozier, G. G. (1970). Compatibility of roommates assigned alphabetically versus those assigned according to educational goals or extracurricular plans. *Journal of College Student Personnel, 11,* 256-260; Pace, L. T. (1967). Roommate dissatisfaction in a college residence hall as related to roommate scholastic achievement, the College and University Environment Scales, and the Edwards Personal Preference Schedule. *Dissertation Abstracts International, 28* (8), 2989A.

16. Carter, T. A. (1967). The effect of roommate ability on the academic achievement of college freshmen. *Dissertation Abstracts International, 27* (10), 3302A; Crew, J. J., & Giblette, J. F. (1966, April). Academic performance of freshman males as a function of residence hall housing. *Student Housing Research: ACUHO Research and Information Committee;* Jackson, G. S. (1984). The impact of roommates on development: A causal analysis of the effects of roommate personality congruence, satisfaction and initial developmental status on end-of-quarter developmental status and grade point average. *Dissertation Abstracts International, 36* (9), 4755B.

17. Zirkle, K., & Hudson, G. (1975). The effects of residence hall staff members on maturity development for male students. *Journal of College Student Personnel, 16* (1), 30-33.

18. Ibid., 32.

19. Ibid., 32-33.

20. Astin, A. (1977). *Four critical years.* San Francisco: Jossey-Bass; Astin, A. (1985). *Achieving educational excellence.* San Francisco: Jossey-Bass; Boyer, E. L. (1987). *College: The undergraduate experience in America.* New York: Harper & Row Publishers; Kuh, G. D., Schuh, J. H., & Whitt, E. J. (1991). *Involving colleges.* San Francisco: Jossey-Bass; National Institute of Education. (1984). *Involvement in learning: Realizing the potential of American higher education.* Report of the Study Group on the Conditions of Excellence in American Higher Education (U.S. Department of Education GPO Stock No. 065000-00213-2). Washington, DC: U.S. Government Printing Office.

21. National Institute of Education, 19.

22. Pascarella, E. T., & Terenzini, P. T. (1991). *How college affects students.* San Francisco: Jossey-Bass, 648.

23. Mortimer, K. (1984). *Involvement in learning: Realizing the potential of American higher education.* Report of the National Institute of Education (U.S. Department of Education GPO Stock No. 065-000-00213-2). Washington, DC: U.S. Government Printing Office: Boyer.

24. Sanford, N. (1962). *The American college.* New York: Wiley.

25. Erikson, E. (1968). *Identity, youth, and crises.* New York: Norton.

Chapter 5: The Growth and Development of College Students

1. Zastrow, C., & Kirst-Ashman, K. (1990). *Understanding human behavior and the social environment.* Chicago: Nelson-Hall.

2. Ibid.

3. Jones, M., & Bailey, N. (1950). Physical maturing among boys as related to behavior. *Journal of Educational Psychology, 41,* 129-148; Mussen, P., & Jones, M. (1957). Self-conceptions, motivations, and interpersonal attitudes of late and early maturing boys. *Child Development, 28,* 243-256.

4. Blyth, D. A., Bulcroft, R., & Simmons, R. G. (1981, August). *The impact of puberty on adolescents: A longitudinal study.* Paper presented at the annual meeting of the American Psychological Association, Los Angeles, CA.

5. Peskin, H. (1967). Pubertal onset and ego functioning *Journal of Abnormal Psychology, 72,* 1-15.

6. Sanford, N. (1962). *The American college.* New York: Wiley.

7. Erikson, E. (1968). *Identity, youth, and crises.* New York: Norton.

8. Chickering, A. W., & Reisser, L. (1993). *Education and identity* (Rev. ed.). San Francisco: Jossey-Bass.

9. Blasi, A. (1980). Bridging moral cognition and moral action: A critical review of the literature. *Psychological Bulletin, 80* (1), 145.

10. Perry, W., Jr. (1970). *Forms of intellectual and ethical development in the college years.* New York: Holt, Rinehart, and Winston.

11. Widick, C., & Simpson. (1978). Developmental concepts in college instruction. In C. Parker (Ed.), *Encouraging development in college students.* Minneapolis, MN: University of Minnesota Press.

12. Ibid.

13. Perry

14. Moore, W. (1982). William Perry's cognitive-developmental theory: A review of the model and related research. In Fernald & Fernald (Eds.), *Introductory psychology* (5th ed.). (prepublication draft).

15. Kohlberg, L. (1969). Stage and sequence: The cognitive-developmental view. In D. A. Goslin (Ed.), *Handbook of socialization on theory and research.* New York: Rand McNally; Kohlberg, L. (1981). *The philosophy of moral development* (Vol. 1). San Francisco: Harper & Row; Kohlberg, L. (1984). *The psychology of moral development* (Vol. 2). San Francisco: Harper & Row.

16. Gilligan, C. (1981). Moral development. In A. Chickering & Associates (Eds.), *The modern American college.* San Francisco: Jossey-Bass, 155.

17. Kohlberg, L., & Kramer, R. (1969). Continuities and discontinuities in childhood and adult moral development. *Human Development, 12,* 93-120.

18. Kohlberg, L. (1973). Continuities in childhood and adult moral development revisited. In Bates & Schaie (Eds.), *Life-span development in psychology* (2nd ed.). New York: Academic Press.

19. Turiel, E. (1974). Conflict and transition in adolescent moral development. *Child Development, 45,* 14-29.

20. Gilligan (1981)

21. Gilligan, C. (1982). *In a different voice.* Cambridge, MA: Harvard University Press.

22. Weidman, J. C. (1989). Undergraduate socialization: A conceptual approach. In J. C. Smart (Ed.), *Higher education: Handbook of theory and research* (Vol. 5). New York: Agathon Press.

23. Coelho, G., Hamburg, D., & Murphy, E. (1968). Coping strategies in a new environment. In Yamamoto (Ed.), *The college student and his culture: An analysis.* Boston: Houghton Mifflin, 338.

24. Chickering, A. (1974). *Commuting versus residential students.* San Francisco: Jossey-Bass, 80.

25. Case, F. D. (1981). Dormitory architecture influences: Patterns of student social relations over time. *Environment and Behavior, 13* (1), 23-41; Priest, R. F., & Sawyer, J. (1967). Proximity and peership: Bases of balance in interpersonal attraction. *American Journal of Sociology, 72,* 633-649; Rubin, Z., & Shenker, S. (1978). Friendship, proximity, and self-disclosure. *Journal of Personality, 46,* 1-22.

26. Sorenson, R. C. (1973). *Adolescent sexuality in contemporary America.* New York: World.

27. Zastrow & Kirst-Ashman, 247.

28. Priest & Sawyer; Rubin & Shenker

29. Feldman, K., & Newcomb, T. (1969). (Eds.) *The impact of college on students.* San Francisco: Jossey-Bass, 236-237.

30. Ibid.

31. Newcomb, T. M. (1966). The general nature of peer influence. In T. M. Newcomb & E. K. Wilson (Eds.), *College peer groups: Problems and prospects for research.* Chicago: Aldine.

32. Feldman & Newcomb

Chapter 6: Adjusting to College

1. Coons, F. (1974). The developmental risks of the college student. In D. DeCoster && P. Mable (Eds.), *Student development and education in college residence halls.* Washington, DC: American College Personnel Association.

2. Rossi, P. (1964, November 28-29). *Effects of peers on socialization of college students.* Paper presented at the Research Conference on Social Science Methods and Student Residence, University of Michigan, Ann Arbor.

3. Ibid., 3-4.

4. Levitz, R., & Noel, L. (1989). Connecting students to institutions: Keys to retention and success. In M. L. Upcraft, J. N. Gardner, & Associates (Eds), *The freshman year experience.* San Francisco: Jossey-Bass.

5. Myers, E. (1981). Unpublished attrition research studies, St. Cloud State University, St. Cloud, MN; Beal, P. E., & Noel, L. (1980). *What works in student retention.* Iowa City, IA: American College Testing Program and National Center for Higher Education Management Systems.

6. Levitz & Noel, 66.

7. Chickering, A. (1974). *Commuting versus residential students.* San Francisco: Jossey-Bass, 80.

8. Harris, T. A. (1969). *I'm OK — You're OK: A practical guide to transactional analysis.* New York: Harper and Row.

9. Powell, J., Plyler, S., Dickson, B., & McClellan, S. (1969). *The personnel assistant in college residence halls.* Boston: Houghton Mifflin. 102.

10. Levitz & Noel, 72.

11. Mussen, P., Conger, J., & Kagen, J. (1969). *Child development and personality* (3rd ed.). New York: Harper & Row.

12. Chickering, A. W. (1972). *Education and identity.* San Francisco: Jossey-Bass.

13. Astin, A. (1977). *Four critical years.* San Francisco: Jossey-Bass.

14. Super, D. E., Crites, J. O., Hunnel, R. G., Moser, H. P., Overstreet, P. L., & Warnath, C. F. (1957). *Vocational development: A framework for research.* New York: Teachers College; Super, D. E., Starishevsky, R., Matlin, R. & Jordan, J. P. (Eds.). (1963). *Career development: Self-concept theory.* New York: College Entrance Examination Board.

15. Ibid.

16. Miller, T., & Prince, J. (1976). *The future of student affairs.* San Francisco: Jossey-Bass, 13.

17. Astin (1977), 135.

18. Pace, C. R. (1984). Historical perspectives on student outcomes: Assessment with implications for the future. *NASPA Journal, 22* (2), 10-18.

Chapter 7: Peer Counseling

1. Lange, A., & Jakubowski, P. (1976). *Responsible assertive behavior: Cognitive behavioral procedures for trainers.* Champaign, IL: Research Press.

2. Fensterheim, H., & Baer, J. (1975). *Don't say yes when you want to say no.* New York: David McKay.

Chapter 9: Mediation

1. Cunningham, M., & Berryman, C. (1976, March 6). *Conflict: How to deal with it effectively.* Speech presented at the First Annual Bowling Green All-Greek Leadership Conference.

2. Miller, G., & Zoradi, S. (1977). Roommate conflict resolution. *Journal of College Student Personnel, 18,* 228-231.

3. Ibid.

Chapter 10: Suicide Intervention

1. Centers for Disease Control. (1997). *Suicide in the United States* [On-line]. Available: *www.cdc.gov*

2. Whitaker, L. C. (1989). Suicide and other crises. In P. A. Grayson & K. Cauley (Eds.), *College psychotherapy* (pp. 48-70). New York: Guilford.

3. Schwartz, A. J. (1990). The epidemiology of suicide among students at colleges and universities in the United States. In L. C. Whitaker & R. E. Slimak (Ed.), *College student suicide* (pp. 25-44). New York: Haworth.

4. Binstock, J. (1974, April), *The futurist.*

5. Pretzel, P. (1972). *Understanding and counseling the suicidal person.* Nashville, TN: Abingdon Press.

6. Coleman, J. (1972). *Abnormal psychology and modern life.* Glenview, IL: Scott, Foresman and Co.

7. Santrock, J. W. (1987). *Adolescence: An introduction* (3rd ed.). Dubuque, IA: William C. Brown.

8. Lee, E. (1978). Suicide and youth. *The Personnel and Guidance Journal, 57,* 200-204.

9. Weiner, I. B. (1980). *Psychopathology in adolescence.* New York: Wiley.

10. Lee, 201.

11. Shochet, B. (1970). Recognizing the suicidal patient. *Modern Medicine, 38.*

Chapter 11: Violence and Crime in Residence Halls

1. Crime on campus. (1988, October 4). *USA Today,* p. IA.

2. Lederman, D. (1993, January 20). Colleges report 7500 violent crimes on their campuses in first annual statements required under federal law. *Chronical of Higher Education, 39,* p. A32; Collison, M. (1993, February 17). Many are skeptical about low crime rates reported by some colleges and universities. *Chronicle of Higher Education, 39,* p. A25.

3. Gibbs, N. (1993, January 18). 'Til death do us part. *Time, 141,* p. 38-45.

4. Council on the Status of Women. Survey conducted July 1992 to December 1992.

5. Pritchard, C. (1988). *Avoiding rape on and off campus.* Wenonah, NJ: State College Publishing Co.

6. Ibid.

7. "Crime on campus"

8. Pritchard

9. Koss, M. (1988). Hidden rape: Incidence, prevalence, and descriptive characteristics of sexual aggression and victimization in a national sample of college students. In A. W. Burgess (Ed.), *Sexual assault* (Vol. 2). New York: Garland.

10. McMillen, L. (1988). Colleges urged to step up efforts to prevent rape, a major menace to students on campus. *Chronicle of Higher Education, 34* (1), p. A1.

11. O'Shaughnessy, M. E., & Palmer, C. J. (1990). *Sexually stressful events survey: Summary report.* Unpublished manuscript, University of Illinois at Urbana-Champaign, Office of the Dean of Students.

12. Leo, C. (1987, March 23). When the date turns into rape. *Time, 77.*

13. Ibid.

14. Smith, C. (1988). *Coping with crime on campus.* New York: Macmillan.

15. O'Shaughnessy & Palmer

16. National Crime Prevention Council (N.D.c). *Be smart. Be alert. A safe campus starts with you.* Washington, DC: Author. [Available at The Woodward Building, 733 15th Street, NW, Washington, D.C. 20005]

17. National Criome Prevention Council (N.D.b). *Being forced into having sex—even if it's by someone you know—is rape, and it's a crime.* Washington, DC: Author. [Available at The Woodward Building, 733 15th Street, NW, Washington, D.C. 20005]

18. Laird, B. (1988, October 4). Facts, figures behind the fears. *USA Today,* p. 6A.

19. New York Times (1993). Chronical of Higher Education.

Chapter 13: Alcohol Abuse

1. NIAAA—DHEW, 1972.

2. Eigen, L.D. (1991). *Alcohol practices, policies, and potentials of American colleges and universities.* Rockville, MD: U.S. Department of Health and Human Services.

3. Presley, C. A., & Meilman, P. W. (1992). *Alcohol and drugs on American college campuses.* Carbondale, IL: Southern Illinois University Wellness Center.

4. Ibid.

5. Harris, L., & Associates, Inc. (1974). Public awareness of the National Institute on Alcohol Abuse and Alcoholism advertising campaign on public attitudes toward drinking and alcohol abuse. In *Alcohol and Health* (Study No. 2355). Washington, DC: U.S. Government Printing Office.

6. Wechsler, H., Dowdall, G. W., Davenport, A., & Castillo, S. (1995). Correlates of college student binge drinking. *American Journal of Public Health, 85,* 921-926.

7. Zucker, R. A. (1968). Sex-role identity patterns and drinking behavior of adolescents. *Quarterly Journal of Studies on Alcohol, 29,* 868-884.

8. Wilsnack, S., & Wilsnack, R. (1982). Sex roles and adolescent drinking. In Chafetz & Blane (Eds.), *Youth, Alcohol, and Social Policy,* New York: Plenum Press, 11.

9. Rachal, J., Williams, J., Brehm, M., Cavanaugh, B., Moore, R., & Eckerman, W. A (1975). *National study of adolescent drinking behavior, attitudes, and correlates.* Research Triangle Park, NC: Research Triangle Institute.

10. Park, F. (1975). Sex-role adjustment and drinking disposition of women college students. *Journal of Studies on Alcohol.*

11. Wilsnack & Wilsnack, 4.

12. Keller, J. E. (1971). *Drinking problem?* Philadelphia: Fortress Press.

Chapter 15: Sexuality

1. Smith, S., & Smith, C. (1988). *The college student's health guide.* Los Altos, CA: Westchester Publishing Co.

2. Hatcher, R.A., Trussell, J., Stewart, F., Stewart, G. K., Kowal, D., Guest, F., Cates, Jr., W., & Policar, M. S. (1994). *Contraceptive technology* (16th ed.). New York.

3. Hatcher, R. A., Guest, F., Stewart, F., Stewart, G., Trussell, J., Brown, S., & Cates, W. (1988). *Contraceptive Technology 1988-89* (14th ed.). Atlanta, GA: Printed Matter, Inc.

4. Sifton, D. W. (1994). *The PDR family guide to women's health and prescription drugs.* Montvale, NJ: Medical Economics.

5. P. Geiger, personal communication, August 1997.

6. Sifton

7. Hatcher et al. (1994).

8. Ibid.

9. Sifton

10. Centers for Disease Control. (1996, May 17). *Abortion surveillance, United States, 1992* [Online]. Available: *www.cdc.gov*

11. Hatcher et al. (1994).

12. Ibid.

Chapter 16: Sexual Orientation

1. Kinsey, A. C., Pomeroy, W. B., & Martin, C. R. (1948). *Sexual behavior in human males.* Philadelphia: W. B. Saunders Publishing.

2. Sex survey surprise. (1993, April 17). *The New York Times,* p. L20.

3. Kinsey

4. Kallman, F. J. (1952). Comparative twin study on the genetic aspects of male homosexuality. *Journal of Nervous and Mental Disease, 115,* 283-298.

5. Evans, N., & Levine, H. (1990, Fall). *Perspectives on sexual orientation.* Macomb, IL: New Directions for Student Services, No. 15, pp. 49-58.

6. Ibid.

7. Cass, V. C. (1979). Homosexual identity formation: A theoretical model. *Journal of Homosexuality, 4,* 219-235.

8. Rhoads, R. A. (1995). Learning from the coming-out experiences of college males. *Journal of College Student Development, 36,* 67-74.

Chapter 17: Issues of Race and Gender

1. College enrollment by racial and ethnic group. (1992, August 26). *Chronicle of Higher Education,* p. 3; College enrollment by racial and ethnic group. (1997, August 29). *Chronicle of Higher Education,* p. 18.

2. American Council on Education. (1990). Racial and ethnic trends in college participation: 1976 to 1988. *Research Briefs, 1* (3), 1-3.

3. College enrollment trends. (1997, August 29). *Chronicle of Higher Education,* p. 5.

4. Treadwell D. (1989, January 15). *Los Angeles Times,* p. 13.

5. Thieblot, B. A. (1989, September). *Currents,* p. 15.

6. Smedley, B. D., Myers. H. F., & Harrell, S. P. (1989, July/August). Minority status stresses and the college adjustment of ethnic minority freshmen. *Journal of Higher Education,* pp. 434, 448.

7. Jackson, G. A. (1992, Spring). Why they continue to fail: Black students in White colleges: The dark side of higher education: A review of the literature. *NCEDA Journal,* pp. 14-17.

8. Ibid.

9. Hughes, M. S. (1987, November). Black students' participation in higher education. *Journal of College Student Personnel,* p. 535.

10. Jackson

11. Hughes

12. Ibid., 541.

13. Mentzer, M. S. (1993, July/August). Minority representation in higher education. *Journal of Higher Education,* p. 417.

14. Ibid.

15. Atkinson, D. R., Whiteley, S., & Ginn, R. H. (1990, March). Asian-American acculturation and preferences for help providers. *Journal of College Student Development,* 155.

16. Zastrow, C., & Kirst-Ashman, K. (1990). *Understanding human behavior and the social environment.* Chicago: Nelson-Hall.

17. Ibid.

18. Marsh, P. (Ed.) (1988). *Eye to eye: How people interact.* Topsfield, MA: Salem House Publishers.

19. Ibid.

20. U.S. Bureau of the Census. (1990). *Statistical abstract of the United States, 1990.* Washington, DC: U. S. Government Printing Office.

Chapter 18: Educational Programming

1. Wilson, W. (1913). The spirit of learning. In N. Fobister (Ed.), *Essays for college men.* New York: Henry Folt.

Chapter 19: Community Development

1. Hillery, G. (1955). Definition of community: areas of agreement. *Rural Sociology, 20* (2), 118.

INDEX

Abdicating, 299
Abortion, 240-41
Academic adjustment, 102-3
Academic boredom, 99
Academic policies, 143-44
Academic unpreparedness, as cause
    of attrition, 99
Accommodation, defined, 81
Accountability, 41
Adaptation, defined, 81
Adjustments to college life
    academic adjustment, 102
    apartment quest, 109
    broken relationships, 107-8
    career planning, 110-11
    child-parent break, 100-101
    conflicts, 102
    dating, 104-5
    extroversion, 103-4
    financial problems, 106
    first year of college, 95-116
    forces of attrition for freshmen, 99
    homesickness, 103
    homosexuality and, 105
    intimacy, 107-8
    introversion, 103
    loss, 111
    RA anxieties, 112
    reaction to freedom, 103
    roommates and, 102
    second and third years, 106-9
    self-confidence, 112
    self-esteem needs, 101
    senior year, 109-112
    separation, 111
    sophomore slump, 108-9
    suicide, 105-6
    support needs, 101
    tolerance, 98
    transition period, 97-98
    value clarification, 107
    value exploration, 101
    value identification, 107
    values, 110

Adult roles, influence of, 64
Advising, 134-35
African-American students, 272-75
AIDS, 241-43
Alarm systems, crime, 189
Alcohol abuse, 203-15
    alcohol education programming,
        212-14
    alternatives to, 213
    beverage type, 205
    binge drinking, 207-8
    body chemistry, 206
    body weight, 205
    causes of, 208
    drinking environment, 206
    drinking games, 208
    drinking history, 205-6
    eating and, 205
    experimentation, 209
    family history, 206
    hangovers, 206
    identifying problem drinker, 210
    influence on behavior, 205
    low-risk drinking, 211-12
    maturity, 209
    with other drugs, 206-7
    party planning and, 211-12
    peer-group influences, 208-9
    problems of, 207-11
    sex roles and, 208
    short-term effects of, 204-6
    sobering up, 206
    speed of consumption, 205
Alcohol education programming,
    212-14
Alcoholism, defined, 210
Allocentrism, Kohlberg's Theory, 85
America, residence hall history in,
    27-40
American Association of Collegiate
    Alumnae, 29
American College Health Association,
    241

American Council on Education,
    33, 35
Analysis, counseling and, 128-29
Angel dust, 220-21
Anorexia nervosa, 199
Antiabortion groups, 240
Anxiety, test-taking, 342
Apartment quest, 109
Application of principles
    adjustments, 114-16
    alcohol abuse, 215
    community development, 317
    crime, 192-94
    discipline and confrontation,
        156-57
    drug abuse, 233
    educational philosophies, 53-54
    educational programming, 306-8
    food abuse, 201
    history of residence halls, 43-46
    influence, 66-68
    mediation, 164-66
    peer counseling, 136-38
    race and gender, 285-88
    roles of RA, 19-22
    sexual orientation, 265-68
    sexuality, 254-56
    study skills, 345-48
    suicide intervention, 176-78
    time management, 328-29
Approach, vs. confrontation, 145
Asian American Student Association,
    277
Asian-American students, 275-76
Assertive confrontation, defined, 150
Assimilation, defined, 81
Association of College and University
    Housing Officers—
    International, 35
Athletic programming, 294
Attitudes, counseling and, 120-21
Attrition, forces of, 99
Autonomy, and Chickering's Theory,
    78

Availability, 12
Avoidance, 162

Barbiturates, 227
Battered women, 180-82
Behavior problems, 141-57
Beliefs, counseling and, 120-21
Beverage type, alcohol abuse, 205
Bicycle theft, 189
Binge drinking, 207-8
Birth control pills, 237
Black Student Association, 277
Body chemistry, and alcohol abuse, 206
Body weight, and alcohol abuse, 205
British collegiate system, residence hall history and, 24
Broken record technique, 151
Broken relationships, adjustments to, 107-8
Bulimia, 197-99
Burglary, 188
Burnout, 17
Bursen, 24

Cambridge University, collegiate system of, 24-25
Campus police, 190
Cannabis, 218-19
Career planning, senior year, 110-11
CAS guidelines, 51
Chickering's Theory of Development, 75-80
  autonomy and, 78
  competence, 76-78
  developing purpose, 79-80
  identity and, 79
  integrity and, 80
  interdependence and, 78
  interpersonal relationships, 78-79
  vectors of, 76
Childhood socialization, defined, 83
Child-parent break, adjustments to, 100-101
Chronicle of Higher Education, 180
Civil Rights Act, 281
Civil War, 26
Classroom behavior, and study skills, 338
Cocaine, 226-27
Cognitive development, 80-83
  Perry's theory, 81-83
College athletics, 28
Coming out, 260-61
Commitment, 161
  Perry's Theory of, 82-83
Communism, 37-38

Community, defined, 309
Community, influence of, 63
Community development, 309-18
  elements of community, 310-12
  establishment of, 312-14
  types of, 312
Competence, Chickering's Theory 76-78
Condoms, 237-38
Confidence, counseling and, 119-20
Confidentiality, 13
Conflict analysis, 161-63
Conflict mediation, 162
Conflict situations, defined, 159-60
Conflicts, adjustments to, 102
Confrontation, 139-94
  assertive, 150-51
  broken record technique, 151-52
  commitment, 151
  intoxicated person, 152-54
  skills of, 150-51
Contraceptives, 236-38
Contracting, 161
Contrition, 147
Controlled substances (chart), 222-25. See also Drug abuse
Coordination, 299
Coping mechanisms, for stress, 17
Council for the Advancement of Standards for Student Services/Development Programs (CAS), 51
Counseling, peer, 117-38
  advising, 134-35
  analysis and, 128-29
  attitudes, 120-21
  beliefs and, 120-21
  complaints about, 118-19
  confidence, 119-20
  developing options, 129
  drug abuse, 230-31
  environment for exchange, 124
  follow-up stage, 129-30
  listening stage, 125-27
  model of, 122
  motivation, 121
  nonverbal clues, 124
  objectivity, 122
  overview, 119-22
  precounseling stage, 122-24
  problem identification, 127
  professional counseling referral, 130-33
  resolution stage, 129
  and sexual orientation, 262-63
  values and, 120-21
Counseling encounter, defined, 118

Counseling minority group members, 279
Counseling model, disciplinary, 144-50
  action, 149
  approaching the student, 145-46
  fact gathering, 144-45
  follow-up, 149-50
  listening, 148-49
Counselors, in 1950s, 37
Crack, 227
Crafts programming, 294
Cramming, study skills, 340
Crime, in residence halls, 179-94
  alarm systems, 189
  battered women, 180-82
  bicycle theft, 189
  rape, 182-88
  robberies, 190-91
  statistics, 179
  theft, 188-89
Crisis management, 139-94
Cross-cultural communication, 277-79
Cultural differences, race, 273-75
Cultural programming, 294
Cultural separateness, 276-77
Custodial care, 49

Dating, adjustments to, 104-5
Defense mechanisms, 148
Defining conflict, in mediation, 159-60
Delegation, 299
Denial, 146
Depo-Provera, 237
Depressants, 227
Depression, 132
Designer drugs, 221
Detectable vs. undetectable drugs, 229-30
Detoxification programs, 230
Developing options, counseling and, 129
Developing purpose, Chickering's Theory 79-80
Development, of students, 71-94
  Chickering's theory, 75-80
  cognitive, 80-83
  Gilligan's Theory, 86-87
  Kohlberg's Theory, 84-85
  moral, 85-86
  Perry's Theory, 81-83
  physical, 72-73
  psychological, 73-74
  social, 87-89
Developmental programming, 294
Developmental tasks, defined, 74

Diaphragm, 238
Direct intervention, influence of, 63
Disciplinary counseling, 144
Discipline, 141-57
    counseling model, 144-50
    recording procedures, 154-55
Discrimination, against women, 280
Discussion, as study skill, 339
Dissonance as cause of attrition, 99
Domus pauperum, 24
Dormitories, residence hall history
    and, 24-25
Dormitory, defined, 24-25
Drinking games, 208
Drug abuse, 217-34
    angel dust, 220-21
    barbiturates, 227
    Cannabis, 218-21
    cocaine, 226-27
    controlled substances, chart,
        222-25
    counseling, 230-31
    crack, 227
    depressants, 227
    designer drugs, 221
    detectable vs. undetectable drugs,
        229-30
    drug enforcement, 218
    Ecstasy, 221
    in educational institutions, 228-29
    hashish, 219-20
    heroin, 227-28
    imitation drugs, 226
    LSD, 220
    marjuana, 218-19
    mescaline, 221
    methamphetamines, 226
    narcotics, 227-28
    opiates, 227-28
    overdoses, 231-32
    PCP, 220-21
    psilocybin, 221
    psychedelic drugs, 220-21
    quaaludes, 227
    role of RA, 229
    stimulants, 221-27
    THC, 220
Drug enforcement, 218
Drugs and alcohol abuse, 206-7
Dualism, Perry's Theory of, 81-82

Eating, and alcohol abuse, 205
Eating habits, 131. See also Food
    abuse
Ecstasy, 221
Educational programming, 291-308
    goals of, 292-93

methods, 296-305
    strategies for programming, 304
    traditional model, 293-95
    wellness programming model,
        295-96
Educational goals, 51-52
Educational institutions, drug abuse
    in, 228-29
Educational philosophies of residence
    halls, 47-54
    blend of approaches, 50-51
    CAS guidelines, 51
    custodial care approach, 49
    educational goals, 51-52
    money management, 48
    moral development approach, 49
    student development approach, 50
    student learning approach, 49
    student services approach, 48-49
    working with students, 48
Educational programming, 294
Educational skills, of RA, 4
Eisenhower administration, 37-38
Emotional control, 131
Emotions, managing, 77
Empathy, in mediation, 163
Encounter programming, 295
Enforcement of policies, 11-12
Environment for exchange, counseling
    and, 124
Environment for study skills, 332-33
Equal Employment Opportunity
    Commission, 281
Essay exams, 341-42
Ethnic interrelationships, 277
Ethnocentrism, 271-72
Evaluative responses, 162
Excessive moodiness, 131
Exchange environment, 124
Expectations of RA, 5-6
Experimentation, alcohol abuse, 209
Experimentation, study skills, 338-39
Extracurricular activities, influence of
    residence hall on, 56-57
Extroversion, adjustments to, 103-4

Faculty interaction, influence of resi-
    dence hall on, 57
Family background, influence of, 58
Family history, alcohol abuse, 206
Federal government, residence hall
    history and, 38-39
Financial problems, adjustments to,
    106
First impressions, 10-11
Follow-up stage, counseling and,
    129-30

Food abuse, 197-201
    anorexia nervosa, 199
    bulimia, 197-199
Football, 28
Forces of attrition for freshmen, 99
Fraternities, 30-31, 59
French Revolution, 24
future of residence hall, 40-41

Gender, 279-88
    discrimination against women, 280
    gender harassment, 282
    sexual harassment, 280-83
Genetics, and homosexuality, 259
GI Bill, 34
Gilligan's Theory of Moral Develop-
    ment in Women, 86-87
Goodness, women and, 87
Gott v. Berea College, 32
Grades, and RA, 7
Guilt, shifting, 148

Hall directors, and RA relationship, 13
Hangovers, 206
Harvard House Plan, residence hall
    history and, 31-32
Harvard University, collegiate system,
    24-25
Hashish, 219-20
Health and safety regulations, policies,
    142
Health, and study skills, 333
Heroin, 227-28
Higher Education Amendments Act,
    38
Higher Education Facilities Act, 38
High-rise residence halls, 41
Hispanic Student Assocation, 277
HIV, 241-243
Hobby programming, 294
Homesickness, adjustments to, 103
Homophobia, 262
Homosexuality. See also Sexual
    orientation
    adjustments to, 105
    genetic factors in, 259
    history of, 257-58
Honesty, and study skills, 343
Hostility, 147

Identity and Chickering's Theory, 79
Identity development, 259-60
Imitation drugs, 226
In loco parentis, 32, 142
Incompatibility as cause of attrition,
    99
Influence of residence hall, 56-57

on extracurricular activities, 56-57
on faculty interaction, 57
on interpersonal relationships, 57
on perception of social climate, 57
on personal growth, 57
on retention, 56
Influence on students, 58-64
adult roles, 64
community, 63
direct intervention, 63
family background, 58
integration of experiences, 62-63
involvement, 62
leaving home, 58
optimum dissonance, 63
peer-group, 58-59
RA influence, 61
role modeling, 63
roomate, 60-61
Information acquisition, study skills,
337-40
Integration of experiences, influence
of, 62-63
Integrity and Chickering's Theory, 80
Interdependence and Chickering's
Theory, 78
Interpersonal relationships, 13-17
Chickering's Theory 78-79
influence of residence hall on, 57
Intimacy, adjustments to, 107-8
Introversion, adjustments to, 103
Involvement, influence of, 62
Irish immigrants, 272
Irrelevancy as cause of attrition, 99

Jewish Student Association, 277

Kinsey Report, 258
Kohlberg's Theory of Moral Development, 83-85
allocentrism, 85
sociocentrism, 84-85
Kolbe, President, 26
Ku Klux Klan, 272

Land Grant College Act of 1862, 27
Landlord-lessee regulations, policies,
142
Language, and race, 276
Leaving home, influence of, 58
Lectures, and study skills, 338
Legal aspects of policies, 142-43
Library, as study environment, 332
Listening, and discipline, 148-49
Listening stage, counseling and,
125-27
Listening techniques, 126

Loss, senior year, 111
Low-cost housing, residence hall his-
tory and, 33-34
Low-risk drinking, 211-12
LSD, 220
Luther, Martin, 24

Manipulative communication, 162
Maturity, alcohol abuse, 209
Maturity, changes at, 73
Mediation, 159-66
analysis of conflict, 161-62
defining conflict, 159-60
empathy, 163
metacommunication, 162-63
roommate conflicts, 160-61
strategies for, 162
Mental health, 41
Mescaline, 221
Metacommunication, defined, 162
Metacommunication, in mediation,
162-63
Methamphetamines, 226
Methaqualone, 227
Middle Ages, universities and, 23
Misdirection, 147
Model of counseling, 122
Money management, 48
Moodiness, 131
Moral development approach, 49
Moral development, women and, 86-
87
Moral reasoning, levels of, 83
Morning-after pill, 237
Movitation, 121, 299
Multiculturalism, 41
Multiple-choice testing, 341
Music
and group living, 118
and studying, 332

Narcotics, 227-28
National Association of College and
Univesity Housing Officers, 35
National Association of Deans and
Advisers of Men, 26
National Association of Deans of
Men, 30, 35
National Defense Education Act
(NDEA), 38
National Science Foundation, 38
Negotiation, 161
Nineteenth century, residence hall his-
tory and, 25-27
Nonverbal clues, counseling and, 124
Nonviolence, women and, 87
Norplant, 237

Objective exams, 341
Objectivity, counseling and, 122
Opiates, 227-28
Optimum dissonance, influence of, 63
Orientation to personal survival,
women and, 86-87
Origins in U.S., residence hall history
and, 25
Outreach, 291-317
community development, 309-17
educational programming, 291-308
Overdoses, drug abuse, 231-32
Overview, counseling, 119-22
Objectivity, and counseling, 122

Paranoia, 132
Parietal policy, defined, 109
Party planning and alcohol abuse,
211-12
Passive programs, 295
PCP, 220-21
Peer counseling. See Counseling
Peer group, 87-89
and alcohol abuse, 208-9
influence of, 58-59
social development and, 87-89
Perry's Theory of Cognitive Develo-
ment, 81-83
commitment, 82-83
dualism, 81-82
relativism, 82
Personal growth, influence of
residence hall on, 57
Personal health, preoccupation with,
132
Personnel, residence hall history and,
36-37
Pharmacological desk reference, 218
Physical (biological) development,
72-73
Planned Parenthood, 240
Policies, university, 142-44
academic, 143-44
health and safety regulations, 142
landlord-lessee regulations, 142
legal aspects of, 142-43
small-group living, 143
Policy, RA opinion of, 11-12
Policy enforcement, 11-12
Precollege acquaintanceships, 98
Precounseling stage, 122-24
Pregnancy, 239-40
HCG test, 239
home test kits, 239
Prejudice, 272-73. See also Race and
Gender
Preparation, study skills, 332-37

Primary peer group, defined, 88
Problem definition, 161
Problem drinker, 210
Problem identification, counseling
    and, 127
Problem recognition, 161
Procrastination, and study skills,
    335-37
Professional counseling referral,
    130-33
Program goals, resident hall
    educational philosophies and,
    51-52
Program objective, defined, 298
Programming, defined, 292
Projection, 148
Prostaglandin, 241
*Prostrollo v. University of South
    Dakota*, 39
Psilocybin, 221
Psychedelic drugs, 220-21
Psychological adaptation to physical
    development, 72-73
Psychological development, 73-74
    Chickering's theory, 75-80
Psychosocial development, 270-71
Public Housing Authority, 35
Publicity, programming, 300
Purpose, 79

Quaaludes, 227
Quadrangle plan, residence hall histo-
    ry and, 27-28

Race, 269-79
    Asian-American students, 275-76
    counseling minority group mem-
        bers, 279
    cross-cultural communication,
        277-79
    cultural differences, 273-75
    cultural separateness, 276-77
    ethnic interrelationships, 277
    ethnocentrism, 271
    prejudice, 272-73
    psychosocial development, 270-71
Rape, 182-88
    acquaintance, 184-85
    counseling victims, 188
    date, 185-86
    reaction to, 186-87
    residence hall actions, 187-88
Rape trauma syndrome, 186
Rationalization, 148
Reaction to freedom, adjustments to,
    103
Reality, women and, 87

Recreational programming, 294
Reference group, defined, 88
Referral
    professional counseling, 130-33
    for suicide intervention, 174-75
Relativism, Perry's Theory of, 82
Relaxation, and testing, 342-43
Reserve Officers' Training Corps
    (ROTC), 34
Residence hall, history of, 23-46
    1930s and, 32-33
    1960s and, 38
    1970s and, 39-40
    1980s and, 40
    American, 27-40
    British collegiate system, 24
    communism and, 37-38
    dormitories and, 24-25
    early twentieth century, 27-28
    federal government and, 38-39
    future and, 40-41
    Harvard house plan, 31-32
    low-cost housing, 33-34
    nineteenth century and, 25-27
    origins in U.S., 25
    personnel, 36-37
    quadrangle plan, 27-28
    residence hall revival, 28-31
    student rebellion and, 39
    traditionless period, 36
    wandering students, 23-24
    WWI and, 31-32
    WWII and, 34-36
Residence hall design, 57-58
Residence hall education, approaches
    to, 48-51
    custodial care, 49
    moral development, 49
    student development, 50
    student learning, 49
    student services, 48-49
Residence hall revival, 28-31
Residence hall and sexual orientation,
    262
Resident Assistant (RA)
    as administrator, 10
    anxieties, senior year, 112
    as counselor, 9
    influence of, 61
    and interpersonal relationships, 13-
        17
    as role model, 8-9
    as student, 7
    as teacher, 9-10
Resolution stage, counseling and, 129
Responsibilities of RA, 3-22
Responsibility, vs. selfishness, 86

Retention, influence of residence hall
    on, 56
Robberies, 190-91
Role modeling, influence of, 63
Role of RA, in drug abuse, 229
Roommate, adjustments to, 102
Roommate, influence of, 60-61
Roommate conflicts, mediation,
    160-61
RU486, 241

Secular trend, defined, 72
Seductive behavior, 282
Selective perception, 162
Self-confidence, senior year, 112
Self-disclosure, 260
Self-esteem needs, adjustments to, 101
Self-sacrifice, women and, 87
Separation, senior year, 111
Sex roles and alcohol abuse, 208
Sexual bribery, 282
Sexual coercion, 282
Sexual harassment, 280-83
Sexual imposition, 283
Sexual orientation, 257-68
    coming out, 260-61
    counseling, 262-63
    homosexual myths, 258
    identity development, 259-60
    lifestyle, 261-62
    residence halls and, 262
    self-disclosure, 260
Sexuality, 235-56
    abortion, 240-41
    AIDS, 241-43
    birth control pills, 237
    condoms, 237-38
    contraceptives, 236-38
    depo-provera, 237
    diaphragm, 238
    HIV, 241-43
    morning-after pill, 237
    norplant, 237
    pregnancy, 239-40
    STDs (chart), 243-51
Sexually transmitted diseases (STDs),
    236, 243-51. *See also* AIDS
Sleeping habits, 131
Small-group living, policies, 143
Social climate, influence of residence
    hall on, 57
Social programming, 294
Socialization, defined, 87
Sociocentrism, Kohlberg's Theory,
    84-85
Sophomore slump, 108-9
Sororities, 59

Speed, and drug abuse, 221
Sputnik, 37
Stereotypes, 271
Stimulants, 221-27
Strategies for mediation, 162
Student development, and residence
        halls, 50, 55-68
    comparisons with non-residence,
        55-57
Student health center, 230
Student learning approach, 49
Student rebellion, residence hall histo-
        ry and, 39
student service, defined, 48
Student services approach, 48-49
Study skills, 331-48
    classroom behavior, 338
    cramming, 340
    discussion, 339
    environment for, 332-33
    experimentation, 338-39
    health and, 333
    honesty and, 343
    information acquisition, 337-38
    lectures, 338
    preparation, 332-37
    procrastination, 335-37
    studying process, 339-40
    test taking, 340-43
    textbook reading, 337-38
Studying process, 339-40
Suicide
    adjustments to, 105-6
    discussions of, 132
Suicide intervention, 167-78
    ambivalence, 169
    causes, 168
    depression, 169
    interviewing students, 170-71

    model for, 171-74
    referrals, 174-75
    symptoms, 168-69
Support needs, adjustments to, 101

Territorial imperative, 311
Test taking, study skills, 340-43
Testing, 340-43
    anxiety, 342
    essay exams, 341-42
    multiple-choice, 341
    objective exams, 341
    relaxation and, 342-43
Tetrahydrocannabinol (THC), 220
Textbook reading, study skills, 337-38
Theft, 188-89
Time management, 321-29
    defined, 321
    discretionary time, 323-25
    other-imposed time, 325-27
    overplanning, 322
    predictable time, 322-23
Tolerance, adjustments to, 98
Traditionless period, residence hall
        history and, 36
Transition difficulties as cause of attri-
        tion, 99
Transition period, adjustments to, 97-
        98
Twentieth century, residence hall his-
        tory and, 27-28

Uncertainty about major as cause of
        attrition, 99
Uneven growth patterns, physical de-
        velopment and, 72
Unrealistic expectations as cause of
        attrition, 99

Value clarification, 107
Value exploration, adjustments to, 101
Value identification, 107
Values, 19-20
    counseling and, 120-21
    senior year, 110
Vectors, of Chickering's Theory 76
Violence, on campus, 41
Vocational preference, 110

Wandering students, residence hall
        history and, 23-24
Wellness programming model, 294-96
Wilson, Woodrow, 292
Women. *See also* Gender
    battered, 180-82
    discrimination against, 280
    goodness, 87
    and moral development, 86-87
    nonviolence and, 87
    orientation to personal survival,
        86-87
    reality, 87
    residence halls and, 32
    self-sacrifice, 87
WPA (Work Projects Administration),
        34, 36
WWI, residence hall history and,
        31-32
WWII, residence hall history and,
        34-36

Yale University, and collegiate system,
        27
    residential quadrangles at, 32